T0313933

MARKET MAOISTS

MARKET MAOISTS

THE COMMUNIST ORIGINS OF CHINA'S CAPITALIST ASCENT

JASON M. KELLY

 Harvard University Press

CAMBRIDGE, MASSACHUSETTS

LONDON, ENGLAND | 2021

First printing

Library of Congress Cataloging-in-Publication Data

Names: Kelly, Jason M., 1979- author.

Title: Market Maoists : the communist origins of China's capitalist ascent / Jason M. Kelly.

Description: Cambridge, Massachusetts : Harvard University Press, 2021. | Includes index.

Identifiers: LCCN 2020043109 | ISBN 9780674986497 (cloth)

Subjects: LCSH: Mixed economy—China—History—20th century. | Markets—China—History—20th century. | China—Economic policy. | China—Economic conditions. | China—Commerce—History—20th century.

Classification: LCC HC430.C3 K58 2021 | DDC 330.951/05—dc23

LC record available at https://lccn.loc.gov/2020043109

For Rebecca and Abigail

CONTENTS

ABBREVIATIONS

AmCham	American Chamber of Commerce
CCP	Chinese Communist Party
CCPIT	China Committee for the Promotion of International Trade
CFEC	Central Finance and Economics Committee
CHINCOM	China Committee of the Coordinating Committee for Multilateral Export Controls
CIA	US Central Intelligence Agency
CNIEC	China National Import and Export Corporation
CNTIC	China National Technical Import Corporation
COCOM	Coordinating Committee for Multilateral Export Controls
CPSU	Communist Party of the Soviet Union
ECA	Economic Cooperation Administration
FYP	Five-Year Plan
GAC	General Administration of Customs of the People's Republic of China
GLF	Great Leap Forward
HSBC	Hongkong and Shanghai Banking Corporation
ICA	US International Cooperation Administration
ICBM	Intercontinental ballistic missile
ITA	China International Trade Association
LDP	Liberal Democratic Party
KMT	Kuomintang, Chinese Nationalist Party
MFA	Ministry of Foreign Affairs of the People's Republic of China
MOFT	Ministry of Foreign Trade of the People's Republic of China
NATO	North Atlantic Treaty Organization
PLA	People's Liberation Army
PRC	People's Republic of China
SAS	Scandinavian Airlines System

MARKET MAOISTS

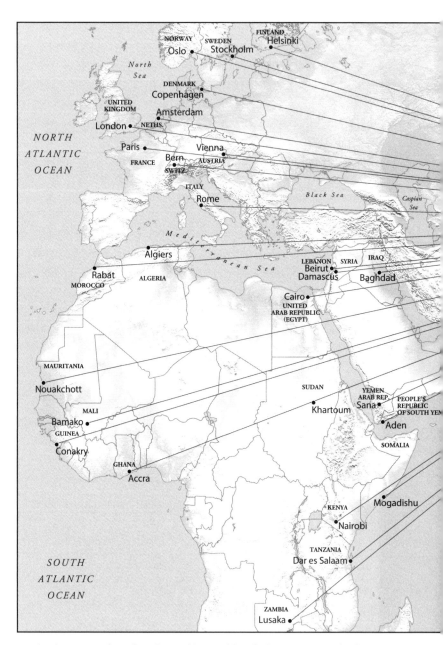

Mao's China in markets abroad: People's Republic of China commercial offices established outside the Socialist Bloc by 1970.

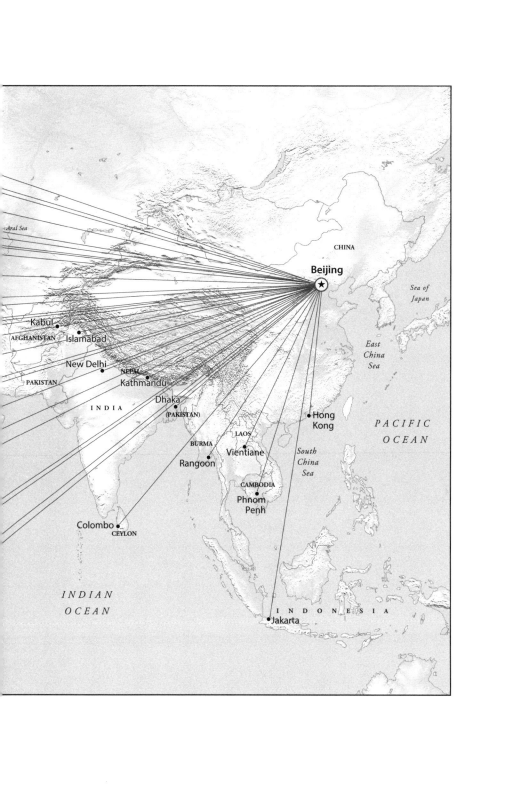

INTRODUCTION

ON A COLD, CLEAR, otherwise ordinary morning in January 1973, officials at China's State Planning Commission in Beijing went to work. Most of them probably rode bicycles or walked to the office—Beijing was a city of few cars in the early 1970s. Some may have taken the bus. Today was a good day to arrive early. It was January 2, and before the workday ended, these planners would submit to leaders in the State Council a formal plan to launch the biggest foray into capitalist markets in the history of the People's Republic of China (PRC). At the heart of this proposal, which these officials had been developing for months, was a colossal buying spree: a staggering US$4.3 billion in new technologies and equipment—including entire production plants—all from the capitalist world, all for Communist China, all within three to five years.[1]

The plan's authors may have felt their nerves that bright morning. The political climate seemed hardly ideal for such a bold proposal. After all, China remained in the grip of the Cultural Revolution. The chairman himself, Mao Zedong, was still very much alive and committed to anti-imperialism and socialist revolution. Evidence of the nation's revolutionary fervor still filled the newspapers each day. Just that morning, the *People's Daily* featured a New Year's address by North Korean leader Kim Il-Sung urging comrades to "hold high the revolutionary banner of anti-imperialist and anti-American struggle."[2] The daily quotation from Mao, in large print next to the masthead, proclaimed, "the 700 million Chinese people are the strong backup force of the Vietnamese people" in their fight against American imperialism.[3] None of this seemed to jibe with a proposal to import billions of dollars' worth of goods produced, packaged, and peddled by capitalists from across the imperialist world, including the United States.

And yet, the proposal, once submitted, sailed through the senior ranks of the Chinese Communist Party (CCP). Vice Premier Li Xiannian backed the program. Premier Zhou Enlai was a vocal advocate. Mao Zedong himself signed off on it. Once approved, the "Four-Three Program" (Si San Fang'An), as it was dubbed, became one of the largest Chinese Communist trade initiatives ever, comparable only to the massive technical and economic assistance that China had received from the Soviet Union during the heyday of the Sino–Soviet alliance in the early 1950s.

How was this possible? Beset by the xenophobia of the Cultural Revolution and devoted to an anti-imperialist, socialist, and revolutionary path to modernity, how was it that *this* China aspired to a multibillion-dollar trade program with the very capitalists who embodied the imperialist aggression that Mao's China aimed to crush?

The Four-Three Program also doesn't seem to fit Mao's founding vision for a "new" China. Just months before the formal establishment of the People's Republic of China in October 1949, Mao argued that the world was cleaving in two and China had to pick a side. "All Chinese without exception must lean either to the side of imperialism or to the side of socialism," he said. "Sitting on the fence will not do, nor is there a third road."[4] This ultimatum seemed to rule out half measures and compromise. The Chinese people would take the road of socialism, a stance hardly conducive to blossoming trade with the capitalist world.

For years, scholars have largely taken Mao at his word. The same Cold War framework of socialist solidarity and capitalist hostility that informed Mao's outlook in 1949 has shaped how the world has thought about the way China came of age on the global stage under Mao's reign. The sensation created by Mao's meeting with Richard Nixon during the US president's historic trip to China in the winter of 1972, a few years before Mao's death, is the exception that proves the rule. Nixon's visit captivated the world precisely because it jarred with the prevailing perception of how revolutionary China fit within the wider world, a perception that still lingers today, long after Mao "left to meet Marx" and the Cold War became history.

The end of the Cold War spurred a new age of scholarship on China's international experience under Mao as previously unseen documents from Communist and post-Communist states became available. This unprecedented access allowed historians to scrutinize aspects of China's foreign relations to a degree unimaginable three decades ago. Yet much of this research has gravitated toward the perspective of Mao and his top lieutenants in Zhongnanhai, the central leadership compound in Beijing.[5] There is a good reason for this. Mao was central to China's foreign relations during the Cold War; his decisions set the course. But the tendency to emphasize Mao's outlook also reinforces the mistaken impression of China during his rule as either raging against the capitalist world or contentedly detached from it.

The reality was less doctrinaire, more nuanced, and often ideologically promiscuous. This book reveals how. It shifts focus away from the wars, alliances, and clean divisions that typically orient studies of China's international experience under Mao and explores instead the commercial relationships that linked the Chinese Communist Party to international capitalism from the early days of the Pacific War to the waning years of the Cultural Revolution.[6] A close examination of these commercial ties breaks apart the established narrative of Cold War binaries to uncover an adaptive mode of CCP engagement with international capitalism that transcended the Cold War and linked Mao's revolution to larger historical currents sweeping the globe. Rather than shun capitalist markets outright, Party traders adapted to them by selectively appropriating commercial practices and norms in an effort to expand access to markets abroad. This sustained interaction and adaptation produced a paradoxical momentum in the making of Chinese Communism: just as China's anticapitalist revolution was coming into full bloom at home, the Chinese Communist Party was also wading deeper and deeper into capitalist markets abroad. Senior Party officials railed against the conjoined threats of capitalism and imperialism, but at the same time, and with less fanfare, Chinese Communist traders diligently sought deals with firms and governments across the capitalist world. These committed revolutionaries scoured global markets for everything from wristwatches and buses to buyers of soybeans, bicycles, and tea. The deals they struck, in places such as Hong Kong, London, Tokyo, and Geneva, reached into the hundreds of millions of dollars each year.

These figures may not surprise some. Economists, economic historians, and seasoned traders have long known that Mao's China never sequestered itself fully from overseas capitalist markets.[7] To some among this group, this capitalist trade might seem inconsequential. Communist China's early foreign trade amounted to just a sliver of the nation's total economy—about 5 percent of China's gross national product as late as 1978, the US Central Intelligence Agency (CIA) once estimated—and trade with capitalists constituted only part of that share.[8] The surge of trade and investment that epitomized the Reform and Opening period of the late 1970s and early 1980s, after Mao's death in 1976, seems to diminish the significance of early PRC trade even more. China's total trade exploded during the last decades of the twentieth century, from just over US\$20 billion in 1978 to over US\$474 billion in 2000—an increase of over 2,000 percent.[9] Compared to this later growth, Mao-era trade can seem trivial.

But statistics tell only part of the story. Beneath the modest tabulations of Maoist trade lie something of more lasting significance—the transactions themselves. More than goods and currencies changed hands between Mao's traders and their capitalist counterparts. These deals also served as sites for the exchange of ideas, habits, and beliefs, and as venues where individuals, institutions, and the logics that guided them formed subtle but lasting legacies.

These legacies took several shapes. Most fundamental were the skills and knowledge that traders developed. Some learned to craft advertisements that would resonate with capitalist consumers. Others mastered contract law, tracked freight rates, analyzed insurance markets, or studied the intricacies of product packaging. A more diffuse legacy was the simple tradition of an unbroken market presence. With each transaction, Party traders retained a foothold in markets around the world, giving the CCP its own slender stake in the global economy throughout the Mao era. Securing this foothold was a system of trade offices designed to foster commercial interaction with foreign capitalists. These institutions ranged in size from entire divisions within the central Ministry of Foreign Trade in Beijing to small-time front companies in Hong Kong's central business district, but all of them operated under CCP mandates that encouraged and expected them to expand trade with foreign capitalists. By pursuing this goal, these institutions upheld the Party's tradition of market presence and served as repositories for the skills, knowledge, and experience that supported each transaction.

But the most consequential of legacies is discernable only in retrospect because it emerged so gradually and inadvertently. Senior economic officials in Beijing and working-level Chinese traders in Hong Kong, Europe, Japan, and elsewhere all had to learn the habits, techniques, expectations, and even the aesthetics of international capitalist commerce to trade productively on behalf of the Chinese Communist Party. As these traders and planners negotiated prices, delivery dates, and other terms, they also negotiated what it meant to be a representative from the "new" socialist Chinese state—how to behave, when to reject capitalist conventions, and when to concede and conform. Although none realized it at the time, these officials were learning to reconcile revolutionary aspirations at home with market realities abroad, an iterative process that required them continually to relate China's emerging identity as a modern socialist state to the practices and mentalities of capitalist commerce. This gradual reconciliation, along with the skills, knowledge, experience, and institutions that sustained it all, helped to lay the groundwork for the Four-Three Program in the early 1970s, and ultimately, China's historic turn to global capitalist markets after Mao's death.

None of this was inevitable. Despite the smooth passage of the proposal submitted by the State Planning Commission in January 1973, the Four-Three Program itself did not unfold smoothly once underway. Nor did Reform and Opening flow inexorably from the legacies that formed during Mao-era capitalist trade. Various Party leaders sometimes raged against trade with capitalists as a threat to the revolution and a dereliction of socialist virtues, imperiling deals and, sometimes, the Chinese traders who negotiated them. The Party under Mao also never wavered from its pledge to root out and destroy capitalism inside China. All of this made the politics surrounding trade with capitalists fitful, unpredictable, and violent, sometimes verging on schizophrenic, as it was during the rampages of the Cultural Revolution. But despite this hostility and capriciousness, China's traders continued to seek out capitalist markets.

Why did they do it? Party officials sought trade with foreign capitalists for various and shifting reasons during the mid-twentieth century. Calculations of revenues and costs often drove the decision making. It was simply cheaper, and therefore more profitable, to export iron to the large and eager Japanese market than elsewhere in the late 1940s, for example. But larger political and strategic considerations also took precedence routinely in debates over CCP trade policy. In the early 1950s, for instance, leaders in Beijing assessed that expanding trade with Britain and capitalist nations on the European continent could drive a wedge between Washington and its NATO (North Atlantic Treaty Organization) allies, thereby furthering China's larger geopolitical aims, a calculation that ultimately proved correct.

Behind the Party's shifting rationales for trade with capitalists, two core convictions never wavered. First, trade always served politics. The CCP's commitment to socialist revolution remained unshakable during the Mao era, and trade policy developed within this political framework. Second, and related to the first, Mao and other top leaders believed that unchecked markets posed an existential threat to the Chinese revolution, and by extension, the Party and the Chinese state. Exposing China to the concentrated wealth of insatiable foreign firms and the governments that served them would undermine the revolution and chip away at China's sovereignty. This conviction, based partly in ideological principles and partly in China's own historical experience, led Party leaders to conclude that the CCP must safeguard its own supreme authority in the face of international markets, a conviction that has not diminished with time. The trick was finding a balance: learning to take advantage of capitalist markets abroad without endangering the Chinese state or the revolution. Embedded in this search for balance was a realization: over time, Party leaders and rank-and-file traders began to see how, with vigilance and strict controls, global markets could be used to fortify socialism in China rather than degrade it, a realization that still shapes the Party's approach to international trade today.

The story of how the Party reached this understanding is part of something larger than China's own twentieth-century history. It also helps to explain a broader, global shift that began in the mid-nineteenth century and continues to this day. This shift, which historian John King Fairbank once called "one of mankind's greatest problems," centers on the question of how to integrate the Chinese people, a full fifth of humanity, into a modern international order stitched together by economic, political, scientific, and technological connections.[10] The scale of this integration, and the magnitude of its influence on world history in the late twentieth and early twenty-first centuries, make it all the more important to understand the

CCP's early engagement with global capitalism as a key plotline in the making of the world we know today.

These factors also make China's case unique. The People's Republic of China was not the only socialist state to conduct business with foreign capitalists during the early Cold War. The Soviet Union traded with foreign capitalists, too. So did Yugoslavia, Cuba, Hungary, Poland, Czechoslovakia, the German Democratic Republic, and others.[11] Yet none of these states went on to remake the post–Cold War world through trade and commerce the way China has. The size of China's market, the scale of its ambitions, and the breadth of its engagement with global capitalism has transformed the world over the past forty years. It's no exaggeration to say the world would be a different place without the entrepreneurs, workers, consumers, and investors that China has brought to global markets.

Few would dispute the importance of these influences, but many have misunderstood their origins. Scholars generally begin the narrative of China's commercial contact with the capitalist world only after Mao left the scene, when Deng Xiaoping took control of the Party, the state, and the economy, and ushered in a new era of reform and opening up to global markets as part of China's larger Reform and Opening agenda.[12] The subtext of this narrative, which the CCP itself has espoused, is redemption. Mao's death is catharsis. He takes with him the Cultural Revolution, the Great Leap Forward, and the many other hardships and tragedies that shape our view of his rule, and the Party is reborn. Outside China, the notion of Reform and Opening as a fresh start resonates also with a persistent expectation that post-Mao China has embarked on a slow and unsteady march to the open markets and democratic principles of liberal capitalism— precisely the road Mao vowed in 1949 that China would never take. This lulling sense of inevitability has come under increasing criticism in recent years, but it nevertheless remains a powerful impression that has long distinguished Mao from Deng and his successors.

The trouble is, this impression obscures the Maoist precedents that helped to make Reform and Opening a possibility. Just as the State Planning Commission's US$4.3 billion scheme for importing fertilizer factories, industrial plants, and technologies from the capitalist world in 1973 did not emerge as a bolt from the blue, so Reform and Opening drew selectively from long-established ideological rationales and policy precedents that developed during the Maoist era. This is not to diminish the magnitude or significance of the transformation initiated by Reform and Opening itself. Rather, the point is that experiences from the Mao era helped to set the stage for what followed. They made it easier for Party leaders to recognize the benefits that might accompany a push to deepen China's ties to global markets in the late 1970s, but also reinforced the notion that this deepening could be achieved without sacrificing fundamental political authority at home.

Placing commerce at the center of analysis offers other insights. In particular, it allows us to see more clearly what Maoist ideas about foreign relations and trade actually looked like in motion. Mao's ideological convictions so dominated policy formulation during the early People's Republic that it can be tempting to conclude that he and other Chinese leaders conceived and dictated foreign policy from the cloistered confines of ideological abstraction, and that the conceptualization of foreign policy in Mao's China was coterminous with its implementation. But this obscures how foreign policy abstractions blended with the everyday practicalities of diplomacy—in this case, commercial diplomacy. Mao knew next to nothing about market economics and less still about the cultures and practices of international business. Many top leaders in Beijing were equally clueless when it came to these subjects. This left a gap in which trade officials at different stations and in different places had to interpret the relationship between political orthodoxies and market exigencies. Tracing this interplay yields new insights into the ways Maoist foreign policy ideas modulated as they passed through different minds and varying political, commercial, and institutional contexts. The result is a broader, richer, more dynamic understanding of Chinese foreign policy during the Mao era.

Tracking this Maoist commerce also forces us to venture beyond the official state-to-state relations that traditionally frame our thinking about Mao's China. A more transnational approach, one that breaks from the nation-state as the sole category of analysis, brings into focus dimensions of Chinese foreign relations that have been largely overlooked. Historians have already examined other aspects of China's transnational ties during Mao's reign, including the influence of Maoism on radical movements around the world and the smuggling activities of fisherman, travelers, and others who ferried goods to and from Mao's China for their own private gain.[13] Missing, however, is a close consideration of how the Party's own traders and planners contributed to the commercial dimensions of this Mao-era transnationalism. The CCP routinely sent cadres abroad to attend expos, tour factories, and meet with banks, firms, and trade groups. Industry reps, importers, and salesmen regularly visited China, too.

Without a doubt, high politics, national leaders, and national interests guided most of this interaction on the Chinese side after 1949. As a result, the Chinese state played a central role in these commercial relationships, and many of the documents that tell the story that follows—some of which have never been used before by historians—are held in central, provincial, and municipal archives in China. But a predominantly state-centric perspective by no means precludes insights from a transnational approach. Advertisements, catalogs, ship manifests, and other commercial documents located outside state archives offer crucial insights into the commercial interactions that linked Mao's China to the capitalist world. This hodgepodge of sources helps to reveal some of the many diverse ways that the People's Republic of China was present in the world during its formative early years.

Important as these formative PRC years are, they make up just part of the story. As this book shows, the commercial links between the CCP and global capitalism did not emerge with the founding of the People's Republic of China in 1949, just as they didn't begin with the advent of Reform and Opening in 1978. They also predated and outlasted the Cold War. Pursuing the history of these links thus requires pushing through the markers that usually partition the history of Chinese foreign relations. This, too, brings another simple but important insight: the Chinese Communist Party, the same Leninist organization that rules China today, has been unceasingly exploring and experimenting with commercial connections between Chinese socialism and global capitalism for decades longer than many assume—gaining experience, adapting, and accumulating legacies with each passing year. The post-Mao phases of this exploration are well known. Uncovering the Mao-era antecedents brings the full arc of this exploration into view.

THE ROOTS OF THESE COMMERCIAL TIES reach back to the 1930s, when the CCP began to build a trade network that linked the "liberated" areas of northeast China to international capitalist markets through the entrepôt of Hong Kong. This network, which the Party inaugurated in November 1947, was a patchwork operation. It strung together Soviet shipping, a North

Korean wharf, port city front companies, a major British bank, and other seemingly incongruous elements of early postwar international commerce. The building of this network reveals an image of the Party struggling to develop its own ways to be present, to participate, and to prosper in capitalist markets well before the founding of the People's Republic of China.

On the eve of China's "liberation" in 1949, as the Chinese civil war drew to a close, a combination of ambitions and anxieties began to drive Party leaders and economic officials to tighten control over foreign trade. In effect, the CCP began to close the Open Door that had long permitted foreign firms and businesspeople to operate freely in mainland China. But the Party was not closing the door to foreign trade entirely. As the CCP stepped into the roles of port city administrators, Hong Kong entrepreneurs, and finally, sovereigns of a new Chinese state, an uncertain and contingent climate emerged in which Chinese Communist leaders, working-level cadres, and foreign capitalists all sought to renegotiate China's relationship to the capitalist world to suit their own interests.

The founding of the PRC brought new institutions designed specifically to manage the state's trade with the capitalist world. During the Korean War, which began for China in the fall of 1950, these institutions came to be imbued with the mobilizing sentiments of China's "War to Resist America and Aid Korea." As these institutions struggled to break through the American-led embargo against China during the war, Chinese Communist traders began to see their mission of expanding trade with the capitalist world as a patriotic duty, one that gained global prominence during the Moscow International Economic Conference of April 1952. Ultimately, these formative years armed Chinese trade officials with new enthusiasm and experience, both of which set China on a new path in its commercial relations with the capitalist world as the 1950s got underway.

This enthusiasm and experience were on full display in the spring and summer of 1954 during the Geneva Conference, a key moment for China on the world stage. Most of the attendees in Geneva were preoccupied with military and political affairs, but Chinese officials, in particular the Chinese Ministry of Foreign Trade official Lei Renmin, arrived with plans to showcase Chinese products and encourage commerce. Lei's mission was to reinforce the image of "new" China as committed to peace, development, and increasing trade, a message Beijing emphasized during the mid-1950s through formal diplomacy, official trade publications intended for capitalist audiences, and international trade fairs.

When the euphoria of the Great Leap Forward swept through China several years later, in mid-1958, it reshaped the institutional and intellectual underpinnings of the nation's trade with foreign capitalists. Against the backdrop of the Sino–Soviet split and Mao's questioning of the Soviet model as China's preferred path to socialist modernity, senior CCP officials and everyday bureaucrats came to see the Great Leap Forward as offering precisely the mix of confidence and commitment China needed not just to surpass many capitalist powers in production and economic growth, but eventually to push the capitalist world off the cliff on which it had long teetered. The logic of the Leap led Chinese traders to conclude that expanding trade with the capitalist world would expedite the victory of Chinese socialism and hasten the collapse of global capitalism.

When the bubble burst and the tragedies of the Great Leap Forward became undeniably clear, the Party leadership turned to trade with the capitalist world for salvation. Chinese Communist officials sought capitalist markets during the early 1960s to purchase food, equipment, and technology that would help to end a dire national famine and return the country to sounder economic footing. In doing so, the Party drew on the practices and rationales that had guided the activities of Chinese communists in capitalist markets since the earliest days of the Pacific War.

By the early 1970s, the Chinese Communist Party was facing a world of new challenges, including the prospect of war with the Soviet Union, rapprochement with the United States, and a yawning gap between what the CCP had long promised from socialism and what it had actually delivered. In the turbulence of this moment, Party leaders and institutions were able to draw from decades of knowledge and experience to consider more expansively the question of how global markets might be used not just to pursue China's revolution, but more important, to achieve the long-term national goals that the revolution had set out to achieve in the first place, decades earlier, before the creation of the Chinese Communist state.

1

OPENING A CAPITALIST WINDOW

SOMETIME IN NOVEMBER 1947, a Soviet freighter called the *Aldan* moored in waters off the docks of Hong Kong. The ship had just arrived from the North Korean port of Rajin and was loaded with herbal medicines, soybeans, and other farm goods from China's Communist-controlled northeast—Dongbei. Before long, four men in vests emerged from the captain's quarters on the ship and prepared to disembark. Their destination was likely visible from the deck of the *Aldan:* a sturdy white building with lines of windows that stretched upward from the waterline like glass colonnades. After a short boat ride to shore, the four men, all members of the CCP, headed for the vault beneath this art deco structure, which housed the deposits of one of Britain's most influential banks, the Hongkong and Shanghai Banking Corporation (HSBC).[1]

The men probably entered the bank's north entrance on Des Voeux Road, nearest the harbor, and passed between the two bronze lions that guarded the entryway before stepping into the air-conditioned building. Then they headed downstairs, beneath the marbled banking hall, and stepped across the threshold of the twenty-ton steel door of the bank's safety deposit vault. Once inside, they huddled around a steel strongbox, one of them recalled years later, and waited for an attendant to open one of two locks on the box and leave the room.[2] The moment they were alone, one of

Figure 1.1   Des Voeux Road entrance to the Hongkong and
Shanghai Banking Corporation (HSBC) in Hong Kong,
where the Chinese Communist Party deposited its gold in
1947. Reproduced with the permission of HSBC Holdings plc.

the men used his own key to open the second lock and the four men emptied hundreds of ounces of gold from pockets concealed in the linings of
their vests. When their pockets were empty, the heavy box was locked again
and secured in the vault, and the men slipped into the humid streets of
Hong Kong. By nightfall, with the gold in the vault and the Dongbei cargo
floating safely in the harbor, the men had completed a historic step toward
plugging the Chinese Communist revolution into global capitalist markets.

These four men, all economic experts within the CCP, were in Hong
Kong to put the final touches on a trade network that linked the "liberated"
areas of Dongbei to international markets through the British colony of

Hong Kong. The soybeans they shipped, the gold they smuggled, and the wireless radios and medicine they bought with the proceeds—all of it signaled a commitment by the CCP to open its own window into markets abroad, an ambition that had been gestating within the Party since as early as the start of the Pacific War in the summer of 1937. To understand the rationales that produced this ambition, and that compelled four Communist revolutionaries into the bowels of the HSBC bank in November 1947, it is important first to appreciate the wartime environment that shaped CCP thinking on trade and revolution in the decade before the arrival of the *Aldan*.

Mobilizing for Trade

"The characteristics of war have determined the features of wartime economic work," observed Li Fuchun, a leading CCP economic planner from Hunan, during a speech just before the *Aldan* arrived in Hong Kong to sell its Manchurian soybeans.[3] His remark captured perfectly the centrality of war in the evolution of CCP thinking on trade between 1937 and 1947. Two entangled conflicts shaped the Party's outlook during the era.

The first was the war with Japan. The Sino–Japanese War began on July 7, 1937, when a dispute between Chinese and Japanese troops near a rail junction outside Beiping, as Beijing was then called, escalated until both sides began shooting. The dispute concerned a missing Japanese soldier, but it was fueled by tensions that had been brewing for years. In September 1931, Japanese troops had invaded northeast China after an explosion destroyed railway tracks owned by Japan in southern Manchuria. The Japanese military blamed Chinese nationalists for the railway "attack," but Chinese observers claimed, correctly, that the Japanese army planned the explosion as a pretext for invasion.[4] Six months later, Japan established a puppet state in Dongbei called Manchukuo and the hostility deepened. By 1935, the Japanese army harbored plans to push deeper into north China to suppress anti-Japanese sentiment in the region, which by then had metastasized in response to years of Japanese aggression.[5]

These antagonisms enflamed the July 1937 skirmish outside Beiping and the fighting spread south to Shanghai, then on to Nanjing, the capital of Nationalist China. There, beginning in December, the enmity and violence reached new heights when Japanese troops murdered as many as three hundred thousand civilians and former Nationalist soldiers who had fled the fighting in Shanghai.[6] Generalissimo Chiang Kai-shek, head of the Kuomintang (KMT) Party and the leader of Nationalist China, had pledged that Nanjing would never fall.[7] Now he and his government fled west, leaving behind any hope that China might repel Japan with a single blow.

Despite these setbacks for China, Mao Zedong sensed opportunity in a war with Japan because of its likely influence on a second conflict, a Chinese civil war, which he believed was more important. The tall, still-slender forty-three-year-old was living with his third wife in a merchant's home on the west side of Yan'an, a dusty market town in the hills of northern Shaanxi Province.[8] Mao and the rest of the Party leadership had been there since January 1937, taking stock. The Communists had already been fighting the KMT for a decade, and Mao understood that this conflict posed the more immediate threat to his revolution. It was the KMT that had driven the CCP into the wilderness of Shaanxi in the first place. In October 1934, the Nationalists had dislodged the Communists from the mountains of southeastern China and hounded them for thousands of miles until they finally reached Shaanxi in late October 1935. The CCP had found temporary safety in the northwest, but throughout 1936 they suffered under KMT blockades designed to strangle Yan'an and the surrounding Shaan-Gan-Ning Border Region, a Communist stronghold that straddled the borders of Shaanxi, Gansu, and Ningxia Provinces. Chiang Kai-shek had erected the blockades to weaken the Communists before attacking and destroying them for good. But just as Mao had hoped, the fight against Japan intervened to thwart Chiang's designs.

On December 4, 1936, Chiang Kai-shek flew to Xi'an to discuss plans with local warlords for breaking CCP resistance, which remained his top priority. But the de facto ruler of northwestern China, a warlord named Zhang Xueliang, believed the greatest threat to China was Japan, not communism. Zhang had been negotiating with the CCP since April and had already agreed not just to refrain from attacking the Communists, but to arm them as well.[9] The Communists' position strengthened even further in the early hours of December 12, 1936, when Zhang Xueliang's troops kidnapped Chiang Kai-shek and pressured him to drop his plans for an assault against the CCP and to join a United Front with the Communists against Japan instead. Weeks of negotiation followed, and on Christmas Day, 1936, Chiang agreed finally to shuffle his priorities.[10]

These crisis weeks in northwest China transformed the CCP's economic prospects. Inside the walls that ringed Yan'an, Party leaders began to recalibrate their thinking away from the challenges of surviving the KMT blockade and toward the prospect of exploiting the new alliance in pursuit of long-term objectives.

Chiang Kai-shek dismantled the blockades in the spring of 1937.[11] Even more promising for the Communists, KMT financing began to arrive. The Nationalist government had agreed to pay the CCP 500,000 yuan each month as part of the new United Front alliance against Japan. Mao grumbled about the sums, but every yuan helped.[12] The Communist bases had scarcely been able to produce enough to feed and clothe themselves before the United Front, let alone churn out surplus goods for export. Aid from the Soviet Union and the Communist International (Comintern) had certainly helped, but this support was neither stable nor sufficient.[13] Now, with regular infusions of KMT cash, the Party could tap a larger pool of capital to finance its trade.[14]

To handle these funds and to coordinate the alliance, in August 1937 the CCP began to open offices in cities across Nationalist-controlled China. The first five sprouted in Nanjing, Xi'an, Lanzhou, Taiyuan, and Shanghai. By war's end, fifty more had emerged.[15] The Party called them "Eighth Route Army" and "New Fourth Army" offices after the two main Communist armies they supported, both of which now fell under nominal KMT control as part of the United Front. The new offices quickly became economic beachheads for the CCP in market cities across China, but they also served a political function as testaments to the growing legitimacy of the CCP. Party officials were now operating offices openly in KMT-controlled cities with financial support from the KMT itself.

Neither party expected the solidarity to last. The United Front had been coerced—literally at gunpoint, for Chiang—and both parties intended to rule China outright, without power-sharing concessions to the other. This made for a shaky alliance from the outset. Already by late 1940, Chiang had halted much of his support to the CCP and had resurrected a blockade along the southern and western perimeters of the Shaan-Gan-Ning Base Area.[16] Still, the cooperative spirit lingered long enough for the CCP to develop the Army Offices it would use for trade with large mainland markets and, ultimately, overseas markets as well.

While the United Front furnished opportunities and institutions for trade, the exigencies of war created new demands for it. Mao and his deputies were busy throughout the summer and fall of 1937 working supply lines to keep Communist troops fed, shod, and fighting. The Eighth Route Army Office network could not have come sooner as far as the Party was concerned. Cables from Yan'an at the time reveal a CCP leadership struggling with shortfalls on numerous fronts. The Huabei region in north China had no money and needed 5,000 yuan to cover expenses, Mao wrote to Ye Jianying in early August.[17] Ye, a Red Army officer then based in Xi'an, had been tied up in United Front negotiations throughout the spring and summer.[18] He received another urgent note from Mao two days later. Yan'an had no food, Mao said, and the cadres there would soon go hungry. On August 17, Mao sent more instructions to Bo Gu and Lin Boqu, both of whom were in Nanjing to negotiate the finer points of United Front arrangements. Mao urged them both to nudge their Nationalist contacts to prepare 600,000 yuan for the CCP before August 21 and added that the Party already lacked money to buy rice.[19] The desperate tone of these requests likely included a dose of theatrics. After all, many of these solicitations coincided with the final stages of United Front negotiations, and ratcheting up the sense of urgency aided CCP negotiators as they tried to pry every yuan they could from KMT coffers under the emerging terms of the United Front.

But Mao's pleas did not end with the United Front negotiations—they persisted for the rest of 1937 and into 1938.[20] Internal CCP communications unrelated to United Front talks also reveal a similar tone of anxiety over supplies and funds. In late August, Mao sent a note to Pan Hannian, chief of the Party's new Eighth Route Army Office in Shanghai. Assistance had begun to arrive, Mao explained, but it was not enough. "Nanjing gave us only 500,000 [yuan] this month, not 1,000,000," Mao told Pan. They also gave "no arms or any other kind of supplement; [there is] only a supplement of clothing and a small amount of ammunition," he wrote.[21] The Party also still needed arms, rain gear, gas masks, and cotton-padded clothes.[22] The weather in the north was already cooler and Red Army troops would soon need blankets and thick clothing made from hides, too.[23]

Despite the urgency of these requests, the Party's top leaders remained wary of the large capitalist markets that were capable of providing the resources they needed. Mao and others had absorbed the Leninist principle that trade with rich capitalists was inherently exploitative. It was driven by monopolists' search for markets to carve up and control for themselves, they believed.[24] This was more than an abstraction for many in the CCP. It was a tangible truth that resonated with personal experience. They had been born into a China that was already divided and occupied by capitalist-imperialist powers, and the indignity of this experience fueled much of the Party's revolutionary nationalism. For them, it was capitalist trade, un-bridled and unwanted, that had sliced open a national wound. Leninism offered a framework that made sense of these grievances.

Yet this wariness was not so doctrinaire that it foreclosed the possibility of doing business with capitalists. Mao argued that context mattered, too. Threats ebbed and flowed with the tide of history, and so did opportunities. At a Party meeting on May 3, 1937, Mao stressed that Japanese imperialism had become the "primary contradiction" facing the Chinese Communist Party. The contradiction between China and what he called "general" imperialism had transformed during the 1930s into a "particularly prominent" and "par-ticularly acute" contradiction between *Japanese* imperialism and China. Tokyo's intentions were clear, Mao told his colleagues. "Japanese imperialism has im-plemented a policy of completely conquering China." To confront this threat, the CCP had to shuffle its ideological defenses. Mao argued that the Party "must relegate contradictions between a number of other [forms of] imperi-alism and China to a subordinate position."[25]

Mao did not arrive at this position on his own. A sense of unease had been growing in Moscow since Hitler's rise to power in January 1933, and this apprehension colored Soviet and international communist assessments of the world situation. In December 1933, the Political Bureau (Politburo) of the Communist Party of the Soviet Union (CPSU) approved a foreign policy outlook that identified the fascist powers of Germany, Italy, and Japan as the main threat to the Soviet Union rather than British, French, or US imperialism. The Comintern was quick to agree. During the organ-ization's Seventh Congress in the summer of 1935, delegates approved a new line calling on communists everywhere to strive for a worldwide front against fascist aggression.[26] The CCP leadership fell into line once it learned of the Comintern's new position sometime in the fall of 1935.[27] At an en-larged CCP Politburo meeting in mid-December, the Central Committee affirmed the need to establish alliances with all countries, parties, and individuals who opposed the Japanese threat—capitalists included.[28] Against this backdrop, Mao's pronouncement in early May 1937 that Japan had become China's "primary contradiction" represented not the chairman's independent analysis, but rather his alignment with an established Comintern line.

Regardless of where this assessment originated, Mao insisted on limits to antifascist cooperation. "To defeat the Japanese aggressors [we should] rely mainly on our own strength," he explained in late July 1937. Regarding trade and aid, he said the CCP must "struggle for sympathy from England, the United States, and France for our anti-Japanese [resistance]," but the Party should also "struggle for their assistance under conditions that do not forfeit China's territorial integrity or sovereign rights." Trade with capitalists was indispensable, but also dangerous. It must be controlled.[29]

This view produced an early and abiding tension in CCP trade policy. On the one hand, the Party must remain aloof from foreign capitalists to safeguard China's independence; on the other, it must "struggle" to engage them. The Party reconciled these divergent aims in the concept of *zili gengsheng,* or "revival through one's own efforts." *Zili gengsheng,* which became a pillar of economic policy in the Mao era, was never just a policy. It was a disposition, a blend of caution and ambition from which Party leaders could derive the orientation and scope of China's economic interaction in a given historical context. The term offered a foundation for thinking about the political implications of trade, especially the dependencies and vulnerabilities that accompanied it.[30] Trade could breed dependency if not carefully controlled, and dependency brought vulnerability. In its broadest sense, *zili gengsheng* meant never trusting one's fate to outsiders and never placing all of one's eggs in a single basket.[31] As long as this condition was met, the conditions were ripe in early autumn 1937 for the CCP to develop its own sturdy connections to capitalist markets. The ideological rationale was in place, the institutional scaffolding stood ready, and the economic incentives were undeniable.

The Hong Kong Foothold

Against this backdrop, the CCP turned to Hong Kong. Throughout the fall of 1937, opportunities to trade with mainland markets dwindled as Japanese troops conquered China's largest cities. By December, the Japanese army controlled Beiping, Tianjin, Zhangjiakou, Hohhot, Shijiazhuang, Taiyuan, Shanghai, and Nanjing, and the Japanese navy was blockading ports along China's coast.[32] As Tokyo consolidated control over these markets, Party leaders pulled together plans for an Eighth Route Army Office in Hong Kong, where the CCP had been running underground operations since before the outbreak of the Sino–Japanese War. An office in the British colony seemed ideal for soliciting donations from anti-Japan sympathizers overseas. It would also provide access to the markets that Party traders would need to transform cash into supplies for Communist bases and the front lines.

The Party had first to consider whom to place in charge of such an operation. Sometime in late 1937, most likely in late September or early October, the Party's keenest observer of foreign affairs, Zhou Enlai, proposed that a cadre named Liao Chengzhi head the effort.[33] The twenty-nine-year-old Liao was an ideal candidate. He came from impeccable revolutionary stock. His father, Liao Zhongkai, had been a renowned modernizer and patriot, a skilled financier, and a founder of the KMT's predecessor, the Revolutionary Alliance.[34] The elder Liao was also a martyr: assassins shot him to death in August 1925, a tragedy that brought the limited solace of conferring on the Liao family unimpeachable revolutionary credentials. Liao Chengzhi's mother, He Xiangning, was a revolutionary in her own right. She joined the Revolutionary Alliance the same year as her husband, making her the second female member of the organization.[35] This distinguished lineage carried weight with Chinese communities in Hong Kong, Macao, Southeast Asia, and farther afield, and the CCP hoped to capitalize on this cachet by assigning Liao the role of heading the office's fundraising in Hong Kong.

Liao had other qualifications. He was cosmopolitan—born in Tokyo, he spoke fluent Japanese, and his American-accented English was so colloquial that he garnished his speeches with "God only knows" and other natural expressions.[36] He had also studied French, German, and Russian.[37] Revolutionary work had taken him to Europe, where he organized strikes in Antwerp, Rotterdam, Hamburg, and Marseilles.[38] By the time Mao sent for Liao in Yan'an one evening in October 1937, the polyglot who turned up was every bit the product of these experiences. But he was also earthy and affable. Liao was a hybrid, equally at home in an earthen hut or a Hong Kong flat. He was the perfect face for an Eighth Route Army Office in Hong Kong.

"Comrade Zhou really knows how to choose people," Mao supposedly told Liao when he arrived for a briefing on his assignment. "[He] knows how to gauge them and assign them to the right positions," the chairman said. He wanted Liao to know that he enjoyed the Party's full support, and that the decision to send Liao south, first to Nanjing for training and then on to Hong Kong, was not Zhou's alone. "I also raised my hand," Mao explained, "this is the Central Committee's decision."[39] It was a vote of confidence from the Party's senior-most ranks, but the subtext was also clear: the Central Committee would be watching.

With Liao on board, the Party pressed ahead. Administrators penciled the future Hong Kong office into the organizational charts: Liao would report to the Central Committee and the Central Yangtze River Bureau, a Wuhan-based organization headed by Zhou Enlai that oversaw CCP work in Hong Kong and Macao. But before moving further, the Party had to clear a major impediment: no one had asked the British yet whether they would permit a Chinese Communist office in the colony. The chance to raise the issue arrived sometime in 1938, when Zhou Enlai convened a forgotten but fateful meeting with Britain's ambassador to Nationalist China, Archibald Clark Kerr.[40]

Zhou had several factors in his favor when he made his case for a Hong Kong office, not least a sympathetic counterpart. Ambassador Clark Kerr had arrived in China in the winter of 1938, fresh from an ambassadorship in Baghdad. His predecessor in China, Sir Hughe Montgomery Knatchbull-Hugessen, cut short his tenure after a Japanese plane strafed his official car as he drove to a meeting with the Japanese ambassador just outside Shanghai the previous August. Japanese Embassy officials expressed "regret" for the maiming of Sir Hughe and blamed the incident on mistaken identity, but the episode did little to endear Clark Kerr to the Japanese position in China.[41] Not that he was likely to favor Tokyo in any case. Clark Kerr had a reputation for sympathizing with the plights of the countries in which he served.[42]

The newly arrived British ambassador was also feeling the weight of Britain's strategic predicament in East Asia. Throughout the summer and fall of 1937, London had struggled to maintain neutrality in the Sino–Japanese War without undermining Britain's strategic and commercial interests in the region, a nearly impossible task that nonetheless created incentives for supporting China's resistance. Among these was a desire to protect the business interests of British firms operating in East Asia. Within weeks of the outbreak of fighting near Beiping in July 1937, KMT orders for tanks, planes, and ammunition had begun to arrive at the offices of British merchants. Many of these goods would have to be transshipped through Hong Kong. For British traders, these purchase orders represented business as usual; military shipments had routed through Hong Kong prior to the outbreak of war as a matter of course.[43] "We consider our function straightforward and as free of political unpleasantness as our previous armaments dealings," the Shanghai office of the Jardine Engineering Corporation explained in an August telegram to Hong Kong colleagues. The Nationalist government had asked the firm to provide British tanks and other armaments, all of which the KMT hoped to receive at Guangdong following transshipment through Hong Kong. Any move to limit these emerging opportunities could, at the least, run contrary to the interests of British firms. "Naturally," wrote the Foreign Office, "Jardine Matheson & Co. Ltd. would like to do the business if it is feasible for them to do so."[44]

Britain's long-term aims played into Zhou's hands as well. Appearing to spurn China in its hour of need risked "alienating the goodwill of China on which the prosperity of Hong Kong ultimately depends," the Colonial Office wrote in September. As far as the Colonial Office was concerned, "a few risks for China's sake would probably be a good investment in that it would reinforce that goodwill after the war."[45] This "investment" created two potential gains for London. First, allowing support to funnel into China through Hong Kong would preserve the colony's position as a shipping and financial hub, contrary to Japan's revisionist aspirations. "Hong Kong herself has nothing to gain by Japanese domination in the south [of China], for they would no doubt attempt to cut out Hong Kong's position as an entrepôt center," the Colonial Office reasoned.[46] Second, circumscribing Hong Kong's position in the China trade could cost British firms market share after the Sino–Japanese conflict had run its course. "I venture to put forward further consideration that if we now cut off arms supply to China through Hongkong, we are unlikely to obtain [a] large share in rearmament of China after the termination of hostilities," the British Embassy in Nanjing wrote.[47]

London's sensitivity to its reputation in China was justified. "The Chinese [Nationalist] Government and the educated classes are watching with the utmost anxiety for the reaction of His Majesty's Government to Japan's suggestion that restrictions should be imposed on the use of Hongkong as an entrepôt for the import of arms into China," the British Embassy in Nanjing wrote to London on August 29.[48] Chinese observers, including CCP leaders, were indeed keeping a close eye on London's moves. In a July 21 instruction, the Party's central leadership lumped the British together with the French to argue that both colonial powers disapproved of China's nationwide resistance effort. London and Paris were clinging to the hope that China and Japan would reach a compromise. "This approach of theirs, objectively speaking, will benefit Japan," Party leaders concluded.[49]

With these pressures churning in the back of Ambassador Clark Kerr's mind, Zhou Enlai was well positioned to make the case for opening a CCP office in Hong Kong. He pointed out to the ambassador that a discreet presence could be used to channel funds and supplies quietly from sympathetic compatriots abroad to anti-Japanese resistance fighters on the mainland.[50] If the CCP managed the office properly, London would be able to retain the appearance of neutrality while still seeing to its own strategic and commercial interests in the region. Clark Kerr agreed, and with his support the CCP received approval from Hong Kong authorities to open the new office.[51]

The CCP did not enjoy carte blanche in the colony. Too conspicuous a support structure for China threatened to undermine London's efforts to retain an air of balanced neutrality. "The Chinese naturally look to Hong Kong as the entrepôt for the supply of war materials," the Foreign Office explained in a September 1937 memorandum. However, "the Japanese will certainly take steps to prevent it being so used should the traffic grow large enough to become a serious menace."[52] London also had little appetite for exacerbating tensions with Japan. War would not break out in Europe until September 1939, but already German expansionism foreshadowed conflict in Europe. Picking a fight with Tokyo raised the possibility of Britain being pulled into two conflicts on two fronts, with little assistance expected from the United States, which remained mired in isolationism.[53] Zhou Enlai fully recognized London's delicate position. He promised Clark Kerr that CCP members operating in Hong Kong would refrain from any displays or activities that might undermine London's official neutrality in the Sino–Japanese conflict.[54]

The CCP moved quickly to establish the new office, which opened its doors in early 1938 at 18 Queen's Road Central.[55] To conceal its activities and affiliation, the Party disguised the office, which was tucked into a thicket of firms in the heart of Hong Kong's central commercial district, to look like a tea shop. Outside the office door hung a sign that identified the shop only as the Yuehua Tea Company.[56]

Despite this attempt at concealment, the bustle at the office began to erode its cover from the outset. Staff at Yuehua recruited hundreds of patriots and skilled workers to join CCP bases on the mainland. Yuehua's "tea merchants" also handled the logistics for moving these progressives to mainland bases. In 1938 and 1939 alone, Yuehua personnel ferried over six hundred people from Hong Kong into China. The office also worked hand-in-glove with the China Defense League to raise funds, translate and distribute CCP propaganda, and publish anti-Japan newspapers. Incomplete records show the Hong Kong Eighth Route Army Office raised roughly 2.2 million yuan during the first few years of the war, much of which it used to purchase blankets, bullets, and everything in between for Communist troops on the mainland.[57] This commotion hardly made for a discreet operation, even under the cover of a busy tea shop.

Little of this activity would have slipped past Japanese officials. Tokyo had been aware of Hong Kong's indispensability to "anti-Japanese" resistance since late summer 1937 and was keeping a close eye on the colony. As early as September 1, the aide-de-camp to the Japanese marine minister expressed his concern over the matter directly to Britain's naval attaché in Tokyo.[58] Japan's frustration only mounted as the months passed and supplies continued to funnel through Hong Kong into China. "Something must be done," the Japanese consul general in Hong Kong told his US counterpart in late March 1938.[59] Many of the goods routing through Hong Kong pushed well past the limits of inconspicuousness. Antiaircraft guns, trucks, and even airplanes passed through Hong Kong's "neutral" shipping facilities bound for China.[60] Most of this traffic represented KMT rather than CCP shipments, but Japanese officials had little incentive to parse between recipients. Nor did British authorities, who continued to wring their hands over how to ensure Hong Kong's neutrality without alienating China, infuriating Japan, or undermining the British merchant houses that dominated the colony's trade routes.

Everything came to a head for the Yuehua Tea Company on March 13, 1939. That morning, the Hong Kong Police Special Branch raided the company, seized documents, and arrested several staff. Local police also arrested Lian Guan, who oversaw daily operations at the company and was nominally Liao Chengzhi's personal secretary. When an alarmed Liao Chengzhi raised the matter the next day with the police chief and the head of the Hong Kong Special Branch, the police chief told him dryly that his office had been unaware that Yuehua had any connections to the Eighth Route Army Office.[61]

The Yuehua staff members were ultimately released and the whole affair chalked up to a mistake, but Liao had little trouble reading between the lines. Hong Kong authorities were becoming queasy with the Party's presence in the colony. On March 16, Liao cabled the Central Committee and the Southern Bureau, which had replaced the Yangtze Bureau in October 1938, to suggest that the raid was an effort to pressure him to leave the colony. For two months, he explained, local authorities had been stepping up investigations into six "patriotic" Chinese organizations in the colony, and not without cause. Liao recognized that affiliates of the Eight Route Army Office had begun to push the limits of acceptable public discourse in the colony. He told the Party leadership that Song Qingling, the founder and public face of the China Defense League, had recently castigated British imperialism in a public speech for having surrendered to fascism.[62] Public displays of this sort did little to endear Liao's operation to local authorities or to Foreign Office staff in London. By late June, "the anti-Party sentiment [in Hong Kong] had heightened considerably," Liao reported.[63] The British had had enough. Hong Kong authorities shuttered Yuehua for good before the end of 1939, but Liao and his staff continued to operate in the colony quietly without a cover office.[64]

The demise of the Yuehua Tea Company was a setback, but the Party learned important lessons from the operation that shaped its trade with capitalists. Foremost among these was the need to tighten security. The Party leadership took seriously the loss of sensitive documents during the Yuehua flap, and within weeks issued new guidance designed to shroud CCP commercial work in secrecy. On April 1, 1939, the Southern Bureau cabled new rules to all offices under its command: do not store secret Party documents inside offices; treat Party financial accounting materials as top secret; burn sensitive cables involving intelligence work and secret affairs immediately after reading them; burn other documents within five days of their arrival; do not allow local parties to borrow office space; and burn this guidance after reading it.[65] The CCP Secretariat followed up on April 12 with similar instructions.[66] The tone of this guidance was unmistakable: commercial work in non-CCP areas was, and must be, secretive—more akin to intelligence operations than open propaganda work.

None of this meant the Party had any intention of curtailing its Hong Kong trade. Communist troops were too desperate for that. If anything, the consensus among the Party leadership leaned in the other direction, toward expanding trade. On April 13, three senior Party officials—Zhu De, Peng Dehuai, and Yang Shangkun—wrote to Nie Rongzhen and other top Red Army commanders to underscore the importance of trade as a vital part of the army's efforts to overcome its economic difficulties.[67]

The challenge, then, was to expand foreign trade while ensuring its sustainability through secrecy. Not coincidentally, the most promising model for achieving these aims stood just a few hundred meters from where the Yuehua Tea Company once stood, on Connaught Road Central. There, a small firm called Liow & Company was doing a brisk business in mainland trade from a cramped office space. The firm looked like any other importer-exporter on the street. Capitalized at just US$20,000, it was run by a man who appeared preoccupied with the same chores that consumed most small business owners. But this company, known in Chinese as Lianhe Hang, took its orders directly from the CCP. In early 1938, CCP operatives in Hong Kong recognized the value of opening another firm in the colony, one that had no discernable ties to the Yuehua Tea Company. Staff at the Eight Route Army Office, which would oversee this secret company, intended to use it as a clean front for opening bank accounts, renting warehouse space, and arranging shipping contracts.[68] The firm, which was up and running by late summer 1938, represented a new, and ultimately more durable, approach to CCP commerce with the capitalist world.

The man at the head of this operation, Qin Bangli, looked the part. He had the budding paunch of a bourgeois climber, an impression he encouraged by wearing suits and ties and slicking his hair with pomade. His background also fit perfectly with the Party's emerging consensus on what kind of cadre could burrow into capitalist markets. Qin was born in 1908 into a family of local notables in Wuxi, a famed commercial center just west of Shanghai. His father died young and left the family poor, a trauma that pushed financial concerns to the front of Qin's mind at a young age. As a teenager, he apprenticed at a local bank, a path that suggested a search for prosperity, but eventually he found purpose in the mission of the Chinese Communist Party.[69]

Figure 1.2   Qin Bangli, pioneer of the Party's underground commerce in Hong Kong, in an undated portrait. Reproduced from *Red China Resources* (Beijing: Zhonghua Book Company, 2010).

Qin seems to have found his way to the Party through his brother, Qin Bangxian, a senior CCP cadre who was known mostly by his pseudonym, Bo Gu. In 1930, Bo recommended his younger brother to Chen Yun, who was then the head of the Party's organization department in Jiangsu. Chen, a former Shanghai typesetter and a rising star who would go on to guide economic policy at the national level for decades, no doubt sensed opportunity in the younger Qin, whose background in banking and trusted elder brother suggested a promising future in secret commercial work. Within a year, Qin Bangli had opened at least five small stores on behalf of the CCP in Shanghai and one in the southern port city of Shantou. These shops sold a range of goods, such as furniture and stationery, but they also provided vital funds and fronts for underground Party members. To Qin, these companies offered experience. He learned how to lay a foundation of commercial legitimacy just sturdy enough to support a host of illicit activities in Shanghai during the 1930s, including the procurement of supplies for the Party's base in the mountains along the Jiangxi-Fujian border.[70]

Qin's success with these shops revealed an aptitude for blending entrepreneurship with underground Party work, and in 1938 Chen Yun sent him to Hong Kong to support Liao Chengzhi by establishing what would become Liow & Company.[71] The assignment came with significant autonomy. None among the senior ranks of the CCP, save perhaps Chen Yun, was in a position to dictate the specifics of how Qin should run the Hong Kong company. No one had the technical skills, the business experience, or the time to manage his activities closely, so the leadership had no choice but to delegate authority for day-to-day business down to Qin and other cadres operating in Hong Kong. But strategic decisions still required approval from the Central Committee, the Yangtze River Bureau, and later, the Southern Bureau. For instance, after local officials decided that "Lianhe Hang" would make a suitable Chinese name for the company, they had to request formal approval from the Party Center before using it. The idea was to allow the Party's central leaders to retain control over strategic decisions, as any disciplined Leninist organization required, without hamstringing tactical operations on the ground, which moved at the pace of markets.

On the ground in Hong Kong, Qin slipped into the rhythms and norms that structured life for much of the colony's entrepreneurial class. He also cultivated relationships with merchants and financiers. But Party needs, not profits alone, drove his agenda. CCP bases were perennially short of Western medicines, for example, so Qin befriended the manager of a Hong Kong pharmaceutical company. He cultivated a relationship with another firm because it sold the wireless communication equipment needed by Red Army guerrilla units fighting in the north.[72]

Qin's networking, his suits, his downtown office—all of it served the revolution. It was a crafted persona. Behind the scenes, he scrimped every Hong Kong dollar he could. His daughter later recalled that the family lived in a rented apartment so cramped that family members shared the only sofa for a bed. Qin passed the early years of the Sino–Japanese War in this blended state, capitalist in practice but communist by conviction. When Hong Kong finally fell to the Japanese on Christmas Day 1941, Liow & Company continued to operate quietly. Qin himself left Hong Kong for the mainland and eventually settled in Wuzhou, a small city in eastern Guangxi Province, but he trekked back to Hong Kong routinely to monitor operations at Liow & Company.[73]

Qin kept busy by expanding his operations into the lucrative tire and tung oil trades in the early 1940s.[74] As he did so, the Central Committee began to consolidate its position on foreign trade. On March 23, 1940, the CCP Secretariat instructed Communist bases to use tax policies and administrative controls to bring trade into line with the Party's wartime goals. The same instructions urged officials to avoid importing goods that were unnecessary or that could be produced locally. The Secretariat also encouraged cadres to facilitate "appropriate" exports to pay for essential imports.[75] More guidance soon followed asking bases to establish trade bureaus to manage these tasks.[76] Behind these instructions lay a deepening conviction that foreign trade with capitalist markets would continue apace—not freely, but in accordance with the Party's objectives. By the time Tokyo surrendered to Allied forces in August 1945, the trade question that most concerned the CCP leadership was not whether trade would continue with capitalists, but how and where.

The Northeast Connection

The end of the Sino–Japanese War in August 1945 left the CCP with new territories, more resources, and pressing demands in north China, all of which encouraged a push for trade on a grander scale. In late summer, the Soviet Red Army rushed into northeast China as part of a strategic offensive designed to crush the Japanese military in Dongbei. For the CCP leadership, the arrival of Soviet forces in Manchuria amounted to a replacement of hostile Japanese interlopers with friendly Soviet ones. The newly arrived Soviet troops were slow to reverse course, waiting until March 1946 to begin withdrawing from the region, but the CCP used this interim to fill the region with units from its own army, which had grown significantly.[77]

Nearly 100,000 Eighth Route Army soldiers converged on Manchuria in late 1945 and mixed with scattered underground forces that began to resurface after the Japanese surrender.[78] By Mao's count, he had 910,000 Chinese Red Army soldiers at his disposal in April 1945. His rural militia forces added another 2.2 million troops to the total. The CCP itself had grown, too. Mao figured the Party ranks had swollen to 1.2 million women and men near the end of the war with Japan.[79] All this expansion brought both relief and anxiety, particularly for the Party's logisticians and economic specialists. More Party members meant more mouths to feed, and more troops meant more men to arm, especially because Mao did not expect the postwar peace to last.

He was convinced that his forces would soon be tested in an all-out conflict with the KMT. Mao harbored no illusions that negotiations with the Nationalists would lead to a lasting peace. "The Kuomintang peace offensive is a complete sham," he cabled the Party's Northeast Bureau on October 22, 1946. "The civil war will not stop, [and we] must make it difficult for Chiang to enter the northeast."[80] The conflict ahead would be "long and arduous," he wrote to the Northeast Bureau a few days later, and the Party must prepare accordingly.[81] This included securing funds and equipment to fight a sustained war. Having witnessed over the preceding eight years how useful trade with capitalists could be during a protracted conflict, the Party had already begun to lay the groundwork for linking CCP-occupied north China to its fledgling commercial operations in Hong Kong.

The Central Committee took a step in this direction on May 3, 1946, when it documented its thinking on the prospects for future trade with capitalists. This was a fluid moment for China, the committee believed. "The United States still does not believe that the CCP can engage in long-term economic cooperation with [Americans]," the Party's leaders wrote. "[They] still suspect we want to conduct economic cooperation with the Soviet Union in order to resist the United States." As a result, American interactions with local CCP units "have an exploratory aspect to them[.]" This was natural, the Central Committee judged, but temporary. "Once they [the Americans] are able to clarify completely our position, then [they] will be able to determine their policies and guidelines with respect to us."[82]

The Central Committee made it clear that under these circumstances, passivity would not do. "We should adopt a guideline of implementing trade and economic cooperation with the United States, England, France, and various [other] countries," the Central Committee wrote. But Party leaders were also apprehensive. Closer contact brought closer threats, particularly when dealing with Americans. The Central Committee told cadres to reject any attempt by Americans to manipulate their way into a military presence on the Shandong Peninsula, where they were active already. "American capitalism wants to control economic activity in China (including the

liberated areas)," the Central Committee wrote. "This tendency is inevitable."[83] The Party was treading a precarious path, which required vigilance.
Still, the Committee judged that the gains would be worth it, and in a few
short months, several cadres would depart from Dalian to prove it.

Tucked north of the Yellow Sea between Korea Bay and the Bohai Sea,
the city of Dalian held the allure of an ice-free port in northern China
linked by sea to Hong Kong. People and goods could also reach Dalian
by rail from the northeastern city of Harbin, which CCP troops had conquered in April 1946 on the heels of the departing Soviets.[84] Perhaps most
important, Dalian was also still firmly under Soviet control. When Moscow
and the KMT government signed a Sino–Soviet Treaty of Friendship and
Alliance in August 1945, the two sides had agreed that Soviet-occupied
Dalian would become a "free port open to the commerce and shipping of
all nations."[85] The agreement soon proved a farce, however, as Soviet military
authorities permitted port access to just a trickle of vessels. By January 1947,
port traffic remained fully under military control.[86] Moscow justified its
lingering presence by observing that the Sino–Soviet Treaty allowed Soviet forces to administer the city and neighboring Port Arthur as long as a
formal state of war existed with Japan.[87] Until a peace treaty was signed
with Tokyo, the Soviets would stay put.

Soviet occupation provided ideal cover for the CCP to establish a presence in Dalian. Party officials gathered in the city just weeks after the Soviets took control. In September 1945, the CCP began to establish "private"
companies in the city, many of which opened factories that produced boots,
uniforms, and materiel; others were used to "receive" enemy property.[88]
None of these outfits could operate openly as organizations of the Chinese
Communist Party. The Soviets' precarious position in the city required ob-
fuscation. The same treaty that Moscow had contorted into justifying Soviet military control of Dalian—the 1945 Sino–Soviet Treaty of Friendship
and Alliance—also recognized the sovereignty of the Nationalist government over China. This recognition, in turn, prevented the Soviets from
collaborating openly with Chinese Communists. Further complicating
matters, a new US consulate general opened in the city in April 1946, which
brought to Dalian the prying eyes of Consul General Merrell Benninghoff
and his staff, all of whom watched intently for signs of CCP activities.

The CCP and the Soviets nevertheless managed to conceal their cooperation in Dalian. Staff at the US consulate general strongly suspected

collaboration between the two but could not confirm it.[89] Maintaining this facade required no small amount of orchestration. Chinese sources reveal that Soviet military authorities generally acquiesced to the CCP's military production near Dalian, but forbade Chinese Communists from producing artillery within the city itself.[90] The Soviets also prohibited the Americans from straying beyond the city limits, an arrangement that effectively separated CCP production from American observation.[91]

Moscow's tacit support for the CCP in Dalian went beyond permitting military production. Li Zhuping, a Party member who arrived in Dalian in 1947 to work in military logistics, recalled nearly forty years later how a Soviet lieutenant colonel once inquired into the markings of the ships that CCP "businessmen" were using for their trade. The Soviet officer explained that if Chinese "old friends" shared identifying details of the ships ahead of time, he could pass the information along to his contacts in the Soviet military, who could then ensure that the arrival and departure of these ships was made "convenient." Naturally, CCP officials passed the information along.[92] Some of these ships arrived bearing medicines, cotton, tobacco leaf, and fuel. Others brought grain, rubber, chemicals, and wood. Once unloaded at Dalian, they were filled again with exports of cotton cloth and yarn, fishing nets, salt, and glass, much of it bound for Vladivostok.[93]

The approvals that kept this trade flowing were quiet testimonials to the international frictions that the Party had to overcome in Dalian. In some ways, commerce there resembled the Party's trade in Hong Kong in the late 1930s. Both environments allowed the Party to exploit international political divisions to carve out space in ostensibly "free" or "neutral" port cities. Both contexts also demanded that the CCP establish and maintain a veneer of independence and commercial legitimacy as a precondition for operating. This requirement, in turn, induced the Party members who worked in these front companies to err on the side of concealment when conducting business. Deception soaked into the otherwise mundane tasks of commerce, a seepage that would leave lasting effects on how the Chinese Communist Party understood the fundamentals of trade in a capitalist context. The key difference between the CCP's experiences in Dalian and in Hong Kong was that the political cleavages of the Cold War had now replaced the regional divisions of the Sino–Japanese War.

In late 1946, the CCP in Dalian began to use its local advantages to pursue the Central Committee's interest in exploratory trade with the

Americans, British, French, and others in the region. The Dalian-Port Arthur Prefectural Party Committee even coined a slogan to capture the spirit of the Central Committee's instructions: "organize businessmen, face overseas, serve the development of production, guarantee reasonable profits!"[94] This new campaign coincided with gathering momentum for trade farther north, in Dongbei's Heilongjiang Province, where Chen Yun was leading another new trade initiative.

Chen had arrived in Harbin in April 1946 to assume control of the Military Control Commission that was overseeing the CCP's first attempt to run a major Chinese city. By late June, he had taken charge of finance, economics, and logistics as a member of the newly established Northeast Bureau Standing Committee.[95] Although Chen would later gain a reputation as a Party conservative, he could be bold when he sensed opportunity, and he already recognized the value of expanding trade with neighboring regions. He had spent the winter negotiating an agreement with the Soviets to export mostly grains in exchange for cloth and other imports, and at a cadre symposium in March he argued that the Party also needed to develop commercial trade as a source of finance.[96] By the summer, he was convinced that trade was vital to stability in northeast China. On July 11, 1946, he announced that the Party had no choice but to open up foreign trade. Only by exporting the region's abundant grains, he argued, would the CCP be able to acquire the goods that people needed for daily life.[97]

Chen envisioned Dongbei's restoration as the bean basket of northeast Asia, a traditional role that reflected the economic geography of the region. Deep, fertile soil blanketed the treeless north Manchurian plains, making for easy cultivation of soybeans and other hardy cereals. The climate was also ideal for such crops—summer months brought sunshine and rain, and the cool, dry autumns were optimal for ripening and harvesting.[98] The region's flat terrain and river systems also made transportation cheap and efficient. Farmers on these plains produced eighteen million tons of grain annually before the Japanese army invaded in September 1931. Of this, three million tons were shipped to mainland Chinese cities or exported to Western Europe and other overseas markets.[99] Much of this went to Japan, which absorbed 40 percent of Manchurian exports in the 1920s. This figure increased to 60 percent during the Japanese occupation in the 1930s and early 1940s.[100]

Northern Manchuria's specialization in grain production left the region dependent on imports for daily essentials. Cotton, which was vital for surviving the frigid winters, grew only in limited quantities in the southern and western reaches of Manchuria, and families in the north tended not to weave or spin. Salt was also scarce in the north, but sea salt was abundant in southern Manchuria. As early as March, Chen Yun proposed addressing these complementarities by shipping soy beans and sorghum from northern Manchuria to Dalian, where it could be traded for salt.[101] By late spring, his trade advocacy had coalesced with the Central Committee's May 3 guidance on trade and the campaign for trade in Dalian. As this momentum built, Chen began to develop a framework that would link Manchuria's grain output to Dalian's port facilities and, ultimately, Hong Kong markets.

Chen Yun set things in motion on September 2, 1946. That day, he instructed the Northeast Bureau's new liaison office in Pyongyang to share with the North Koreans a lengthy list of goods that he hoped to import in exchange for Chinese grain.[102] Chen also ordered the liaison office to propose opening joint factories and a CCP-run shop in North Korea. To ensure the safety of any future Chinese shipments involving North Korea, Chen instructed the liaison office to stress the importance of safeguarding the shipping and communication lines that linked North Korea to Dalian and to the Sino–North Korean border town of Andong (known today as Dandong). The liaison office wasted no time in carrying out Chen's instructions; just over a month later, during a Party meeting on October 15, 1946, Chen announced that the Northeast Bureau had "opened up foreign trade."[103] The next two steps were to purchase and ship local grain for export.

As Chen pushed foreign trade in the northeast, Zhou Enlai contributed his own momentum several hundred miles to the south, in Shanghai. At his temporary residence in the city one evening in August 1946, Zhou briefed Liow & Company founder Qin Bangli on a new, three-part mission that required him to relocate to Hong Kong once again. First, Zhou instructed Qin to establish a seaborne shipping route along China's coast that the CCP could use to develop its trade operations more fully. Qin's second objective stemmed from the first. Zhou told Qin to carry out various "financial tasks" in Hong Kong, which included arranging insurance, exchanging currencies, coordinating shipping, and other trade-related activities. Finally, Zhou ordered Qin to groom a cohort of cadres skilled in the techniques of foreign trade work.[104] The Party needed more Qins, Zhou recognized, cadres who were versed in the ins and outs of the Party's brand of secretive trade and who could not just handle the urgent needs of today but also contribute to the longer-term aim of building a new, socialist China.

Qin moved back to Hong Kong in the fall of 1946 and resumed his role as a successful merchant. He moved with his family into a stately home at 6 Sau Chuk Yuen Road in Kowloon across the harbor from his Hong Kong Office.[105] Qin's visitors would naturally have assumed that he had purchased the impressive home himself. In fact, his father-in-law had it built for his own family years earlier.[106] Qin's houseguests also would not have known that their host lived on a CCP income—a stipend just large enough to play the part of a young merchant family. He earned HK$700 each month; his wife received only HK$500. These sums took you only so far in Hong Kong, but it was enough to blend into bourgeois circles.[107]

The villa and other trappings represented more than just posturing. This was a tacit acknowledgment on the part of Qin and the CCP that participation in capitalism abroad was contingent on certain aesthetics and practices. It required investments in infrastructure and acquiring certain mannerisms; it depended on conformity, the placing of at least one foot on the foundation that fostered coherence and stability in capitalist markets. Embedded in this recognition was the deeper lesson that the ostensible incompatibility between the Chinese revolution and the capitalist status quo could be reconciled. There were ways of sanding the edges of these two hostile worldviews to make them fit together enough to conduct business.

Qin expanded operations at Liow & Company as soon as he settled back into life in Hong Kong. The firm moved to an office just a few blocks from Victoria Harbor on Des Voeux Road Central and adopted a new name: the Lianhe Import-Export Company.[108] Qin also registered a branch office in Guangdong, called Tianlong Hang, to facilitate trade between Hong Kong and the Chinese mainland.[109] As these operations expanded, the CCP leadership began to send skilled Party members south to serve as staff.

These cadres brought valuable experience. The group included veterans of the Eighth Route Army Offices, people like Yuan Chaojun. Before Yuan arrived in Hong Kong in April 1947, he had run an Eighth Route Army Office communication station in Guiyang and traded clandestinely in Shanghai.[110] Another arrival that summer, Liu Shu, was an expert in accounting, finance, and shipping, a skill set he had developed while working at the Eighth Route Army Offices in Guilin and Chongqing.[111] When another member of this experienced group, Qian Zhiguang, embarked for

Hong Kong in 1947, his long trek to the colony helped cinch together the trade initiatives then sprouting up in Dalian, Manchuria, Pyongyang, and Hong Kong.

Qian's route took him east by land from Yan'an to Yantai, a port city on the northern edge of the Shandong peninsula. From there, he boarded a steamboat and headed north across the bay to Dalian, where he met with Chen Yun and other Party leaders to discuss next steps. While Qian was in town, two developments brought the CCP closer to establishing sturdy trade ties to overseas markets. First, the Party in Dalian established the Zhonghua Trade Company, which the CCP intended to use as a front for handling customs declarations and insurance for imports and exports transiting the port.[112] Second, Qian Zhiguang dispatched two cadres from Dalian to finalize arrangements for a maiden shipment of exports from Manchuria to Hong Kong. He sent Wang Huasheng, a nominal employee of the Zhonghua Trade Company and an Eighth Route Army Office veteran, east to Pyongyang to work with the local Party liaison office and the Soviet Embassy to charter two Soviet ships, one of which was the *Aldan*.[113] Qian dispatched the second cadre, Zhu Hua, north to Harbin to coordinate with the Northeast Bureau on a shipment of one thousand tons of soybeans, a cache of gold, and other assorted agricultural exports.[114]

In early November 1947, Zhu Hua and these exports left Harbin on a train bound for the North Korean port of Rajin.[115] The southern branch line of the Chinese Eastern Railway was the more direct route from Harbin to Dalian, but the Red Army controlled neither Changchun nor Shenyang, both of which were major junctions along that line. This left the overland route from Harbin across the Tumen River to Rajin as the safest, most reliable path to the sea. When the goods arrived in Rajin, they were loaded aboard the Soviet-flagged *Aldan*. Wang Huasheng also boarded the vessel to oversee the shipment, and the *Aldan* promptly set sail for Hong Kong, where it arrived unscathed and with cargo intact.

Wang Huasheng met with Qin Bangli, Yuan Chaojun, and Liu Shu not long after arriving in Victoria Harbor, and the four men smuggled the gold from the captain's quarters of the *Aldan* to the vault below HSBC. The remainder of Wang's mission was uneventful. The group sold the soybeans for a good price, but had less luck finding buyers for weasel pelts. Few in Hong Kong's humid climate were in the market for fur. The group used the proceeds from the sales to purchase medicine, newsprint, vacuums, filters, and other supplies needed in the north.[116] Wang and his associates then loaded these items onto the *Aldan,* and the ship left Victoria Harbor for its return voyage north.

Legacies of Exchange

The anticlimactic conclusion of the *Aldan* mission belies its historic significance. The ship's maiden voyage marked the completion of the CCP's own network for exchanging cadres, cash, and goods with international markets undetected and unobstructed. The Party had built front companies in Dalian, Pyongyang, Hong Kong, and Guangdong that furnished space, letterhead, customs declarations, and other markers of commercial legitimacy and conformity. Even if much of this was only skin deep, it was enough to permit the CCP to be present, and to participate, in markets abroad.

This—the very act of sustained participation—mattered. It mattered because it demonstrated over time, in different places, and under varying circumstances that the CCP could trade with foreign capitalists without relinquishing its revolutionary goals. Party ideology stretched to accommodate this realization, just as the skill sets of cadres in front companies stretched to link ideology to practice. The expertise these cadres developed made it easier still for senior Party officials to turn to foreign markets for solutions to new economic problems as the Communists expanded their control over the Chinese mainland in the years ahead.

2

CLOSING THE OPEN DOOR

ON JUNE 30, 1949, less than two years after the *Aldan* arrived in Hong Kong, Mao Zedong delivered his famous lean-to-one-side address, in which he explained that "all Chinese without exception" must "lean" either toward socialism or imperialism: there was no "third road."[1] The speech left no doubt which path China would choose, which raised questions about the durability of the Party's trade with capitalists just months before the founding of the Chinese Communist state. In line with Mao's vision, China's trade began to lean toward the socialist world in the months and years that followed. In 1950, the first full year of the People's Republic, China transacted roughly 74 percent of its trade with capitalist countries, according to internal CCP figures. Just two years later, socialist trade had already surged and the capitalists' share of China's trade had plummeted to 21 percent.[2]

The scale of this realignment and the certainty behind Mao's pronouncements might suggest there is little to be gained from examining the Party's capitalist trade on the eve of the founding of the People's Republic. If capitalist trade was fading, and socialist trade flourishing, why dwell on the rump end of this historic shift? More socialist trade brought more contact, and more contact created more opportunities to observe how the CCP conducted itself, and changed, through interactions with outsiders.[3]

But a closer look at the Party's trade with capitalists during this pivotal moment reveals an aspect of CCP foreign policy that is otherwise easy to overlook: contrary to the starkness of Mao's vision in June 1949, the Party was not steeped in an unalloyed aversion to global capitalism in the late 1940s. Party leaders were still eager for access to overseas capitalist markets. The chairman himself suggested as much in his June 30 speech when he turned to the subject of commerce. There is always business to be done, he said. "We only oppose the internal and external reactionaries who are preventing us from doing business," he explained.[4] Regardless of whether Mao truly believed this claim, as a matter of policy this stance raised a difficult question for the Party's trade officials: if Communist China was open for business to all, what did it mean to *lean* to the side of socialism, in theory and in practice, while trading with capitalists? The Party struggled to answer this question on many levels and in different environments during the two years before the founding of the People's Republic of China.

Successes on the battlefield made this question all the more urgent. Party administrators followed Communist troops as they pushed from Manchuria south into China's cities and ports in 1948 and 1949. Once there, these officials had to balance the Party's need for control over trade with the flexibility demanded by businesses and markets. Their goal was not to sever trade with capitalists but to renegotiate the terms under which China did business with them and to make trade serve the revolution. This was an iterative and highly contextual process. Party officials drew from past experience and ideological convictions to redefine China's relationship to capitalism, but they also took cues from events on the ground. The institutions they built, and the guidelines they developed, helped to lay the foundation for the trade policies of the future Chinese Communist state.

Tightening Trade Controls

By the summer of 1948, the *Aldan* was just one among many vessels ferrying goods between Communist bases and capitalist markets in China. Many of these operations were no larger than a man on a junk. In Dalian, Culver Gleysteen, a first-tour diplomat working at the US consulate, uncovered how this trade worked despite Soviet restrictions on his movements in the city. Gleysteen's parents had been missionaries, and he grew up in Beiping speaking fluent Chinese. He liked to chat up the locals, and during a conversation one day in early July the topic of trade arose. His contact, a local priest, explained that traders could export goods from Dalian without problems as long as they paid the required taxes, but certain products, deemed "vital" to the local economy, could not be exported. Nor could citizens leave the city at will. In practice, this meant locals exported mostly seafood and sea products. Junks making the return trip were permitted only to import food and medicine.[5] Still, the boats came and went, and business seemed brisk enough.

Small-time smugglers added to the flow of goods. The evidence for this was ubiquitous. Local shops carried British cloth, clocks, and American cosmetics. They sold lightbulbs and pens—not just any pens, Parker 51s, the envy of any social climber in postwar East Asia. According to the American consul in Dalian, Paul "Zeke" Paddock, the glint of a Parker pen cap could be seen in the shirt pockets of many CCP cadres at the time.[6]

Party officials had mixed feelings about these products. On one hand, fresh imports proved that supplies were piercing the KMT blockades that now stretched from the mouth of the Pearl River in the south to the Bohai Sea in the north, throwing "liberated" regions a supply lifeline. On the other hand, many of the goods that slipped into Communist areas, such as the Parker pens, were little use to soldiers who lacked ammunition or factories desperate for supplies. In the eyes of Communist planners, lipstick and pens represented loose ends, economic inefficiencies they could ill afford.

This was especially true now that the Party's position in northeast China was improving steadily. By mid-1947, Communist forces were gaining momentum on the battlefield and Party officials sensed a shift in the revolution. In June, Communist troops pushed south through Nationalist lines along the Yellow River near Kaifeng and into southern Shandong Province. From there, they marched south to establish a base in the forests of the Dabie Mountains, north of the Yangtze River along the Henan-Hubei border. The maneuver forced Chiang Kai-shek to siphon some of his own forces away from the front lines in the north down to the central plains to defend KMT-controlled cities along the Yangtze River.[7] With the Dabie distraction diverting KMT resources to the south, Chiang could no longer commit fully to stamping out the Communists in the north. On September 1, 1947, Mao vowed to drive his forces into KMT-held areas as part of a nationwide counteroffensive that would take the form of conventional warfare rather than targeted guerrilla strikes.[8] This would require substantially more soldiers and equipment, as well as a changed mind-set.

The Party had to broaden its thinking under these changing circumstances. It had to consider the needs of a vast "liberated" expanse when formulating economic policies, argued Li Fuchun, a Hunanese economic specialist with a mind for logistics.[9] Li had managed supplies for the Red Army during the Long March in the mid-1930s. Now, as a top planner, he analyzed scarcities on a larger scale. He had good reason to worry about the resources required to mount the nationwide campaign Mao envisioned. In late 1946 and early 1947, the military was consuming over 80 percent of the Party's budget.[10] With military commitments this large, and poised to grow, Li viewed all economic decisions in the context of military affairs. "The war decides everything," he said. "All work, especially economic work, must embark from this [maxim]."[11]

In Li's mind, this meant tightening control. He believed regulation was the only route to efficiency, especially in trade, and efficiency was vital to supplying the war effort as it expanded. Li explained his thinking in a report to the Northeast Bureau in October 1947. The central policy for foreign trade was "unified control," he told the committee.[12] As he saw it, firm control over foreign trade would allow the CCP to pursue a focused and efficient development agenda. "We will strive to export our surplus products and import essential materials for the development of production and construction," he explained.[13] The influx of Parker pens would have to stop. The Party "will strictly forbid the importation of consumer goods and luxury items," Li vowed, which had produced "unrestricted" and expensive deficits.[14] Three-quarters of the provincial governments under CCP control by the winter of 1946–1947 were running deficits.[15]

None of this meant the Party intended to smother all private commerce *within* the territories it controlled, at least not for the time being. Li's colleague and future minister of trade, Ye Jizhuang, clarified the Party's position on internal "free trade" during a meeting of the standing committee of the Northeast Political Committee in February. "As for private trade within liberated areas, under the government's policy of free trade, as long as there is no hoarding or profiteering, and no manipulation of prices or contraventions of government decrees, [we will] always permit freedom," he explained.[16] Freedom, but with limits—and the Party set the limits. This was the crux. True to the spirit of *zili gengsheng,* the range of permissible trade could expand or contract depending on the exigencies of the moment. Today, wartime necessities and the looming counteroffensive informed the Party's trade calculus, but tomorrow might bring new considerations altogether. The CCP retained the right to delimit trade for itself—not markets, not firms, and certainly not businesspeople abroad.

On a deeper level, Li was concerned about more than efficiency and supplies. He worried that unfettered trade could invite foreign domination. Like other Party leaders, he believed that a century of imperialism had crippled China's economy and consigned its people to semicolonial subordination. The old China, where imperialists, feudalists, and bureaucratic capitalists conspired to control the economy for their own gain, was precisely what the Party sought to overthrow.[17] Unless the Party remained vigilant, unrestricted commerce could poison the revolution just as it was beginning to breathe in new life.

In November 1947, a month after Li called for centralizing control over foreign trade, Communist forces conquered Shijiazhuang, an industrial city 185 miles southwest of Beijing. The Party concluded that Chiang Kai-shek's troops were unlikely to retake the city, which encouraged economic planners there to adopt a long-term perspective.[18] Control of Shijiazhuang also encouraged the Central Committee to think more carefully about how it expected to govern medium and large cities—Shijiazhuang was one of the earliest large cities to fall under CCP control. The Central Committee hoped to adopt a systematic approach to urban governance, one informed by the Party's own experiences in smaller cities and towns. "Over the years, we have captured many cities," the Central Committee noted in February 1948, "and [we have developed] rich experience as well." The problem was that local officials had failed to record and circulate their experiences for the benefit of cadres elsewhere.[19] This had left Communist officials largely blind as they took over cities, with little to go on beyond narrow personal experiences.

The Central Committee began to address this shortcoming in early 1948 by ordering all central bureaus and branches, and all Party committees on the front lines, to compile summaries of their experiences in cities with at least fifty thousand inhabitants. Local leaders were instructed to submit these reports, one for each city, to the Central Committee within three to four months.[20]

As the deadline for these reports approached, Party leaders turned their attention to preparations for China's "liberation" on a national scale. On

June 11, 1948, Zhou Enlai and Dong Biwu, who was then head of the newly created Central Ministry for Finance and Economics, initiated a program to collect economic data in anticipation of the Party's national takeover. "We need nationwide, systematic investigation materials concerning national resources, banking, factories, mining, communications, trade, agriculture, forestry, animal husbandry, fisheries, financial revenues, the activities of bureaucratic capitalists, etc.," they wrote to Xu Dixin, a Party propagandist and economist then living in Hong Kong.[21] In December 1947, Xu had established a small office called the Jianhua Economic Information Research Office. Now, he was overseeing a priority assignment straight from Zhou Enlai and Dong Biwu, who authorized Xu to permit cadres with an interest in research to forgo political activities temporarily if it freed them up for economic research.[22]

Xu Dixin organized six groups, five to seven cadres in each, to investigate banking, remittances, taxation, and other aspects of the Chinese economy. The Party also needed better information about how China's trade worked, particularly in port cities such as Tianjin in the north and Shanghai in the south, so Xu ordered one of the groups to study international trade.[23] Soon, Party members in Hong Kong were collecting information on an array of subjects related to the Chinese economy.

Hong Kong Special Police officers once stumbled into evidence of this collection drive when they raided a suspected Communist front in the spring of 1949. When the officers searched the organization—another ostensibly private company called Kin Yuen Hong in Central Hong Kong—they found a cache of reports and internal Party documents on economic affairs. One report examined remittances in south China; another analyzed British and American economic interests in China.[24] The police also found bulletins that outlined CCP guidelines on trade and financial operations in south China, including the establishment of a new regional trade bureau.[25] This mix of economic analysis and Party guidance revealed that cadres in Hong Kong were not just gathering information, they were also relating that information to directives that arrived from the CCP central leadership. New policies on trade and economics had to connect sensibly to conditions on the ground, and these underground Party members contributed to that process on the frontlines.

British intelligence saw the raided office as a platform for collecting economic intelligence, but Hong Kong colonial authorities also recognized a more important point. The thrust of the documents suggested that the CCP fully expected trade between Hong Kong and south China to continue, at least in the near term. The first step toward preserving that trade was to investigate how it worked.[26]

The colonial officials in Hong Kong were right. CCP leaders did plan to use pre-liberation trade patterns to stabilize the economy under Communist rule. But the Party hoped for more from trade than just stability. Commerce would also supply the military and drive postwar reconstruction. "We now have cities," the Northeast Bureau proclaimed on June 10, a day before Zhou Enlai and Dong Biwu ordered Xu Dixin to begin collecting economic data. "[We] should cherish cities, [and] give full play to the role of cities, [so that] cities produce more military supplies and everyday goods to support the war and enrich the economies of liberated areas."[27]

This straightforward recommendation glossed over a host of stubborn questions that the CCP would face as it began to take over China's largest cities. How would the Party exert control over the thousands of foreign firms and businesspeople living and working in places like Tianjin, Shanghai, and Guangzhou? Would all of them be permitted to continue operating, or only some? If not all, how would the Party determine who could stay, under what circumstances, and for how long? What about Chinese entrepreneurs? How much autonomy should they be granted? As 1948 drew to a close, the Party had yet to develop the policies that answered these increasingly urgent questions.

The Search for Policy Coherence

The road to Beijing was opening up for Mao Zedong as 1949 began. He and the rest of the Central Committee were hunkered in Xibaipo, a village of mud-brick homes and cypress trees some two hundred miles southwest of the future capital, but it must have felt closer than that. After twenty-seven years of struggle, the CCP was poised for victory over Chiang Kai-shek and the Nationalists. And with national "liberation" nearly within reach, Mao's mind turned to the task of governance. Economic affairs loomed particularly large. During a Politburo meeting in early January, he tried to temper expectations about the pace and scale of China's economic transformation. He assured his colleagues that the "new democratic economy" that would emerge in China would be planned and that it would develop toward socialism, but he also cautioned that if China tried to pursue socialism too quickly, everything would collapse.[28]

Mao had expressed similar gradualism in years past. Almost exactly nine years earlier, in a speech outlining what he meant by "new democracy," he mused that China must pass through two stages of revolution. First, China would undergo a democratic revolution. This would be a relatively inclusive stage—the proletariat would lead, Mao said, but it would ally with diverse groups and individuals from across society. Only after this stage culminated in a "new" democratic society, ruled by a joint dictatorship of all revolutionary classes, could China embark on the second stage of its revolution, which would lead finally toward socialism.[29]

This two-stage formulation placed China at the vanguard of a new type of revolutionary process in colonial and semicolonial contexts, but it also anticipated the inevitable disjuncture between the promise of socialist transformation and the persistent realities of daily life in China following "liberation." In this way, the concepts of "new democracy" and "new democratic economy" helped to justify the economic continuities that might otherwise jar with expectations of what China's transition to socialism should actually look like.

Mao did not expect the same continuities in foreign affairs. He was adamant that China repudiate its passive relationship to foreign imperialism and that it reclaim the nation's full sovereignty and confidence on the world stage. In early 1949, he crystallized his thinking on foreign affairs into two expressions: "making a fresh start" (*lingqi luzao*) and "cleaning the house before entertaining guests" (*dasao ganjing wuzi zai qingke*). Both concepts embodied his emphasis on sharp breaks with the past in foreign affairs and his insistence that the Chinese people had "stood up" under the Party's leadership.

Mao had used the phrase *lingqi luzao* in the context of foreign affairs as early as the spring of 1949, according to Zhou Enlai, but the spirit of the expression, which literally means "building a new stove," had emerged earlier.[30] On January 19, 1949, the Central Committee circulated a directive written by Zhou and approved by Mao that sketched the contours of the idea: the CCP would abolish all standing treaties with the West rather than renegotiate terms after national "liberation." China's new leaders would then set their own terms for restarting diplomatic relationships and would forgo formal relations with any nation that rejected the terms of the new Chinese state.[31]

"Cleaning the house before entertaining guests" dovetailed with the idea of a fresh start. Mao believed that starting off on the right foot required cleansing China of its imperialist vestiges—to "clean house," as he put it in February 1949—before inviting "guests" to return.[32] Like "making a fresh start," "cleaning the house" was a defensive concept. It was designed to carve out domestic space in which to purify the Chinese revolution and to build a strong, independent state free from the encroachment of foreign imperialists. Both concepts resonated with the Party's push for decisive control over trade and the economy, and they reflected Mao's conviction that Western capitalist powers posed an inherent threat to the Chinese revolution if left unchecked. But neither concept was so rigid that it demanded severing China from all contact with the capitalist world, even if some capitalist states refused to accept the Party's new terms for official relations. Instead, Mao intended to redefine terms so that existing trade relations could be aligned with China's emerging new identity.

Behind this philosophizing was a growing pressure to develop concrete policies that would guide trade in China's largest cities—not in months or weeks, but now. On January 15, Communist troops conquered the city of Tianjin, the largest port in north China and home to some two million inhabitants, many of whom were foreign born. The next day, when the KMT navy withdrew from the area, the Party found itself for the first time in charge of a sophisticated economy with long-standing ties to overseas markets. That same day, January 16, all American-financed flour and wheat shipments to China stopped. Shippers found it "physically impossible" to unload cargo at Tanggu harbor, the major port that served Tianjin. Ports farther south were already clogged or oversupplied. The US Economic Cooperation Administration (ECA) announced it might divert flour shipments originally intended for China to other destinations, possibly Korea.[33]

If the ships stopped arriving, Tianjin would sink into crisis. A. T. Steele, a longtime China correspondent in Beiping, wrote, "foreign trade is Tientsin's life blood." Until the Party restored the city's commerce with the outside world, Steele believed, it would remain "a serious liability" for the CCP leadership.[34] Mao also recognized the dangers of a floundering economy in Tianjin and hoped to minimize the disruptions. On January 3, he had cabled his commander Lin Biao to ask for an investigation into ways to avoid damaging the city's industrial sector and to minimize damage during the invasion itself.[35]

The CCP also began to develop policy solutions to these problems. On January 19, the Central Committee issued its directive on foreign affairs, which touched on the subject of trade. The document, which Mao edited before release, sought to instill prudence in cadres operating in Tianjin and Beiping. "Concerning trade with capitalist nations, do not busy [yourselves] establishing or restoring routine trade relations," the Central Committee instructed. There was no need to rush things. "Especially do not busy [yourselves] concluding common [*yi ban*] trade contracts." Instead, "[cadres] can only engage in temporary, individual localized import and export trade with these countries when it is advantageous to us and [when it concerns] urgently needed [goods]."[36] Working-level cadres could trade with foreign capitalists, in other words, but they should not appear eager to do so. Nor should they create the impression that ad hoc local trade reflected larger CCP policy. These deals were temporary expediencies, scaffolding for a wobbly economy.

Despite these instructions, Mao still worried that overzealous officials might complicate the Party's relations with local communities of foreigners. The following day, January 20, he sent instructions to the municipal Party committees in Tianjin and Beiping and to senior military commanders in the area to explain that they were not permitted to interact with foreigners freely. "[For] every specific step you take when handling foreigners," Mao ordered, "[you] all should submit your recommendations to the Central Committee in advance, and you may act only after securing approval from the Central Committee."[37]

The Party continued to refine its positions on trade and foreigners in the weeks that followed. On February 16, the Central Committee issued two directives that applied a broader perspective to trade policy.[38] The first, addressed to the North China Bureau and the leadership in Tianjin and Beiping, explained that ideology would guide trade. The Central Committee said that the CCP's "basic principle of foreign trade" was to satisfy China's needs as much as possible by doing business with the Soviet Union and the "new democracies" of Eastern Europe. The CCP would trade with capitalists only when socialist partners did not need goods China wanted to sell, or when socialist partners were unable to sell China what it needed.[39] Mao had already shared the outlines of this position with the Soviet Union in late January 1949 during talks with the visiting Soviet official Anastas Mikoyan.[40] In this spirit, the CCP's Central Committee concluded its instructions with advance approval for officials in Tianjin to initiate talks with local Japanese businesses about the possibility of maintaining commercial relations.[41]

That same day, February 16, the Central Committee sent a second cable that reached a wider readership and offered a more comprehensive statement on CCP trade policy.[42] The document noted that many businesses operating in Nationalist-controlled areas had already approached CCP officials in Tianjin with requests to trade. The Central Committee explained that local trade like this was necessary for the speedy recovery of the Chinese economy, but any such trade must adhere to three core principles. First, it must benefit China. Second, it had to safeguard China's independence and sovereignty. Third, it must be controlled strictly by the new Chinese Communist government.[43] This last point—the need for control—set the tone for the Central Committee's directive, just as it had framed Li Fuchun's report on trade to the Northeast Bureau in October 1947. It conveyed to cadres across north China in no uncertain terms the central importance of exercising full sovereign authority when doing business with local capitalists.

To provide an institutional foundation for this control, the same instructions also ordered the North China People's Government to establish a foreign trade bureau immediately in Tianjin. Private businesses wishing to operate in the city would have to secure permits and approvals from the new bureau. So would visiting delegations interested in developing trade with Communist China. The new bureau would also take responsibility for drafting a trade plan that used import and export controls and tariffs to bring Chinese trade into line with the Party's larger industrialization goals. This push for control reached down even to the level of the local junk trade, which the new foreign trade bureau was also instructed to oversee.[44] For traffickers in lipstick and pens, it was an ominous development.

Yet just four days later, the Party softened its guidance. On February 20, 1949, the Central Committee issued more instructions on trade work, this time presenting a more accommodating position. The earlier guidance concerned matters of "principle," the Central Committee explained, and officials in Tianjin and Beiping were expected to study these principles systematically. The Central Committee nevertheless expected cadres working in these cities to "approach businesspeople who previously conducted export and import trade" and others who worked in related industries. During these meetings, cadres were expected to conduct "detailed inquiries" to develop an understanding of the business environment and then "propose ways to conduct foreign trade in the future."[45] Principles mattered, the Central Committee seemed to be saying, but not so much that they should stand in the way of developing a functioning trade regime in Tianjin and other large commercial centers. Nor did principles absolve local cadres from examining capitalist trade practices in search of methods and techniques that might profitably inform future CCP policy.

The tension running through this guidance—firm control on the one hand, selective accommodation on the other—placed working-level cadres in a bind. How could one recognize the proper balance between sternness and openness, or principle and practice, in any given moment during exploratory talks with any given local business owner? What consequences might befall the unlucky cadre who strikes the wrong balance between these contradictory impulses? Nobody seemed to know. The Central Committee made clear its own ambivalence, if nothing else, in yet another set of instructions on March 1, 1949. Local officials "should continue to adopt a stern [yanzheng] manner" when interacting with foreigners from capitalist nations, the Central Committee instructed. But foreign trade authorities should adopt an "energetic and friendly [youhao] stance" with any foreign businessperson, agency, or organization willing to conduct business. As an example, the Central Committee explained that local officials were authorized to help foreign businesses with minor difficulties, such as procuring vehicle licenses and travel permits. However, cadres "also must not [be] excessively friendly or excessively energetic, to the point of creating the misimpression among foreigners that we are eager [jiyu] to seek trade with them."[46]

This tortuous effort to relate policy to principle produced widespread confusion in Tianjin, which soon squeezed the life from the city's business community. The British consulate general in the city catalogued commercial grievances in a memorandum in September 1949, nearly eight months into the CCP's occupation of the city. Complaints ranged from lack of access to local trade authorities and restrictions on personal movement to oppressive security regulations, discriminatory banking regulations, and arbitrary and aggressive taxation.[47] Many traders were frustrated by issues beyond CCP control. Nationalist blockades along the Chinese coastline prevented all ships from reaching Tianjin during the first months of CCP control, and it wasn't until March 1949 that the first fully loaded

British-flagged freighter arrived from Hong Kong.[48] Still, the Party's muddled position on trade with foreign capitalists only made matters worse.

As officials in Tianjin wrestled with implementing the Central Committee's guidance, the Party's senior-most leadership convened in Xibaipo for the Second Plenum of the Seventh Central Committee. The meeting, which began on March 5, was a critical moment in the founding of the Chinese Communist state. Over the course of eight days, attendees staked out the policy positions that would become the foundation of the People's Republic of China. When the subject of economics arose, the top leadership articulated a clearer sense of what they expected foreign trade to accomplish for Communist China. The final resolution of the plenum identified the key obstacle to China's revolutionary transformation as the "backward" character of the Chinese economy. Agriculture accounted for 90 percent of China's national production, the Party estimated, and industry comprised only 10 percent.[49] For Chen Yun and others who helped draft the resolution, trade was a means for transforming China from a backward nation into a modern industrial state. The Party would trade away China's backward farm goods in exchange for advanced technology, chemicals, fuels, and equipment—the building blocks of industrialization.

The Party had already begun this transformation-through-trade with the Soviet Union. On March 29, after fifteen rounds of talks in Shenyang, the CCP's Northeast Administrative Council signed a major trade contract with Soviet representatives in Harbin. The agreement committed the CCP to exporting 663,800 tons of grains and cereals—mostly soybeans, but also corn, rice, wheat flour, and vegetables. The Party would also export soybean oil and eggs, pelts and furs, frozen seafood, meats, and over one million tons of coal. In exchange, the Soviets agreed to provide 10 million meters of cotton cloth; nearly 3,000 trucks; fuels and oils; 200 tractors; and lathes, milling machines, and other manufactured goods.[50]

The March deal was the latest in a string of contracts CCP representatives had been signing with Soviets based in Manchuria since 1946, including at least one export deal with the quasi-private Qiulin Company, a Dongbei-based firm founded by Russians, absorbed by HSBC, overtaken by the Japanese government, and then finally returned to Soviet control again in 1945.[51] As the Central Committee's February 16 guidance made clear, the CCP fully expected more contracts in the future as Soviet trade became a priority for the new Chinese state. Party leaders made even their most personal decisions based on this expectation. The Politburo member Ren Bishi urged his daughter in October 1948 to take up Russian studies as part of her schoolwork in north China because, as he explained in a letter, "[those who] will aid China's construction in the future will not be [from] England or the United States, but rather the Soviet Union; much of [China's] construction work will inevitably have to be learned from the Soviet Union."[52] And much of this learning and cooperation would occur in the context of bilateral trade.

But even Ren's vision was not confined to Sino–Soviet trade. Like his colleagues on the Politburo, he also believed capitalist markets could benefit China's development, even if China could not expect "aid" from the Americans or the British. On March 13, the final day of the Second Plenum, he pointed to wartime Japan as an example of how China might achieve its industrialization goals. He explained that the Japanese managed to industrialize Anshan and Benxi, two northeastern cities in Liaoning Province, by selling agricultural products abroad for hard currency, then using the currency to import technology and equipment. If Japan could do it, surely the CCP could, too.[53]

Of course, any such program would require firm control and tight orchestration to ensure China imported the proper modernizing equipment and exported the right produce. As Mao put it in his own report to the plenum, not having a policy of controlled trade was "not possible."[54] Mao continually emphasized this point not just because he believed control over trade would protect China from infiltration by capitalist-imperialists. He also thought control would give China a unique advantage in global markets. He remained convinced that capitalist states stood always on the brink of economic crisis. As a result, capitalist foreign policy was guided by a ceaseless quest for fresh markets abroad, the only means for staving off collapse. By this logic, China enjoyed outsized clout because of the sheer size of its market, which represented the prize among prizes in the minds of ravenous capitalists. Mao drew this inference not just from Lenin but also from a deeper tradition in Chinese thought—a central kingdom sense of superiority, which presumed that foreign "barbarians" needed China more than China needed them. This imbalance gave China leverage. Mao believed capitalists had begun already to jockey for a share of the China market in March 1949, when he told Party leaders that several capitalists had been competing to do business with China's liberated areas.[55]

And Mao was right, to an extent. In April 1949, when the US ambassador to Nationalist China, Jonathan Leighton Stuart, proposed a unified commercial policy against the CCP—whereby Western capitalist powers would refuse to trade with the Communists unless all capitalists received equal and fair treatment—other representatives of capitalist nations rejected the idea diplomatically.[56] Some noted that no legal or moral justification prevented firms from accepting deals offered by the CCP. Others said it would be difficult for businesses to refuse a profitable transaction simply because other firms did not enjoy the same opportunity. Still others pointed out it would be hard to ensure compliance with such an arrangement, especially in cases of barter trade. Nobody liked the idea. Too many firms were too eager to claim their share of the Chinese market no matter who was in charge, just as Mao expected.

DESPITE THE CLARITY OF the CCP's larger principles on capitalist trade, Party leaders remained uncertain how to link these ideas to a policy framework nuanced and consistent enough to inform the daily work of cadres in Tianjin, Beiping, and elsewhere. As the urgency for coherent policies mounted in the spring of 1949 and national "liberation" seemed increasingly imminent, the CCP began the process of creating a national-level bureaucracy capable of consolidating economic decision making. At the center of this process was the veteran economic specialist Chen Yun.

On May 9, 1949, Chen boarded an overnight train to Beiping from Shenyang, where he and Li Fuchun had been leading regional economic planning for Dongbei.[57] Just after Chen arrived in Beiping, he turned his attention to trade. On May 11, he departed the city center for the Western Hills just outside town, where the Party's Central Military Commission was hosting a three-week conference on finance and economics. The retreat offered a chance to exchange views with the Party's leading thinkers and policymakers on a range of economic issues, including problems associated with foreign trade in Tianjin, Shanghai, and Tangshan.[58]

The list of trade problems to discuss seemed to lengthen by the day, and Chen understood the urgency of them all. He recognized that the Party had little time to develop a national policy framework to guide foreign trade, particularly if Communist forces soon took control of Shanghai, by far China's largest, richest, and most sophisticated urban economy. Already

Chen was worried about Shanghai. On May 23, while still at the conference, he wrote to Zhou Enlai about the scarcity of cotton in the city, which he believed threatened the textile industry and, indirectly, the entire city's economy. In a letter to Zhou just two days earlier, with Shanghai no doubt foremost in his mind, Chen had also discussed the idea of buying cotton from Hong Kong to shore up supplies.[59]

Pressures like these kept trade at the front of Chen's mind as he spoke with the other conferees, but much of the conversation focused on institution building and the question of how to centralize economic decision making. On May 31, after weeks of internal discussions and consultations with the Soviet Union, Liu Shaoqi drafted a summary outline on behalf of the Central Committee to propose the creation of a new central economic governance body called the Central Finance and Economics Committee (CFEC).[60] After Mao and Zhou tinkered with the text, the Central Committee released the document to announce the immediate creation of the CFEC, which was empowered to oversee all financial and economic work at the national level, including matters related to foreign trade. The document made no mention of who would lead the CFEC, but on June 4 Zhou Enlai announced that Chen Yun and Bo Yibo would take charge. Most important, the CFEC was meant to be a lasting institution, a point Zhou made clear by explaining that the CFEC would remain intact after the founding of the People's Republic of China.[61]

Chen Yun emphasized the nationwide jurisdiction of the CFEC when he accepted the position. He explained that in the past, economic work had taken its cues from regional Party organizations. But now economic problems were taking on an increasingly national character. Entirely new problems were emerging, too. International trade was a case in point. "Previously, [we] didn't have major cities," he said, "but now [we] have major cities, [and] now we have the problem of international trade." He explained that production in places such as Jiangsu, Zhejiang, Anhui, Jiangxi, Hubei, and Sichuan all depended on Shanghai as a conduit for imports and exports. Tianjin was similarly bound to regional markets in the north. Consolidating control and managing growth in the context of these complex interdependencies would be difficult, but "these issues must be resolved by the Party Center's financial institutions," he argued.[62]

No doubt Shanghai weighed heavily on Chen's mind as he spoke. Communist troops had taken control of the city in the final week of May 1949 while he was still at the economic conference in the Western Hills, creating a daunting new responsibility for the emerging CFEC. Shanghai was in a class of its own: more trade flowed through Shanghai each year than the rest of China's ports combined.[63] To keep the city afloat, the Party had to resolve a host of problems. For example, the American-owned Shanghai Power Company burned one thousand tons of oil every day to supply 87 percent of the city's power needs, but virtually all the oil reaching Shanghai arrived from British and American sources. Even if the Party could secure agreements for steady oil supplies into the city from these traditional sources, it was expensive. Shanghai Power spent much of its US$3.5 million monthly budget on oil imports, and most of this sum—nearly US$3 million—was paid in foreign currency. Still, the city had to have power. Without it, much of Shanghai's vast textile industry and many of its 9,700 factories would have no choice but to shut down, bringing the city's economy to a halt.[64]

Food was another concern. The Nationalists had scorched miles of market gardens that surrounded the city in preparation for the city's defense.[65] To offset the disruption in food supplies, the US government had been providing nearly 60 percent of the city's basic food needs through a rationing program run by the ECA. The Party might be able to feed the city by bringing in Chinese grains from elsewhere, but this would take time. Large rice shipments from the interior wouldn't reach Shanghai until September. Shortfalls in other commodities also worried the Party leadership. Local textile factories, for example, the city's largest industry, were running on cotton supplied by the ECA.[66]

Even if the Party could secure cotton shipments from Hong Kong, as Chen Yun had proposed to Zhou Enlai, local officials had first to clear the harbor. Sunken junks and half-submerged ships cluttered the city's waterways—a grim parting shot by fleeing Nationalist soldiers in the last days of the siege. The Nationalists had also drained the city's banks and emptied its warehouses of stockpiled raw materials and pending exports.[67]

Beyond these urgent challenges, Chen Yun also had to consider longer-term factors as the CCP took control of Shanghai. Government officials, banks, and trading firms throughout the city, across East Asia, and around the world were watching closely to see how the CCP would reconcile its pursuit of revolutionary transformation with the need for stable ties to China's traditional import and export markets. Shanghai was a "proving ground for communist relations with the Western world," A. T. Steele observed.[68]

The Party understood this point and instructed its officials to be professional. On May 10, before the campaign to "liberate" Shanghai had begun, Chen Yi, the future mayor of the city, ordered his troops to be careful when interacting with non-Chinese residents in the city. Not all of them were the same, he explained. "There are [some from] imperialist nations, [and some from] democratic nations," he pointed out. But it was important to notice even finer distinctions when interacting with them. "Within imperialist nations there are also government officials and peaceful citizens, [and] we must treat the two distinctly," he said. All this parsing could be confusing, so Chen erred on the side of caution as he summed up his orders: "Aside from designated persons, no one is permitted to converse with foreigners."[69]

Chinese locals were also watching how the Party managed its takeover of Shanghai and other urban economies, and the CCP knew it. "If we lack wisdom in production work," the Central Committee cautioned in its Second Plenum resolution in March, "[if we] cannot quickly learn production work, [if we] are unable to make production enterprises recover and develop as quickly as possible, [thereby] achieving true results, [namely] first improving the lives of workers, as well as improving the lives of everyday people, then inevitably we will be unable to preserve power, we won't have a leg to stand on, we will fail."[70]

On June 4, just after Communist troops took control of Shanghai, the Central Committee instructed Party leaders in Shanghai, Hankou, Nanjing, and Jiujiang—all market towns along the Yangtze River—to establish trade supervision offices.[71] Two days later, the Party announced regulations for Shanghai that offered traders there new liberties, such as a provision allowing them to use their own foreign currency to finance imports. This broke from a KMT policy that required merchants to surrender their foreign money and use it for imports only through Chinese government banks, the effect of which was to reduce imports while traders stashed cash in US banks.[72] The CCP Military Control Commission in Shanghai also ordered the release of all imports that had been detained by KMT customs agents and permitted exporters to fulfill previous contracts.[73] In some cases, Party officials themselves stepped in to complete pending transactions. A US diplomat posted to Shanghai recalled years later that Communist officials confiscated stores of tungsten, hair, and tung oil to fulfill several standing export contracts held by Nationalist trading companies. To complete the orders, the local Party branch dispatched an official to the US consulate to pay the required fees and collect the consular invoice required for goods intended for export to the United States, which the consulate provided.[74]

Alongside these relaxations, the Party also wrote new regulations designed to establish control over the direction of trade in the city. Like the KMT, the CCP initiated a permit system that categorized different imports and exports.[75] All imports were divided into three categories: permitted goods, items permitted for import only by state-owned firms, and forbidden imports, which required special authorization. The Party then compiled lengthy lists of items in the first two categories. Permitted imports included metals, chemicals, medical supplies, production equipment and machinery, and other goods that would support industrialization. Items permissible for import only by state-owned firms included vehicles and aircraft, communications equipment, tobacco, industrial explosives, and photography supplies. Anything not included on these two lists fell into the third category requiring special permits to import. Exports received similar treatment. The Party intended to use exports to earn foreign exchange without creating shortfalls of raw materials or daily necessities at home. With these domestic needs in mind, the CCP forbade private traders from exporting grains or grain products, animals, birds, gold, and silver, whether coins or bullion.[76]

The CFEC and the new trade office in Shanghai aided the Party in monitoring and enforcing these new policies, but trade in the coastal cities remained unsteady and often frustrating. This was not always the fault of ambiguous CCP policy. Beginning in March, Party leaders contacted foreign capitalists several times to explore trade opportunities, but they often received only tepid replies. On March 30, the US consulate in Tianjin reported that the local CCP foreign affairs group had invited the chairman of the city's American Chamber of Commerce (AmCham) to discuss foreign trade. According to the AmCham chairman, the talks were cordial, and the Communists showed heightened interest in trading with the United States. But the exchange produced little beyond smiles and courtesies.[77]

In April, cadres in Beiping put out trade feelers as well. Yao Yilin, a senior official then working in the CCP's North China regional Ministry of Commerce and Industry, directed a subordinate to make contact with the US consul general in Beiping, Oliver Edmund Clubb. When the two met, Yao's emissary explained that the CCP wished to propose trade between north China and US-occupied Japan. Clubb reported that the Party's North

China region was prepared to offer Japan one hundred thousand tons each of coal and salt in exchange for machine parts, especially components that could be used in the textile and steel industries. Yao's emissary also said the CCP was interested in purchasing newsprint and medicines. To facilitate these trades, Yao's representative explained that the Chinese side planned to rely on a mix of established and newly formed local Chinese firms, all of which would be overseen directly by the North China government. He also said his boss was willing to restore Sino–American trade to prewar levels.[78]

Yao's initiative almost certainly originated higher up in the CCP hierarchy. His office in Beiping routinely reported to Zhou Enlai, who often issued orders to Yao and his staff directly.[79] This close connection to Zhou, in conjunction with the political significance of a CCP emissary's visit to a US diplomatic mission in the future capital of the Communist state, suggests that Yao's outreach was backed by Zhou himself. The meeting with Clubb may also have been prompted by the Soviets. On April 19, Stalin instructed Ivan Kovalev, his representative in China, to advise Mao not to refuse foreign loans or abstain from trade with capitalist nations, unless a proposed deal infringed on China's sovereignty or strangled its national industry. One week later, and three days before the meeting with Clubb, Stalin ordered Kovalev to inform Chen Yun that Moscow encouraged the "trading activities" of China's national bourgeoisie, by which he meant small-scale entrepreneurs. This included trade with Hong Kong and foreign capitalists living elsewhere. Stalin left it up to CCP leaders to decide which goods could be bought and sold, and which capitalists could be approached for trade, but his message to Chen Yun made it clear that he supported trade between areas controlled by the CCP and capitalists abroad.[80]

Regardless of where Yao's initiative began, if it was an effort by Zhou to gauge the feasibility of securing a US agreement to allow a resumption of trade between Japan and Communist China, the response was not reassuring. Clubb reported the proposal up the chain, but the deal ran into opposition from General Douglas MacArthur, whose position as supreme commander, Allied Powers, in Tokyo gave him the final word on any potential trade arrangement. MacArthur's office quietly killed the idea with a mix of delays and bureaucratic obstacles.[81]

Despite the rebuff, the CCP continued to probe for trade elsewhere. On May 25, 1949, the Northeast Bureau reported to the Party's central leadership that several foreign firms and some private companies run by ethnic Chinese had expressed interest in serving as intermediaries for re-kindled Sino–Japanese trade. These firms proposed to buy soybeans, salt, and other goods in China for resale to Japanese buyers. In Japan, the firms would purchase textile equipment, steel, and US cotton on behalf of the CCP. The proposal intrigued Party leaders in Northeast China enough that they urged the Central Committee to support it as long as the whole operation remained hidden—no documents should denote Japan as the final destination of Chinese Communist exports, and there should be no direct contact with the Japanese.[82]

When Zhou Enlai wrote the Central Committee's response to the pro-posal on June 2, 1949, he urged the Northeast Bureau to adopt a nuanced perspective.[83] "Under conditions of mutual benefit and equality, we need not reject direct trade with Japan; on the contrary, we should welcome Japa-nese ships and firms to Chinese ports to conduct trade relations," he wrote. Zhou explained that inviting closer ties to Japanese businesses offered a chance to enhance new China's influence among the Japanese people. It would also create opportunities to exploit latent contradictions between the United States and Japan. China's democratic parties and national bour-geoisie didn't oppose trade with China, he continued. MacArthur did. American monopoly capitalists did. The Americans wanted the Japanese market for themselves, Zhou argued. American coal and salt exporters in particular connived to prevent cheaper Chinese supplies from breaking into the Japanese market.[84]

That the Northeast Bureau proposed clandestine trade with Japan, rather than the more open approach proposed by Zhou, is understandable in light of the ambiguous and imprecise guidance the Central Committee had is-sued throughout the spring. When faced with the choice of adopting a "stern" posture or a "friendly" and "energetic" one, few sensible officials would opt for the latter in a report to suggest trade with foreign imperial-ists. This was doubly so for cadres proposing a commercial arrangement with Japanese imperialists just four years after the fall of the Japanese em-pire and the end of its occupation in China. Zhou seemed to understand this caution. He reassured the Northeast Bureau that if they had proposed indirect trade because of "concerns about Chinese political reasons"—in other words, fear of straying from the Party line—then they should know that "these concerns no longer exist."[85]

Despite Zhou's reassurance, the political climate surrounding trade in China's coastal cities felt uncertain, and not just for Party cadres. Many businesses chose to keep their heads down. They did their best to survive and hoped that prospects would improve once the new regime was in place. "Our situation [is] deplorable[,] prognosis bad but not hopeless," wrote one agent for the Chinese Engineering & Mining Company in Beiping.[86] Some sought to restore stability by communicating with the CCP directly, often using the most politically antiseptic language they could muster.

"Dear Sirs," began one letter to the East China Foreign Trade Office from Leo Wertheimer, an agent representing firms in New York and London. "We have pleasure in acknowledging receipt of your esteemed letter of June 29th," he wrote. Mr. Wertheimer faced an uphill task. Soliciting business from Communist revolutionaries on behalf of American and British imperialists posed special challenges and required a delicate touch. After some respectful scene setting, he came to the crux of the matter: "It goes without saying that in our capacity as China correspondent of both of the companies as printed on the head of this letter sheet, we would be very pleased to continue business connections," he explained. "Please take it as granted that you will have our whole hearted cooperation and you would, indeed, oblige us if you would give us too your best cooperation and assistance, thus, enabling both of us to carry on our old established connections to the benefit of China," he proposed.[87] The reference to "the benefit of China" was the closest the letter came to politics. Mostly, Mr. Wertheimer stuck to commerce. Like many others, he was trying to insulate business from the revolution that surrounded it.

Chinese traders hoping to import goods from the United States and other capitalist countries took a similar approach. Importers and exporters commonly resorted to blind solicitation letters during the early postwar period because firms and agents were often unfamiliar with distant markets. To find partners, businesses turned routinely to foreign embassies and consulates, which kept directories of manufacturers, importers, exporters, insurance agencies, and other trade-related businesses.[88] For entrepreneurs such as Mr. M. Han, of Health Products, Inc., who wanted to import chemicals from the United States, finding suitable exporters meant drafting a letter to the US consulate in Hong Kong. "Gentlemen," he began. "We, as a factory chartered recently and permitted to import chemicals and raw materials for the manufacture of drugs, are interested in getting the necessary supplies from your port," he wrote. Mr. Han then came to the point: he wanted a list of US suppliers.

It was a routine letter of solicitation, but what stands out is what the letter leaves out. Nowhere did Mr. Han invoke the Chinese Communist Party, the very authorities who granted his firm permission to import chemicals from the United States. He made no reference to liberation or imperialism. His only brush with Party rhetoric was an allusion to "mutual benefit," a term that eventually became a staple of Party propaganda. The letterhead was simple and professional; aside from the city listed under the firm's street address—Peiping—nothing distinguished the document from any other commercial inquiry received by the US consulate. This otherwise unremarkable professionalism suggested an effort to preserve the customs of routine business, despite the political upheaval—to keep commerce moving.[89]

In July, Yao Yilin again tested the waters for trade, this time with the British, when he held talks with Leo G. Frost, a manager of the Tianjin branch of the venerable firm Jardine, Matheson & Company.[90] In keeping with the Central Committee's March guidance, and with explicit backing from Chen Yun, Yao invited Frost and his associates to Beiping for quiet talks on trade and shipping.[91]

Yao's timing was perfect. There was ample time—months—until the Party would be prepared to announce the founding of the PRC, which meant Yao could exchange views with British merchants and possibly sketch the outlines of a working commercial agreement well before the details became wrapped up in the intractable politics of formal diplomatic relations. But the proposed talks were also not too early. The recently established CFEC now gave the Party a stable institution capable of distilling from the talks the rudiments of a working policy on CCP trade with foreign capitalists.

Yao's choice of Jardines was also shrewd. Leo Frost soon looped in the director of Jardine's Shanghai office, John "The Younger" Keswick.[92] Keswick was more than the office director of an esteemed firm in China. He was also chairman of the China Association, a league of leading merchants and officials dedicated to lobbying in London on behalf of British commercial interests in China and Japan. As chairman of this influential group, Keswick offered a direct line into Shanghai's powerful foreign commercial community. British sources also make clear that Yao Yilin expected the

British delegation to include two or three additional executives beyond Keswick, including the Shanghai agent of HSBC, George H. Stacey.[93]

The timing was perfect, the participants ideal, but Keswick never made it to Beiping. Neither did Stacey. An unfortunate delay and a capricious note conspired to foil both trips, a prime example of how unanticipated events can disrupt an otherwise seemingly inevitable flow of events. Part of the problem was that Keswick seemed to feel no urgency in scheduling the talks. By the second week of August 1949, he still had not finalized his travel arrangements. Frost wrote to Yao on August 11 with apologies and explanations for the delay, telling Yao that Keswick remained unable to travel because of difficulties facing his firm in Shanghai. Keswick hoped to make the trip as soon as he could, Frost explained.[94]

But sometime in the weeks that followed, John "The Younger" undermined the talks further by committing a tragic blunder. For reasons that remain unclear, he took it upon himself to draft a preparatory memorandum to Yao Yilin. Inexplicably, he appears to have shared the note with no one before mailing it to Beiping—not any of his contacts at the British consulate, none of his colleagues at Jardines, not even George Stacey, his fellow delegate to Beiping.[95]

The memorandum was a disaster. In the words of the British consul general in Shanghai, who saw the note after it had been sent, it was "not a good document."[96] Others in the Shanghai business community who got wind of the memo's content thought it calamitous.[97] Keswick began his letter with an effort to clear the air. In a tone of confidence verging on imperiousness, he announced his own ambitions and expectations for commercial operations in China, and then alluded to an assortment of shortcomings that businesses had already encountered while operating under CCP authority. This opening gambit almost certainly irritated CCP officials. Keswick then presented eleven questions that, by his own assertion, were "of great importance because successful cooperation between the Chinese people and the British depends upon the initial agreement on certain broad principles." Nearly all of the questions were hopelessly broad, fraught with political sensitivity, and more than a touch demanding: "What is the Government policy on taxation of both foreign and Chinese private enterprise?" he wanted to know. "What is the Government's general policy regarding trading?"[98]

It may have been possible for Keswick, or some other influential figure, to minimize the damage caused by the impulsive memo had Keswick sent it earlier in the summer. But his delays had shifted the entire sequence of events closer to the founding of the People's Republic, which ultimately ensnared the talks in the politics of diplomatic recognition. When Keswick was finally ready to make the trip to Beiping in late October, his invitation was off the table. Keswick and Stacey received word that if they still intended to travel, they would have to apply for permits the ordinary way, from the Commerce Department of the Shanghai Military Control Commission, and without official sponsorship from Beiping.[99] Frost tried valiantly to salvage the visit by working his own channels from Tianjin, but the trip was over before it had begun.[100] So, too, was any hope of reaching an early agreement on commercial relations between the CCP and the major trading houses operating in China's ports.

It was a missed opportunity, but even if Keswick had been able to meet with Yao Yilin in Beiping during the summer, John "The Younger" would not have altered the CCP's long-term plans for foreign businesses in China. The Party still wanted to scrub away the stains of imperialism in China— to "clean house," as Mao had put it. In practice, this meant diminishing, and eventually eliminating, the independence of foreign-owned banks, custom houses, shippers, insurers, and other firms on Chinese soil—not right away, but after the Party had squeezed them for the expertise, capital, and connections it needed to stabilize the Chinese economy. After this transition, however, the new Chinese state would determine who could trade, under what terms, for what goods, and at what prices.[101]

By wresting control of the economy from foreign businesses, the Party was repudiating the Open Door framework proposed by the United States nearly a half century earlier, in 1899 and 1900, under which foreign powers agreed not to deny others commercial access to their own spheres of influence in China. Mao was closing the Open Door to enable the Chinese themselves to determine how much to open China's market to foreign capitalists. Although Mao never stressed the connection, this new agenda echoed the age when Qing officials also tightly regulated foreigners who came to China for trade. Mao's approach was steeped in Marxist-Leninist rationales, but the sentiment behind it resonated with China's own historical experience to such an extent that, to many, it seemed faintly familiar, almost natural.

A meeting between Keswick and Yao in mid-1949 would have changed none of this, but it may have been useful nonetheless to Keswick and others. At the very least, it could have provided insights into CCP thinking on trade and commerce at a time when the business community in China had more rumors than facts. Without these insights, firms in Shanghai could only fumble along, like their counterparts in Tianjin and Beiping, unsure of what the future might hold.

Setting the Stage for PRC Trade

Chen Yun was in Shanghai as the Keswick visit began to unravel. The city was still reeling under the grip of a Nationalist blockade and Chen was in town to meet with economic leaders to discuss the blockade and chart a path forward. In a speech on August 8, 1949, he told a gathering of CCP economic planners from around the nation to brace themselves for a long-term blockade. Prepare, he counseled, but don't give up. The imperialists "cannot completely blockade us to death." The Party had its own methods for seeing to that. Already, Chen reminded his audience, the CCP had taken control of links to foreign markets in the north, in places like Tianjin, Dalian, and the inner-Mongolian trading town of Manzhouli. Once Communist troops "liberated" Guangzhou, the Party could lay claim to yet another commercial conduit in the south. CCP traders could also "export and import some [goods] to and from Hong Kong," he suggested.[102]

Although Chen didn't say so at the time, Qin Bangli's Hong Kong firm, now called China Resources, was already slipping past the Nationalist blockades routinely, and just three days earlier Chen had cabled Zhou Enlai to propose that the CCP expand the Dalian–Hong Kong shipping route to include a stop in Shanghai, which would allay his concern over the city's cotton shortages. Soviet ships could transport upward of one hundred thousand quintals—approximately five thousand metric tons—of cotton to bolster Shanghai's textile industry.[103] The new Shanghai stop would also relieve other strains and shortages in the city. Despite these promising developments, Chen Yun remained uneasy about the missed opportunities and lukewarm exchanges between Party officials and foreign capitalists during the spring and summer.

Mao saw things differently. To him, this was an opportunity. Capitalist aloofness and KMT blockades prepared the ground for mobilizing the rank and file. "The blockade is extremely beneficial to us in the current period," he wrote on September 2.[104] It offered something to lean against, a common hardship to unite the masses, fuel for China's revolution. If Chen Yun squinted, he could also see advantages in the Party's predicament. Chinese traders could exploit the contradictions among the imperialists, he told officials in Shanghai.[105] This may have been true, but it was hardly ideal footing on which to begin the task of founding a new state and rebuilding a devastated economy.

In late September, Chen Yun was back in Beiping to join the rest of the Party leadership and representatives from "friendly" political parties in finalizing preparations for the founding of the new state. The assembled leaders approved a new national flag and chose a national anthem; Beiping also became "Beijing" to reflect its status as the new nation's capital. Less symbolic, but critically important, the group also ratified a document called the "Common Program," which served as a de facto constitution that laid out the new state's official positions on a host of domestic and international policy issues, including foreign trade. Large questions still loomed over the Party's position on trade with capitalists, so Chen Yun and his fellow delegates faced the challenge of writing around unresolved issues while still establishing a position sturdy enough to serve as an enduring foundation for the emerging state. Their efforts took the form of Article 57 of the Common Program, which read:

> The People's Republic of China may[,] on a foundation of
> equality and mutual benefit, restore and develop commercial
> [and] trade relations with the governments and people of indi-
> vidual foreign countries.[106]

This flexible formulation established two essential prerequisites for doing business with the new Chinese state: "equality" (*pingdeng*) and "mutual benefit" (*huli*), both of which left wide latitude for interpretation. Naturally, the Party reserved for itself the right to determine whether and when business agreements had satisfied these requirements, depending on the historical, political, and economic context of each deal; the identities and political persuasions of the parties involved; and the nature and substance of the transaction itself. By using Article 57 to affirm the Party's position as final arbiter of the political propriety of trade transactions, Chen Yun and others were simply codifying the flexibility that the CCP had grown accustomed to over the preceding years.

The Party underscored its flexible authority by using *ke* in its characterization of whether the new state would recover and develop commercial relations with foreigners. *Ke,* which can be translated as "may" or "can," left open the possibility that the CCP could refuse commercial relationships with the outside world even if the conditions of "equality" and "mutual benefit" existed. *Ke* also captured perfectly the cultivated veneer of distance, bordering on aloofness, that had been evident in CCP policy on trade with capitalists since at least as early as the Central Committee's February 1949 guidance to cadres in Tianjin.

This was no accident. Chen Yun had used language similar to Article 57 to describe China's trade policy at a separate forum that also convened in late September. But on that occasion, Chen stated that the new People's Government "wished" or "desired" (*yuan*) to recover and develop trade relations with various governments and peoples.[107] The difference may seem trivial, but it mattered. As it was written, Article 57 restored to China the fundamental right of determining whether China opened its door to foreign trade only a crack or wide enough for all. Restoring this authority was part of the CCP's larger claim to legitimacy—the Party had led the Chinese people to victory, and China was now "standing up" for its own rights, as Mao put it.[108] On October 1, 1949, two days after the Common Program was formally approved, Mao Zedong proclaimed the founding of the People's Republic of China.

IN THE MONTHS THAT FOLLOWED, the Party's attention turned north, toward Moscow. Mao expected to sign a treaty with the Soviet Union that would bring security and substantial aid to the new Chinese state. The leadership had been laying the groundwork for this assistance since the preceding winter, when Stalin's secret envoy Anastas Mikoyan arrived in Xibaipo for talks.[109] Mao, Zhou Enlai, and several other Party leaders requested various types of economic assistance from Mikoyan during his visit, ranging from paper for printing banknotes to outright loans.[110] Even before Mikoyan arrived in Xibaipo, Mao had written to Stalin to ask for help in restoring China's railroads. On January 8, 1949, he had requested loco-motives, oil, and various instruments and machines, all of which Mao hoped to obtain on credit.[111]

Despite these entreaties, the CCP failed to secure a large commitment from the Soviets for months. Finally, on June 27, Stalin told Liu Shaoqi, who had arrived in Moscow the previous day for secret talks, that Moscow had decided to provide the CCP with a loan of US$300 million, which could be disbursed over five years in the form of equipment, machinery, and commodities.[112] Stalin instructed a group, led by Mikoyan and Ivan Kovalev, to prepare a draft of the loan agreement while Liu was still in Moscow, and the two sides signed a preliminary memorandum regarding the loan and its terms in late July.[113] Less than six months later, in De-cember 1949, Mao was preparing to board a train for Moscow—his first trip abroad—where he would meet Stalin for the first (and only) time in person and sign the treaty that would secure the loan and consummate re-lations between the Soviet Union and the new Chinese Communist state.

When Mao left Beijing on December 6, economic aid remained a top objective.[114] But even as he was preoccupied with securing assistance from the leader of the socialist world, Mao was also attuned to prospects for trade with capitalists. On December 22, the day after Stalin's birthday, Mao ca-bled Beijing to urge the Central Committee to adopt a comprehensive perspective while preparing for a Sino–Soviet trade agreement. He re-minded them that China had already done business, or was going to do business, with Britain, Japan, the United States, India, and other nations, and that China must therefore take trade with these capitalist states into account when preparing for future trade with the Soviet Union.[115]

Mao recognized that China's relationship to international markets re-mained unsettled, and he was firm in his conviction that China would "lean" toward socialism in its foreign affairs, but he also presumed that for the time being China would continue to trade with its traditional trade partners, most of which were capitalists. For Mao, the question remained not whether to continue this trade, but how. How would the CCP synthe-size its budding relationship to the Soviet Union with China's long-standing ties to capitalist markets, all while redefining the terms of China's trade with capitalists to suit the Party's own economic and political objectives? All of this remained uncertain as Mao's train crossed Siberia, and maybe this was for the best. If he had held too tightly to a fixed vision of China's future trade, he almost certainly would have been disappointed. Too many of the elements that shaped the Party's trade agenda were beyond his control. He couldn't control Stalin or the Soviets. Markets and businesses had their own agendas. Access to hard currency and financing remained uncertain.[116] Changes in regional and international politics were even more elusive and unforeseeable. Unbeknownst to Mao as he sat smoking in his train car, war would break out in Korea in just six months, a development that surely would have upended a clear and comprehensive trade plan, had he developed one.

3

THE KOREAN WAR AND THE FIGHT FOR TRADE

JUST OVER A WEEK INTO THE NEW YEAR, on January 10, 1950, Zhou Enlai also boarded a train for Moscow. Mao had been in the Soviet capital since December 16, and late in the evening on January 2 he sent a cable to Beijing instructing his premier to spend several days preparing for talks with the Soviets, then to rendezvous in Moscow for negotiations on the new Sino–Soviet treaty.[1] Zhou had ten days to organize his thoughts—the length of time it would take him to cross Siberia and reach the Soviet capital. He knew trade and economic affairs would figure prominently in the upcoming negotiations. On January 7, Mao had again cabled from Moscow ordering Zhou and the Central Committee to develop a comprehensive trade plan for 1950, one that included not just trade with the Soviets and fellow socialist states but also Great Britain, France, the Netherlands, Belgium, Australia, Japan, Canada, and the United States.[2] By the time Zhou's train passed into Soviet territory, he had been joined by Party experts who understood China's economic needs. Li Fuchun was there; so was Ye Jizhuang, China's new minister of trade. Also joining the delegation were experts in finance, steel, and coal; trade officials from Manchuria; and diplomats from the Ministry of Foreign Affairs.[3]

Planning for peace, stability, and growth preoccupied the delegation, just as it did Mao in Moscow. "The most important question at the present time is the question of establishing peace," Mao had told Stalin during a brief welcome reception. "China needs a period of 3–5 years of peace," Mao explained, "which would be used to bring the economy back to pre-war levels and to stabilize the country in general." A central component of this reconstruction effort, he believed, and a priority for the Chinese delegation in Moscow, was Soviet financial aid. "We would like to decide on the question of Soviet credit to China, that is[,] to draw up a credit agreement for 300,000,000 dollars," he told Stalin on December 16, his first day in the Soviet capital. When Stalin offered to formalize the agreement right then and there, if the chairman so wished, Mao responded in no uncertain terms: "Yes, exactly now," he said.[4]

The Soviet loan was just one aspect of the bilateral negotiations, however, and it took several weeks to reach an agreement on the substance of the new Sino–Soviet treaty. Much of this time was consumed by posturing rather than discussions. After Mao's first exchange with Stalin on December 16, he saw the Soviet leader again at the Bolshoi Theater on December 21, Stalin's birthday, but several weeks passed before the two met again. During the first weeks of the new year, before Zhou Enlai's arrival on January 20, Stalin toyed with Mao by neglecting him, an unsubtle reminder to the Chinese leader of his rank on the socialist totem. Mao understood perfectly; the inhospitality insulted and infuriated him.[5] Despite the slight, which Mao would never forget, larger political and economic imperatives ultimately prevailed, and the two sides eventually signed a new Sino–Soviet Treaty of Friendship, Alliance, and Mutual Assistance on February 14, 1950.

The new treaty was by no means an unalloyed success for the Chinese delegation. The Soviets insisted on larding the agreement with secret protocols that gave them economic privileges in Manchuria and in the northwestern autonomous region of Xinjiang. But by the time Mao and Zhou left Moscow to return to Beijing on February 17, they had nevertheless achieved two consequential successes: they had cemented Communist China's first strategic alliance and they had secured an economic lifeline for the fledgling state. The new treaty committed both parties to the development and consolidation of bilateral economic ties and to undertaking all possible economic cooperation. But more important, the two sides also finally signed the loan agreement that the CCP had been seeking since the previous winter, which China would use to purchase supplies for building and upgrading hydropower stations, metallurgical plants, railroads, factories, and coal mines.[6] China promised to repay the loan with a mix of strategic materials, agricultural produce, and cash.[7]

In China, state propagandists heralded the treaty as a historic achievement. The front page of the *People's Daily* commemorated the event with large portraits of Mao and Stalin above the fold, each leader turned toward the other, both gazing slightly upward. Page 2 spelled out the many successes achieved by the CCP leadership in Moscow, including the terms of the new loan. An editorial on the following page explained that the new agreements had "brought the relationship between the two great powers of China and the Soviet Union into a new era," a development that carried "great political importance and historical significance for the entire [Far] East and the world."[8]

All of this seemed promising, the loan in particular, and it came at a welcome moment for Chen Yun, who was in Beijing when the news broke. He was presiding over a national conference organized by the CFEC, where officials were grappling with scarce funds and mounting expenditures at the level of the central government.[9] Chen was also troubled by a litany of other economic issues. He worried about capital flight—some of the bourgeoisie were moving their money to Hong Kong and the United States. He had concerns about inflation and the stability of commodity prices. He was uneasy about the health of state economic institutions, especially the chronic threats of corruption and waste. He also worried about provincialism in the ranks, which might tempt his bureaucrats to neglect broad national gains in favor of narrow institutional ones.[10] More broadly, he worried about how to instill confidence in the new state and its ability to stabilize and grow the economy, particularly given the dearth of economic experience among Party officials.

News of the Soviet loan and the bilateral treaty offered a shot of encouragement as Chen stewed over these concerns. He had spent much of early 1950 delivering speeches, writing op-eds and reports, and convening meetings devoted to finding solutions to his economic concerns. A common refrain in his work was the need to instill discipline—in spending, in revenue collection, in commitment to shared national goals—always by means of centralized government control over the economy. By early spring, he was feeling more confident. He reported to the Politburo on March 29 that the nation's financial situation had improved. Last year, the nation's deficit stood at 65.8 percent of revenue. Now, three months into the new year and following a national campaign to unify control over finance and economics, the budget was nearly balanced.[11] There were still problems—many private businesses remained shuttered, for example, especially in Shanghai, which was reeling under the Nationalist blockade, and the Party had yet to resolve persistent grain shortages and lags in industrial production—but on the whole the economy seemed to be moving in the right direction.[12]

Chen emphasized this point during a June 15 meeting of the National Committee of the Chinese People's Political Consultative Conference. "Our nation's economy is now at a major turning point in history," he said, and he was righter than he knew.[13] Chen's theme was the domestic economy, and his point was that China had finally begun its long-awaited transition from a "feudal" and "semicolonial" backwater into an industrializing, modern power. His remarks concentrated on the policies that would achieve rapid recovery and growth in a peaceful climate after years of civil war. Yet just ten days after the speech, on June 25, 1950, a massive force of North Korean tanks and troops crossed the thirty-eighth parallel and invaded South Korea. In less than thirty-six hours, the United States government decided to send forces to support its South Korean ally.[14] In another four months, China itself would become embroiled in the conflict, which by then had expanded considerably.

When Chinese "volunteer" troops entered the Korean War in October 1950, they found themselves stuck in a protracted conflict with the world's most powerful "imperialist" nation and its United Nations allies.[15] Without question, the war upended Chinese Communist leaders' expectations of the kind of international environment in which they would pursue China's development. Rather than the three to five years of peace and rebuilding that Mao and Chen Yun had hoped for, China was mired in a conflict that, if it continued to escalate, would not only siphon precious resources away from rebuilding the domestic economy but could also threaten the very survival of the Chinese state. The new wartime environment also changed the way senior Party officials and working-level traders thought about the global economic system and China's place within it. By extension, the war also shaped the strategies and tactics that China used to achieve its economic objectives on the world stage. The People's Republic of China would still do business with its socialist allies and much of the capitalist world, as Mao had anticipated in January, but it would do so under vastly different circumstances.

Laying a Foundation

On a steamy day in mid-July 1949, when Mao's trip to Moscow was still five months into the future, a middle-aged cadre named Lin Haiyun arrived in Beiping with a major task ahead of him.[16] He had been in Tianjin for months, preoccupied with the challenge of taking control over the city's commerce without strangling it. Now, in Beiping, he was responsible for thinking of commerce on a national rather than municipal scale. Lin made his way toward his new office in the leafy legation quarter at the corner of Zhengyi Road and Dongjiaomin Alley. He walked up the stone steps, beneath the Romanesque archway, and into the brick European revival building that was originally the Peking branch of the Yokohama Specie Bank.

One of Lin's first orders of business was to map out the bureaucracy that would become the backbone of Communist China's trade with the capitalist world. That summer, the CCP Central Organization Department had appointed Lin director of the Foreign Trade Business Office (Waimao Yewu Shi), a post he held concurrently with his role as deputy director of the Central Commerce Office (Zhongyang Shangye Chu). These titles gave him the authority to help create offices capable of conducting business with capitalists abroad, and to staff these offices with competent civil servants and Party cadres. Lin had other trade responsibilities, too. It was his job to encourage state-owned and private firms in China to cultivate trade with businesses abroad. He was also responsible for developing ties between the future Chinese state and the foreign firms that remained in China after "liberation." But his core mandate in the summer of 1949 was to help organize a new trade bureaucracy, a task he would tackle in close coordination with Yao Yilin, who was now director of the Central Commerce Office and Li's immediate supervisor.[17]

Lin and Yao began by writing down the responsibilities of a new Central Ministry of Trade (Zhongyang Maoyi Bu) that would oversee all trade in China, foreign and domestic. In August, Lin oversaw the drafting of a second set of regulations, this time for a unit within the Ministry of Trade called the Foreign Trade Division (Guowai Maoyi Si), an organization designed to guide all of China's foreign trade after the founding of the People's Republic of China.[18] Both documents underwent minor revisions in late September to bring them into line with the spirit of the Common Program, and by mid-October the Central Committee was prepared to announce the formal founding of both institutions.

Figure 3.1   Ye Jizhuang, known as the "red housekeeper," was the PRC's first minister of trade. Wikimedia Commons.

On October 21, 1949, the government formally established the nation's new Ministry of Trade. From the outset, experienced trade officials staffed the ministry's top echelons. Ye Jizhuang, a Guangdong native and Red Army veteran in his late fifties, left his post in northeast China as head of the Foreign Trade Department of the Northeast People's Government to become the PRC's first minister of trade.[19] Ye was a meticulous man, a tidier and taskmaster, so much so that colleagues called him "the red housekeeper." He was also good with numbers and a stickler for precision. He bristled at words such as "roughly" (*dagai*), "maybe" (*keneng*), and "more or less" (*chabuduo*) during meetings. Numbers are critical in economic work, he told his staff. The Party used those figures to make policy decisions and to carry them out, so there was no room for slipshod work.[20]

Yao Yilin became one of Ye Jizhuang's three vice ministers at the Ministry of Trade, alongside Lei Renmin, an economic specialist from Sichuan, and Sha Qianli, a Jiangsu native who would go on to work at the People's

Bank of China.[21] Lin Haiyun was appointed head of the ministry's General Office (Bangong Ting), a position that entailed working with ministry leaders to develop internal policies and procedures, many of which were based on suggestions from the Soviet Union.[22] But Lin soon gravitated toward foreign trade, and on December 26, 1949, he was reassigned to lead the ministry's Foreign Trade Division, which placed him at the center of the Party's plan to institutionalize its trade practices and embed them within state policy.[23] This ministry-wide mandate required working across several offices that were organized along both geographical and functional lines.

Lin's new role put him in touch with the ministry's Office of European and American Trade, which was responsible for drafting a plan for trade with capitalist nations in Europe, the Americas, and Africa that supported the national trade agenda. Staff in the office researched various aspects of the markets in these regions. They studied industrial production, for example, and they monitored market prices. They also tracked the supply and demand of goods and materials. These officials also performed the routine procedures that kept international commerce flowing, from preparing background materials before negotiations to scheduling meetings and drafting contracts on behalf of Chinese state trading companies. Staff members in the Office of Asian Trade did similar work for state firms trading with capitalists in East and Southeast Asia.[24]

Workers in these regional offices coordinated with colleagues in an office called the Administrative Division (Xingzheng Guanli Ke), which fell under the Trade Management Office (Maoyi Guanli Chu) of the Foreign Trade Division. The Administration Division worked with the export and import branches of the Foreign Trade Division and the experts in the Offices of European and American Trade and Asian Trade to propose responses to market developments abroad.[25] Staff in the various functional offices of the Foreign Trade Division also analyzed developments in capitalist markets around the world, just like their colleagues in regional offices. Officials in the Plans Office (Jihua Chu), for instance, monitored the prices of hog bristles, eggs, tea, tin, and other global commodities. They also published reports that described market trends for state trading companies.[26] The Foreign Shipping Office (Guowai Yunshu Chu) researched port fees and freight rates around the world.[27] In all of these offices, whether functional or regional, workers collected and analyzed information about various aspects of business and capitalism abroad. All of this required knowledge and prior experience, which created a recruiting challenge for the Foreign Trade Division.

Lin Haiyun recognized that his employees must understand finance. They had to be conversant in markets. Foreign language skills were also a must. He looked first for cadres who had learned about trade as staffers in the various financial offices of the Party's North China People's Government. But ministry vacancies far exceeded the number of experienced cadres, so Lin had no choice but to abandon the Party's unwritten rule, in place since the 1930s, that commercial work must remain in the hands of trusted Party functionaries. He hired holdovers from the Nationalist regime, the same technical experts who had overseen China's foreign trade before "liberation," but who had decided to stay on to help build a new China. Many of these former KMT officials had studied abroad. Wang Yanling was educated in the United States before joining the Nationalist government. After the founding of the People's Republic of China, Lin appointed him to head the Commodity Inspection Department of the Foreign Trade Division. Elite Chinese universities also yielded new talent, and Lin recruited recent graduates of Beijing University, Qinghua University, and Fu'er University, which later became Beijing Normal University.[28]

Soon Lin was casting an even wider net for talent. Using the resources of the Party's Central Organization Department, the Ministry of Foreign Affairs, and the Hong Kong office of the Xinhua News Agency, he sought out Chinese abroad who might be willing to return to China to help rebuild the nation through trade. This is how Lin identified people like Zhou Shiyu, who joined the Foreign Trade Division after completing his doctorate in the United States. Zhou was one of many returnees who used their graduate training on behalf of the Foreign Trade Division. This influx of fresh talent lent a cosmopolitan, technocratic air to the Foreign Trade Division.[29]

But the CFEC was not content to rely solely on the in-house expertise of the Ministry of Trade to develop the nation's trade portfolio. In July 1950, the ministry convened a nationwide conference in Beijing to discuss import and export business in China. During the conference, a consensus emerged that more had to be done to raise the level of knowledge among workers and researchers involved in international trade. Conferees decided to establish a forum—the China International Trade Association (ITA, or Zhongguo Guoji Maoyi Yanjiuhui in Chinese)—that would serve as a network for state workers, academics, bankers, customs officials, and others with an interest in foreign trade. Through the ITA, these professionals could share insights and exchange ideas in support of the state's efforts to boost trade and spur economic construction.[30]

By recruiting and connecting these professionals, Lin Haiyun and the CCP were creating space within the nation's bureaucracy for people who were proficient in many of the skills sought by firms in capitalist nations. These specialists shared the same professional interests and analytical frameworks as their counterparts in New York or London, but they were meant to use their skills for fundamentally different aims—not for profit alone, but for the good of the nation and the glory of the revolution. For them, profit was framed as a means to larger ends rather than an end in itself. The ITA was designed to support these political goals by spreading knowledge and expertise across trade-related industries in China, but before the association managed to draft its founding charter, events in Korea transformed the work that the nation's trade experts were supposed to perform.

Chinese troops crossed the Yalu River into North Korea on the evening of October 19, 1950, setting in motion a series of events that changed the environment in which Chinese trade officials operated. In response to China's decision to join the fighting, on December 3 the US Department of Commerce announced what amounted to a complete embargo on American exports to mainland China, Hong Kong, and Macao. Technically, any American who wanted to export products to these destinations could apply for an export license, but the Commerce Department had no intention of issuing these licenses broadly.

A few days later, on December 8, the Commerce Department took the unprecedented step of prohibiting American ships and planes "anywhere in the world" from carrying "strategic materials" to proscribed countries, which included the People's Republic of China. It no longer mattered which ports an American carrier used to load or unload goods—if a US shipper carried cargo anywhere in the world that was bound for final delivery to the PRC, the shipment violated US Commerce Department regulations. Anyone caught defying the order faced a fine of US$10,000, a year in prison, and the possibility of having their operating privileges revoked.[31]

These measures were part of a larger US trend toward tightening restrictions on trade with Communist China. Beginning in early 1950, the United States had pushed to subsume PRC trade under the mandate of the

Coordinating Committee (COCOM), a multilateral organization of US allies established in November 1949 to stem the flow of strategic goods into the Soviet Union and Eastern Europe.[32] COCOM lacked the authority to enforce export restrictions because it was a voluntary organization, but in October 1951 the United States would pass the Mutual Defense Assistance Control Act, known as the Battle Act, which empowered the US president to withhold economic and military aid to any nation that allowed the sale of US-embargoed goods to a prohibited destination. This meant anyone who violated COCOM restrictions risked losing US aid.[33] The war in Korea also led COCOM to establish in 1952 a related organization called the China Committee, or "CHINCOM," which enforced restrictions on exports to China and North Korea.

CHINCOM offered a starker, less forgiving approach to trade controls than COCOM, one that the Truman administration believed was commensurate with China's belligerence in Korea.[34] Both COCOM and CHINCOM kept lists of banned exports, but the latter's list was longer. It included not just weapons and goods that could be used to fight a war, but also tools, equipment, and technology that would support China's broader industrialization efforts. The difference between COCOM and CHINCOM controls became known as the "China differential," and it reflected not just list lengths, but also more nuanced differences between the two control regimes. In addition to a list of prohibited exports, for example, COCOM also maintained an index of products permitted for export to the Soviet Union and Eastern Europe in limited quantities. COCOM also kept a list of goods for "surveillance." Items on this list could be exported, but had to be monitored so that shipments could be halted quickly if strategic considerations demanded. CHINCOM lacked these nuances; it was simply a catalog of products off-limits to China and North Korea.[35]

IN AUGUST 1950, just two months after the start of the Korean War, the Bureau of Foreign Trade in Guangdong saw early signs of these exclusionary trends when it observed that US and Japanese agencies had begun to scrutinize the activities of four Party-run companies and two banks in Hong Kong. Zhou Enlai and others began to suspect a further tightening of US and Japanese controls on trade with China.[36] To preempt any such moves, the Party directed these organizations to prepare to cease Hong Kong operations and ordered senior personnel to evacuate.[37]

When the embargo finally did arrive, its impact was immediate. The US Commerce Department ordered the off-loading and detention of shipments already en route to Hong Kong pending further instructions from Washington. Panic spread through Hong Kong business circles. Local shipping agents, insurers, and banks besieged the staff of the US consulate in Hong Kong with inquiries. Colonial officials in Hong Kong, responding to anecdotes collected by local chambers of commerce, were indignant at what they described privately to US officials as a "hysterical" approach to export control.[38]

Officials in Beijing were also indignant, and alarmed. A week after the December 3 order, the CFEC still had not received a formal note explaining the details of the new American restrictions. Still, Chinese officials quickly pieced together an understanding of what they were facing. On December 12, the CFEC prepared a report for Mao, Zhou, and the Central Committee that outlined the American embargo and proposed countermeasures to minimize losses.[39] The report also observed that Japan had announced its own ban on exports to China, Hong Kong, and Macao, beginning December 6, although this ban was slated to last only until January 15.[40] Four days after the CFEC wrote its report, the US government froze all Chinese assets in American financial institutions. Communist China was being pushed out of international markets.

As the details of the US embargo became clear, Beijing salvaged as much as it could of the nation's trade.[41] Employees at China Resources in Hong Kong went on a buying spree, snapping up bicycles, cigarette paper, and anything else employees believed would become more difficult to obtain as the US embargo tightened.[42] They moved quickly, draining overseas bank accounts before they could be frozen by the Americans. Still, despite these efforts, the CFEC estimated that the United States was able to seize roughly US$42.5 million worth of PRC assets, a staggering sum equal to 10 percent of the total value of China's imports from capitalist nations in 1950.[43] Without a doubt, the embargo was a crippling blow to the nation's trade.

And yet, beyond these short-term losses, Party leaders also sensed opportunity. The embargo forced the Ministry of Trade to think carefully about how it could turn the fighting in Korea, and even the embargo itself, to China's advantage. On October 7, 1950, the ministry observed that "frenzied preparations for war" by imperialist nations had changed the old forms of foreign trade, and not all for the worse. Flourishing markets were causing prices to surge for some goods, and the ministry's analysts saw signs that this bullishness would continue, so they called for a break from some of the usual restrictions on exports and marketing.[44] There should be more flexibility when setting price controls for some exports, the ministry said, which would allow traders to take advantage of the surge in global commodity prices. If the state's price caps could rise alongside prices in the marketplace, China's exporters would be better positioned to maximize earnings from sales of goods such as hog bristles and tung oil.

The Ministry of Trade realized that the wartime environment also required heightened caution, and its October 7 guidance revealed an underlying wariness. The ministry encouraged traders to strive for barter transactions and to avoid long-term contracts. They should also avoid exporting on consignment, a practice in which a firm is paid for its exports only after they are sold abroad by a foreign distributor.[45] These moves would all lower the risk of selling goods abroad in an uncertain climate. Barter contracts lessened exporters' reliance on international banking and eased the demand for scarce capital, short-term contracts minimized the risk of major market swings, and avoidance of exporting on consignment ensured that payment for exports arrived in China promptly.

This mix of uncertainty and opportunity led the Ministry of Trade to conclude that it needed closer coordination and better communication within the trading community. Import and export companies would have to integrate more tightly and trade professionals needed to cooperate closely in pursuit of barter trade agreements. The ministry asked its Foreign Trade Bureaus in port cities to "strengthen" joint meetings and requested meetings between importers and exporters to exchange information and improve research. Ministry officials in Beijing also asked lower-level officials in the ports to provide updates whenever possible.[46] The CFEC reinforced the ministry's request on November 6 by ordering all foreign trade management offices in China's main ports to report directly to the Ministry of Trade in Beijing.[47] The ministry even installed long-distance telephone lines and required trade officials in Tianjin, Shanghai, Wuhan, Guangzhou, and elsewhere to call the ministry headquarters nightly with reports on local conditions.[48]

The phone reporting was an improvement, but only so much information could be conveyed through nightly calls. And even if lower-level officials could keep the leadership abreast of everything they observed from their offices, the trade scenes in places like Shanghai and Tianjin were simply too big and too complex, and the wartime climate was too uncertain, for cadres to follow all the trends, much less analyze them and propose policy responses. To keep up, the ministry needed the eyes and expertise of the entire trading community in China—not just officials in state-run firms and Ministry of Trade offices, but private firms, bankers, entrepreneurs, and even academics.

The ITA was an obvious venue for bringing together these constituencies. In January 1951, trade officials from around the nation converged on Beijing for a conference on trade management and to discuss the future of the ITA.[49] The decisions they reached dovetailed perfectly with the push from the Ministry of Trade and the CFEC to unify China's national trade community and pool its expertise. The conferees first sought to clarify the aims of the ITA and to organize a structure. They drafted a constitution, which headquartered the ITA in Beijing and planned for branches in Tianjin, Shanghai, Qingdao, Guangzhou, Hankou, Kunming, Dalian, and several smaller markets.[50]

The constitution also established research as a core mission. The association expected its members to analyze tariffs, trade management practices, product standards and specifications, foreign currencies, commercial treaties, and other elements of international commerce. Members were encouraged to collect and analyze data on the supply, demand, and production of goods at home and abroad, to research distribution systems, and to track prices. But research was only part of a member's responsibilities. Affiliates were also expected to help increase exports and enable growth. They were tasked with raising the quality of exports and improving substitutes for goods that previously had been imported but were no longer available because of the American-led embargo. None of this work mattered unless information circulated efficiently within the community, so the ITA committed to organizing symposia, lectures, and reports to share insights and findings.[51]

ITA membership was not compulsory, so the Party had to entice practitioners and experts to join, many of whom may have been wary of leaning too far into the embrace of an organization underwritten by the state and, ultimately, the Party. Delegates to the Beijing conference identified several benefits that might entice prospective recruits. Members could contact other professionals through the ITA network for assistance when researching international trade, for example, and they could circulate their own research and analyses with other members. They also enjoyed discounts on association publications and special access to lectures and symposia.[52] These perks appealed to professionalism, and by framing the benefits of membership in purely professional terms, the ITA underscored its intention to assemble a mass of engaged experts and practitioners, all committed to using their expertise to support the larger goal of boosting economic growth through foreign trade.

This is precisely the expertise that the Ministry of Trade needed to augment its capabilities, but the ITA also created political risks. Recruiting experts from all walks of life opened the door for reactionaries, closeted capitalists, and other dubious elements to seep into the organization. To guard against this, the ITA wrote admission guidelines that would screen out undesirables. Any individual wishing to join had to present introductions from at least two standing ITA members, for example. They also needed a formal approval from the association council before they could be admitted.[53] Quality controls like these ensured that ITA members were not just trade specialists but also politically palatable.

In its first year, the ITA succeeded in assembling experts from across industries, public and private. In Shanghai, by far the largest ITA branch, individuals working in private firms and in the "cultural sector"—most likely at universities—accounted for roughly half of the 730 individual memberships.[54] A closer look at the branch roster reveals that the ITA drew in professionals working for the Shanghai Customs Office, the Minsheng Transport Ship Company, Fudan University, the Bank of Shanghai, and the China Insurance Company, as well as government officials from the municipal Bureau of Trade and Industry and the East China Regional Trade Office.[55] Collectively, these people brought a wealth of expertise just when the Ministry of Trade needed it most.

As the American-led embargo tightened in 1951, the central government had to find new ways to make inroads into overseas markets. The Japanese government followed its decision in December 1950 to join the China embargo with an announcement on February 28, 1951, that Tokyo would no longer permit barter trade with mainland China.[56] More Sino–Japanese trade began to flow through Hong Kong as a result. Roughly 80 percent of the US$38 million in hog bristles, peanuts, tung oil, coal, and other Chinese goods destined for Japan looped south through Hong Kong in 1951 before being shipped north again to Japan.[57]

These indirect shipments allowed the CCP to conceal elements of Sino–Japanese trade, but they also reflected the Ministry of Trade's growing inclination to turn to Hong Kong as a solution to China's broader embargo woes. On May 25, 1951, the ministry drafted instructions on behalf of the CFEC calling for national trade flows to shift south, toward the South China region. The instructions explained that trade with capitalist nations would become increasingly difficult, and China should strive to use Hong Kong and Macao as springboards into these markets.[58] That same year, the South China Finance Committee opened a string of "joint offices" near the borders with Hong Kong and Macao to handle the increase in trade.[59]

Anticipating that the United States might try to squeeze the Party in Hong Kong, Beijing had already taken steps to conceal its activities there. Months before the United States announced its embargo, Zhou Enlai and Bo Yibo had ordered officials in Guangdong to "organize mass smuggling" in Hong Kong and Macao. They instructed South China customs officials, trade bureaus, and border guards to coordinate reception stations for smuggled goods in small ports along the Chinese coast.[60] Soon, these stations had plenty of work. By late 1951, the CIA estimated that China was smuggling between two hundred and three hundred tons of strategic materials from Hong Kong to mainland China via Macao every night.[61]

Some of this smuggling resembled the Party's pre-1949 trade patterns. One CCP-controlled company was shipping salt and soybeans from north China to Hong Kong by sea, just like the *Aldan* had several years earlier. The firm then bought medicines and metals in Hong Kong to ship north to Tianjin.[62] Other operations extended beyond Hong Kong and Macao to markets farther afield. In August 1951, the CIA reported that Beijing was smuggling "strategic war materials" into China from Malaya by way of Bangkok, Hong Kong, and Macao, using a network that operated with the tacit approval of Thai officials.[63] Once these goods arrived in Hong Kong, the CCP used multiple conduits to funnel them across the Guangdong–Hong Kong border. The CCP-controlled company Wu Fu, or "Five Blessings," smuggled tires and gasoline from Hong Kong into Guangdong under the protection of Hong Kong police officers who received kickbacks. Every night after dark, Wu Fu ferried two thousand gallons of gasoline and fifty sets of tires across the Sham Chun River at Lo Wu while police at the border looked the other way.[64] Gasoline and tires also made their way into Guangdong at Lok Ma Chau, two miles west of Lo Wu. So did kerosene, telephones, car parts, and electrical supplies. The CIA also reported cases of boats smuggling medicines, lubricants, and electrical supplies into Guangdong farther east, from an inlet near Sha Tau Kok in the New Territories.[65]

These smuggling operations flowed in both directions. The CIA reported in May 1951 that Chinese opium flowed into Hong Kong and Macao from Guangdong and Tianjin. In the latter case, ships carrying the drug were often accompanied by Chinese naval escorts for part of the journey before being unloaded onto junks at prearranged points. According to the CIA, these opium sales generated an important source of income for the Chinese state.[66]

The proximity of Hong Kong to Guangdong and the Party's long experience trading there made the colony an obvious conduit for Chinese trade during the early years of the embargo, but as detailed CIA reporting suggests, it was becoming more difficult for Party traders to operate clandestinely in the colony. As the US government deepened its commitment to shutting down PRC trade, the size of the staff at the Hong Kong consulate increased significantly—well beyond its consular needs. Between October 1949 and late 1951, the size of the staff at the consulate swelled from sixty-seven to ninety-six employees, a conspicuous growth spurt. The office of the governor of Hong Kong observed that a staff of ninety-six seemed hardly necessary to look after the affairs of an American community that numbered scarcely 1,000 people.[67] It was obvious, wrote one British bureaucrat, "that if these officials in fact earn their pay, they must be doing other work—i.e. work concerned with China."[68]

He was right. US officials at the consulate began monitoring CCP trade through Hong Kong in late 1949, just after the founding of the PRC. They regularly collected statistics and compiled monthly reports on Chinese Communist trade for policymakers and analysts in Washington.[69] These reports, which were based mostly on shipping manifests, became a staple of consular correspondence.[70] The consulate was churning them out weekly by December 1950 to chronicle the activities of shippers and trade agents with ties to China, including CCP front companies such as China Resources and long-standing pillars of East Asian commerce, such as Butterfield & Swire.[71] The reports, which offered more data than analysis, were both exhaustive and exhausting. Karl Rankin, the US consul general, estimated that his staff spent between thirty and forty man-hours preparing each report.[72] On top of this, many of the consulate's ninety-six employees were also busy enforcing the embargo, chasing down rumors of violations wherever they led.[73]

Hong Kong authorities soon began to suspect that the American consulate's zeal for the embargo was leading to strong-arm tactics. On April 23, 1951, the Hong Kong colonial secretary, J. F. Nicoll, reported to London anecdotes of US officials summoning local businessmen to the American consulate on various pretexts, then dropping heavy hints that these businessmen might not be permitted to continue serving as agents for US exports. Mostly, the Americans threatened agents who exported American products to China, Nicoll observed, but not always. He had heard of at least one case in which a US official warned a non-American firm that it might lose its right to export a popular American cigarette brand unless the company dropped its business exporting Swiss drugs to the PRC. It did not seem to concern the US official that Switzerland was not a member of COCOM. The American official also hinted that the firm's director might have problems obtaining a visa for a planned visit to the United States. Nicoll admitted that evidence to support such allegations was sparse, but an American official had admitted to him privately that the consulate did in fact use such tactics.[74]

Pressures like these, along with the expanding American presence in the colony, began to eat away at Hong Kong's allure as a pipeline for Chinese goods to overseas markets. One former employee of China Resources who worked in Hong Kong during the Korean War, Zheng Chinan, recalled years later that some firms wouldn't dare meet with him during business hours. They were afraid of "spies," he explained. Others refused to sell Zheng large quantities of goods, such as oil, forcing him to pool products through piecemeal purchases before shipping them to the mainland. The Americans targeted PRC shipping, too. Huaxia, a Party front company, had to use multiple cutouts to ship goods from Hong Kong to mainland ports, sometimes using a company for a single shipment before closing it down to evade American scrutiny.[75]

All of this raised the costs and risks of trade in the colony, and officials at the Ministry of Trade in Beijing realized they would need multiple channels into foreign markets if trade was going to develop under the embargo. The ministry took a major step in this direction in 1951 when it expanded its presence into Europe by setting up commercial offices inside several PRC embassies where China had already established diplomatic relations. These offices were meant to be permanent, rooted in the new state's bureaucracy, rather than ad hoc arrangements. The representatives who staffed them did not pose as private businessmen the way employees of China Resources and other front companies did. Nor were they diplomats working under the Ministry of Foreign Affairs (MFA). The Ministry of Trade appointed these representatives directly, paid their salaries, and funded the offices. The representatives reported directly to the Ministry of Trade in Beijing and to local embassy management, which was appointed by the MFA. This dual chain of command ensured that the activities of these commercial representatives synced with the diplomatic objectives of the MFA.[76]

Yet the decision to expand into Europe raised the question of political reliability. Leaders in Beijing had reservations about stationing trade officials overseas so close to rich, capitalist markets. While this was not a new concern in the context of CCP trade, the offices in Europe did pose unique challenges. In the 1930s and 1940s, close personal ties between Party leaders on the Chinese mainland and CCP traders in Hong Kong helped to allay anxieties about the corrupting influences of money and markets on cadres. Chen Yun and Mao Zedong could trust specialists like Qin Bangli to live in Hong Kong and to work on the Party's behalf because he was a known quantity. Chen Yun could vouch personally for Qin's ability to operate in the heart of capitalist markets without being seduced by the glitz of materialism.

By 1951, however, the Party's capitalist trade had outgrown these early personal networks. The Ministry of Trade was an institution, and the impersonal nature of appointments raised the odds of working-level cadres straying from the revolutionary path, particularly given the nature of their work. Not only did these officials arrange insurance, shipping, and other administrative aspects of trade but they also negotiated deals directly with trade departments and businesses from capitalist countries in Europe. They were permitted to sign contracts, arrange cargo inspections, and charter shipments with local transportation companies.[77] These interactions brought trade workers into the orbit of capitalism daily, and too much time in this ideological swirl could be disorienting, so the ministry felt it had to develop controls to keep its cadres tethered to the state and its commercial agenda.

One such measure was the requirement that Ministry of Trade officials in Europe report back to Beijing regularly with updates on how all negotiations were proceeding. They were also expected to maintain the same spartan existence as all PRC diplomats despite their routine contact with nearby business communities. The ministry ordered that the expenses and "cadre lifestyles" of its overseas staff must also adhere to embassy protocols. The budgets of trade officials had to be approved by embassy management, and any issues that arose locally concerning "principles" had to be reported to the embassy leadership.[78]

Establishing these commercial offices may have been a political risk, but this was outweighed by the potential gains from direct access to Europe's capitalist markets. In addition to representing the Chinese government in business transactions, Ministry of Trade officials in Europe also conducted research that dovetailed with efforts back home to deepen China's understanding of capitalist trade. They conducted investigations and collected materials on the local commercial climate, market trends, and product technologies—all in consultation with the CFEC and the ministry headquarters in Beijing.[79] They served as an appendage of the new state capable of reaching straight into European markets and, as far as top CCP officials were concerned, they would serve as a beachhead for a trade program that would grow significantly in the years ahead. As these cadres were still settling into life in Europe, their colleagues in Beijing were pushing to expand trade with capitalists elsewhere. In the fall of 1951, Zhou Enlai seized an opportunity to press this agenda through a much more conspicuous, multilateral approach.

The Moscow Conference

On October 27, 1951, a group of left-leaning entrepreneurs from England, France, West Germany, the United States, and other capitalist nations met in Copenhagen with commercially minded citizens from several socialist states. For two days, they talked about trade.[80] The group had gathered in Denmark to seek ways to increase trade across the Cold War divide. By the time the meeting adjourned on October 28, the group had settled on the idea of convening an international economic conference as its next step.[81]

The group's agenda fit perfectly with Beijing's commitment to developing trade with the capitalist world, and Zhou Enlai was quick to see its potential value. He instructed the CFEC in Beijing to assist the preparations for the conference, and he sent an unofficial delegation—"the Chinese People's Committee in Defense of World Peace"—to participate in a series of preparatory meetings abroad.[82] The Chinese delegation included Wu Juenong, the general manager of the China Tea Company, Peking University president Ma Yinchu, and Ji Chaoding, a Columbia University–trained economist and director of the Bank of China.[83] But the group excluded representatives from the Ministry of Trade, an omission likely intended to preserve the nongovernmental image of its mission. Both Wu and Ji attended a subsequent planning meeting in Moscow in January, during which planners settled the specifics of the conference, which would convene in Moscow from April 3 to 12, 1952.

Organizers expected 443 delegates to attend the conference: 314 from capitalist nations and 129 from the socialist bloc—including 25 from the People's Republic of China.[84] Participants agreed beforehand not to discuss the merits or deficiencies of different economic systems.[85] After all, they claimed, the point was to discuss business, not politics—this was an apolitical gathering. No one believed this.

Zhou Enlai saw the conference for what it was: a highly visible venue where China could rebuff the embargo publicly and negotiate trade deals. When he reviewed the list of Chinese delegates to the conference prepared by the CFEC, he observed that the banking and financial sectors seemed well represented, but the group needed a trade expert. He asked about Lei Renmin as a possibility.[86]

Lei was a logical choice. The forty-two-year-old Shanxi native was from Pingyao, a famed financial center during the late Qing empire. He had studied economics as a graduate student at Waseda University in Tokyo before the outbreak of the Pacific War, and now, as a vice minister at the Ministry of Trade, he oversaw China's trade with the capitalist world.[87] He was also comfortable around foreigners. British officials found him "an agreeable personality, who is quite forthcoming in conversation."[88] Lei's character and training made him a good fit for the Moscow mission, but he was preoccupied with other concerns at the moment. In late 1951, the Party had launched a campaign that aimed at rooting out corruption and consolidating CCP control over the economy. The "Three Anti Campaign," as it was called, targeted the vices of corruption, waste, and obstructionism within the Chinese bureaucracy. It took aim at three groups in particular: CCP cadres, state bureaucrats, and managers of factories and firms. The campaign ran on allegations of corrupt and wasteful deeds, browbeaten confessions, mass meetings, and propaganda designed to stir up enthusiasm for eliminating corruption and vice.[89]

While the Three Anti Campaign was still unfolding, in January 1952 the Party launched a second movement, called the Five Anti Campaign, which used similar tactics but had a broader mandate. The Party mobilized workers and officials in cities across the country with parades, loudspeakers, newspaper editorials, and radio broadcasts, all calling on the masses to participate in an assault on China's corrupt bourgeoisie. The campaign took aim at the five depravities of bribery, tax evasion, theft of state property, abuse of government contracts, and theft of state secrets. But the real theme of the movement ran deeper: the CCP was demonstrating it would no longer protect private businesses in China. Entrepreneurs who stayed on in China, and those who returned home after "liberation" in 1949, would face the same antagonisms as foreign capitalists operating in China. The Party organized group criticism sessions, demanded confessions from business leaders, and encouraged industrialists and other presumed capitalists to report on one another to root out past transgressions and break apart economic hierarchies that had survived "liberation."

All of this cast a shadow over the Ministry of Trade, which had been recruiting precisely the individuals who were now being targeted by the campaigns. It was a fraught moment for Lei Renmin, given his role as coordinator of China's trade with the capitalist world. When Zhou Enlai proposed that Lei join the delegation to Moscow, the vice minister already had his hands full managing the campaigns inside the ministry and had little time for additional responsibilities.[90] The Party's Central Organization Department mentioned this to Zhou, but the premier was firm. "Let him go, let him go make friends, [and] have a look around," Zhou reportedly responded.[91] His insistence that Lei attend the conference offered backing at a sensitive moment not just for Lei himself but also for the kind of work he was overseeing at the Ministry of Trade.

On February 21, 1952, Zhou met with Lei Renmin and several others to review remarks for the coming conference and to scrutinize the delegation roster again. The group selected Nan Hanchen, governor of the People's Bank of China, to lead the delegation, with Lei and Ji Chaoding serving as deputies.[92] A few weeks later, on March 15, Zhou met with the entire delegation on the eve of its departure to offer some final guidance. "Opportunities to attend this kind of international economic conference are hard to come by," he told them, "[we] can't let it pass."[93] Zhou reminded them that most of the attendees would be progressives, "but there will also be reactionaries," he warned. Don't avoid them, he instructed. "You must make friends widely, don't just make friends with progressives; make reactionary friends, too."[94] It was a bold order, especially in the context of the Three and Five Anti Campaigns, but it underscored how important it was to the premier to fight the American-led embargo and to develop working relationships with capitalists abroad. The Moscow Conference was only a starting point. Zhou recognized that it wouldn't destroy the embargo. But by attending, he told the group, you "can expand our influence, [you] can open up a gap in the barrier."[95]

With these instructions, the group left for Moscow, where it was greeted by China's ambassador to the Soviet Union on March 27, five days before the conference opened.[96] The group had arrived early to confer with Soviet counterparts, but Lei was not among them. He was still preoccupied with the Three and Five Anti Campaigns back home, and wouldn't arrive until April 2, the day before the conference opened.[97]

When the conference began, nearly every detail seemed choreographed to showcase the modern sophistication of both the attendees and the host. Soviet sedans shuttled participants between the grand Sovietskaya Hotel and the conference site, a former nobleman's estate that the Soviets had repurposed into a trade union complex called the House of Unions. One of the halls inside the club, a former ballroom called the Hall of Columns, had been updated with modern features for the event, including the installation of blond birch desks and a simultaneous translation system like the one used at the United Nations, with headphones for each delegate, to allow attendees to follow the proceedings in English, French, German, Russian, Spanish, or Chinese. The Soviets also emplaced movie cameras and soundproof translation booths along the balcony that ringed the conference floor. Attendees could read special editions of *Foreign Trade, Currency and Credit,* and *Problems of Economics* in English, French, German, or Chinese.[98] All of these touches reinforced the deliberate cosmopolitanism of the conference. The Soviets and their guests, including the Chinese delegation, sought to present an image of inclusivity, openness, modernity, and transcendence across different economic and social systems.

The message underlying this ambiance—a shared desire to expand trade across the Cold War divide—became a common refrain among attendees. Oskar Lange, a Polish economist and diplomat who taught economics at the University of Chicago before renouncing his US citizenship to serve as the Polish People's Republic's first ambassador to the United States, reported during an April 9 plenary session that members of the conference group he chaired, the International Trade Group, had discussed the low volume of international trade, which he attributed to the decline in trade between the countries of the East and West. Delegates were anxious about this state of affairs, Lange reported, and many members of the International Trade Group attributed this "disruption" to "artificial obstacles" rooted in "discriminatory restrictions" of a noneconomic nature. The solution was obvious. Using another refrain that would become common during the conference, the International Trade Group proposed the "removal of all restrictions on foreign trade based on non-economic considerations."[99]

Dean Acheson was following these developments, and the American secretary of state thought the entire conference was "spurious." It was a spectacle. Conference organizers had concocted a program to "confuse and weaken" the "free world," he told prospective attendees in a press release. "They [the Soviets] wish to organize pressures in non-Communist countries against current restrictions on the export of strategic materials to the Soviet bloc," he explained. By chipping away at COCOM and its embargoes, the conference intended to undermine the strength and solidarity on which the present peace depended, he believed.[100] Spurious or not, the conference touched a nerve in the United States. American newspapers were derisive, but also captivated. The *New York Times* took interest in which Americans had declined invitations to the conference. These "men of good reputation," as Acheson called them, included former treasury secretary Henry Morgenthau, the Harvard economist John Kenneth Galbraith, and the chairman of the University of Chicago Economics Department, Theodore Schultz.[101] Supreme Court Justice William O. Douglas received a letter inquiring whether the United States would participate in such a conference, but did not receive a personal invitation. Even if he had, he told the *New York Times,* "I would of course decline it because I share the suspicion concerning the use of such paraphernalia by the Soviets."[102]

Justice Douglas's suspicion was warranted. The Soviets, and the Chinese, had every intention of using the conference to champion free trade and the principles of equality and mutual benefit. It was all counternarrative to COCOM embargos and blockades. Lei Renmin worked this message with particular flair during the conference. "I am firmly convinced," he concluded during a working group meeting on the morning of April 7, "that the nations being interconnected as they are, the artificial barriers could be removed and international trade would be able to develop normally."[103] His message was plain enough: trade was normal, a natural pursuit for all nations no matter their ideological predisposition, and the Americans were preventing it. Another claim, although tacit, must also have rankled Justice Douglas and Dean Acheson: the suggestion that socialism offered a shortcut to modern prosperity. The sleek cars, the opulence of the Sovietskaya Hotel, the modern communications technology, and the other "paraphernalia"—all of it reinforced the notion that socialism was bounding toward prosperity. Officials at the CIA also understood this message, the conference, and "the atmosphere" it created as a propaganda threat deserving of some kind of response. "Lacking any definitive lines of counter-propaganda and countermaneuver," the CIA deputy director of plans concluded glumly in a letter to the CIA director, "our side can be expected to sustain loss after loss."[104]

But the conference was more than just theater. Like many others, the Chinese were there also to do business. "We propose to discuss not only general principles, but definite business arrangements," Nan Hanchen explained during the April 4 plenary session.[105] Lei Renmin framed China's appeal for more trade with the capitalist world largely in terms of economic gains and market logic rather than ideological solidarity or political sympathy. Chinese coal is cheaper for Japanese than coal from elsewhere, he said during a meeting of the Development of International Trade group. A rekindled Sino–Japanese coal trade would therefore help lower production costs for Japanese industries.[106]

The Chinese delegation signed its first contract of the conference—with Great Britain—on April 8. Over the next four days, the Chinese signed agreements with representatives from Holland, France, Belgium, West Germany, Italy, Pakistan, Ceylon, Finland, Switzerland, and Indonesia.[107]

The value of these contracts totaled more than US$220 million, a substantial sum for the Ministry of Trade in 1952. The euphoric delegation reported after the conference that the total value of the deals they signed in Moscow accounted for 36 percent of China's planned state imports from capitalist countries in 1952 and a full 50 percent of planned state exports to the capitalist world.[108] These were impressive figures, but many of the deals ultimately fell through, often because conferees from capitalist countries found it difficult or impossible to navigate the thicket of COCOM restrictions. After a year of delays, for example, only 5 percent of the business China had negotiated with Japan in Moscow had come to fruition.[109]

The collapsing deals were a disappointment, but not entirely unexpected. The real value of the contracts lay in their symbolism. Just as Dean Acheson had suspected, the Chinese leadership used the Moscow agreements as a catalyst for Chinese propaganda. The contracts represented cracks in the embargo, and the CCP began to exploit them not long after the conference concluded.

In particular, CCP propagandists used the Moscow deals, and the conference itself, for two key purposes. First, and most publicly, they continued to champion the cause of internationalism. "This historic conference has already achieved glorious success," Xinhua declared on April 16. The success stemmed not just from the trade deals concluded but also, Xinhua explained, "because 471 businesspeople, economists, union workers, and workers in cooperatives from 49 countries with different social systems shared a common confidence[,] despite maintaining different ideas and beliefs[,] in using international economic cooperation to improve the lives of individuals living in different countries."[110] This was panideological internationalism rather than the standard proletarian variety. The delegates in Moscow were "unanimous in their view" that current abnormalities in international trade required urgent correction.[111] Of course, as Dean Acheson recognized, "internationalism" at the Moscow Conference was a euphemism for opposition to American imperialism. Chinese newspapers occasionally made this point explicit. A Labor Day editorial in the *People's Daily* stated that the Moscow Conference contributed to the "smashing [of] the American imperialist policies of embargo and blockade."[112]

The second propaganda line to emerge from the conference was more domestically focused. The CCP began to champion the Moscow deals in internal communications to mobilize domestic institutions. In July, the statistics department of the General Administration of Customs (GAC) framed the Moscow Conference as a crowning moment in China's second-quarter trade with the capitalist world. If nothing else, the GAC stated, the "great achievements" of the conference "reflected opposition to the American imperialist 'blockade' [and] 'embargo' on the part of a great many businessmen from capitalist countries, as well as [their] urgent demands to reinvigorate normal trade relations with the peaceful democratic camp, especially with new China."[113] Each deal with a representative from a capitalist nation (and the GAC listed all eleven countries) testified to the world's shared opposition to American imperialism. And these contracts marked just the beginning, the GAC said. "This is a good start to the restoration and development of our international trade with the capitalist camp on a foundation of equality and mutual benefit."[114]

The Ministry of Trade recited its crowning numbers again in a report on August 21: contracts with eleven capitalist countries worth over US$220 million. The report, which was sent to trade officials at the central, provincial, and municipal levels, argued that these and other deals with capitalists, alongside the deepening economic crisis within the capitalist camp, "make it easier for us to smash the American imperialist blockade, [and] to struggle to develop trade with capitalist nations."[115] The Ministry of Trade and the CFEC were still touting these successes six months later, nearly a year after the Moscow Conference, and the significance of the event seemed only to have grown. It was a milestone, a "turning point in our struggle to develop trade with capitalist countries," the ministry claimed in March 1953.[116]

Zhou Enlai himself took up these themes and placed them into the larger context of China's transformation under Communist rule. On April 30, 1952, just a few weeks after the Moscow Conference concluded, he gave an internal speech on diplomacy to Party members. Over the past two years, he told the audience, the strength of imperialism in China had weakened substantially. In the past, China had a "comprador economy," he explained, a term that described the practice of foreign companies hiring Chinese agents to run their business operations in China. Foreign firms once conducted 80 percent of China's foreign trade, he continued, but China had changed. Now, foreign firms only handled 10 to 20 percent of China's foreign trade. For Zhou, the Moscow Conference symbolized this shift. "[During] the international economic conference [in Moscow]," he explained, "our nation negotiated trade [worth] over US$220 million with Britain and ten other capitalist nations, [and as a result,] Britons in China gorged on jealousy, saying[,] why didn't we [China] talk with nearby foreign firms in China[?]"[117] The foreign firms that once dominated China, many of which still clung to outposts in Shanghai and other cities, were now marginalized, reduced to carping on the sidelines. China did still want to do business with the foreign firms remaining in China, Zhou said, "but we absolutely will not grant them monopolies, because monopolies are the privilege of imperialism."[118] The Chinese people now enjoyed the privilege of deciding how much to trade and with whom through their own representative, the Chinese Communist Party, and the Moscow Conference gave concrete expression to this restoration of China's sovereignty over its own trade, both at home and abroad.

BEYOND THE PROPAGANDA AND THE DEALS, the Moscow Conference left subtler and more lasting legacies. Not long after the conference concluded, the CFEC and the Ministry of Trade began to use decisions taken at the conference to reconfigure the Chinese trade bureaucracy itself. During the final plenary session in Moscow, on April 12, attendees voted to establish a "Committee for the Promotion of International Trade." Delegates agreed to establish national committees that would continue the work begun in Moscow along two lines: they would disseminate information about the Moscow Conference itself, and they would expand trade among nations "on a basis of equality and with due regard to the needs of the industrialization of underdeveloped countries."[119] The Chinese government began to implement these commitments a few weeks later, in early May, when it created the China Committee for the Promotion of International Trade (CCPIT) and designated Nan Hanchen as its first president.[120]

Rather than develop the CCPIT entirely from scratch, the Ministry of Trade grafted it onto existing institutions, beginning with its most obvious domestic counterpart, the ITA. The ITA had been limping along since its founding in July 1950. Despite the enthusiasm behind its creation, the association had yet to congeal into the expansive clearinghouse for trade-related knowledge that the Ministry of Trade had envisioned. Some offices seemed to thrive. Shanghai, Wuhan, and Xiamen published newsletters, organized lectures and workshops, and even, in the case of the Xiamen branch, opened a local trade library that housed two thousand volumes. But other cities had trouble following suit. The distractions of the Three and Five Anti Campaigns had created delays.[121]

Now, the CCPIT offered a chance to breathe new life into the original ITA mission. In August 1952, the Ministry of Trade and the CCPIT agreed to subsume all ITA offices under the CCPIT, a merger that essentially hitched existing ITA offices to the CCPIT mandate. That very month, the CCPIT began to coordinate all work at the ITA offices.[122]

As the CCPIT absorbed the ITA, it also began to coordinate trade-related research in China more broadly. On June 16, 1952, members of the CCPIT Research Committee committed to identifying and assigning research responsibilities to a collection of organizations in China.[123] Rather than a loose confederation of trade expertise, as envisioned two years earlier by the ITA, the CCPIT proposed an explicit division of labor for trade promotion. On July 1, the Research Committee assigned various trade topics—including shipping trends, country studies, foreign currency, and trade theory—to six different groups: import and export companies, the Foreign Trade Division at the Ministry of Trade, the Foreign Operations Bureau at the People's Bank of China, the GAC, the People's University, and the CCPIT itself.[124] This division of labor would allow different segments of the national trade community to take responsibility for developing expertise in different fields.

A redoubled research effort was only part of the CCPIT's ambitions. The organization also turned its attention overseas, toward a transnational network of trade associations and private businesses that shared an interest in trade across the Iron Curtain, whether for commercial or ideological reasons. Other delegates to the Moscow Conference also established trade promotion committees in their own countries. In the first two years after the conference, the CCPIT maintained contact with counterparts from fifteen such committees, many of which were based in capitalist countries, including France, Britain, and Italy. The CCPIT used these relationships to push for trade in various ways, including regularly hosting capitalist trade delegations. By 1954, the CCPIT could claim to have established ties to foreign businesses and trade associations from fifty-nine different states and regions.[125] Each of these relationships represented a blow against the American embargo, just as each supported the Party's growing desire to increase trade with the capitalist world.

The Moscow Conference was not the sole animating force behind the CCPIT's agenda. In fact, the conference and the CCPIT both emerged in the context of a larger economic agenda that was underway in China. When the Moscow Conference convened in April 1952, the CCP had already begun to prepare for China's first Five-Year Plan (FYP), a tightly scripted economic agenda modeled after Soviet planning practices. The Politburo had decided in February 1951 that China's own FYP would commence in 1953, which left economic officials just twenty-two months to produce a plan.[126]

China's Five-Year Plans were herculean undertakings. Each one compelled planners to fill tables with forecasted statistics that inevitably added up to inspiring milestones of future progress. The plans always anticipated long-term growth. They nearly always brimmed with confidence in the future of socialism. But planners also had to demonstrate how the nation would achieve this growth. They had to demonstrate, in overwhelming detail, how vast inputs would converge to yield an equally complicated array of outputs, all of which pushed the national economy toward greater production, industrialization, and material prosperity. This meant distilling order from the messy realities of daily economic life—and not just the realities of today, but those of the future as well. In the realm of capitalist trade, planners had to estimate the quantities of remittances from abroad each year. They had to forecast shipping rates, insurance premiums, and packaging costs. They had to predict revenues from the sale of rice, tea, and other commodities, which meant accounting for shifting market trends.

Accuracy mattered because planners were committing the nation to goals that had to be met. Each forecasted figure for export revenue was a postdated check. If the country came up short, the consequences—such as a lack of hard currency—could ripple through the entire plan. Under these conditions, the Party could ill afford a haphazard approach to foreign trade. The systematic mind-set adopted by the CCPIT would help to wring some of the uncertainty out of trade by organizing state efforts to study and understand foreign markets.

The Party soon made other institutional changes to account for the necessities of the first FYP, the most dramatic of which was the dissolution of the Ministry of Trade itself on August 7, 1952. China needed more specialized entities to oversee trade once the FYP had commenced. In its place, the Central Committee established the Ministry of *Foreign* Trade and placed it under the leadership of the CFEC. The Central Committee simultaneously established the Ministry of Commerce, which took charge of the nation's domestic trade.[127] From that moment forward, the CFEC had a central ministry dedicated solely to overseeing all of China's foreign trade, including direct control over China Resources in Hong Kong.[128]

The new central ministry was based in Beijing. Like all Chinese bureaucracies inspired by the Soviet Union, it oversaw a hierarchy of subordinate organs, called Foreign Trade Bureaus, one for each province, autonomous region, and centrally administered municipality. Many localities also had branch offices. The central ministry set the agenda for these subordinate offices by coordinating with the State Planning Commission to draft import and export plans, monitoring ongoing trade, and signing new trade agreements.[129] Just as important, the central ministry shaped the culture of trade work by disseminating guidance and, beginning in 1954, running the ministry's own training institute in Beijing, which offered a five-year program for budding trade officials.[130]

The Ministry of Foreign Trade also managed the nation's foreign trade corporations. These monopolies controlled the trade of different categories of goods, called "lines." Most lines were self-evident: the China National Silk Corporation exported precisely what one would expect. Other lines were less clear. The China National Sundries Export Corporation "specialized" in products as varied as its name suggested: building materials, stationery, textiles, even sporting goods. Each foreign trade corporation had a central office in Beijing; many also had offices throughout China. Import corporations tended to open offices near China's major ports. Some export corporations had branches where their products were primarily produced. The National Native Produce Export Corporation had a branch in Guangxi, for example, where pears, plums, peaches, and other produce was grown.[131] All of these offices, no matter their locations, operated under the direction of the new Ministry of Foreign Trade.

THE PARTY LEADERSHIP NEEDED experienced officials to help run the new ministry, so they turned to Lei Renmin, the Moscow Conference veteran, to play a critical role. On August 15, the CFEC appointed him vice minister of foreign trade in charge of all commerce with capitalist countries, a clear sign that the Party leadership expected China's trade with capitalist markets to increase as the Five-Year Plan took effect.[132] Lei had long been a quiet advocate for expanding trade with capitalist Europe. As a former vice minister at the Ministry of Trade, he would have known about the rising costs and security concerns caused by American scrutiny in Hong Kong. He also knew that Switzerland, Sweden, Finland, and other European nations were willing to trade with China. Chinese firms were already trading with these European nations through an East German intermediary based in East Berlin called the China Export Corporation.[133] The company was struggling, however, and Lei believed China could do more. He envisioned an arrangement in which PRC agents marketed Chinese exports directly to customers from Western Europe and purchased European products without the help of middlemen.[134] Before the Moscow Conference, Lei had failed to gain support for his vision. But he clung to the view that China had to expand its presence in European markets if it wanted to accomplish its development goals.

Now, as Lei took up his new role as vice minister of foreign trade, the context had changed. His earlier ambitions for European trade aligned perfectly with the goals expressed at the Moscow Conference, and they offered a promising framework for achieving the trade goals the Party was developing as part of the Five-Year Plan. Beijing had already sent a member of its Moscow delegation to East Berlin, a cadre named Shi Zhi'ang, to establish the China National Import and Export Corporation (CNIEC), which was meant to be a temporary expansion of China's trade presence in Europe on the heels of the conference. But soon after arriving, Shi sensed longer-term potential, so he asked for more time and more cadres. By May 1953, the CNIEC had reached an agreement with East German officials that China could establish, fund, and operate its own commercial office independently in East Berlin.[135]

The point of the new office was to increase contact with capitalists in Western Europe, so the staff made themselves as accessible as possible. European companies could communicate with the office via cable or telephone.[136] They could also visit the office in person, according to the British Council for the Promotion of International Trade. The CNIEC was a short flight from London to Tempelhof Aerodrome in West Berlin, and from there it was a quick trip to the eastern sector of the city. No visa was necessary. The new office also established a relationship with the London Export Corporation, which acted as the CNIEC's correspondents for trade in the United Kingdom.[137]

Within a year, as many as four hundred people were working at the CNIEC office in East Berlin.[138] The CIA observed that this staff consisted "mostly of young [people] who are Moscow indoctrinated, lack business experience, and who are terrified of making any mistake." Still, the CIA predicted that as the staff gained experience, it would become more efficient and the office would grow as a center for negotiating trade between Europe and China.[139]

This is precisely what the leadership in Beijing envisioned. The CNIEC office represented a tangible commitment to durable ties between Communist China and overseas capitalist markets. Zhou Enlai, Chen Yun, and Lei Renmin anticipated a future in which development and industrialization at home would eventually eliminate China's reliance on these markets, but that was a distant vision. In the meantime, the Party leadership believed that China's economic and security interests were best served by building sturdy institutions for capitalist trade. These institutions—from the CNIEC and the CCPIT to the central Ministry of Foreign Trade and its subordinate offices and trade corporations—embedded a structural validation in China for continued trade with the capitalist world. Cadres and experts who worked within these institutions thought about the finer points of capitalist trade without needing—for the time being, at least—to grapple with the larger ideological question of whether such trade was appropriate in the context of China's Communist revolution. Instead, the bankers, economists, and officials who staffed these organizations understood China's trade with foreign capitalists as a sanctioned pursuit. It was simply their daily work. For them, trade with capitalists became revolutionary praxis.

The Korean War took this validation a step further, and not just for officials working inside the nation's trade bureaucracy. As Zhou Enlai realized, the COCOM embargo could be more than a practical encumbrance. It was also a cause ripe for mobilization. Mao had grasped this dynamic during the Nationalist blockade of Shanghai in 1949. Now, the Korean War and COCOM had globalized this mobilizing function. In both public propaganda and internal communications, Chinese trade institutions developed a new narrative for China's place in global markets, one that centered on the theme of trading with capitalists as an anti-imperialist struggle.

Trading with foreign capitalists became not only patriotic but also inter-
nationalist, as Lei Renmin argued at the Moscow Conference. No longer
did CCP traders fully conceal their presence in capitalist markets, as Qin
Bangli had done in Hong Kong during the 1930s and 1940s. Gone was
the incoherence that hindered the Party's capitalist trade during the fluid
months of early 1949. By the early 1950s, capitalist trade did more than
support China's economic development; it also constituted an essential
pillar of China's struggle against American imperialism.

4

COMMERCE IN THE MAKING OF "PEACEFUL COEXISTENCE"

AT 10:00 ON THE MORNING OF JULY 27, 1953, representatives from the United Nations High Command, North Korea, and the People's Republic of China signed an armistice that halted the fighting on the Korean Peninsula. Although the end of combat in Korea opened the door to subtler forms of conflict in East Asian politics, the armistice still dampened tensions in the region significantly.[1] This shift was particularly promising for the Ministry of Foreign Trade. The cease-fire presented new opportunities for the ministry to pick apart the American-led embargo, which still hampered China's trade agenda, and officials there had every intention of making full use of the postwar change in climate.

At the bottom of the Korean Armistice agreement, beneath a lengthy discussion of prisoners of war and just before a concluding "Miscellaneous" section, a single line recommended that the signatories convene a high-level political conference within three months to "settle through negotiation" the fundamental questions that fueled the fighting in the first place: peaceful settlement of the "Korean question," the withdrawal of foreign forces from Korea, "et cetera."[2] The signatories missed the three-month deadline, but representatives from the United States, the Soviet Union, Britain, and France—the "Big Four"—met in Berlin in January 1954 for four weeks of acrimonious talks over European and Asian affairs. Little was settled beyond an agreement to meet again, this time in Geneva, in April, to continue discussions about the "Korea question" and the ongoing conflict between French forces and the Viet Minh in Indochina.

The talks in Geneva would be broader and more inclusive than those in the Berlin meeting. In particular, the summit would include representatives from the PRC, a decision that thrilled the CCP leadership. For the first time, world leaders had formally invited "new" China to join them in consequential discussions on the future of world affairs. Zhou Enlai had no trouble recognizing this larger significance. "The People's Republic of China's participation in the [Geneva] conference alone has already marked a big step toward relaxing international tensions," he wrote in March, a month before the conference began.[3] For Zhou, China's very participation in the meeting signaled a major shift for both China and the world.

John Foster Dulles agreed, but the US secretary of state saw this shift in a very different light. He was outraged that Chinese Communists had been invited to Geneva. In a joint radio and television address to the American public after the Berlin Conference, he tried to downplay the significance of the PRC's participation in the coming talks. Ultimately, he explained, delegates from China "will not come to Geneva to be honored by us, but rather to account before the bar of world opinion."[4] He believed the regime in Beijing was simply "evil," and it galled him that US negotiators would sit across the table with its representatives. He knew the summit created political problems at home, too, as some on the Right began to level charges of a "Far Eastern Munich" at Geneva.[5]

The history of China's participation in the Geneva Conference has largely been written with these political and diplomatic stakes in the foreground.[6] Previous accounts show that the conference was a diplomatic coup for Zhou Enlai and the rest of the PRC delegation, just as Dulles had feared. It marked the PRC's acknowledged entrée into great power diplomacy and heralded the start of a new phase in Chinese foreign policy, one in which China committed to crafting a national identity committed to fostering peace and stability in international affairs rather than fomenting violent revolution. But there was a commercial mission embedded within the conference that has been largely overlooked.

Zhou Enlai was determined to use the summit to develop China's economic relations with other participating nations, a strategy he believed would reinforce the larger aims of reducing tension, fostering geopolitical stability, and undermining the American-led embargo.[7] As he put it in March 1954, "we should adopt a policy of actively participating in the Geneva Conference, of enhancing diplomatic and international activities, in order to undermine the policy of blockade, embargo, and expanding armaments and war preparations by the U.S. imperialists, and of promoting the relaxation of the tense international situation."[8] In essence, the Geneva Conference offered a chance for Zhou and the rest of his delegation to continue what Nan Hanchen and Lei Renmin had begun in Moscow two years earlier. By embedding trade into his diplomatic offensive at Geneva, Zhou intended to link the spirit and tactics of the Moscow Conference of 1952 to the emerging post-Korea peace offensive in Chinese diplomacy. Ultimately, his aim was to challenge not just the US-led embargo but also the American presumption to dictate the rules of global commerce, particularly the fundamental question of who can participate, and who cannot.

Business on the Margins

Over two hundred PRC officials arrived in Geneva with Zhou Enlai in late April 1954 for the summit.[9] Among them was Lei Renmin, whose mission in the Swiss city was straightforward: market Chinese goods, meet capitalists, seek trade. Unlike his work at the Moscow Conference, however, he planned to conduct the bulk of his Geneva business on the sidelines of the summit. The list of Chinese delegates identified Lei as a "chief counsellor" (*shouxi guwen*) rather than "delegate," a title that freed him up to participate in activities outside of the Palais de Nations, where the plenary sessions convened.[10]

Lei arrived in town with the rest of the Chinese delegation on April 24, but he did not stay with Zhou Enlai at the Grand Mont-Fleury, a luxurious estate several kilometers outside of the city.[11] Instead, Lei checked into a suite at Le Richemond, an elegant hotel on the Quai du Mont Blanc, a lakeside promenade just a few minutes' walk from the Rue du Rhone business district. The central location was Zhou's idea, prompted in part by the recognition that Lei's work required him to be accessible to other delegations and visitors during the conference.[12] The downtown location limited Lei's contact with Zhou and the rest of the senior members of the Chinese delegation, but the trade-off was necessary and it reflected the subtle ways that trade and commerce supported the CCP's larger foreign policy goals at the time. The contact with capitalists sought by Lei would produce the increase in trade that would substantiate China's new national identity as committed to peace and development. At the same time, the trade deals that emerged from Lei's interactions would undermine the solidarity of the American-led embargo against China and enable the PRC to use capitalist markets to achieve the goals outlined in the nation's first Five-Year Plan, which lasted from 1953 to 1957.

All of this made Lei Renmin a member of the Chinese delegation, but not an official delegate. He had real work to accomplish in Geneva, but much of it would take place away from the cameras. None of these arrangements meant Lei had been let loose to write his own program in Geneva, or that his responsibilities were marginal concerns to the leadership in Beijing. On the contrary, Zhou Enlai believed Lei's activities were vital. "[Regarding] our [strategy for] improving relations with Western nations," the premier explained in August 1954, "in politics there is 'peace,' in economics there is 'trade.'"[13] Accordingly, Zhou attached great importance to Lei's mission.[14]

Lei preferred quiet sidebar meetings for his "struggles" with capitalists, and he convened many in Geneva during the spring and summer of 1954. Most important among these was a series of private discussions with Humphrey Trevelyan, the British chargé d'affaires in Beijing who was in Geneva as an official member of the British delegation, and Peter Tennant, the overseas director of the Federation of British Industries, an organization that claimed to represent 90 percent of British industrial manufacturers. Zhou Enlai instructed Lei to seek out interactions with British officials specifically during the conference because he believed Britain offered the most promising prospect for breaching the embargo against China.[15]

Lei first met with Trevelyan and Tennant in Geneva on May 6, 1954. At 10:00 A.M. that morning, he escorted his British counterparts into a sitting room within a private suite occupied by the Chinese delegation at the Beau Rivage Hotel, just steps from Le Richemond where Lei was staying. By Tennant's account, Lei was an accommodating host who straddled the line between apparatchik and businessman, stylistically at least, by wearing a standard-issue Mao suit and dapper brown shoes. Alongside him at the meeting was Shi Zhi'ang, the deputy manager of the China National Import and Export Corporation (CNIEC), and a secretary, Chu Siyi.[16]

From the start, Lei took every opportunity to showcase Chinese wares. He decorated the suite with Chinese products—a cabinet displayed ivory and jade bric-a-brac, Chinese art was conspicuously displayed, and a carved blackwood lamp with tassels of orange silk lit the room. "Stage props," Tennant called them. Chinese tea filled the cups on the table, and smoke from Chinese cigarettes filled the lungs of the six men as they exchanged greetings.[17] Both parties sought to set a conciliatory tone during the opening pleasantries. Lei expressed "delight" at meeting with Trevelyan and emphasized that China welcomed British efforts to develop Sino–British trade. Trevelyan made it clear that the sentiment was mutual. He replied that British businesses hoped to "expand Sino-British trade, [and] to broaden channels for contact, [so that] in the future it will include industry, commerce, and banking."[18]

But no sooner had the two men begun to stoke this sense of shared purpose than fissures began to emerge. "At present," Lei told his visitors, "Sino-British trade relations are not normal." He did not need to explain why. The embargo hung over the meeting as thickly as the cigarette smoke. "It is entirely possible," Lei continued, "to launch trade, to restore [it] to the conditions of the past, and [even to achieve] greater development [amid] China's [current] period of economic construction and the steady improvement in the lives of the Chinese people.[19] Lei's point was unmistakable: demand for trade existed on both sides of the negotiating table, but the American-orchestrated embargo, to which the British government had acquiesced, was obstructing this shared goal. For bilateral trade to reach its full potential, London would have to reconsider its stance on the embargo.

Trevelyan and Tennant expected Lei to link the morning's talks to the embargo. They also anticipated that he would connect trade to China's larger foreign policy aims. Ultimately, the fight over these linkages drove the conversations that followed, which centered on three issues dominating Lei's agenda in Geneva. The first concerned lists of goods, a subject that arose as soon as Lei and Trevelyan—the two senior-most negotiators—withdrew from the suite to allow Tennant and Shi to delve into the details. Shi asked for a list of the goods that United Kingdom producers could supply to the People's Republic of China, but Tennant responded by suggesting that Shi, or the CNIEC, provide their own list of the goods they hoped to import from Britain.[20]

Both sides had clear rationales for their positions. Tennant said he wanted to avoid the burden of compiling vast lists of potential exports, and he worried about the "trainloads" of paperwork that would inundate Shi if they chose this approach. Lei Renmin countered during a follow-up meeting on May 7 that Chinese planners needed to know what products were available as they drafted plans for imports and exports.[21] Beneath these rationales lurked political calculations that both sides understood but neither expressed. A list of goods from either party would invite detailed comparisons to existing embargo restrictions and neither side wanted to show its hand on this subject first. Tennant and Shi knew they held starkly different views on the issue of how future trade would relate to the China embargo. British officials and businessmen hoped to achieve as much trade as possible without being dragged into the political morass of the embargo, while Lei and Shi intended to use the trade talks as a fulcrum for prying the embargo apart.

Tennant eventually agreed to provide a list of potential exports on May 26. When he slid the document across the table, Shi seemed "favorably impressed" with its length, according to Tennant, despite the fact that it included not a single item banned for export by the embargo. Still, Shi explained he would have to share the list with officials in Beijing before the talks could proceed. The two sides decided to reconvene the following day, May 27, at 2:30 in the afternoon. When the appointed hour arrived, Shi had to ask for an extension. The Chinese side had been reviewing the list throughout the night and needed more time. An hour later, Shi was ready. When the meeting began, he declared bluntly that Tennant's list was inadequate for China's planned industrialization. It also failed to accord with both sides' expressed desire to expand trade. Tennant was unimpressed. He wrote afterward that Shi had "revealed himself as very inexpert in all our talks." Tennant was frustrated, but hardly surprised.[22]

With Tennant's list on the table, Shi began to use it to pick apart the embargo exactly as the British had expected. He asked whether Tennant could expand the lists of chemicals, medicines, and scientific instruments in the draft. He reiterated China's interest in heavy electrical equipment, steel, nonferrous metals, ships, heavy vehicles, locomotives, and wagons—all "strategic" items expressly prohibited for export to the PRC under the current embargo regime. Shi said he realized the difficulties surrounding trade in such goods, but he hoped nonetheless that progress could be made by "looking ahead," Tennant recalled. After all, Shi concluded transparently, he hated to think that the British "would be less forthcoming than Western Germany and France" had been in their talks with China.[23]

"Looking ahead" might also allow the two parties to see an intergovernmental trade agreement, Shi Zhi'ang believed. This was the second issue on Lei Renmin's agenda. Shi broached the subject with Tennant on May 6, and the way he raised it—with "studied casualness"—implied to Tennant that this was a topic of considerable prestige and interest to Lei and Shi.[24] Trevelyan assessed that Lei and Shi hoped to achieve an agreement similar to recent PRC deals with Burma and Indonesia.[25] Both parties knew that Beijing would certainly tout a formal Sino–British trade agreement as a break in the American-led embargo, but neither side addressed this issue directly in the talks.

Instead, Shi framed his request in commercial terms. Any agreement that bore the imprimatur of both governments would boost the "confidence" of traders in both Britain and China, he argued. Tennant explained that an official agreement would have the opposite effect in Britain, where traders typically looked askance at governmental endorsements and associated them with trade restrictions rather than expansions.[26] Lei pushed the issue on May 7 by explaining that Chinese state planners needed assurance that imports would arrive on schedule to ensure domestic production remained on track.[27] But Trevelyan was firm. Her Majesty's Government did not support such agreements except where they solved "practical," that is, commercial, problems.

Lei let the issue drop. He had a third subject to pursue anyway, one that promised to undercut the embargo just as much and to boost China's cachet in the process. On May 6, Lei had proposed that the two sides discuss bilateral commercial visits. Trevelyan seemed open to the idea. He replied that London "very much welcome[d] the Chinese side to visit us."[28] Seizing the moment, Shi followed up later in the day with Tennant. A trade fair was actually underway in Britain that very moment, Shi observed. Tennant caught the hint. He understood that Shi was angling for an invitation sooner rather than later.[29]

Lei returned to the subject of bilateral visits the next day, May 7. He told Trevelyan and Tennant that the most suitable moment for trade delegations in either direction was sometime in May or June. June was, after all, the midyear mark for Chinese planners, who operated on the calendar year. China would certainly welcome a British trade delegation to the PRC within the next two months, he continued, and Beijing would be glad to send a delegation of its own to Britain.[30]

Lei and Shi continued to work out the details for a Chinese delegation visit to Britain, and by late May Shi was anxious to schedule dates.[31] Both

Trevelyan and Tennant supported the request in principle, but it raised troubling questions for Foreign Office officials in London, who rightly suspected that the Chinese planned to make "political capital out of the visit and to weaken the embargo."[32] Many in the Foreign Office questioned the wisdom of retaining the embargo as a cornerstone of British trade policy, especially following the cease-fire in Korea, but no one doubted Washington's commitment to the policy or its vigilance for signs that allies might be straying from the cause. Roger Makins, the British ambassador in Washington, wrote to the Foreign Office on May 20, 1954, to remind everyone of this point. The very act of holding trade talks with PRC officials on the sidelines of the Geneva Conference, he said, "will presumably cause an unfavorable reaction in this country."[33]

Appearances mattered. The British had to tread carefully to avoid creating the impression that they were undercutting the embargo or diluting their solidarity with the United States. Already Lei and Shi had begun referring to the potential Chinese trip to the United Kingdom as a "trade delegation" rather than a business trip, a clear nudge toward formal diplomacy.[34] Torn between the desire to host PRC visitors as a prelude to export growth, on the one hand, and concern over how Washington might perceive such a trip, on the other, the Foreign Office sought a middle position. On June 2, 1954, the British government agreed that a PRC visit should proceed, but that the visitors should be restricted to factories that produced goods on the lists already passed during talks in Geneva, rather than a general tour of British industry. Offering tours of shipyards and other "strategic" production sites would only cause "misunderstanding" in the United States. Also, the delegation should be small—about six or seven people, none of whom should be Lei Renmin.[35]

The Chinese delegation received an invitation to visit Britain on behalf of the Federation of British Industries, the China Association, and several other nongovernmental trade associations on June 3, 1954.[36] Despite the limited scope of the visit, and the exclusion of Lei, whose senior rank would have lent an official air to the delegation, the proposed visit represented a commercial and diplomatic success for Beijing. As it turned out, it was one among several in Geneva.

In between negotiations at the Beau Rivage hotel, Lei had also been orchestrating a public diplomacy campaign meant to cultivate China's image as a peaceful and promising business partner. The idea to use the Geneva

Conference for public diplomacy originated with the Soviets, who suggested in early April that the Chinese delegation consider "showing movies, organizing speeches, small-size exhibitions, and cultural performances." Zhou Enlai liked the idea and instructed his subordinates to "immediately consider work on this."[37]

Lei Renmin's major contribution to this effort occurred on May 15, when he hosted what the *Times of India* called a "veritable trade-cum-cultural exhibition." Some two hundred reporters sipped Chinese tea and wandered Le Richemond, eyeing painted scrolls and other treasures shipped from China. Photographs on the walls and in albums testified to China's economic development under CCP leadership. Any prospective trade partner would have little trouble envisioning the mechanizing agricultural nation China proclaimed to be, the industrialized power it aspired to become, or the kind of foreign trade it sought in support of its development goals.[38]

Lei convened a press conference the same day to underscore his message. He told reporters that rising standards of living and industrial development had opened up "vast potential" for foreign trade. This wasn't an abstraction; it was already happening. Lei recited statistics that suggested gathering momentum: China's overseas trade volume in 1953 reached its highest level since 1930; PRC trade with capitalist countries last year was up 29 percent over the year before; British exports to China increased by a third in 1953, and imports from the PRC were up 350 percent. But Lei expected more. China's industrialization demanded it. China welcomed Europe's machinery and consumer products, he made clear, and Beijing was willing to offer silks, handicrafts, and produce in return.[39]

The tone of Lei's remarks harkened back to the Moscow Conference two years earlier. His mantra remained "equality and mutual benefit," and he suggested that neither political nor ideological differences would shake these principles loose from China's trade policy. "China will trade with any[,] and I emphasize, any country," he vowed, "as long the principle of equality and mutual benefit is observed." This image of commercial openness contrasted starkly with what he framed as a petulant embargo policy enforced by Western governments, and it was this contrast that brought together the Communist government in Beijing and capitalist traders in Europe in a politically agnostic alliance. After all, Lei argued, the trade embargoes imposed on China by Western governments hurt Chinese and capitalist traders alike.[40]

Reporters from mainstream newspapers read weakness into Lei's press conference. They sensed that the capitalist embargoes were taking their toll on "Red" China's economy. Robert Alden of the *New York Times* wrote, "The economy of Communist China has been seriously hurt by the United States trade embargo."[41] The press conference was an "olive branch," Alden believed, a softer side of the Beijing government designed to contrast with "the vilification that his [Lei's] colleagues have been heaping on the United States."[42] Though the *New York Times* reporter never said so directly, the whole spectacle smacked of propaganda: the "rosy picture" of PRC economic development, Lei's assurances that China's door was open wide to American and other capitalist businessmen, his willingness to trade with businessmen of any ideological stripe. All of it came from a place of pain and weakness. The embargo had cut into the Beijing regime, and so Lei had to reach out—for machines, for equipment, for help. If this was the true impetus behind Lei's accommodating stance on trade, then the whole affair at Le Richemond was disingenuous, more trade carnival than fair. It was a plea, not a welcome.

Some merchants sensed an opportunity in Geneva, regardless of the motivations behind Lei's showmanship. The chairman of HSBC wrote in his annual statement to the board that the mere presence of Zhou and the PRC delegation in Geneva seemed to thaw the East–West commercial divide. The summit offered a chance for "a clearing of the air," he believed, between Asian Communists and capitalist counterparts.[43]

But regardless of whether one agreed with the *New York Times* or HSBC, Lei Renmin's interest in signing contracts in Geneva was genuine and the Ministry of Foreign Trade was prepared to substantiate the message with real transactions. An internal Ministry of Foreign Trade report from 1956 shows that the PRC was conducting hundreds of millions of dollars in trade with capitalists during the first half of the 1950s, including over US$320 million worth of imports and more than US$264 million in exports in 1954 alone (see Figure 4.1). The report is as authoritative as they come: a preface explains that the ministry used the data to brief Mao himself in April 1956.[44]

The same report also confirms what economists have long suspected from non-Chinese sources: that the capitalist world's share of total PRC trade shrank substantially during the first half of the 1950s to a nadir of below 18 percent in 1955 (see Figure 4.2). Taken together, however, Figures 4.1 and 4.2 also show that the PRC's surging trade with the socialist

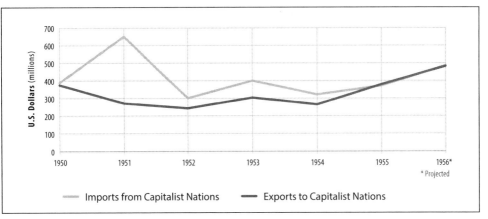

Figure 4.1   Early PRC trade with capitalists. *Data Source:* Ministry of Foreign Trade, *Duiwai Maoyi You Guan Ziliao Huibian, Di Yi Fen Ce* [Compilation of Information on Foreign Trade, volume 1], May 1956.

world in the early 1950s did not *replace* China's trade with capitalists; it simply overshadowed it. PRC trade with the capitalist world remained surprisingly steady throughout the early 1950s despite the embargo, while socialist trade, which was financed with the help of Soviet loans, shot upward.

At the same time, the PRC's share of total trade within the capitalist world had declined. The US International Cooperation Administration (ICA), an office within the Treasury Department that helped administer the embargo, calculated in November 1955 that the PRC accounted for just over 2 percent of world trade in 1938. In 1948, that portion had declined to 0.9 percent, and by 1954–1955, the PRC's share of "free world" trade had shrunk to 0.4 percent. But these percentages could be misleading. The ICA also observed that annual foreign trade within the "free world" increased from $41.2 billion in 1938 to $158.3 billion in 1955.[45] Much of China's shrinking share of global capitalist trade thus reflected breakneck expansion in foreign trade throughout the capitalist world rather than contractions in the PRC's own trade with capitalists.

Still, no one knows how much PRC trade with capitalists might have grown without the embargo during the 1950s. The obvious corollary is also unclear: whether China had been "seriously hurt" by the embargo, as Robert Alden of the *New York Times* presumed.[46] What is clear is that Lei's public diplomacy in Geneva and his push for trade had the full backing of the

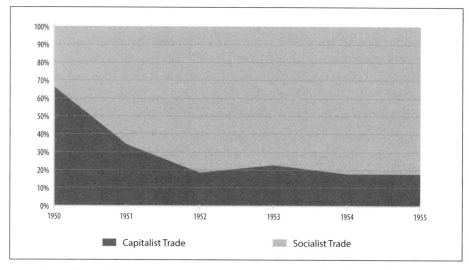

Figure 4.2   Relative trade volume, capitalist versus socialist. *Data Source:* Ministry of Foreign Trade, *Duiwai Maoyi You Guan Ziliao Huibian, Di Yi Fen Ce* [Compilation of Information on Foreign Trade, volume 1], May 1956.

CCP senior leadership, who, like Lei, saw increased contact with the capitalist world as a critical dimension of PRC foreign relations in the post–Korean War climate. Zhou Enlai thought of the Geneva conference, and China's interactions with the British in particular, as a proving ground. Success there, both political and commercial, could illustrate that nations of different political systems and ideologies could indeed coexist peacefully.[47]

Zhou contributed his own talents to crafting this message. He met privately for over an hour in Geneva on May 30 with two members of British Parliament, Harold Wilson, a Labor Party member and former president of the Board of Trade, and William Robson-Brown, a member of the Conservative Party. The two men had come from London to meet with members of the Chinese delegation, and both men also held private talks with Lei Renmin and Shi Zhi'ang while in town. These meetings soon produced results. On June 1, Zhou cabled the leadership in Beijing to report a breakthrough: Wilson, Robson-Brown, and Foreign Secretary Anthony Eden, who was heading the British delegation in Geneva, had jointly welcomed the PRC to establish a permanent office in London to facilitate future trade.[48] Zhou fully supported the idea, believing that a trade office in

London could serve as a fulcrum for political objectives. He proposed raising the issue formally with the British government and suggested that the new office be permitted to enjoy full diplomatic rights and privileges. The office would really function as a diplomatic mission, he told Mao and the rest of the Central Committee.[49]

Harold Wilson and William Robson-Brown emerged from the meetings with a vastly different interpretation. Both men downplayed the political significance of the talks. The British delegation reported back to London that Wilson and Robson-Brown both "seemed impressed that the Chinese wanted trade to develop and were not primarily out for political capital."[50] The two parliamentarians had left Geneva both correct and wildly wrong in their assessment of Beijing's aims. China did want trade to develop, but it also wanted political capital in equal measure.

Lei Renmin left the conference more certain than ever that capitalists wanted trade with China. In Geneva, he had also met with officials and businessmen from Switzerland, West Germany, the Netherlands, Italy, and France. All of them said they wanted to expand trade with China.[51] But progress with Britain seemed to outstrip all the rest. Lei's talks with Trevelyan and Tennant achieved another breakthrough on June 28 when, with the Geneva Conference still in session, representatives from the CNIEC departed for London on Lei's sought-after "trade mission." The trip offered Chinese officials a chance to mingle with British manufacturers and merchants in London, Sheffield, and Birmingham. It also gave the official host organization, the Sino–British Trade Committee, the opportunity to demonstrate its own zeal for trade with China, which it did with talks, factory tours, meals at the Savoy, and a coach tour of London.[52] Even more important, however, was the momentum created by this London trip. Before the Chinese delegation departed from Britain, they invited the Sino–British Trade Committee to send a group of entrepreneurs and industrialists to visit Beijing in November 1954 for a reciprocal visit.[53] For Lei Renmin, the Geneva Conference was bearing fruit even before it had concluded.

Coexistence through Commerce

The talks in Geneva confirmed Zhou Enlai's sense that a new international climate was taking shape. Before the conference was underway, in late December 1953, he articulated for the first time a new theme in Chinese diplomacy called the "five principles of peaceful coexistence," a concept geared more toward preserving stability within the existing international system than forcing change.[54] Zhou's positive experiences in Geneva reinforced his conviction that China had the wind at its back, and that a peaceful international climate favored China's industrialization and empowerment. Three months after the conference concluded, on October 18, 1954, Zhou provided a broad assessment of world affairs to senior Party officials. He explained that China's diplomatic activity in recent years had yielded a clearer understanding of the world situation. The socialist world remained a postwar juggernaut, he believed, an irresistible force that held the future in its grip. The capitalist world, by contrast, was "old," riddled with contradictions, and dying. Still, it was dangerous. He warned that the imperialists could lash out anytime to forestall their own demise. The PRC must strive to preserve peace in the world to guard against such aggression.[55]

Zhou argued that peace would allow the forces of historical development to strengthen the socialist world quickly, thereby hastening the demise of capitalism. He told the Party leadership that China could expedite these trends by nourishing rifts within the capitalist world. Capitalist nations could be divided into three groups, he explained: war mongers (*zhuzhan pai*), a faction epitomized by American imperialism; status quo preservationists (*weichi xianzhuang pai*), such as Great Britain and France, which were committed to peace but relied misguidedly on the United States to provide it; and a peace-and-neutrality faction (*heping zhongli pai*), which was a shifting group of colonies, postcolonial states, and other subjugated nations with impermanent commitments to "neutrality" in world affairs.[56]

Having divided the world into these three camps, Zhou advocated a three-part strategy. First, China should gird for conflict by strengthening its defense capabilities. Second, it should promote peaceful forces. And third, China should avoid provoking conflict.[57] In terms of more concrete proposals, Zhou called for continued "work" on the status quo preservationist group, with an emphasis on Britain and France in particular. He calculated that fostering ties with these nations would lead to a united front that was committed to international peace. This commitment, in turn, would isolate and contain American imperialism.[58] Trade could be made to serve this strategy as a tool for building a united front with "status quo preservationist" states.

This playbook differed little from what Zhou, Lei Renmin, and other trade officials had in mind during the Moscow Conference in 1952. But the new strategic climate, and the vindication and strength that followed China's "victory" in the Korean War, made this strategy all the more credible to China's leaders. And the conference in Geneva had allowed the CCP to test its principles.[59]

Peaceful coexistence and trade with capitalists also served Party needs closer to home. The entire agenda Zhou outlined in October 1954 was predicated on a foundation of economic and military strength—"using power as a backup force," Zhou called it—and a peaceful international environment was essential to strengthening that foundation.[60] Zhou had in mind a sort of virtuous cycle of peace and strength: more peace brought more strength, and more strength brought still more peace. Li Fuchun touched on this connection between external peace and internal strength in a July 1955 report to the National People's Congress, in which he identified the wartime climate of the Korean War as a major contributor to China's delay in adopting its first Five-Year Plan.[61] A return to tension and conflict could easily disrupt economic planning again and thwart China's plans for strengthening its industries and defenses. Mao seemed to share this perspective. In December 1954, he explained to Burmese prime minister U Nu that China wanted to transform into an industrial nation and this was "long-term work" that required a peaceful international environment.[62]

Mao's enthusiasm for peace may have struck U Nu as ironic under the circumstances. A crisis in the Taiwan Strait, largely of Mao's own making, raised fair questions about the earnestness of the PRC's commitment to peace in the region. On September 3, Chinese People's Liberation Army (PLA) shore batteries had attacked Jinmen, also called Quemoy, a Nationalist-held island about one mile off the coast of Fujian Province. The bombardment, which was unprovoked, lasted roughly an hour and killed two American military officers. Then, on September 22, PLA batteries on the Fujian coast unleashed another hour-long barrage. PRC aggression near the Taiwan Strait did not stop there. A month after Mao's meeting with U Nu, in January 1955, PLA troops landed on Dachen and Yijiangshan, both KMT-controlled islands off the cost of Zhejiang Province.[63]

Mao likely had several reasons for these attacks.[64] But a key rationale, as the historian Chen Jian has written, was his desire to use the tension in the Taiwan Strait to mobilize the Chinese people for reconstruction and socialist revolution at home. Like Zhou Enlai, Mao believed the relaxation of global tensions following the Korean armistice offered a chance to focus resources on building a material foundation for socialism in China, just as he had explained to U Nu. But he had also come to believe from his experience during the Korean War that the Party needed a threat to rally the masses for a burst of reconstruction work. This placed Mao in a bind: he wanted tension to mobilize the masses for rebuilding, but he also wanted a peaceful international environment to free up resources for the same rebuilding effort.

Mao gambled that provocations in the Taiwan Strait would create enough tension to incite the people's revolutionary enthusiasm without sparking a larger conflict with the United States, but the gambit came at great cost. Taipei had been raising the idea of a mutual defense treaty with the United States since March, but Washington had not been receptive. Once the shelling began, however, the Americans changed their position.[65] On December 2, 1954, Washington and Taipei signed a formal defense treaty that committed the two sides to "act to meet the common danger" should either be attacked in the western Pacific.[66] The new treaty effectively doomed any prospect of a PLA invasion of Taiwan to force reunification with the mainland. This was a major setback for the CCP, but the outcome could have been worse. The PLA did manage to "liberate" a few offshore islands near Zhejiang in the event, which did improve security on the Chinese coast. And while the United States aided Nationalist forces as they withdrew from Dachen and Yijiangshan in early 1955, Washington otherwise did not intervene directly in the conflict.[67] Ultimately, the crisis never spread beyond the Strait, and the PRC managed not to soil the peaceful international climate it required for rebuilding. But American imperialism was still a threat, as far as Beijing was concerned, and increasing trade with "status quo preservationist" states remained important for cultivating a united front to contain the United States.

ALTHOUGH CCP LEADERS AGREED THAT increasing trade served the state's strategic interests, Lei Renmin and his colleagues at the Ministry of Foreign Trade faced a number of practical obstacles beyond the embargo.

Foreign exchange shortfalls topped the list. Ministry officials worried throughout 1954 that China's need for foreign currency would outstrip its supply. This concern stemmed in part from the assumption that overseas remittances, a mainstay of the state's hard currency earnings, would dwindle in the years ahead. But other dynamics also fed this anxiety. The Party's long-standing policy of satisfying the import needs of the Soviet Union and Eastern Europe first, for example, ensured that socialist markets claimed the lion's share of China's exports, leaving less to sell for cash in capitalist markets.[68]

These currency troubles were locked into the nation's economic planning through the Five-Year Plan. The State Planning Commission calculated that exports to capitalist markets would have to earn more foreign currency each year to offset overseas remittances, which were projected to contribute a declining share of the nation's earnings. This increased the burden on the Ministry of Foreign Trade and state exporters, but the Party had no choice. The State Planning Commission had earmarked future foreign currency earnings for a multitude of anticipated expenditures. Much of it would be spent on equipment, raw materials, and other goods to support industrialization and to address domestic needs.[69]

The Party also planned to spend currency on foreign policy initiatives, things like embassy buildings and diplomats' expenses, which were paid for in local currencies. Each year, the Ministry of Foreign Trade also spent millions of US dollars, Swiss francs, Hong Kong dollars, and British sterling on insurance and shipping.[70] By weaving these expenditures into the Five-Year Plan, the State Planning Commission had pledged the Ministry of Foreign Trade to earnings targets for years to come.

The ministry had several solutions to this problem. They launched campaigns to conserve foreign cash and proposed tighter and more centralized management over the use of foreign currencies. But the obvious solution was to ramp up exports, which became a mantra for the ministry. Party leaders instructed trade officials to "actively discover new types of export products, improve the quality of export goods, [and] strengthen the [domestic] procurement and export of secondary commodities," which were commodities that had not yet been exported but might find willing markets overseas.[71] They realized that Chinese exports had to be more abundant, better synced to market demands, and more salable abroad if they were going to generate the currency that state planners expected. These themes took root in the Ministry of Foreign Trade during the first Five-Year Plan, but they would persist well beyond it.

Cognizant of these challenges and determined to make the most of peaceful trends, Zhou Enlai pushed for more exchanges with foreign experts, which would stimulate production at home. "[We] must open the doors," he told an assembly of professional organizations on March 4, 1956. "From now on [when] inviting visitors, [we] won't simply invite progressives and moderates to come have a look, we can also allow [political] laggards and even reactionaries to visit," he said. China must "dare to be in contact with people." By this he meant more than simply meeting foreigners inside China. The PRC "must actively carry out work abroad," he told the audience.[72]

Zhou had in mind exchanges like the CNIEC visit to Britain in the summer of 1954. International meetings like this, including exchanges with experts from the capitalist world, would allow China's technicians and managers to enhance production and expedite industrialization.[73] Chairman Mao concurred. In a report to an enlarged Politburo meeting on April 25, 1956, he urged cadres to learn from the capitalist world's "exceptional" science, technology, and management techniques. He also claimed that China could benefit from studying the efficiency of capitalist businesses.[74]

This push for contact, trade, and expansion went beyond rhetoric. By the end of 1955, the Ministry of Foreign Trade had over 33,000 specialists working in 382 different offices at home and abroad. Most staff worked in China, where they served as customs inspectors, municipal trade officials, workers in state-owned trade firms, and instructors at the ministry's Foreign Trade Institute in Beijing. But hundreds were posted overseas in China's nineteen foreign commercial offices—not just in Europe, but also in East and Southeast Asia, the Middle East, and North Africa.[75]

When these officials communicated with each other internally about trading with capitalists, they relied on the revolutionary discourse of the era, using language and concepts that diverged from Zhou Enlai's emphasis on peace. Trade with capitalists was characterized as a "struggle" (*douzheng*), for example, part of a "commercial war" (*shangzhan*).[76] But this struggle was unfolding according to the rules and within the norms of international capitalism. It was a struggle from the inside, in other words, and the aim of the struggle was greater participation. Briefings and memos produced by the ministry in the mid-1950s measured success by pointing to metrics of expansion. In 1956, the ministry touted that it had developed commercial ties to over fifty different nations and regions, and had signed trade agreements with the governments of over twenty countries. This same report encouraged the ministry to push onward—to continue to expand trade with capitalist nations in the years ahead.[77]

As the Ministry of Foreign Trade was encouraging its cadres to reach these new heights, the nation's second Five-Year Plan was coming into focus. The second plan, which would last from 1958 to 1962, also expected China's trade to push past previous quotas. The ministry predicted that trade volume with the capitalist world would rise more than 75 percent above the figures from the first FYP.[78] Ministry leaders argued that higher-quality goods and better marketing would help to meet the new targets, and they urged workers to employ marketing techniques used by capitalist businessmen.[79]

Some of the nation's trade officials had already begun to do this. Marketing had become sleeker, and trade exhibitions more sophisticated. In May 1956, the CCPIT launched a catalog, *Foreign Trade of the People's Republic of China,* the chief aim of which was to sell products, the editorial board wrote in the first issue. "It is a magazine intended to let readers, especially traders and manufacturers who are interested in China's foreign trade, to get as much information as possible on anything in relation to it, particularly her export commodities," the board explained.[80] The Ministry of Foreign Trade, which oversaw the CCPIT, was savvy enough to realize that to sell Chinese goods, the magazine also had to sell China. This meant reconfiguring perceptions of what Communist China was, and what it represented, within markets and consumer communities in the capitalist world.

Three themes in *Foreign Trade* show how the ministry sought to reconfigure these perceptions. The first, and most apparent, was the image of the PRC as a peaceful and already-accepted member of international markets. On page after page, photographs showed Chinese officials signing contracts and touring factories around the world. The editors used statistics to reinforce this picture of engagement: China was trading with over sixty countries and regions by May 1956; during one ten-day period, 870,000 people visited a Chinese expo in Lyons; approximately 9,000 firms in Europe, the United States, Australia, Asia, and Africa had trade ties with Communist

China in 1955.[81] Nearly every article seemed to have some metric or anecdote attesting to China's presence in capitalist markets around the world.

A second theme was the magazine's deliberately depoliticized language, a technique rooted in the Moscow Conference of 1952. The genial tone in *Foreign Trade* contrasted with the discourse of "commercial war" that appeared in internal Ministry of Foreign Trade documents at the same time. When the magazine did acknowledge ideological differences between Communist China and foreign capitalists, it usually emphasized the economic advantages that these differences brought, particularly the benefits of trading with a command economy. "China's economy is a planned economy," the May 1957 issue explained. "Both her industry and agriculture grow in a well-coordinated manner." This steady growth produced incentives for Chinese traders to ensure an "uninterrupted supply of materials" from "reliable sources," the magazine continued, summoning the myth of the inexhaustible China market that had lured Europeans and Americans to China for centuries.[82] The heart of the pitch was that China's brand of Communism—stripped of its revolutionary aesthetic and considered in purely structural terms—could be a boon to business for readers.

This depoliticized image supported a third theme in *Foreign Trade*—the proposition that trade with China was normal, a claim that bolstered the larger argument that the embargo against China was corrupting the natural workings of global markets. "Trade between China and Western countries has not been developing as it should be on account of the trade discrimination policy adopted by some countries," explained an article in the second issue. Many in the West realized that the China embargo was "stupid and impracticable," the authors argued, yet the embargo continued to obstruct "normal economic intercourse in contravention of the interests of all people in the world."[83] On the same page as this argument, above the text, a photograph showed Lei Renmin clinking glasses with a group of Italian businessmen, a testament to the shared desire for "normal" economic relations.

The layout and style of *Foreign Trade* also presented a cosmopolitan sensibility, more like a *Spiegel* or *Sears & Roebuck* catalog, or even pre-1949 advertising in China, than standard Communist propaganda. Each cover featured a color image of economic activity—ships at a quay, or the facade of a trade expo. Back pages displayed products from state export firms. Inside the magazine, advertisements touted the virtues of Chinese products great and small, from sewing machines to peaches.

Orthodox Marxism-Leninism spurned advertising as wasteful, a stimulant that goaded people into buying what they didn't need and couldn't afford.[84] But here ads served the revolution. They smoothed the edges between socialism and capitalism in the interest of expanding trade. An advertisement in May 1957 for Ma Ling food products, for example, attempted to make braised fish with onion palatable to bourgeois consumers in more ways than one (see Figure 4.3). The depiction of the woman in the ad hints at how revolutionary workers in China imagined capitalist consumerism abroad—stylish dress and jewelry, lots of makeup, and alcohol. The ad suggested sophistication and abundance, an attempt to minimize the cultural and aesthetic distances between the revolutionary workers who produced Ma Ling fish and the capitalists abroad who consumed it.[85]

Similar techniques appear in an advertisement for "Kool" and "Rose" shirts (see Figure 4.4). This ad appeared in September 1958—during the fever pitch of the Great Leap Forward. Yet there are no traces of backyard furnaces or people's communes. The aim here was to appeal to the expectations and desires of capitalist consumers.

The fifth issue of *Foreign Trade*, which also appeared in 1958, drew readers to another dimension of China's program to expand its presence in capitalist markets: trade expositions. The cover featured the face of the Canton Exhibition Hall, China's own facility for trading with foreign capitalists. "New" China had participated in international expositions since as early as 1951, when Chinese officials attended the Leipzig Trade Fair, a venue for socialist producers to exhibit products to capitalist buyers. By 1956, the CCPIT could claim that Chinese goods had appeared at exhibits in France, Sweden, Iceland, Denmark, and across Asia—twenty-five expositions in fifteen countries since 1951. The CCPIT estimated that officials had shown Chinese products to more than 19 million potential customers at these fairs.[86]

Alongside this participation in fairs abroad, Party leaders also began to build exhibition halls inside China. On December 28, 1953, Zhou Enlai approved a request from Pan Hannian, then the vice mayor of Shanghai, to build the city's own exhibition center.[87] In 1954, the Ministry of Foreign Trade broke ground on an exhibition hall in Beijing.[88] Both structures, vast monuments to socialist architecture, celebrated the importance of China's trade and cultural contact with the socialist world. But on June 20, 1956, a trade official in Guangdong named Yan Yijun proposed

Figure 4.3   The Party's vision of how capitalists might consume China's braised fish with onions. Reproduced from *Foreign Trade of the People's Republic of China* 3 (May 1957).

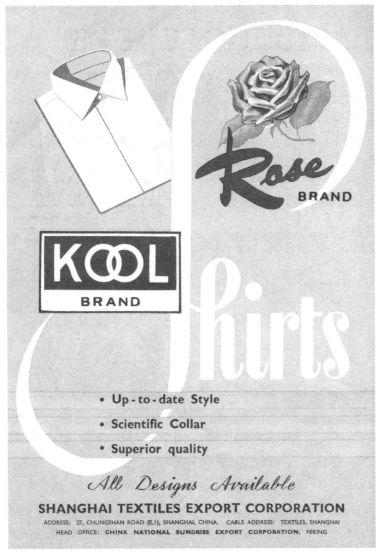

Figure 4.4   Selling white-collar shirts to capitalists during the Great Leap Forward. Reproduced from *Foreign Trade of the People's Republic of China* 5 (September 1958).

building an exhibition hall in Guangdong to support China's capitalist trade.[89] Yan suggested holding the first fair in September or October 1956, just a few months away, so it would have to be held in a temporary venue. His proposal circulated in Beijing until it reached Zhou Enlai, who approved it.[90]

Zhou took a special interest in the project. According to one source, he made recommendations on the location, policies, responsibilities, and even the name of the new facility.[91] He almost certainly realized how much China stood to gain from the new venue. Southeast Asian markets had become increasingly important to officials at the Ministry of Foreign Trade. An internal report in March 1956 singled out Asian and African markets as particularly significant to China's capitalist trade.[92] Yan Yijun's proposal three months later represented a promising opportunity to expand ties to some of these markets, and on a permanent basis.

Guangzhou was an obvious choice for the new facility. Less than two hundred kilometers from Hong Kong, the capital of Guangdong Province offered proximity to the British colony's mature markets and global connections. Regular fairs in Guangzhou might allow the Ministry of Foreign Trade to take advantage of these resources without subjecting itself to British or American oversight.[93] Operating in Guangzhou was cheaper than Hong Kong, too. It required less foreign currency. The Ministry of Foreign Trade would pay for fewer hotel stays, plane tickets, and restaurant meals abroad, all of which required dollars and pounds that could otherwise be spent on imports.[94] Because the facility would be permanent, the Ministry of Foreign Trade could also build on a scale large enough to yield more display space than the cramped pavilions of overseas expos.

The construction went rapidly, and the Canton Exhibition Hall opened less than a year after Yan's proposal, on April 25, 1957. The new building was square and orderly, just like the business inside was supposed to be. Silks, teas, fruits, handicrafts, and equipment spread across 140,000 square feet inside, space enough for 14,000 different commodities, CCPIT officials calculated.[95] The official mission of the fair was to develop "normal international trade based on the principle of equality and mutual benefit," as one catalog explained, and to promote "mutual understanding and friendship between the Chinese people and the peoples of other nations." More than 1,200 people from nineteen countries and territories attended the first fair, which lasted from April 25 to May 25.[96]

The grand opening of the Canton Exhibition Hall coincided with an even more promising development for China's capitalist trade. For the past two years, Beijing had been noticing cracks in COCOM and CHINCOM solidarity. In late 1955, the powerful Japanese steel industry pressured the government in Tokyo to grant exemptions for limited exports of steel to Communist China. British steelmakers, concerned about idle capacity, also pushed for exemptions, which London soon granted.[97] These exemptions generated pressure from others for similar treatment, and it was only a matter of time until the China differential collapsed. Two days after the Canton Exhibition Hall concluded its first fair, during a committee meeting in Paris, Britain announced that it had decided unilaterally to eliminate the differential.[98] Within weeks, France, West Germany, Italy, Holland, Luxembourg, Belgium, Denmark, Norway, and Portugal had followed suit.[99]

The news elated many British firms. The British Council for the Promotion of International Trade estimated that trade with Communist China could quadruple. Businesses would still face challenges, the council acknowledged. For example, most Chinese factories were using equipment produced by other nations because London had restricted exports during China's first Five-Year Plan. This meant workers in Chinese factories were unfamiliar with British machinery. Also, the collapse of the China differential did not mean trade had opened entirely. COCOM restrictions remained in effect. The demise of the China differential simply meant that trade with China now faced the same controls as trade with the Soviet Union. Still, these seemed like minor grievances given the general trend, small ruts in the road to bigger deals and new opportunities.

5

A "GREAT LEAP" IN TRADE

NOT LONG AFTER THE CHINA differential began to fall apart, Mao Zedong launched the Great Leap Forward (GLF), one of the most catastrophic campaigns in modern Chinese history. His goal was to boost production and accelerate modernization in China. He produced widespread starvation instead. For over two years, the GLF nurtured reckless ambitions that crippled the economy and upended Chinese society. The Ministry of Foreign Trade was not immune from the tumult. Among other effects, the GLF sabotaged the ministry's painstaking efforts to cultivate relationships with firms and governments throughout the capitalist world. Despite the ministry's best efforts, the hard work of the early and mid-1950s began to unspool.

But the GLF seemed a timely and auspicious step at first. Mao believed the Leap would push China into modernity. His core proposition was that human will, if sufficiently stoked and properly organized, could overcome material limitations, and the Great Leap Forward was his program to test this proposition on a national scale. He intended to use the GLF like an electric current, charging the people to produce an explosion of agricultural and industrial growth. Farms and factories would produce more than ever, and the PRC would leap to the fore of the industrial age. Trade with foreign capitalists was a vital part of this program. The Party leadership expected to sell a portion of China's newfound abundance to markets abroad in exchange for even more of the fuels, fertilizers, equipment, and technology China needed to accelerate its modernization. At first, this reasoning seemed sound to many, even intoxicating. But reality ultimately pulled China in a different and tragic direction.

A New Environment

In early December 1957, the Ministry of Foreign Trade summoned its senior and midlevel cadres from around the country to Beijing for a conference. When the minister of foreign trade, Ye Jizhuang, addressed the group on December 14, he recited a list of "serious weaknesses" that still plagued Chinese exports. He complained that some goods were failing to keep up with market preferences. Fountain pens, radios, and bicycles were often out of step. Designs were off and colors weren't right. Ye had more systemic complaints, too. Rigid management practices were disrupting transactions, he said. Also, unsteady supply lines were sabotaging deals.[1] Still, the point of the meeting was to inspire officials, not berate them, so he framed these shortcomings as reasons for the ministry to redouble its efforts.

And the ministry did have much to be proud of at the end of 1957. China now had trade relationships with eighty-two different countries and regions.[2] Foreign trade was also becoming a pillar of China's foreign relations, according to Chen Yi, the future foreign minister. "Before, we first conducted diplomacy, and then conducted trade," he told ministry officials on December 13. "[N]ow, we want first to conduct trade, and then conduct diplomacy." Signs of the importance of foreign trade could be found in the list of dignitaries attending the conference—Premier Zhou Enlai was there, so were Vice Premier Bo Yibo and Vice Chairman Zhu De.[3]

Ministry officials hoped to make trade even more important by continuing to expand. Zhang Ping, the chief executive of China Resources, believed China had ample room to grow in overseas markets. From his office in Hong Kong, he saw potential for Chinese exports not just in Hong Kong, but also in Singapore and Malaya. He conveyed this optimism to other ministry officials on December 10, while he was in Beijing for the conference. He also told them China was well positioned to break into markets in Canada, Australia, and Africa.[4]

Ye Jizhuang shared Zhang's optimism. "We must make full use of this opportune moment," the minister of foreign trade said in Beijing, "[and] expand our trade activities." He proposed deepening ties with "neutral" capitalist nations, such as Norway, Finland, Denmark, and Sweden, but he also hoped to increase trade with England, France, and West Germany by manipulating "contradictions" among these nations.[5]

Mao was also feeling optimistic, if not euphoric. Weeks earlier, on November 18, he had declared during a trip to Moscow, "the East Wind [was] prevailing over the West Wind," by which he meant socialism was now overtaking capitalism.[6] He made this remark as China stood at a crossroads in its development. The first Five-Year Plan had been a success, but the Party's decision to model its economic development after the Soviet Union had created problems. The Stalinist playbook encouraged massive investment in heavy industry to build an industrial foundation in China as rapidly as possible. In an overwhelmingly agricultural economy like China's, economic planners turned to surplus grain to pay for this investment. This required heavy extractions from rural areas—grain taxes—which the CCP could earmark for export or deliver to cities to feed the growing urban population. But PRC farmers were not producing enough surplus grain. Per capita grain output in China in 1957 was only half that of the Soviet Union's in 1928, when Moscow initiated its first Five-Year Plan.[7] To follow the Stalinist blueprint, Chinese farmers had to produce more grain.

Chen Yun believed the solution lay in reforms that introduced material incentives. He argued that if you pay good prices for produce and stock stores with affordable consumer goods, then farmers will throw themselves into their work with renewed vigor. But a political flaw marred Chen's logic. To produce consumer goods, the state would have to siphon investment away from heavy industry, which meant lowering industrial growth targets, and this ran afoul of Mao's enthusiasm for rapid industrialization.

Mao was in no mood for half steps in the fall of 1957. Recent breakthroughs in the Soviet Union had heightened his enthusiasm and diminished his patience.[8] In August, the Soviets had launched the world's first intercontinental ballistic missile (ICBM). Then, in October, the Soviets launched Sputnik, the first artificial satellite to orbit the earth. These successes prompted the Soviet leader Nikita Khrushchev to boast in November that the Soviet economy would surpass the US economy within fifteen years. Mao, caught up in the moment and not to be outdone, countered by claiming that China would surpass Great Britain in the production of steel and other industrial goods within the same fifteen-year window.[9]

Mao summed up his plan for accomplishing this feat with a short phrase that identified four new cardinal aims of production: "more, faster, better, more economical" (*duo kuai hao sheng*). This was not a new slogan. The *People's Daily* had used it in an editorial during the Lunar New Year in 1956, when the Party was exhorting the population to complete the first Five-Year Plan ahead of schedule.[10] But now, in late 1957, Mao was resurrecting the phrase after it had been "swept away," he claimed, by moderates who worried that overemphasis on expansion could lead to unbalanced growth.[11]

Mao committed the nation to "more, faster, better, more economical" growth in early October 1957, during the Third Plenum of the Eighth Central Committee.[12] He told Party leaders that there were two ways of doing things, "one way is a bit slower, a bit slipshod, one is a bit better, a bit faster."[13] Framed this way, by Mao himself, it was clear that China would soon go a bit faster. It was a simplistic formulation, but it gave Mao what he wanted. He could have the rapid growth he demanded without the politically dubious concessions to material incentives that Chen Yun and other "conservatives" had proposed.

Mao moved quickly to build support and silence opposition to his new line. The *People's Daily* sanctified the slogan on December 12, 1957, while Ye Jizhuang and his colleagues were still meeting in Beijing. The front page of the newspaper that morning featured an editorial entitled "[We] Must Adhere to the Construction Policy of More, Faster, Better, More Economical."[14] Mao had edited the article himself.[15] A few weeks later, in early January 1958, Mao lashed out at the "right-deviationist conservative" thinking of cadres who opposed a "rash advance" (*maojin*) in economic development, by which he meant Party leaders who advocated for more moderate and balanced growth.[16] He took his attacks further the following week, in Nanning, when he criticized Chen Yun, Zhou Enlai, and Politburo member Li Xiannian by name during a major internal Party forum for their conservative thinking, an unprecedented move in elite Party politics at the time.[17] By mid-March, Mao had collapsed the debate over China's development into a simple binary between so-called anti-rash advance advocates and his own "rash advance" approach. On March 9, he declared at a Party conference in Chengdu that "rash advance" development was

Marxist and "anti-rash advance" was "un-Marxist."[18] This was a dubious claim, but by framing the discussion as a fundamental ideological dispute, Mao was pulling the rug out from under his opponents.

As Mao quashed opposition to his new line in early 1958, he was also quietly refining his views on the relationship between economic development and political consciousness. On January 31, he circulated his thoughts on political economy in an internal Party document entitled "Sixty Articles on Work Methods."[19] The two longest articles in the document, the 21st and the 22nd, carried the most relevance for cadres working at the Ministry of Foreign Trade.

Article 21 explained Mao's concept of "continuous revolution" (*buduan geming*). He wrote that China's revolutions emerge one after another—revolution was perpetual, and revolutionaries never stood still. Each victory in the revolution brought new challenges, and Mao believed that this interminable succession was the lifeblood of the Chinese revolution. Each revolutionary wave bonded the masses together with shared purpose, filled them with fervor, and staved off conceit (*jiao'ao*).[20]

Mao also wrote that China's current revolution was a "revolution in technology" (*jishu geming*), and it was this revolution, he claimed, that would allow China to surpass Britain in steel production within fifteen years. He explained that everyone in China would study technology and science; even Party cadres would have to become proficient in science and technology if they were to lead the nation. But the Chinese people, and cadres in particular, had to strike a balance. An overemphasis on technology ran the risk of neglecting politics, so the Party and the people must "integrate technology with politics."[21] Mao's argument was not simply that technology and politics must be studied simultaneously but that the two pursuits were fundamentally linked—the development of technological competency itself must be a political process at its core. He believed this was true at the national and individual levels. Just as China must industrialize while maintaining its socialist identity, so must cadres become experts in science and technology without relinquishing their "redness."

Mao elaborated on the tension between technology and politics in Article 22. He explained that "red and expert" (*hong yu zhuan*) constituted a unity of opposites; each depended on the other, and successful cadres needed both. The CCP opposed "phony politicos" (*kongtou zhengzhi jia*)—apparatchiks who lacked proficiency in science and technology. But he believed a greater threat came from experts in scientific and technical fields who lacked political consciousness. These "lost" experts, as he called them, were "dangerous." They risked losing touch with the political moment. Lose that and you squander the soul of the revolution.[22]

Mao was characteristically vague about the relationship between "red and expert." He wrote that it was important for cadres to understand "a little" about technical affairs, but what did this really mean?[23] How much was "a little" expertise? Did the balance between red and expert shift depending on context, or was it universal and static? How should one locate this balance in the course of daily work? At the Ministry of Foreign Trade, these were not just philosophical questions for the officials who supported trade with foreign capitalists. For them, every negotiation, every contract, every transaction, at any moment carried the danger of appearing to lose the proper balance between redness and expertise.

The Central Committee circulated Mao's Sixty Articles broadly within the Party on February 8, 1958. In its cover letter, the Committee explained that the document was a draft and invited recipients to submit proposed revisions by April 1.[24] But even if officials at the Ministry of Foreign Trade had concerns about how the Sixty Articles might impact their work, they were in no position to take issue with the document. For months already, since the summer of 1957, officials at the ministry had been struggling under the pressure of the Anti-Rightist Movement (Fanyou Yundong) precisely because their views and behaviors had supposedly clashed with the "correct" political line. According to one ministry report in October 1957, 188 cadres at the Ministry of Foreign Trade had been dismissed recently because of political or ideological problems. Seventy-eight of these cadres lost their jobs because of "serious rightist sentiments" (*yanzhong youqing qingxu*) and another eighty-six had been sacked for "serious individualism" (*yanzhong geren zhuyi*), a shorthand for general selfishness or materialism. Others lost their jobs for malfeasance, "sleeping around," "hedonism," generally "degenerate" behavior, and other political and social transgressions.[25] By February 1958, those who had survived these purges had little incentive to request clarifications, much less voice opposition, when they read Mao's Sixty Articles. Instead, they had ample reason to align the ministry with Mao's emerging new line.

The opportunity to do so came in the form of yet another campaign, called the "Double-Anti Movement" (Shuangfan Yundong), in early 1958.

The Double-Anti Movement took its name from its two themes: "anti-waste" and "anti-conservative thinking." Opposing waste and "conservative thinking," it was thought, would help to boost production. The *People's Daily* described the campaign as a "free airing of views," implying that an organic, spontaneous spirit was behind the movement.[26] In truth, it was a surrogate for Mao's "more, faster, better, more economical" concept, with "anti-conservatism" representing "more and faster," and "anti-waste" a proxy for "better and more economical."

The Ministry of Foreign Trade had embraced the Double-Anti Movement by early March. At the ministry's training institute in Beijing, students plastered the campus with more than 16,000 big-character posters denouncing waste and conservative thinking.[27] Administrators began to adjust the curriculum, too. Since its founding in August 1954, the institute had trained cadres in the practical aspects of foreign trade; instructors taught subjects such as trade economics, accounting, and foreign languages.[28] Now, political activities began to encroach on coursework. The institute's Senior Education Office reported that instructors wanted to achieve a "great leap forward" in the curriculum by assigning more homework and demanding higher-quality studies.[29] But the students were turning to extracurricular pursuits, such as writing big-character posters and chasing vermin to support the national drive to eliminate the "four pests," all of which distracted them from their formal coursework.[30]

The central ministry remained committed to demonstrating its embrace of the Double-Anti Movement, but the divergent views of the faculty and students brought the practical and institutional challenges of "red and expert" into sharp relief. More was at stake than pedagogy. The question of how to allocate time and resources when training new trade officials touched on the fundamentally political question of how "red" China's future trade officials should be. At what point should they cultivate redness at the expense of expertise? Facing these questions, the institute's Party Committee sought middle ground. It reduced the number of "self-study" hours each week from twenty-two to sixteen and reserved ten hours per week for participating in "rectification and reform" (*zhenggai*) activities. To address the faculty push for a curricular "great leap forward," the Party Committee also reserved two hours every morning and evening for students to complete coursework and study.[31]

But the Party Committee could trim the students' studies only so far given the pressure to achieve breakthroughs in trade in the coming years. Just one month earlier, in February, the ministry had adopted the slogan "[achieve] large-scale imports and exports" (*dajin dachu*), which aligned with the "more" and "faster" elements of Mao's aggressive expansionism.[32] If the ministry wanted to expand imports and exports, its officials would need to find a way to combine expertise with the expansionist spirit of *dajin dachu*.

That same month, February 1958, the ministry began to articulate how its officials could contribute to the goal of rapidly expanding commerce with capitalist markets. In a report sent to the directors of various foreign trade bureaus, the ministry argued that it was important to increase contact with overseas markets. "[We] must dispatch capable cadres overseas to operate, to immerse themselves energetically in markets, [and] to strive to strike deals on the spot," the ministry wrote.[33] This included sending small groups abroad to "knock on doors" and seek out business. Trade officials should also strive to establish additional business "strongholds" (*judian*) in key locations. Officials working in PRC commercial offices overseas were expected to delve into the economies of their host nations and to write reports on economic trends, foreign currency developments, and policy shifts.[34] The ministry had proposed many of these steps before, but familiar ideas had begun to meld with the urgency of "more, faster, better, more economical." In this new environment, long-standing goals began to take on new energy, new tensions, and soon enough, new flaws.

A Great Leap

The CCP leadership formally endorsed the spirit of "more, faster, better, more economical" during the second session of the Eighth Party Congress in May 1958. The conference began on a cloudy day, with Party luminaries gathering in the Hall of Embracing Compassion, the CCP headquarters inside the walled compound of Zhongnanhai in central Beijing. The scripted meeting would last three weeks, and it would be dominated by Mao's enthusiasm for growth. During the opening proceedings on May 5, Liu Shaoqi read a Central Committee work report that established formally a new general line: go all out; aim high; more, faster, better, more economical (*guzu ganjin, lizheng shangyou, duokuai haosheng*).[35]

Once the new general line had been canonized, Party leaders demonstrated their support for its principles. One by one, economic leaders took the stage to repudiate their previous "anti-rash" views. Zhou Enlai had already admitted "anti-rash" tendencies earlier in the spring. On March 25, at a conference in Chengdu, he acknowledged having "thrown cold water" on the growing enthusiasm for production among the masses between 1956 and 1957. He had espoused a policy of "less, slower, worse, and wasteful," the premier confessed in Chengdu.[36] This was a start, but Mao expected more. In Beijing, Zhou acknowledged again his "anti-rash" mistakes by reciting Mao's argument: "[when] undertaking socialist construction, there are two methods: one is to do it a bit faster and better; the other is to do it a bit slower and worse." He admitted that he had been wrong to take an "anti-rash" stance. "I am the main person responsible for this error," he confessed.[37]

Other leaders presented their own self-criticisms at the Party congress. Bo Yibo was unequivocal: "The 1956 anti-'rash advance' [stance] was entirely a mistake," he conceded, "a policy error." "I also am responsible for this mistake," he said.[38] Chen Yun delivered a similar confession.[39] So did Li Xiannian.[40] These performances demonstrated the Party's full commitment to the new general line. By renouncing their "conservative" approaches to economic planning, the leadership left little top cover for opposition to the new line at the working level and eliminated any room for resistance to the emerging GLF from within the Ministry of Foreign Trade.

Minister of Foreign Trade Ye Jizhuang witnessed this pageant as it unfolded inside Zhongnanhai. He was there to brief senior leaders on trends in China's foreign trade, but also to demonstrate that he had aligned his own ministry with the general line, which he did by blending the line with established ministry policy. Since 1952, the Ministry of Foreign Trade had relied on metrics of growth, such as expanding trade volume and contract values, to showcase its progress, an approach that already fit well with the expansionism of "more, faster, better, more economical." Much of Ye's address had the ring of briefings from years past. He said he saw great potential for expanding trade in the future, just as he usually did. The reasons for his optimism, such as looming crises in capitalist economies or the inevitable collapse of the US-led embargo, also fit the pre-GLF mold of ministry briefings.[41] But Ye departed from his standard script in key ways.

Most noticeably, he grounded much of his analysis in the concepts of the new line. "In a global situation where the East Wind continues to prevail

Figure 5.1   Chen Yun in Beijing during the Great Leap Forward, June 1958. Wikimedia Commons.

over the West Wind," he told the leadership, "the world standing of the United States and other imperialist nations will continue to weaken."[42] Party officials had been making similar arguments about the coming collapse of imperialism for years, but Ye was now invoking the language of the Great Leap to make the point.[43] He also used the logic of the general line to discuss changes in ministry leadership. The time had come for leading cadres at the ministry to reconsider the balance between red and expert, Ye argued. He said ministry leaders would henceforth put greater emphasis on political work. "Overall, in the past few years, we have generally paid attention to the leadership of political thought," he explained, "but this is still not enough."[44] They would have to do more.

Ye vowed, "from today forward, the leaders of the [Ministry of Foreign Trade] Leading Party Group must achieve seven parts politics, three parts professional work; [they must] overcome the pathology of excessive practical professional matters [and] minimal discussion of ideological principles." They would devote 70 percent of their time in meetings to politics and 30 percent to practical work issues. Ye pledged that ministry leaders would also spend more time each day on political reflection, including at least one hour every day reading political materials.[45]

Ye also proposed institutional reforms to bring the ministry into line with Mao's thinking. Two years earlier, in April 1956, Mao had pushed to carve out space for lower-level officials to contribute their own initiatives to governance and growth in China. "Central authorities must take care to bring into play the initiative of the provinces and municipalities," he had demanded.[46] By mid-1958, his growing distaste for bureaucratic centralism and his faith in grassroots initiative had worked their way into the logic of the new general line. Ye Jizhuang incorporated this theme of decentralization into his remarks. In a move that would come to haunt him before the year was out, he proposed several decentralization measures for the Ministry of Foreign Trade. He said that responsibility for export production, purchasing and pricing of domestic goods intended for export, product processing, packaging, storage, and shipping should all be transferred from central ministry authorities to the localities. He suggested that local authorities take responsibility by overseeing their own accounting and passing profits up to higher levels as appropriate. Foreign exchange earnings should also remain at the local level. He also proposed that leaders at the provincial, municipal, and autonomous region levels draft their own balanced import and export plans and then report these up to the National Economic Commission and the Ministry of Foreign Trade. Then, based on the domestic and international situation, the National Economic Commission and Ministry of Foreign Trade should implement a unified, comprehensive, and balanced plan.[47]

Ye cautioned that unity remained central to foreign trade work. He was not calling for wholesale decentralization of the Ministry of Foreign Trade. He stressed that the ministry must maintain a united front when negotiating with foreign traders, and officials at the central Ministry of Foreign Trade would retain the authority to negotiate deals with capitalist and communist foreigners.[48] Still, his push for decentralization marked a significant break from the ministry's long-standing commitment to centralization.

Ye's speech reflected months of internal reviews and discussions about the future of the ministry and the nation's trade. The ministry's Leading Party Group had convened over twenty meetings since the Nanning Conference in January 1958 to discuss past work and future trends, roles, and policies in the context of the emerging GLF.[49] On May 11, while the second session of the Eighth Party Congress was still in session, the ministry submitted a report that read like an action plan to the Central Committee. It expanded on Ye's proposals in more detail and made clear to the Central Committee that the Ministry of Foreign Trade fully supported the Great Leap Forward.[50]

OUTSIDE OBSERVERS SOON DETECTED signs that the PRC was planning an expansion in foreign trade. Analysts noticed infrastructure projects on the mainland during the spring of 1958 that suggested a major increase in cargo traffic. In mid-April, Jardine, Matheson & Company estimated that Chinese workers would soon finish work on a deep water wharf at Zhanjiang, in southern Guangdong, which would transform the small fishing port into a modern, mechanized facility capable of handling 46 million tons of cargo annually. The PRC was completing similar projects in Guangzhou and Tianjin. In Shanghai, work was underway to increase the city's port capacity to handle nearly 2.4 million tons of additional cargo each year.[51]

There were other signs of growth. On March 29, the *Washington Post* reported that a PRC trade mission visiting France had signed deals worth US$12 million, including contracts for locomotives, hydroelectric machinery, and patent rights to manufacture French-type railroad engines.[52] On April 12, Jardine, Matheson & Company reported in its confidential *China Trade Bulletin* that China's push for exports had gained so much momentum that it "has now become a drive."[53] British diplomats in Beijing reported that PRC export corporations appeared "ready to seize any opportunity to increase, or diversify, China's exports."[54]

With the China differential already abandoned by most of Western Europe, this trade drive faced fewer hurdles from foreign governments and firms. Still, the world's largest market remained off limits. US Treasury Department regulations, issued under the authority of the Trading with the Enemy Act of 1917, still barred Americans from most trade and finance involving the People's Republic of China.

Technically, these regulations did not prohibit *all* trade with the PRC. American firms could legally trade with Communist China if they secured a license from the Treasury Department.[55] For years, few actually received these licenses, but this began to change, too, in the spring of 1958. On April 1, the *New York Times* reported that China Resources had purchased forty-five thousand tons of wheat from the Canadian subsidiary of an unnamed US firm.[56] The US$2.25 million deal prompted many American exporters to wonder whether the US embargo against China also applied to foreign-based subsidiaries of American firms.[57] If not, these subsidiaries might offer an indirect route into the mainland China market. In July, following a summit in Ottawa between President Dwight D. Eisenhower and Canadian prime minister John Diefenbaker, the US Commerce Department announced that automobiles and other "nonstrategic" goods could indeed be exported to the PRC by subsidiaries of US firms if Canadian authorities approved.[58] As the *Los Angeles Times* put it in a headline on Saturday, July 12, the decision represented "A Break in the Chinese Trade Wall," a wall the United States itself had constructed.[59]

Many US firms hoped it was a break. The very next working day— Monday, July 14—the president of Chrysler Canada told the press that his company was prepared to accept *any* order for automobiles or trucks as long as it followed government policy. A senior representative at Ford Canada also told the press his company was open to trading with the PRC if it did not violate US or Canadian law.[60] Other companies soon began to probe for opportunities. On September 3, 1958, the Export Division of the Studebaker-Packard Corporation wrote discreetly to the US Embassy in Ottawa for details on how to use its Canadian car factories to break into the mainland China market while sticking to the letter and spirit of US law.[61] On September 22, the New York office of Scandinavian Airlines System (SAS) called the State Department to inquire about selling transport planes produced by Douglas Aircraft to buyers in the PRC.[62]

As prospects brightened for trade with North America, Beijing's export drive also made headway in markets closer to home. On March 5, 1958, the CCPIT signed a fourth long-term bilateral trade agreement with Japanese nongovernmental organizations.[63] The signatories committed to US$196 million in total bilateral trade for the coming year—US$98 million in each direction.[64] Leaders in Tokyo, including Prime Minister Nobusuke Kishi, saw the deal as an opportunity to push for balanced trade. The nation had accumulated a US$20 million deficit with the PRC the year before, in addition to a deficit of over US$1 billion with the United States, Japan's largest trade partner.[65]

The Sino–Japanese deal suited the Ministry of Foreign Trade's needs as well. The leadership saw Japanese markets as a keystone in the PRC's program of expansion. On February 3, 1958, ministry leaders had urged the directors of the nation's foreign trade bureaus to "vigorously expand trade with Japan." The two nations were natural economic counterparts. The ministry observed that Japanese producers sold many of the industrial goods China needed most, such as ammonium sulfate to produce fertilizer, rayon, steel plating, and nonferrous metals. Chinese soybeans, rice, cashmere, and coal also had a ready market in Japan. The text and terms of the bilateral agreement captured this complementarity.[66]

None of these promising developments signaled a CCP decision to relax its grip on political or ideological prerogatives in trade work. Party leaders still believed trade with foreign capitalists was fundamentally political. Negotiations leading to the March 1958 Sino–Japanese deal had dragged on for months—since September 1957, far longer than anyone had expected. Behind the delays lay disagreements over protocols and rights related to the establishment of reciprocal trade missions in Tokyo and Beijing.[67] Negotiators struggled especially with the issue of whether, and under what legal pretense, the Chinese trade office in Tokyo would be permitted to fly the PRC national flag.[68]

Politics continued to plague the Sino–Japanese agreement after it was signed. The government in Taipei denounced the deal. Nationalist officials particularly resented a memorandum attached to the agreement that ultimately granted the right of the PRC trade mission in Tokyo to fly Communist China's national flag on its building, in addition to other quasi-diplomatic courtesies.[69] On March 12, an editorial in the KMT's official newspaper, the *Central Daily News,* worried that the agreement represented a step toward diplomatic relations between Tokyo and Beijing.[70] The next day, the Nationalist government abruptly halted a trade conference underway with Japanese visitors in Taipei to await Tokyo's clarification of the matter. Taipei officials then raised the stakes by suspending all commercial negotiations and contracts with Japan and calling on supporters at home and abroad to boycott Japanese goods.[71]

As this firestorm was building, US secretary of state John Foster Dulles arrived in Taipei for an official visit. On the evening of March 14, Chiang Kai-shek told Dulles and the US ambassador in Taipei, Everett F. Drumright, that the situation in Japan was developing badly. Chiang expressed fear that Japan had charted a "neutralist" course, meaning the Kishi government had begun to stray from the capitalist camp. Chiang assessed that the Communist regime in Beijing was facing pronounced economic and fiscal difficulties.[72] Under the circumstances, a near US$200 million Sino–Japanese trade deal seemed to throw the CCP a lifeline.

Taipei's objections were just the beginning of the problem. In April, CCP officials also began to emphasize the politics surrounding the agreement. At an opening ceremony for an exhibition of Japanese goods in Wuhan on April 1, Lei Renmin told an audience that the Japanese government had tried to sabotage the agreement and decried the meddling of the US and KMT governments.[73] On April 4, he announced that Beijing was suspending plans to send an advance team of trade representatives to Japan, as called for by the agreement. Still at the expo in Wuhan, he told Chinese and Japanese journalists that the Kishi government had no plans to recognize the right of the Chinese mission to fly the PRC flag in Japan. It made little sense to send the group, he reasoned, until Tokyo clarified its position. He also announced that plans to hold Chinese expos in Fukuoka and Nagoya later in the year were now on ice.[74]

Kishi scrambled to salvage the agreement from cross-strait politics. On April 9, he issued a statement expressing support for the trade agreement, but also underscoring that Japan would not officially recognize the CCP regime in Beijing. Japan's foreign minister, Aiichirō Fujiyama, reiterated separately that any flying of a national flag by the PRC trade mission in Tokyo "will not be recognized as a right, but will be protected under the domestic laws of Japan."[75] The announcement seemed to placate the KMT government, which accepted Tokyo's position and resumed normal business ties with Japan.[76] Chiang had the political reassurance he wanted, but Beijing did not.

On April 13, CCPIT chairman Nan Hanchen condemned Tokyo's statements. He reiterated Lei Renmin's earlier accusation that the Japanese government was colluding with the United States and the Nationalists to sabotage the trade agreement. "Although the Japanese Government has done everything possible to resort to sophistry in the reply [i.e., its recent statement on the draft trade agreement], it cannot succeed in hiding its intention to throw the fourth Sino-Japanese trade agreement overboard," the *New York Times* quoted Nan as saying. Beijing radio took aim at Kishi personally, accusing him of "collusion" with the United States and Chiang and denouncing the leadership in Tokyo as "two-faced."[77]

Any hope of salvaging the Sino–Japanese agreement evaporated on May 2, 1958, when two young men strode into the Hamaya Department Store in Nagasaki, where the Japan–China Friendship Association was hosting a postage stamp and paper-cutting exhibition, and tore down one of the PRC national flags on display.[78] Such a public desecration enraged the CCP leadership in Beijing. Liao Chengzhi, who did so much to launch the CCP's trade program in Hong Kong during the late 1930s and was now serving as deputy director of the State Council's Foreign Affairs Office, was reportedly beside himself with anger. When Liao briefed Zhou Enlai and Foreign Minister Chen Yi on the matter, he recommended that the Party leadership strike back hard.[79] On May 10, they did. Beijing suspended all trade with Japan. The Ministry of Foreign Trade would no longer issue import or export licenses for trade with Japan, and major Japanese firms involved in the China trade received cables from Shanghai informing them that their contracts had all been canceled.[80]

The leadership at the Ministry of Foreign Trade expressed solidarity with these measures. The flag incident in Nagasaki occurred just three days before the opening of the second session of the Eighth Party Congress on May 5, leaving Minister of Foreign Trade Ye Jizhuang no choice but to address the issue explicitly in his report to the Central Committee. He said that on the one hand, China must trade with Japan. Commerce fostered friendly relations between the people of the two countries. It also helped to wean Japan from its reliance on the United States. On the other hand, trade must always serve political struggle, he acknowledged. This may have been a truism within the Party, but it bore repeating in the context of the ongoing discussions about redness and expertise. Even if Ye had had private reservations about the rashness of severing all bilateral trade with Japan, this was not the time to express them. The ministry had been through too much during the recent Double-Anti Movement. As a result, Ye was unequivocal on the matter: the Central Committee's decision to suspend trade with Japan was "completely correct," he declared.[81]

Many outsiders saw the severity of Beijing's reaction as a case of the CCP simply placing politics above commercial gains. Saionji Kinkazu, a longtime China hand from Japan and onetime Soviet informant, held this view. Saionji assessed that Beijing's reaction to the flag incident reflected simmering frustration over Prime Minister Kishi's pro-Taiwan stance. He observed that anti-Japan sentiment remained high on the Chinese mainland just thirteen short years after the end of Japanese occupation. He also suggested that the CCP had grounds for feeling slighted. He pointed out that PRC officials had not only permitted Japanese trade missions to fly the Japanese national flag at recent trade exhibitions in Wuhan and Guang-zhou; they had also assigned People's Liberation Army soldiers to guard the flag.[82]

Politics did play a central role in Beijing's handling of this crisis, but internal CCP documentation suggests that the Party's response to the Na-gasaki flag incident was more nuanced than a simple choice of politics over commerce. In October 1957, just as talks were beginning in Beijing for the fourth Sino–Japanese trade agreement, the CCP Central Investigation De-partment (Zhonggong Zhongyang Diaocha Bu) concluded in an internal report for the Central Committee that the Japanese government was facing fierce economic headwinds. Tokyo was grappling with challenges to its market share in the United States, the report explained, and Japan was dealing with a foreign currency crisis. As a result, the Kishi government was "eager and anxious" (*jiyu*) to expand trade with China.[83]

Similar internal assessments reiterated this point in the months that fol-lowed.[84] On April 26, 1958, the Central Investigation Department as-sessed that Japan's hopes for a larger slice of the China market would only increase with time.[85] The logic of this narrative suggested that Beijing had the upper hand in bilateral economic relations. It also created the possi-bility that the PRC could have its cake and eat it too: it could take a prin-cipled stand on the flag incident with sufficient confidence that, sooner or later, Prime Minister Kishi would diffuse the tension unilaterally because he was so desperate for a solution to Japan's economic woes.

For months after the Nagasaki flag incident, internal CCP reporting un-derscored the wisdom of cutting off trade with Japan. On June 4, a CCP intelligence analysis reported that Japanese officials and members of the governing Liberal Democratic Party (LDP) seemed "worried" that the bi-lateral break in trade would become a long-term affair.[86] On June 12, an-other report claimed that the Japanese had become anxious that capitalist traders from Western Europe would take advantage of Japan's absence in the Chinese market to strengthen their positions there. The report observed that in early June, these concerns had prompted the Japanese Ministry of Foreign Affairs to instruct Japanese diplomats in England and France to probe their local counterparts on their trade positions and plans in the PRC.[87]

All of these reports suggested to policymakers in Beijing that China had the upper hand in the dispute, that Japan was eager—anxious, even—to restore trade with China, and that the Kishi government would eventually show contrition for its handling of the flap. These assessments resonated with the larger sense of confidence, bordering on hubris, that had been thickening the air in Beijing since the fall, when the "East Wind" had begun to prevail over the "West Wind." With time and history on the Party's side, why not punish Japan in the short term? Given Tokyo's presumed desperation for trade with China, the flag incident offered a golden opportunity for the leadership in Beijing not to champion politics *over* trade, but rather to pursue politics through trade, and trade through politics. In the near term, this strategy called for applying commercial leverage, which the ministry did with flair. Sino–Japanese trade plummeted after the flag incident and would not begin to recover until the early 1960s.[88]

A Great Unraveling

The CCP's confidence seemed justified in the spring of 1958, when the Great Leap Forward still seemed full of possibility. But as the Leap evolved from inspiration to perspiration, the trade officials responsible for applying "more, faster, better, more economical" to capitalist trade found themselves facing two challenges. The first arose from the GLF's push for decentralization; the second, from a growing zeal for increased trade volume.

The Party leadership debated problems associated with decentralization during its annual summer conference at Beidaihe, a seaside resort about a half day's train ride from Beijing. The top items for discussion during the August 1958 conclave included industrial production and people's communes, but concerns over decentralization in foreign trade work could not be ignored. A few weeks before the conference, the Ministry of Foreign Trade's Leading Party Group sent an alarming report to the Central Committee that explained how the ministry's push for decentralization had begun to wreak havoc on China's trade with foreign capitalists. The report warned that during the first six months of 1958, local officials had placed orders for imports from capitalist markets that would cost a total of US$94 million, over twice the US$45 million that the ministry had budgeted to localities for the entire year. Even more alarming, the ministry had not yet achieved its export targets for the first half of 1958, which meant foreign exchange earnings had fallen behind schedule. The ministry warned the Central Committee that its holdings of dollars and other hard currencies would dwindle in the third quarter, and if local authorities continued to place foreign orders directly, China would run the risk of defaulting on import contracts.[89]

As a stopgap measure, leaders at the Ministry of Foreign Trade proposed a moratorium on local orders for imports from capitalists during the third quarter. The ministry also suggested a further increase of exports to generate the revenue needed to make up for the surge in import orders during the first half of the year. The Central Committee approved these proposals on August 10, one week before the Beidaihe conference.[90] But the Party leadership would have to make further adjustments to ensure that similar dislocations did not arise in the future.

On August 15, two days before the opening of the Beidaihe conference, the Central Committee circulated a draft resolution that outlined the decentralization problem in the nation's foreign trade work. In short, the Central Committee wrote that decentralization had to be walked back at the Ministry of Foreign Trade. Since Ye Jizhuang's call for decentralization in May, disunity and even "chaos" (*hunluan*) had crept into China's foreign trade system. In some Chinese ports, for example, local foreign trade offices were competing with one another for customers and market share rather than cooperating to strengthen China against foreign competitors. Some trade offices undermined national unity by "casually" (*suibian*) inviting foreign businessmen into China for talks or visits. In a few cases, local authorities had gone so far as to circumvent the Ministry of Foreign Trade entirely by negotiating deals with overseas capitalists directly.[91]

This kind of disarray triggered the deep fear among officials that the PRC might descend into the same "free competition" that plagued the capitalist world. The Central Committee believed that chaos of this sort threatened serious losses, and not just in an economic sense. China could also suffer political losses from unruly commerce with capitalists.[92] Trade with foreign capitalists was a political struggle, after all, as Ye had reminded the ministry's leadership just a few weeks earlier, and internal unity was essential to China's victory.[93]

The Central Committee proposed several measures to ensure that decentralization did not weaken the Ministry of Foreign Trade's grip on capitalist trade. Only headquarter offices subordinate to the ministry, acting as a united front, were permitted to sign deals with private capitalist firms for goods and commodities that traded in monopolistic markets. Trade with capitalists in other goods must be conducted under the unified leadership of the ministry and in accordance with a port-by-port division of trade responsibilities that the ministry had worked out ahead of time.[94]

The Central Committee also ordered that unauthorized contact between domestic trade offices and foreign capitalists must stop. The Ministry of Foreign Trade had to approve any invitation issued to foreign businesspeople to visit the People's Republic of China, just as all PRC trade missions overseas also required ministry approval. In a sign that some cadres had resorted to questionable methods when courting business partners, the Central Committee's resolution specifically forbade Party members from offering "free entertainment" to visiting foreign capitalists.[95] Officials also could not deviate from price lists mandated by the head offices of the Ministry of Foreign Trade. Some officials had schemed to poach capitalist trade partners from competing PRC offices by offering better terms. The thrust of the guidance was that decentralization would continue, but national unity in trade work was essential. The Central Committee vowed that it would "absolutely not permit" (*juebu rongxu*) cracks in China's united commercial front.[96]

But the push for expansion and decentralization had grown too much and resistance had been too bullied for a single resolution from the Central Committee to restore order. China's trade continued to unravel into the fall of 1958. On October 15, a banker from Chartered Bank in Shanghai told a British diplomat that he planned to spend the day renewing over ninety letters of credit to cover Chinese exports, all of which were due to expire by the end of the day. The extensions were needed because the chaos at Chinese ports had produced crippling delays. Trade vessels sometimes arrived in Shanghai two weeks behind schedule because of confusion in north China ports. These same vessels often encountered still more delays in Shanghai.[97] This was hardly the smooth, unified trade mandated by the Central Committee.

Overseas, Chinese commercial activity and diplomacy also seemed to unravel on all fronts, creating an arc of tension that stretched from China's neighbors in Southeast Asia up to its border with the Soviet Union in the north. In late spring 1958, cheap Chinese leather products, cotton textiles, canned foods, and other goods began to flood Southeast Asia and Hong Kong.[98] The influx of affordable goods was welcomed by shoppers, but rival exporters viewed the rapid increase in Chinese products with alarm. Political tension soon followed, with Japanese traders leading the charge. Japanese firms followed market trends in Southeast Asia closely because the region accounted for a third of the nation's exports.[99] On July 17, 1958, the *Japan Times* reported that the volume and variety of Chinese exports to Southeast Asia had spiked since the beginning of 1958. The newspaper reported that Chinese exports to the region had been sporadic in the past, but they had become continuous in recent months and the quality had improved.[100]

Japanese businesses were particularly concerned by the tactics that Chinese exporters used to gain larger shares of Southeast Asian markets. In early summer 1958, newspapers were reporting allegations of PRC price "dumping." In June and July, Chinese cotton piece goods were selling in Southeast Asian markets at 1 to 2 percent below Japanese prices.[101] Other Chinese goods were as much as 15 percent cheaper than Japanese competitors.[102] By fall, the difference had widened. Sometime in late September or early October, Koichi Mishi Katsu, head of the cotton textile section of Dainippon Textiles, reported that China was offering textiles in Southeast Asia at prices 20 percent below those quoted by Japanese manufacturers, and this was for textiles of comparable quality, according to Koichi.[103]

Dumping was easy to charge, but hard to prove. For the allegation to stick, competitors had to show that China was offering goods at prices either below the price charged for the same goods at home or below the cost of production. Evidence of these tactics would indicate China's intention to drive competitors out of the market, capture their market share, and then raise prices to profitable levels once the competition had been eliminated. But because the People's Republic of China was a command economy, calculating the domestic prices of goods and production costs was more art than science. Even if these figures could have been calculated with confidence, dumping was only part of the problem. China's competitors also accused Beijing of other unfair practices.

Some claimed that Chinese exports pirated Japanese designs, especially cotton cloths and ceramics.[104] Others alleged China was freely copying

Western patents.[105] Special financing and payment terms also helped Chinese exports gain market share. In Jakarta, rumors circulated that the Bank of China had offered advance loans to merchants covering 70 percent of the cost-and-freight (C&F) value of goods imported from China.[106] Some Chinese exporters provided delayed-payment terms or offered to deliver goods to Southeast Asian markets without waiting for letters of credit.[107] In Bangkok, a local representative of China Resources negotiated special deals with ethnic Chinese merchants and a local bank offered plum credit terms to merchants who agreed not to place orders from other suppliers.[108]

Some of the frustration with Chinese exports was sour grapes. The spat with Beijing over the flag incident in May had predisposed Japanese businesses and the press to scrutinize Chinese trade for slights. Still, Beijing did nothing to soothe the resentment. Instead, it fanned the flames. CCP leaders encouraged ethnic Chinese in Southeast Asia to boycott Japanese goods in support of Beijing's dispute with Tokyo.[109] Consumers in the region didn't seem to pay much attention—British diplomats reported scant evidence of anti-Japanese boycotts in Vietnam, Laos, Cambodia, Thailand, Burma, the Philippines, or Indonesia.[110] But Beijing's combativeness irritated its neighbors and heightened tensions.

Beijing also faced diplomatic problems to its north. Sino–Soviet relations had been fraying since as early as February 1956, when Premier Khrushchev launched a "de-Stalinization campaign" at the Twentieth Congress of the Communist Party of the Soviet Union (CPSU). Khrushchev had castigated Stalin and his personality cult in a speech during the congress, which blindsided the CCP and greatly offended Mao, who was not consulted beforehand.[111] Smaller tensions flared during the spring and summer of 1958, including misunderstandings over a Soviet proposal to construct a joint Sino–Soviet naval fleet and the building of a Soviet radio transmitter on Chinese soil.[112] But the deeper problem in the relationship was that Mao sensed "great power chauvinism" emanating from Moscow and was no longer content to defer to Soviet primacy in the world socialist hierarchy. On July 22, Mao exploded at the Soviet ambassador to China, Pavel Yudin, with a barrage of vitriol and condescension.[113] Khrushchev visited Beijing the following week, arriving on July 31, hoping to clear the air in a meeting with Mao. But the trip degenerated into a diplomatic circus. Mao disparaged and belittled his guest, and by the time Khrushchev left Beijing, relations had not improved.

Mao then heightened tensions with the United States and its Nationalist ally in Taiwan. On August 23, under direct orders from Mao, the Chinese PLA launched an artillery attack on the KMT-occupied island of Jinmen. Within ninety minutes, over thirty thousand PLA shells struck the tiny island, destroying KMT military facilities, killing hundreds of troops, and engulfing the Taiwan Strait in tension.[114] The PLA continued to shell intermittently for weeks, ensuring that tension remained high until at least mid-October.[115] Mao believed that a circumscribed attack on Jinmen and the KMT-controlled island of Mazu, both just a few miles off the mainland coast, would again create helpful tension at home by rallying the masses and focusing their energy on production and reaching the targets of the Great Leap Forward.[116]

This tension may have been useful for domestic mobilization, but it combined with diplomatic stress elsewhere to jeopardize the Ministry of Foreign Trade's efforts to build on its successes of the mid-1950s. Disruptions in PRC trade, in turn, threatened to undermine the Great Leap Forward and the revolution itself, as Ye Jizhuang and other trade officials knew. Zhou Enlai recognized this threat, too, and in late 1958 he intervened to address it.

On November 8, 1958, at 10:30 in the morning, Zhou convened a meeting with Ye Jizhuang, Foreign Minister Chen Yi, Vice Premier Li Xiannian, and a handful of staff to discuss international trade. Zhou was frustrated. To him, it must have seemed like no one in the Ministry of Foreign Trade was minding the fundamentals. It was as if the GLF had swept away all the nuance and prudence in the ministry's work. His concerns clustered around three interrelated issues.

First, Zhou expressed frustration at slack in planned export procurement work. He asked for an update. Ye Jizhuang explained that the provinces had stepped up their efforts to fulfill export contracts, especially after the Beidaihe conference in August, but problems still remained. When Zhou asked how well the ministry was fulfilling its annual export plan, Ye told him the picture was mixed. They would be able to meet the year's overall export targets, he explained, but imbalances remained when it came to bilateral trade relationships and individual products. Ye told Zhou frankly that exports to capitalist markets were not going well. Similar problems plagued socialist trade: there were shortfalls of thirteen different products owed to the Soviet Union, including cement, pork, and poultry.[117]

This raised a second issue that troubled Zhou: was the ministry on the verge of reneging on contracts? "What's the situation with exports to capitalist markets?" he asked. Ye told him that China would only export around US$600 million in goods to capitalist nations instead of the full US$674 million that the ministry had planned. Zhou responded by insisting that all signed contracts be honored.[118] He had stressed this point before, in July at a meeting of Ministry of Foreign Trade officials, but he clearly felt the message hadn't sunk in.[119] The Ministry of Foreign Trade itself had for years committed to fulfilling all trade contracts, believing that failure to do so would damage China's credit (*shixin*) and constitute a violation of the law (*fanfa*), neither of which benefited the development of China's foreign trade.[120] Still, the issue bothered Zhou enough that he instructed the ministry to compile a list of all export shortfalls, including the quantity of goods promised in signed contracts, how much of each contract had been fulfilled, how much was still owed, which nations were owed, and the provinces and departments that were responsible for providing the goods. Zhou then said that a national conference of provincial and municipal Party secretaries had just begun in Zhengzhou. He ordered the Ministry of Foreign Trade to give the list to an official and put that official on a plane to Zhengzhou, where the shortfalls could be brought directly to the conferees' attention.[121]

Zhou was deadly serious about honoring these contracts. He was willing to risk his compatriots' lives for it—though not necessarily his own. He told the meeting attendees, "[we would] rather ourselves not eat or eat less, not use or use less, and fulfill the contracts already signed." Chen Yi agreed. He had already seen signs of trade problems affecting diplomacy. He told his colleagues that the East German ambassador himself had recently asked for help collecting thirteen hundred tons of frozen poultry before Christmas, part of a trade contract with China that remained unfulfilled.[122]

When Li Xiannian turned to the subject of cotton, Zhou launched into a critique of the Ministry of Foreign Trade's activities on the global cotton market, a third issue that concerned him that morning. Recent figures showed an increase in China's cotton exports by the end of the year, he noted, but revenues from cotton sales were in decline. The reason was obvious, Zhou said: the price of cotton had dropped. The American imperialists engage in price dumping, he said curtly. Turning to Zhao Zhongde, a Ministry of Foreign Trade official, he asked, "are you or are you not also dumping?" Zhao offered a cautious but honest reply: global cotton markets were not great this year, and prices were down. To export cotton, which served as a vital source of foreign currency, China had to lower its prices. Ultimately, though, this was indeed dumping, he acknowledged.[123]

Zhou responded, "this is actually dumping, [and] it has influenced Sino–Indian relations." India, one of the world's largest cotton exporters, paid close attention to trends in global cotton prices. Zhou pointed out that the Ministry of Foreign Trade recently increased exports of cotton yarn, outside the official plan, by thirty thousand units. The ministry had also raised exports of cotton cloth—again, outside the plan—by six million bolts. All of this placed additional downward pressure on global cotton prices. "Who approved this?" the premier demanded.[124] An official sheepishly explained the rationale behind the decision. China desperately needed foreign currency, he said. China had a bumper cotton harvest this year, too, and the Ministry of Foreign Trade faced heavy export responsibilities. Given these considerations, ministry officials did not believe increasing cotton exports would cause major problems, so they never sought senior approvals outside the ministry. If they had, they would have learned that much of China's cotton production that year had already been spoken for, and that officials elsewhere were becoming increasingly concerned that China might actually run out of cotton stock.[125]

To Zhou, a recently reformed "anti-rashist," it must have seemed that the Great Leap Forward had completely upended the discipline and control that the Ministry of Foreign Trade had developed throughout the 1950s. "The products we export, what we export, how much, where, at what price, all of it [means] we must discuss policy," the premier told Chen Yi.[126] It was as though everyone had forgotten that trade was a political act. Zhou believed certain forms of commerce, such as dumping and monopolizing markets, lacked socialist virtue. Ironically enough, they violated capitalist norms, too. Rather than stoop to such techniques, he argued, China aspired to a virtuous path (*wangdao*) in its commercial dealings.[127] This required nuance. Zhou acknowledged that international trade with capitalists was a form of class struggle, but China could not afford to struggle blindly. The Ministry of Foreign Trade had to differentiate among different types of capitalists to pursue agreements that served China's diplomatic goals. This meant developing trade with certain capitalists and avoiding behavior that might undercut the PRC's relationships with these trade partners. Chen Yi piled on. "We cannot take the 'leap forward' spirit and use it as our foreign policy," he said, "[and we] especially cannot oversimplify methods."[128]

Zhou instructed Ye Jizhuang to take these and other points back to the Ministry of Foreign Trade, convene a meeting, and pass them down the ranks.[129] Ye likely shared Zhou's frustrations. Both men had spent years building up a global trade program for the PRC and now it was unraveling. But the problems Zhou identified during the meeting were symptoms, not the disease. The Great Leap Forward, with its insistence on rapid expansion, its demand for decentralization, and its valorization of redness over expertise all pushed the Ministry of Foreign Trade, an institution already cowed into compliance by the Anti-Rightist and the Double-Anti movements, away from the nuance that the premier demanded.

Zhou remained troubled by the direction of foreign trade. He returned to the subject at a meeting of the Central Foreign Affairs Leading Group on the afternoon of November 23, during which he reiterated that the foundation of China's foreign policy was socialism, not capitalism. China's foreign trade must serve politics, he said. Capitalists chased profits blindly, whereas PRC trade was conscious (*zijue de*); it served the interests of the great majority of the world's people.[130] He explained that China's trade sought to help developing nations industrialize, fortify their independence, and raise their own political consciousness, all of which shrank capitalist markets and weakened imperialist economies. He acknowledged that it might appear that socialist trade temporarily strengthened the capitalist class in developing countries by aiding their development, but it also strengthened the working class.[131]

Despite this theoretical clarity, China's socialist trade seemed adrift. Zhou observed that the Ministry of Foreign Trade had undertaken a rectification campaign and now "opposed conservative thought."[132] This aligned with the spirit of the Great Leap Forward, but still the ministry struggled to find its own coherence and direction. What mind-set is "in command" of foreign trade policy? Zhou wondered aloud. "It's still not clear," he said. The ministry had not researched its own policies very well.[133] This critique was unfair. Zhou knew the Ministry of Foreign Trade was being pulled in two directions, caught between the aspirations of the Great Leap Forward and the persistent realities of the world outside China. His criticisms that afternoon sounded like his own search for coherence, as if he were trying to conceive of some way to bridge the gap between the Great Leap's ambitions for change and the practices and proficiencies essential to productive trade.

Zhou continued to wrestle with this challenge, and by late December 1958 his thinking had congealed into a fourteen-point treatise, which he shared in Beijing on the morning of December 23, during a symposium with foreign trade bureau chiefs. In his remarks, Zhou repeated the mantras of *zili gengsheng* and "equality and mutual benefit," but he also raised new propositions that might enhance cooperation and instill order inside the Ministry of Foreign Trade.[134] He repudiated the concept of "commercial war" (*shangzhan*), which had appeared throughout the 1950s in internal ministry documents that discussed trade with capitalists.[135] Instead, Zhou emphasized "peaceful economics" (*heping jingji*) and the PRC's commitment to the enrichment and economic development of the people of the world. This contrasted with imperialists, who sought to impoverish the world's people.[136]

Zhou also disavowed the slogan "import and export on a large scale" (*dajin dachu*), which the ministry had adopted only ten months earlier, in February 1958. He argued that such a mind-set failed to consider the views and positions of China's trade partners, an observation prompted almost certainly by the dumping fiasco in Southeast Asia. He pointed out that *dajin dachu* ignored "objective laws" (*keguan guilü*). The reality was that imperialism still existed and trade was a mutual undertaking. These facts couldn't be willed away, a point that brought the discussion back to the dispute between Mao and much of the top leadership over the fundamentals of political economy. Could China transform itself through subjective will alone, as Mao believed, or would hard realities help to define the limits of China's development, as Zhou Enlai, Chen Yun, and other "anti-rash" advocates had once argued? Zhou was unequivocal: "The Great Leap Forward must also accord with objective realities," he said. "Foreign trade cannot jump 40–50 percent all at once," he told ministry officials.[137]

Ever the conciliator, Zhou tempered this bold assertion by claiming to embrace fully the spirit of expansionism in foreign trade. This included trade with foreign capitalists. He called for more trade with "peaceful, independent" capitalist nations such as Sweden, Switzerland, Finland, and Austria. He told the audience that China bought 1.6 million watches from Switzerland in 1957. In 1958, it bought only 90,000. This was no good, he said. China wanted to buy more in the future. The PRC would also continue to trade with imperialists as long as it served political objectives. The Ministry of Foreign Trade would not rely on trade with these nations, but it could buy things from their markets. After all, he conceded, some did sell quality products.[138]

Zhou's call for a more moderate trade policy in late 1958 proved too nuanced for the brute force of the GLF. The national campaign rolled on despite evidence that local officials were sending exaggerated production figures to Beijing and that famine had emerged in some rural areas.[139] On January 23, 1959, the Ministry of Foreign Trade Leading Party Group responded to Zhou's call for temperance by requesting permission from Mao and the Central Committee to reduce the overall export and import targets set by the original plan for the year. But the ministry's new, lower targets, which the Central Committee approved, still exceeded the actual 1958 values by 19 percent and 3 percent, respectively.[140]

The provinces couldn't keep up. Signs of trouble were already appearing. In February 1959, the US Embassy in Belgrade reported that the PRC had failed to provide additional goods to the Yugoslav government to balance out Beijing's bilateral deficit. The PRC also reneged on contracts to ship cotton waste to Great Britain.[141] Hong Kong imports from mainland China during February 1959 sunk to the lowest monthly total since July 1955.[142] In March, Beijing canceled an agreement with Finland to deliver twenty thousand tons of sugar because the Ministry of Foreign Trade could not fulfill its side of the deal.[143] West German diplomats in Hong Kong told their American counterparts in early April that Beijing had reneged on a number of major export contracts for bristles, textiles, and other goods.[144]

Officials at the Ministry of Foreign Trade wrote candid assessments of their failings in the first half of 1959. One report, written for the Central Committee on March 11, stated bluntly that export procurement during the first quarter of 1959 was "not good."[145] On May 12, Li Xiannian admitted that certain export quotas could not be met. The ministry was still leaning into Great Leap expansionism and it was distorting production quotas. The situation was becoming absurd. Regions without a single walnut tree had been ordered to harvest the nuts for export. Factoryless backwaters had been told to produce goods before they had the means to make them.[146]

The problems were easy to identify, but practicable solutions remained scarce as long as the orthodoxy of the GLF kept moderation at bay.

Minister of Defense Peng Dehuai did his best to challenge the reigning orthodoxy during a leadership conference at the mountain-top retreat of Lushan, in northern Jiangxi Province. On the afternoon of July 12, the blunt marshal marched to Mao's cottage to discuss the problems of the Great Leap, which by now included reports of bottlenecks, hasty construction, chaotic communes, wasteful steel drives, mishandled harvests, and, most troubling of all, famine.[147] But Mao's guards turned Peng away, purportedly because the chairman was asleep, so Peng wrote a fateful "letter of opinion" to Mao in which he laid bare his critiques of the Great Leap Forward.[148]

Mao became enraged when he read Peng's criticisms, and by the time the chairman and the rest of the CCP leadership descended the mountain in August, Peng stood accused of heading an "anti-Party clique."[149] Worse still, the rest of the leadership had been cowed into submission by the force of Mao's furious response, and the Great Leap Forward had been reinvigorated. Hu Qiaomu, who had worked with Mao for twenty years, captured the mood: "The wind is blowing harder now," he said."[150]

That wind swept through the Ministry of Foreign Trade while cadres there labored under contradictory guidelines.[151] Surrender fully to the exuberance of the Great Leap Forward, the Central Committee commanded, but remain practical and prudent, as Zhou Enlai had ordered. On October 7, 1959, the Central Committee urged ministry officials and cadres across the country to "go all out, [and] by any means conceivable" fulfill the nation's plan for annual foreign trade.[152] Even if everyone did "go all out," the ministry had little time left to meet its annual obligations. Ministry leaders reported to Mao and the Central Committee on September 30 that although two-thirds of the year had already lapsed, the nation had fulfilled only half of its annual export commitments.[153] Prospects were even grimmer when it came to certain products. The ministry calculated that by September 1, 1959, only 42 percent of rice export agreements had been fulfilled. Just 38 percent of frozen pork contracts had been satisfied, and barely a fifth of committed wheat exports.[154]

On October 26, the Central Committee and the State Council jointly established a temporary "export office" to coordinate a nationwide export blitz, and placed the veteran trade official Yao Yilin in charge.[155] As much as the new office demonstrated the Party's commitment to meeting China's export targets, it also exposed the inability of the Ministry of Foreign

Trade to accomplish its responsibilities without resorting to ad hoc measures. So did an urgent message from the ministry leadership on November 4, which ordered trade workers to "take emergency action" and declared a "sixty-day battle" to ensure that China met its export responsibilities before the year ended.[156]

The depth of dysfunction was on display when the heads of the ministry's foreign trade bureaus met in Beijing on November 17 to discuss work for the coming year. For a week, trade officials from nineteen different provinces, municipalities, and autonomous regions pitched ideas and requested support for schemes to boost exports. Cadres from Guizhou proposed building a production base for mercury and sulfur. Qinghai officials wanted to construct facilities for producing borax, asbestos, and mercury. Bureau heads from Sichuan, Inner Mongolia, Shanxi, and Liaoning all had their own grand plans for expansion, but little idea how to pay for them or whether they would produce viable exports. Officials at the meeting also requested to buy more goods from abroad. Anhui officials asked to import four sets of chemical fertilizer equipment; Jiangsu wanted thirty. No one seemed to have given any thought to where the funding would come from. Lin Haiyun, who cochaired the meeting with Lei Renmin, had to remind officials repeatedly that the nation's foreign currency holdings would remain tight as ever in the year ahead, but he was swimming against the current.[157]

The Ministry of Foreign Trade submitted its plan for 1960 to Mao and the Central Committee less than a month later, on December 20. In true Great Leap fashion, projections for the coming year were rosy. The report claimed, "current foreign trade, like the entire national economy, is in a good situation."[158] Challenges still existed, the ministry admitted. The United States remained committed to the Cold War, for example, and "Western nations" still made excuses that discriminated against China and limited its ability to trade. Some PRC exports might not reach Western markets as a result, the ministry explained, and some imports would be difficult to obtain. But the "East Wind" still prevailed over the "West Wind," and the future promised more growth ahead. The ministry planned an 11.7 percent increase in imports from capitalist nations in 1960, for a total of US$756 million. Exports were projected to leap even higher, 16.7 percent above 1959 levels, to US$700 million.[159] As in years past, the ministry also expected the Soviet Union to play a central part in the nation's trade agenda in 1960.[160]

The Central Committee approved the plan on December 26, 1959. For officials at the Ministry of Foreign Trade, the plan suggested that 1960 was likely to bring more of the same: more pressure to grow, more enthusiasm at the grass roots, more anxiety at the top. It seemed cadres would also continue to bend expertise to suit redness, the safest path politically, rather than treat the two synergistically, as Mao had instructed but never practiced himself. The Great Leap Forward and the race for "more, faster, better, more economical" output had convulsed the country for two years despite signs of rashness, recklessness, frenzy, and famine. Along the way, the GLF had uprooted the discipline and control that the Ministry of Foreign Trade had long sought to instill in its work, with disastrous consequences for the ministry and the nation, many of which had yet to fully appear.

6

TRADING FOR SALVATION

ON JANUARY 21, 1960, the *New York Times* reported that the PRC had missed its production target for grain in 1959. The news was thirdhand. The *Times* had picked up the story from the Hong Kong newspaper *Ta Kung Pao,* which had already reported the shortfall based on information from the Chinese Communist Party's own *Red Flag* magazine. The author of the *Red Flag* article had tried to put a positive gloss on the figures by claiming that the PRC had produced 270 million metric tons of grain in 1959, a full 8 percent increase from the previous year. But the *New York Times* observed that this total still fell short of the state's announced goal by nearly 5 million metric tons.[1]

Despite the shortfall, the government managed to collect enough grain not only to meet its export targets for the year but to exceed them. A few weeks before the *New York Times* article, on January 6, the Chinese State Council reported to Mao and the Central Committee that the last-ditch campaign to achieve the procurement and export targets set by the Ministry of Foreign Trade had been a success. The State Council boasted that ministry officials had collected 112 percent of the nation's total procurement target for the year, which was enough to export 102 percent of the PRC's total adjusted export target for 1959.[2] In other words, the ministry had collected more than it planned for the year, despite signs that farm yields couldn't keep up.

This disjuncture between what farmers produced and what the state exported revealed a crack in the foundation of the Great Leap Forward, but it wasn't the only sign of problems. Troubling internal CCP reports were flowing into Beijing. One after another, local grain bureaus reported that food stocks had declined precipitously in late 1959 and early 1960, and that a crisis was imminent.[3] People were already starving in some places.[4] The bottom was falling out of the Great Leap Forward.

Serious problems were also emerging in foreign policy, especially in China's relations with the Soviet Union. The tensions that had been building for years between the world's leading socialist powers would finally rupture in the summer of 1960. Almost overnight, the Soviet Union transformed from an ally to a threat, a development that prompted changes in the way the PRC's trade and diplomatic officials understood China's place in the world. In this fluid international environment, China now had to contend not just with capitalist imperialism but with Soviet "revisionism" as well.

These crises in the early 1960s convinced Party leaders that the world was changing and that China had to adapt. Economic catastrophe at home pushed the CCP to look abroad for salvation—for grain to save lives from the famine, first and foremost, but also for technology and equipment to salvage the Party's legitimacy, which still rested in part on the promise to modernize the nation and improve the lives of everyday people. Yet the break in Sino–Soviet relations left officials at the Ministry of Foreign Trade with nowhere to turn for certain vital imports but capitalist markets. As a result, for the first time since the founding of the People's Republic, the bulk of mainland Chinese trade began to turn toward the capitalist world, bringing to an end the brief predominance of Sino-socialist trade.

A Hard Landing

Li Xiannian was anxious throughout the winter and spring of 1960. A member of the Politburo and an acknowledged expert on trade and economic affairs, Li was also an inveterate worrier who had a keen sense of his own limitations. When he first met with Mao in 1954, following his appointment as minister of finance, Li reportedly blurted out that he wasn't up to the task. He lacked the required skills, he told Mao, and he hoped the Central Committee would consider someone else for the post. Mao admonished Li for his hesitation, and Li dropped his objections to the job, but he kept his nervous outlook.[5]

Li was worried in early 1960 because he was reading reports of short-falls as they arrived in Beijing and he recognized the potential for food shortages to wreck the Chinese economy. Grain, cotton, edible oils, meat, and vegetables were the primary provisions of stable markets, he told trade and finance officials during a speech in February.[6] Without these essentials, the people would have nothing to eat and nothing to wear, hardly a stable foundation for economic growth. He was worried enough to take his concerns to the top, and on January 13 he informed Mao that some provincial reports suggested between 10 and 20 percent of rural communes were facing food shortages.[7] A month later, on February 18, he reported to Mao and the Central Committee that several major cities, including Beijing, Tianjin, and Shanghai, lacked adequate grain stocks. Specific "disaster areas" (zai qu) were also contending with serious food shortages, he warned.[8]

It took courage to express these concerns directly to Mao and the rest of the leadership in the context of the anti-rightist hysteria that still dominated in early 1960. Peng Dehuai's ignominious fall during the Lushan conference in the summer of 1959 was still fresh on senior cadres' minds. This dangerous environment helps explain Li's tepid proposals for resolving his anxiety over food supplies. He recommended a coordinated grain transportation "assault" that would ship food from areas with relatively abundant grain stores to regions in need.[9] This was a step in the right direction, but it left untouched the larger Great Leap framework that had produced the shortages in the first place.[10] Li's "assault" also suggests that he still viewed the emerging crisis as a domestic snarl that could be untangled with logistical adjustments alone.

Most Party leaders agreed with Li's impulse to fiddle at the margins, but by late spring a deeper sense of unease had taken root. On June 14, the CCP convened a five-day expanded Politburo meeting in Shanghai to discuss the final three years of the second Five-Year Plan (1958–1962).[11] On the first day of the conference, Mao called for a general cooling off in economic affairs. "[We] can leave a bit more slack," he said. Zhou Enlai agreed and suggested that the CCP lower its production targets for grain, cotton, and pork.[12] Lower the production targets, he reasoned, and the procurement targets also drop, leaving more food in bowls and in stomachs across the countryside. Liu Shaoqi added that the people must have food if socialist construction was to continue. "[We] must safeguard the barest standards of living," he reminded everyone on the afternoon of June 17.[13] By this time, the CCP had no choice but to "leave a bit more slack," a point made clear by the Party's economic planning czar, Li Fuchun, when he addressed the group. The public grain figures for 1959 were bogus, he told the Politburo. The totals had been inflated. Real grain production for 1959 stood at 240 million metric tons, not the 270 million reported in the press.[14] Li did not know it at the time, but the "real" grain totals he was reporting that day were also inflated. Party officials would later discover that China had produced only 170 million metric tons of grain in 1959, not nearly enough to feed the population and keep up with export plans.[15]

Despite these troubling signs, the Party continued to pressure lower-level authorities to ensure that export procurement work remained on track for 1960. The year was already off to a lackluster start. Shaanxi Province had met only 74.6 percent of its export quota for the first quarter, and this figure obscured more severe deficiencies at the level of individual products, such as eggs, oil, and poultry—the types of goods that starving farmers prefer not to collect and ship elsewhere for export. The Central Committee urged provincial authorities to improve their export operations on April 10, 1960, starting with candid investigations of local procurement practices. The Provincial Party Committee in Shaanxi offered a model for how this process might work. Officials there had just completed an internal investigation of export procurement work, which had uncovered shoddy goods and disregard for approved procurement plans, among other serious issues.[16] Similar problems likely existed elsewhere.

Party officials at the Ministry of Foreign Trade also warned on June 3 that imports were outstripping exports. As of May 20, China had exported only 523,000 of the 1.8 million tons of rice that the ministry had committed to exporting, according to its own calculations. In other words, nearly halfway through the year China had met less than 30 percent of its annual rice export commitments. Shortfalls had caused embarrassing and costly effects, just as they had the previous year. The Polish government, for example, had leased two ships outfitted with refrigerated storage in anticipation of receiving frozen pork from China late that spring. When China failed to fulfill its end of the deal, Polish authorities requested US$275,000 in compensation for the ship leases, a significant outlay for China's cash-strapped government.[17] The Ministry of Finance had expected to have earned roughly US$65 million by midyear, but by late June exports had yielded only US$25.5 million.[18]

As Li Xiannian and others at the ministries of Foreign Trade and Finance were contending with these issues, China's diplomatic position worsened. Tension with the Soviet Union continued to build. In late 1959 and early 1960, several issues contributed to the souring of bilateral relations, including the challenge of relations with India. Chinese and Indian troops had fought limited border skirmishes in August 1959, just months after the Dalai Lama fled Tibet for India in March following Beijing's quashing of a popular Tibetan uprising. Mao could stomach the fighting with India, but he was furious to learn that Moscow claimed neutrality in the quarrel, a stance he interpreted as tantamount to Soviet betrayal.[19]

With Mao still fuming, Soviet and Chinese representatives met in Moscow at a February 1960 conference of Warsaw Pact members. During the meeting, the two sides aired their differences over the Soviet Union's advocacy of "peaceful coexistence," a policy that stressed disarmament, peaceful decolonization, and economic competition with the capitalist world rather than anti-imperialist conflict.[20] CCP leaders viewed the policy as capitulation to imperialism. The exchanges in Moscow, many of which occurred in front of other Warsaw Pact members, became so heated that at one point, during a banquet, a drunken Khrushchev cursed Mao personally in the presence of Kang Sheng, a senior official with direct ties to Mao. The Soviet premier called Mao a pair of worn-out "galoshes," using a term that also meant "condoms" in both Chinese and Russian. Mao was like a "defective product," Khrushchev also said, "good for nothing."[21]

The CCP responded a few weeks later with a propaganda broadside. On April 22, the *People's Daily* celebrated Lenin's birthday with a front-page editorial arguing that "peaceful coexistence" was a sham. The article reminded readers that Lenin himself maintained that imperialism was the root of modern war.[22] Wherever imperialism existed, the threat of war loomed. CCP propagandists then published more attacks to drive the point home.[23] By early summer 1960, Sino–Soviet relations had been flayed raw. During a June meeting of Communist party leaders at the congress of the Romanian Workers' Party in Bucharest, Khrushchev denounced Mao as an "ultraleftist," an "ultradogmatist," and a "left revisionist."[24] All signs pointed to a fallout, a prospect that could spell disaster for China's ties to its largest trading partner.

Only a few months earlier, economic relations between the PRC and the Soviet Union seemed as though they might weather the deepening crisis. In late March, Xinhua even celebrated a new Sino–Soviet trade protocol that envisioned a 10 percent increase in trade with the Soviet Union above the previous year. But signs of cooling trade were evident beneath the propaganda. The American consulate in Hong Kong observed in a report to Washington that the 10 percent increase envisioned by the 1960 Sino–Soviet trade agreement was less than the planned 25 percent increase in bilateral trade from 1958 to 1959. Even more telling, Moscow had already claimed that actual Sino–Soviet trade volume in 1959 was 35 percent higher than in 1958, not 25 percent as first projected. On the heels of such rapid growth, the 1960 announcement of a 10 percent increase seemed tepid.[25]

In private, the Central Committee in Beijing was anxious about these trends. On Sunday evening, June 26, 1960, Li Xiannian, Tan Zhenlin, and a small group of top officials discussed trade and economics on a conference call. Tan tried to strike an optimistic note. The overall environment for China at home and abroad was quite good, he told the others. But he had to admit that the congress in Romania had been troubling, especially the unfriendly attitude on display by the Soviets. China had to redouble its efforts (*fafen tuqiang*), by which he meant China would have to strive to achieve *zili gengsheng,* particularly in agricultural production, which would ensure that China's fate remained entirely in the hands of the Chinese people.[26] Tan didn't spell out the connection between the souring Sino–Soviet relationship and the need for *zili gengsheng* because he didn't need to. Everyone on the call must have seen the potential for political tension to corrode bilateral trade and aid.

Li Xiannian took a darker view of events. It was becoming increasingly clear that his plan for domestic grain distribution was inadequate. He suspected municipal authorities in Beijing, Tianjin, and Shanghai were concealing the depth of their food crises. Some cities have only two days' worth of grain in storage, he warned.[27] A June 15 internal report from the State Council's Finance and Trade Office, which Li had likely seen, concluded that neither Beijing, Tianjin, nor any of the major cities in Liaoning Province had enough grain to last two weeks. Shanghai had nearly used up its rice stores entirely.[28] Li also worried about lagging exports to capitalist markets and sluggish foreign currency earnings. Exports to the Soviet Union had fallen behind for the year, too, which threatened to exacerbate the fraying relationship. He understood that, under the circumstances, a cynic might ask a troubling question; as Li put it, "You took a Great Leap Forward, why is it that 'more, faster, better, more economical' export products cannot fulfill the [plan]!"[29] More was at stake than the credibility of the Great Leap Forward. In the context of the increasingly public dispute with the Soviet Union over the very nature of socialism, the legitimacy of the Chinese Communist Party and the Chinese revolution itself were on the line.

With these concerns unresolved, Li Xiannian departed Beijing in early July for the annual Party leadership retreat at Beidaihe. Top CCP leaders planned to spend much of the summer, from July 5 to August 10, deliberating international affairs and China's precarious economic footing. As it turned out, both subjects took on greater urgency not long after the conference began. On July 16, the Soviet Embassy in Beijing dropped a bombshell on the CCP in the form of a short diplomatic note. Addressed to the Chinese Ministry of Foreign Affairs, the document stated that Moscow had decided to withdraw all Soviet technical and economic advisors from China immediately.[30] A second note arrived on July 25 to explain that all Soviet advisers would be gone from China by September 1.[31] Most would walk away from active construction sites and half-completed projects; two-thirds of the 304 Soviet aid projects remained incomplete as of that summer.[32]

Chinese leaders asked the Kremlin to reconsider the decision, but Khrushchev refused.[33] Mao may have welcomed Moscow's decision, given his long-standing faith in the generative powers of self-reliance, but the move alarmed many in the CCP leadership. Li Xiannian and others at Beidaihe began immediately to devise policies that would mitigate the damage.

When the conference concluded on August 10, the Central Committee circulated an internal directive that mapped out the Party's response to the nation's troubling trade prospects in the context of the Soviet withdrawal. To start, the Central Committee placed control over foreign trade into the hands of a powerful triumvirate: Zhou Enlai, Li Fuchun, and Li Xiannian.[34] This group would personally supervise China's foreign trade. Li Xiannian also took charge of a "Foreign Trade Headquarters" (Duiwai Maoyi Zhihuibu), a newly created organization tasked with curbing imports, managing procurement, and streamlining exports.[35] In essence, his responsibility was to reassert central control over China's trade program.

Li had a massive project before him. Just before the Foreign Trade Headquarters was established in August 1960, the Ministry of Foreign Trade had collected only 43.3 percent of its original procurement goal for the year, and only 38 percent of China's planned exports had actually left China. Yet imports were still streaming into China from overseas markets. By July, the Ministry of Foreign Trade had already met 52.7 percent of its annual import goal. To address this imbalance, the Central Committee announced a moratorium on additions to the current year's import schedules unless they were approved personally by the Li-Li-Zhou commission.[36]

The Soviet decision to break off support prompted longer-term calculations. The Party leadership concluded that China's debts to the Soviet Union and its satellites in Eastern Europe now represented an urgent concern. The CCP's own statistics suggested that the nation's debt to the socialist world could reach as high as two billion *yuan* by the end of the year. "This is a serious political problem before the entire Party," the Central Committee wrote. The leadership wanted to wipe the debt clean, the sooner the better. According to the Central Committee, everyone at the Beidaihe conference agreed that China must reduce its debts to the Soviet Union and Eastern Europe in the remaining months of the year, and it must strive to repay "basically" all of its loans to socialist partners in 1961.[37]

This commitment, buried on the second page of a top-secret CCP directive, revealed a seismic shift in the minds of top officials. Paying off China's debts to the socialist world was more than simply a matter of socialist economic construction. Alongside the need to fulfill export commitments and balance the budget, zeroing out socialist debts impacted China's "international reputation" (*guoji shang de shengyu*), the Central Committee explained.[38] This connection, linking socialist debt to international political stature, revealed the entanglement of commercial affairs with China's increasingly complex struggle against imperialism—a struggle no longer against reactionary capitalist-imperialists alone, but now also against "modern revisionists" and their lackeys in the Soviet Union and Eastern Europe. The persistence of China's debts to the Soviet Union represented an economic vulnerability, but it also suggested a political deficiency in this complex environment.

Moscow's withdrawal of Soviet assistance clearly struck a nerve with the Chinese leadership. Wittingly or not, Khrushchev had also activated the same deep ambivalence that could be seen a decade earlier, when Mao signed the Treaty of Friendship, Alliance, and Mutual Assistance with Stalin in February 1950. That agreement brought US$300 million in desperately needed Soviet loans, but the size of the loan was curiously small—the Soviets had provided Poland a credit line of up to US$450 million a year earlier.[39] Mao said in January 1950, while treaty negotiations were still ongoing, that the CCP requested only limited financial aid because it was better "to borrow less than to borrow more at present and for several years," a position corroborated by Soviet evidence and rooted squarely in the framework of *zili gengsheng*.[40] Debt was always a potential threat, no matter the creditor, as far as Mao was concerned. China had no choice but to borrow from its socialist allies in the early 1950s, but the loans still left Mao uneasy. Now, ten years later, Khrushchev's revocation of support appeared to confirm Mao's suspicions.

This apparent confirmation modified CCP thinking on international political economy. Since the 1930s, *zili gengsheng* had served as a coherent framework for reconciling the ostensible contradiction between keeping foreign imperialists at bay, on the one hand, and doing business with them, on the other. By emphasizing the need to control all commercial contact with foreign imperialists, *zili gengsheng* indirectly sanctioned the continuation of such trade. Now the Party leadership was adding a corollary to this framework by linking the "modern revisionists" of the Soviet Union and Eastern Europe to the imperialist world as joint targets of "struggle" (*dou zheng*).[41] In this new formulation, *zili gengsheng* urged a reduction in economic vulnerability to the socialist world by paying off debts early, while still legitimizing controlled commercial engagement with the capitalist world.

The immediate implications of this evolving position were clear for Sino–Soviet trade. China's trade with the Soviet Union, already slipping from the inflated highs of the Great Leap Forward, fell further.[42] As it did, the balance of China's trade volume shifted away from the socialist world back toward capitalist markets, where it would stay for the remainder of the Cold War. No one recognized it at the time, but this turnabout marked the beginning of the end of the brief predominance of the socialist world in China's global economic engagement.

On a deeper level, these changes raised new and difficult questions about the theoretical principles that guided the PRC's trade agenda. Mao and the CCP had long embraced the Leninist argument that monopoly capitalists sought to dictate the terms of trade with poor nations as a means for dominating them. CCP orthodoxy also saw monopolists' quest for higher returns in new markets as the fundamental force animating capitalist trade.

By definition, then, the capitalists' zeal for foreign trade was driven by exploitative designs.[43] But as Chinese trade officials turned increasingly toward the capitalist world for trade rather than to socialist allies, the clean lines that distinguished capitalist from socialist trade began to blur. If economic exchange with socialists was no longer inherently an expression of solidarity and mutual assistance, and if commercial ties to the Soviet Union could now threaten China's independence, could economic exchange with the capitalist world become less inherently pernicious, too? If so, what did this mean for future thinking inside the Party on the dangers and opportunities of capitalist commerce in a fluid environment?

Few had time to ponder these questions in the summer of 1960. Too much was unraveling and people were starving. At Beidaihe, Li Fuchun had begun to reorient economic planning away from the Great Leap mentality toward a program of "adjustment, consolidation, and rising standards."[44] When the conference ended in August, the Party's economic leaders scrambled to restore order in time for the fall harvest. Most recognized the difficulty of the task. During a telephone conference on the evening of August 25, Li Xiannian seemed to think the nation's economy was up against a wall. The food situation had deteriorated to an alarming degree. He explained that in the past two years, the Party could pull from its stockpiles whenever it encountered a crisis. Now, working grain stores stood at their lowest levels, supplies of cooking and vegetable oils were alarmingly depleted, and working cotton reserves were practically nonexistent.[45]

Desperate for grain, Party planners began to consider turning to capitalist markets for food.[46] Chen Yun raised the possibility informally to the Ministry of Grain, and after considering the matter internally, Party leaders at the ministry decided to discuss the possibility with the Central Committee and to bring Li Xiannian into the conversation.[47] This was hardly a novel proposition in the larger context of Chinese foreign trade during the twentieth century. Rice usually fetched a higher price than wheat on international markets, and the Nationalist regime routinely exploited this difference by exporting rice and importing wheat, which allowed it to feed more people at lower cost.[48] But in Mao's China, such trade veered dangerously close to "rightism." China must feed itself, the Party had long insisted, and since 1949 mainland China had maintained positive net exports of grain amounting to roughly 2.3 million tons per year—until, that is, late 1960.[49]

A New Path?

By October 1960, after most of the fall harvest had been collected, any hope of a miraculous turnaround had flickered out. The food situation remained bleak, and winter lay ahead. Several top officials had already seen the grim countryside firsthand. Li Xiannian had conducted inspections of "disaster" areas in Hubei, Hebei, Henan, and elsewhere in late September. Chen Yun had embarked on his own multiprovince inspection tour in August.[50] Still, Party officials showed no interest in turning to the Soviet Union for help. Quite the opposite. On October 23, 1960, Zhou Enlai wrote to Mao and the Central Committee to explain that he, Li Fuchun, and Li Xiannian were in agreement that representatives from the Ministries of Foreign Trade and Foreign Affairs should meet with the Soviet Embassy in Beijing to discuss Sino–Soviet trade relations.[51] Minister of Foreign Trade Ye Jizhuang's draft remarks for the meeting left little doubt that China had no intention of sacrificing pride or principle for the sake of assistance.

By turns defiant, accusatory, and appreciative, Ye's remarks encapsulated the schizophrenia that had come to characterize Sino–Soviet relations. He insisted that the Chinese economy had leapt ahead during the past three years, but he also acknowledged recent "temporary" setbacks. And while he expressed appreciation for Soviet assistance over the years, which he said the Chinese people would never forget, he also pointed to Soviet perfidy as one of two reasons for China's current economic difficulties, the other being natural disasters.[52] He recited a list of grievances: Moscow's unwillingness to accept supplemental Chinese exports that would address China's bilateral deficit for 1960; a continuous flow of partial or incomplete sets of products from the Soviet Union outside of existing contracts, despite China's explicit request not to send deliveries unless a formal contract had been signed; and repeated Soviet refusals to accommodate urgent Chinese orders for imports, despite China's need for many of these imports, such as petroleum products and trucks, to fulfill its standing export contracts with the Soviet Union.[53]

Ye charged that these were not oversights or misunderstandings. He accused Moscow of "willfully making things difficult" (*guyi weinan*) in some cases.[54] He lashed out at Moscow for violating the socialist principles of equality, mutual benefit, and mutual cooperation, and for failing to adhere to the norm of friendly relations among socialist nations. In a sanctimonious flourish, Ye committed Beijing to repaying all of its standing debts to the Soviet Union in accordance with the original terms of the loans, which stipulated repayment between 1961 and 1965, but China would have to reconsider contracts for the current year and for 1961. He then capped his tirade with a string of platitudes about the unbreakable bonds of friendship between the people of the Soviet Union and China.[55]

Lest there be any doubt that the enmity was mutual, on November 14, the PRC Embassy in Moscow reported to the Ministry of Foreign Affairs and the Ministry of Foreign Trade headquarters in Beijing that China seemed to have been sidelined from Soviet trade planning for the coming year. The embassy reported that according to an unnamed Soviet source, the Soviet Central Committee had met in early November to discuss foreign aid and trade, and had excluded the PRC from its 1961 plans.[56] By December 1960, officials at the Chinese Embassy in Moscow were confident that the Soviet leadership intended to cut trade with China. PRC embassy officials recognized that Moscow expected weaker growth in overall foreign trade in 1961, but they also knew that Moscow planned to expand trade with nationalist (*minzu zhuyi*) states, newly independent countries, and most socialist partners. Taken together, these trends revealed "that the Soviet side has already prepared to reduce greatly [*dada suojian*] foreign trade with our nation," the embassy concluded.[57]

With Sino–Soviet economic relations crumbling, and facing the prospect of mass starvation at home, Chen Yun's suggestion that China import capitalist grain began to gain traction. Li Xiannian supported the idea, and on November 29, 1960, he sent a letter to Mao, Zhou, Li Fuchun, Tan Zhenlin, and Bo Yibo to propose it formally. He stressed that this was a temporary expedient, meant only to help China cross a difficult stretch in its economic development. But it was nonetheless a vital and urgent measure. Li proposed that China import just over 12 billion *jin* (roughly 800,000 tons) of grain to start. Zhou agreed with the proposal and lent his support on December 5. Mao chimed in the following week, on the morning of December 12, with a few penciled characters on the margins of Li's proposal. "Return to Comrade Xiannian. Agree completely. [If we] can import 20 billion *jin,* [that would be] better."[58]

With Mao's approval, trade officials got to work. Three days later, on December 15, the Ministry of Foreign Trade established a new office to coordinate the effort, the Grain Import Leadership Small Group Office (Waimao Bu Liangshi Jinkou Lingdao Xiaozu Bangongshi). The ministry placed Chen Ming in charge of the office, a cadre with long experience in capitalist markets.[59] Chen had immigrated to China from Malaya in 1938 as a teenager, and after 1949 he had worked at the Ministry of Foreign Trade and the Bank of China.[60] As head of the new Grain Import Office, he worked for Li Xiannian, who oversaw the grain import program.[61]

On its first day in operation, December 16, Chen's office confronted one of the most pressing challenges—logistics. Buying and rapidly shipping hundreds of thousands of tons of grain from capitalist markets to Chinese ports required expertise and close contacts in capitalist markets, so the Party turned to China Resources. The Grain Import Office instructed China Resources to arrange meetings with Australian grain exporters and to push for a deal, with the goal of importing one hundred thousand tons of wheat before Christmas. The office also instructed China Resources to dispatch two of its representatives to Canada to secure a similar import agreement by January 10, 1961. To ship the grain, the firm planned to use Far East Enterprising, a China Resources subsidiary founded by Qian Zhiguang and Qin Bangli in 1948. By mid-January 1961, just weeks after the Grain Import Office was formed, Far East had signed charters for forty-nine vessels to carry grain into China.[62]

As these preparations were underway in Hong Kong, finance and trade officials in Beijing grappled with the question of how to pay for the grain. Officials at the Ministry of Foreign Trade concluded in a report on November 14, 1960, that China needed to earn US$93 million in exports to capitalist markets in November and again in December to meet its annual plan commitments. But during the first ten months of the year, the nation had earned an average of just US$45 million each month in exports to capitalists.[63] China would have to double its monthly export earnings in the final two months of the year just to complete is preexisting trade plan, and this was before the grain import program was even underway.

The financial prognosis seemed bleaker still when looking ahead to 1961. On December 22, the Finance and Trade Office of the State Council calculated that the PRC would need US$810 million in foreign exchange to pay for imports from capitalists in 1961. This figure did not include aid to China's allies, which State Council analysts expected to cost an additional US$40 million. Yet the Finance and Trade Office expected China's exports to earn only US$660 million in 1961, far short of the total US$850 million it needed.[64] Finance officials had few ideas for how to cover this US$190 million shortfall.

Sales of precious metals would close some of the gap. The Central Committee had already approved the sale of 80 million *liang* of silver in 1961 to raise US$72 million.[65] Now, the PRC planned to sell an additional 60 million *liang* of silver and 400,000 *liang* of gold, which was expected to yield an additional US$68 million. But even with these sales, Beijing would still need an additional US$50 million to cover imports for the year, and this was where the economic planners left off. They could stretch the numbers only so far. China would simply have to find a way to sell more gold and silver, export more goods, or cut imports.[66]

Even if the State Council had been able to find the US$850 million it needed for capitalist trade in 1961, this figure was only a starting point. Estimates of the size of the grain import program continued to grow through the end of 1960 and into 1961.[67] By March 1961, the figure had swollen to 5 million tons. A program of this magnitude would push the cost of capitalist imports for 1961 to US$1.03 billion, according to Li Xiannian's calculations. Even an increase in exports to US$720 million for the year would leave China facing a shortfall of US$310 million, Li explained in March, a gap too wide for gold and silver sales alone to close.[68] Debt was the only way to make the numbers work, Chinese officials had begun to realize.

Beyond logistics and finance, the leadership also confronted the difficulty of situating massive grain imports from capitalists into the Party's ideological framework. The problem was not how to rationalize trade with capitalists; CCP traders had been doing that for decades. The real hurdle was that conspicuous grain imports cut against the CCP's long-standing commitment to self-sufficiency in food. Anticipating this challenge, Beijing began in early 1961 to stress two rationales for its departure from Party orthodoxy.

First, the leadership insisted that grain imports were only temporary, even though this would turn out not to be the case. Li Xiannian made this point to workers in the State Council's Finance and Trade Office on

January 27, 1961. The current situation was "exceptional," he explained. It didn't even matter how long the imports lasted, he told them. In the end, "no matter how many years [we] engage in grain imports, generally speaking, this is only temporary."[69] Nobody knew how long "temporary" meant. The point, he seemed to suggest, was that the program presumed transience, and that was enough.

The second rationale embraced the theme of victimhood. Two years of natural disasters had afflicted China, Li said, laying the groundwork for an argument about the causes and consequences of the Great Leap Forward that survives in official CCP literature to this day. These natural calamities—flooding along the Yellow River in the summer of 1959, for example, and droughts in the north—left the PRC no choice but to seek aid widely. Li said that the Party was forced (*pobu deyi*) to import grain from abroad, a decision that was both "completely necessary" (*wanquan biyao*) and "correct" (*zhengque*).[70] This was true, as far as it went. But for obvious reasons, Li skipped over the Party's own responsibility for the state of the Chinese economy. In Li's telling of events, grain imports became an example of CCP vigilance, of deft trade work and nimble policymaking in the face of exogenous shocks. It became a tale of heroics rather than an indictment of ineptitude.

As Li Xiannian crafted this narrative in Beijing, traders in Hong Kong managed logistics. China Resources staff established two negotiating groups: one for Canadian grain, one for Australian. The Ministry of Foreign Trade identified these markets because both Canada and Australia were major grain producers, and both nations had bumper harvests in 1960. North America and Australia also had alternating growing seasons, which meant it would be possible to sign contracts that would allow grain to flow into China throughout the year. Also, China Resources staff in Hong Kong already had relationships with Canadian and Australian contacts.[71]

To follow these developments in Hong Kong, the Ministry of Foreign Trade sent Chen Ming to Shenzhen. From there, he worked at a local branch of China Resources and kept leaders in Beijing informed. Nobody trusted the confidentiality of the telephone lines in Hong Kong, so each day the China Resources office in the colony sent a courier across the border into Shenzhen to brief Chen on developments in person. Chen would then relay the details using a secure phone line from Shenzhen to Beijing.[72] The entire operation was wrapped in secrecy. Figures relating to grain amounts or sales of gold and silver were particularly sensitive; in early 1961, the Central Committee reminded cadres not to circulate this kind of information outside relevant Party organs and central bureaus.[73]

These precautions grew partly from the Central Committee's desire to prevent the disclosure of statistics that might raise questions about the degree to which China had actually "stood up" on its own two feet under CCP rule. But these measures also reflected a realization that leaked information about such large transactions could affect China's bottom line. News of China's plans for a succession of large contracts could easily generate upward pressure on international grain prices and shipping rates.[74]

In the end, Chinese trade officials could conceal the import program for only so long. Reporters from the Canadian *Globe and Mail* were on hand to take pictures of two China Resources employees and badger them with questions as they arrived in Canada for negotiations on December 29, 1960. "I can't tell you anything," one of the negotiators said when asked about his trip. "We have a lot of friends and we want to visit them," he said, and left it at that. But the mere arrival of China Resources negotiators in Canada was enough to incite speculation, and the next day's headline read, "China Trade Team Arrives: Wheat Considered Principal Interest."[75] A few weeks later, on January 23, the *Globe and Mail* announced that the China Resources team had signed a contract to import nearly 5.6 million bushels of grain, and this was just the beginning.[76]

On February 2, the wires reported that Beijing had reached another deal with Canada to purchase forty million bushels of grain, one of the largest single commercial grain sales in Canadian history at the time.[77] News also broke from Australia, where PRC negotiators had reached a deal to buy one million tons of wheat for US$60,500,000. This figure included three hundred thousand tons of wheat that Beijing had agreed to buy from Australia in December, but which had not been announced previously at Beijing's request.[78] By the time news of this deal broke, Australian grain was already in mainland China. The first shipment from Australia arrived at a Chinese port roughly thirty-five minutes after midnight on February 2, 1961.[79]

More deals followed. In the spring of 1961, the Canadian Wheat Board and China Resources reached an agreement for grain sales from June 1, 1961, through December 1963. The deal called for a total of six million tons of wheat, barley, and flour to be shipped to mainland China in exchange for approximately US$362 million.[80] The specifics of shipment quantities and prices would be worked out in future negotiations, but the aggregate sums involved made this again one of the largest grain sales in Canadian history. The contract also turned China into Canada's second largest consumer in the global grain market, behind only Great Britain.[81] In September, figures from the Commonwealth Bureau of Agricultural Economics revealed that the PRC had purchased more wheat from Australia in 1960–1961 than any other nation.[82] These were just the largest of China's new import contracts. CCP negotiators also signed grain contracts with other capitalist nations, including France, Argentina, West Germany, and Italy.[83]

Financing this spree required a bold political precedent: compromising on the CCP's principled avoidance of capitalist debt. China Resources negotiators needed credit from Ottawa to seal the long-term agreement with the Canadian Wheat Board; without financing, the talks were a waste of time. Negotiations ultimately led to an agreement for China to pay 25 percent in cash up front for each individual contract and the remainder of the balance within 270 days. The Canadian government, eager to off-load its massive grain surplus, agreed to guarantee credit up to a ceiling of US$50 million.[84] These arrangements, routine commercial minutiae, marked a historic departure for the Party. Since the founding of "new China" in 1949, the CCP's unwillingness to take on capitalist debt had kept a lid on the scope and scale of trade with the capitalist world. Now, the lid was coming off, precisely when Beijing was hoping to pay off Soviet and East European debts ahead of schedule.

CCP traders continued to reach grain deals for the rest of 1961 and throughout the first half of the 1960s. The influx of grain brought partial relief to many millions. But it also induced queasiness at the Ministries of Foreign Trade and Finance, where officials recognized that the current mode of financing these purchases—capitalist debt, gold and silver sales, and limited cash reserves—was both unsustainable and, in the case of debt, politically perilous.

Even when the financing came through, the national balance sheet was worrying. On January 18, 1961, the Office of Finance and Trade at the State Council estimated that if international grain prices held at US$70 per ton, and if China stuck to the Ministry of Foreign Trade's export targets for the year, the nation would accrue a deficit of US$243 million from its capitalist trade. Budgeters at the State Council proposed that the Ministry of Foreign Trade trim its import plan by cutting back on nonessential goods, such as steel, to help close the expected gap. They also stressed the importance of squeezing every last exportable good from Chinese production capacity. China must keep the big picture in mind, the office counseled. People certainly need to eat, but walnuts, almonds, melon seeds, and other consumables produced for overseas markets had to be exported. If farmers ate these products in the field, it would erode China's hard currency earnings, which would decrease the amount of grain China could afford to import.[85]

The Office of Finance and Trade had a point. China needed cheap grain to feed millions of people, so it needed foreign currency to buy the grain on international markets. This meant China must export everything it could, especially produce such as walnuts and almonds, which earned higher prices on international markets than grains. By selling high-priced produce and importing cheaper grains, China could purchase more calories than it sold. But the terrible truth behind this logic was that it required senior Party officials in Beijing to order starving peasants in the countryside to fill baskets with walnuts for delivery to state export companies on the thin promise that someday this contribution would be returned several times over as grain. The bitter irony of the planners' logic was that it demanded illogical faith from local farmers.[86]

Still, trade officials in Beijing saw no other option. Even if these belt-tightening measures succeeded, China would cut its projected capitalist trade deficit down to US$106 million, but not eliminate it. Once again, the planners could push the numbers no further. The Office of Finance and Trade simply hoped that PRC traders would be able to export more and negotiate some sort of credit arrangement or installment plan that would paper over this gap as talks progressed.[87]

While grain from Canada, Australia, and other capitalist nations arrived at Chinese ports during the winter and spring of 1961, the urgency of the crisis began to subside. The relief made Li Xiannian almost euphoric. On July 30, he wrote to Mao and the Central Committee that "grain days are here," thanks to the chairman's guidance and the quick work of the Party center. He also remarked on the absence of any domestic unrest and "relatively good" social order, a telling remark about his priorities, given the context.[88]

Despite the congratulatory tone at the start of Li's letter, he still harbored doubts. He also worried about next steps. After accounting for the influx of capitalist grain, Li calculated that China still faced an aggregate grain shortfall of 5.35 million tons for the rest of 1961 and into 1962, a sum so large that it would be impossible to correct with imports by the first half of 1962. China didn't have the money, nor was it clear where CCP traders would find the grain to purchase. Reports from Canada and Australia raised the possibility that grain prices might rise in the near future and that neither Canada nor Australia would be as forthcoming with financing and deferred payments as they had been with initial deals.[89] Any practicable solution to these problems required steady increases in hard currency earnings.

The Ministry of Foreign Trade had already begun to make institutional and ideological changes that would place the import program on sounder footing. In June 1960, the ministry approved funding and plans for the development of permanent export production "bases" (*chukou shangpin shengchan jidi*), a concept that would intrigue trade officials for years to come. The purpose of these bases was to expand and stabilize the supply of exports to overseas markets.[90] As Chen Yun described them in May 1961, these bases would operate with international competition in mind. "[When] doing business on international markets, it's not just us, but many [others], too," he said. The only way to beat the competition is to listen to customers' demands. Quality mattered. Price mattered. Stability mattered. These were the keys to commercial success, he said. Export production bases would enable China to organize production around the needs of foreign markets rather than subjective internal mandates. When Chen made these points in late spring 1961, his goal was to have the bases operating as soon as possible, ideally by the end of 1962.[91]

The Ministry of Foreign Trade also began to reorient propaganda work at this time. The ministry abandoned *dajin dachu*, which had done so much to unhinge the nation's trade agenda. In its place stood *yijin yangchu*, which translates loosely as, "use imports to cultivate exports." The slogan meant China should import raw materials that domestic producers could use to produce higher-value-added goods, which China could export to earn hard currency. The concept was not new in China. In March 1961, Zhu De recalled that coastal cities in "old China" also practiced *yijin yangchu*. The difference now, however, was that foreign imperialists no longer exploited this process in China; the Party controlled the production. This distinction helped to inoculate the concept against questions about its pre-"liberation" roots.[92]

Yijin yangchu offered a strategy for earning hard currency that did not require squeezing the population ever more tightly, and it was a long-term vision, Zhu De explained. It was "not a one-year plan for this year, nor something undertaken only during a crisis," he said. Rather, it was a "historical [phenomenon] in the formation of global markets," and it was impossible to seal oneself off from it.[93] The Ministry of Foreign Trade had actually been practicing *yijin yangchu* quietly since 1957, when processed exports and other re-exports comprised 13 percent of China's exports. In 1960, that share had climbed only slightly, to 15.8 percent. By 1961, however, it reached 27 percent, and in 1962 it climbed to 32.2 percent of China's total export volume.[94]

The growth of *yijin yangchu* carried a significance beyond hard currency. For one, it was a strategy oriented mostly toward the capitalist world.[95] The Ministry of Foreign Trade's adoption of the strategy in 1961 represented a tacit acknowledgment by top Party officials that China's trade would continue to drift away from the Soviet Union and Eastern Europe and toward capitalist markets, precisely as it did. The concept also posited a tight, lasting link between global commodity markets and global consumer markets via China's own production bases. This represented an adjustment in the way the CCP conceived of Communist China's relationship to global markets, a turn toward a perspective characterized increasingly by calibrated and continuous connections rather than tightly scripted, discrete transactions conducted at arm's length. In this sense, *yijin yangchu* marked a turning point. It presaged a much more consequential shift in China's relationship to the global economy that would occur during Reform and Opening.

From 1962 to 1965, PRC trade appeared to have turned a corner. The hunt for grain, unprocessed goods, and new consumers led Chinese traders to strengthen existing trade relationships and to seek new ones. At the same time, a new initiative was also taking shape that suggested other significant changes in China's commercial interactions with capitalist markets. As Li Xiannian had argued in January 1961, the grain import program was a temporary expedient, no matter how long it lasted. But by late 1962, officials at the State Planning Commission and the Ministry of Foreign Trade had developed a program that promised to help wean China from this ex-

Figure 6.1   Li Xiannian (center) chatting with Zhou Enlai (right) and Deng Xiaoping (left) in March 1963. China.org.cn.

pedient eventually by entering into new, more complex contracts with foreign capitalist firms. The key, planners believed, was finding new sources of technology in capitalist markets. China would strive to import technology and equipment from capitalist firms to boost its own productivity, another signal that China was already looking past socialist markets and considering more carefully how capitalist markets might contribute to China's socialist modernization.

Planners were particularly interested in using imported chemical technologies to boost agricultural yields. Higher yields per hectare would enable farmers to produce more with less, bolstering the state's ability to provide China's growing population with enough food, clothing, and other basic necessities for daily life, a long-standing goal of revitalized importance after the recent failures of the Great Leap.[96] Better to enhance China's own ability to produce these goods by importing technology, the officials reasoned, than to rely on foreign goods indefinitely. *Zili gengsheng* had preached this logic for decades, but it was now operating in a changed environment. The break in relations with Moscow and the demise of the China differential (but not COCOM itself) in the late 1950s led state planners to pursue new sources for these technologies. Naturally, they turned to two of the most promising markets at the time: Japan and Western Europe.

On October 13, 1962, the State Planning Commission and the Ministry of Foreign Trade submitted a joint proposal for fifteen large import projects, all "urgently needed," which would help to modernize China's production of chemical fertilizers and synthetic fibers. The Chinese chemical fertilizer industry was built with 1940s technology, the planners noted. Even the factories built by the Soviets were out of date.[97] Based on interactions with several capitalist nations, officials argued that it was possible for China to import natural gas chemical plants, precision machine tools, oil-refining equipment to help power factories, and other technology that would help China's chemical industry achieve a badly needed "leap forward" in development.[98]

None of this would be cheap, and with scant foreign currency through at least 1963, the proposal recommended dividing the list of fifteen projects into two tranches. Planners suggested signing six contracts, worth about US$20 million, before the end of 1963. The remaining nine contracts, estimated to cost around US$52 million, could wait until 1964.[99] Zhou Enlai approved the proposal on November 24, and within a year, China began to sign contracts.[100]

The first was with Japan, an obvious choice given the rapid reconciliation between Beijing and Tokyo in the early 1960s. The resignation of Japanese prime minister Nobusuke Kishi in July 1960 had opened the door to rekindled trade with Japan following the two-year hiatus that began with the Nagasaki flag incident in May 1958. Zhou had seized this opportunity on August 27, 1960, when he told the visiting director of the Japan–China Trade Promotion Association that if China and Japan could restore trade relations, it would benefit the people of both nations. He proposed three types of commercial exchanges: government accords (*zhengfu xieding*), people-to-people contracts (*minjian hetong*), and individual deals negotiated under special considerations (*gebie zhaogu*).[101] The first type reflected Beijing's continuing pressure on Tokyo to move in the direction of formal recognition of the PRC. The second two, however, signaled a willingness to allow private Japanese firms, mostly left-leaning ones, to trade with China as well.[102]

Zhou's "three trade principles" (*maoyi san yuanze*), as they were called, set the stage for a renewed push for trade with Tokyo. On November 9, 1962, Liao Chengzhi and Takasaki Tatsunosuke signed a trade memorandum that further normalized bilateral trade. The Liao–Takasaki Memorandum created a stable framework in which a wider range of Japanese firms could trade with China's official trading corporations. Now, Japan's largest conglomerates, companies such as Mitsubishi and Sumitomo, could trade with Chinese state trade agencies. The agreement also permitted companies to sign contracts for as long as three to five years, reinforcing stability in the trade relationship. The new agreement permitted Chinese traders to import certain "badly needed" Japanese goods using a deferred-payment structure that operated on credit from the Bank of Japan.[103] The bilateral relationship soon stabilized further when, on April 19, 1964, the two sides signed an agreement to establish trade missions in each nation's capital, a long-standing CCP goal.

China linked this warming trend to its new import initiative on June 29, 1963, by signing a nearly US$20 million contract with the Kurashiki Rayon Company in Japan. The firm promised two chemical plants, both to be built on the outskirts of Beijing: one to make organic chemicals and another to produce vinylon, a synthetic fiber that could be used as a substitute for cotton. The final cost for both projects was just under US$23 million, after accounting for just over US$2.7 million in interest payments, which China would pay as part of an eight-year payment plan.[104]

As Sino–Japanese trade relations were returning to sturdier ground, Vice Minister of Foreign Trade Lu Xuzhang was also exploring options in Western Europe. For three weeks in the spring of 1963, Lu visited Britain to meet state officials and leading industrialists and to discuss future Sino–British trade. He also toured factories and shipyards, and even stopped to visit Oxford University. The full slate of business meetings on Lu's schedule offered a chance to show his hosts that his trip was more about expanding trade than grandstanding, but the political symbolism of his trip was undeniable.[105] His visit was the first to Britain by any minister of the PRC government at the invitation of Her Majesty's Government.[106]

In truth, Lu *was* after publicity. Grandstanding could spur trade, a point Lu Xuzhang recognized as much as Lei Renmin had in Geneva nearly ten years earlier. After Lu left Britain, he also stopped in Switzerland and the Netherlands, where he met with a group of European businessmen to discuss trade prospects.[107] Not long after Lu's trip, between September 1963 and January 1964, Chinese trade officials signed six large contracts with European firms, including companies in Britain, Holland, Italy, and France.[108]

China was represented in all of these agreements by the China National Technical Import Corporation (CNTIC), a state company managed by the

Ministry of Foreign Trade that specialized in importing technical designs, factories, plants, and equipment.[109] CNTIC officers continued to negotiate throughout 1964, and by the end of the year, they had signed a total of fifteen large contracts. The total cost for these programs exceeded US$131 million, only about a quarter of which would be paid up front. China would pay the balance over time, an arrangement that cost nearly US$10 million in interest.[110]

These were considerable sums for a struggling economy, but there was something else noteworthy about these transactions. The internal reports that discussed these deals reveal that senior officials recognized the beginnings of a new level of commercial interaction between China and foreign capitalists. One report, written in March 1963, made clear that shopping for large, highly complex technologies in a global market was a multiphase process that required new levels of technical, logistical, and financial sophistication. The report, written by two working groups formed by Zhou Enlai to explore imports related to fertilizers and chemical fibers, outlined the many phases of each transaction.[111] Any one transaction could require Chinese officials to solicit bids from multiple firms in various countries, visit foreign production facilities, compare the terms and technical specifications of each bid, conduct technical talks, and negotiate contract terms, all while considering the political implications surrounding each prospective deal. The whole process generally lasted about a year, the report said, sometimes longer.[112] All of this required mastering a bewilderment of details, but also managing the steady coordination that moved these deals toward consummation.

As Chinese trade officials learned more about these transactions, they made some pleasant discoveries. Firms in Japan and Western Europe promised faster delivery schedules than socialist traders, for instance. With capitalist firms, China generally had to wait only six months between the first shipment of products until the last, and never more than a year. Orders from the Soviets usually took two to three years. Capitalists also offered more assurances. Contracts guaranteed the quantity, quality, and resource consumption rates of products; any shortcomings obliged the seller to pay fines to the buyer. Another benefit was the chance to nose around capitalist factories. Most contracts stipulated that Chinese officials had the right to send people to the seller's factory to inspect and accept final products—a prime opportunity, MOFT officials noted, to examine foreign technology up close.[113]

Perks aside, adapting to these types of transactions took time. In March 1965, officials from the New Technology Import Group in Beijing, an office under the State Economic Commission, documented stubborn flaws in technical trade work, revealing just how much work still had to be done almost two years after China's contract with the Kurashiki Rayon Company in 1963. Many technical import projects were unclear, the report said, or showed inadequate preparation. Some cadres were too timid during negotiations and when soliciting proposals.[114] Yet by analyzing these shortcomings, and urging corrections, Chinese officials were also revealing a marked self-awareness and a commitment to learning how to change behavior and practices to trade with capitalists more successfully.

Among these proposed changes, a clear theme was the need for more interaction with capitalist firms. The New Technology Import Group encouraged Chinese traders working on large projects to solicit bids widely and to negotiate with multiple firms simultaneously. Cadres should also be willing to walk away from talks; not every negotiation had to conclude with a signed agreement.[115] All of this would require broader contact and more negotiation with foreign capitalists.

This push for interaction was not limited to large industrial and technical imports. Beijing also pursued more commercial interaction beyond specific projects, including at trade fairs outside of the semiannual Canton Fair. In July 1963, Britain's first official trade exposition opened in Beijing. Visiting businessmen stayed at the Xin Qiao Hotel, which the CCP had built originally to house Soviet advisers. But for nearly two weeks in the summer of 1963, it was occupied by imperialists from the British crucible manufacturer Morganite, the industrial firm R. H. Windsor, and Jardines. The British mission in Beijing viewed the exhibition as a valuable opportunity, particularly because it offered a chance for UK industrialists to meet potential Chinese "end-users" and CCP officials. Chinese interlocutors also seemed to value the chance to interact. Chen Ming, Ji Chaoding, and other officials spent four hours one evening after the expo at the Summer Palace, having dinner and whiskey sodas at an event hosted by the De La Rue Company, a printing and paper manufacturing firm.[116] Gatherings like this, designed to mix socializing with business, produced few deals, but they did pave the way for a much larger exhibition in the fall of 1964, when representatives from 230 different firms visited Beijing for the PRC's largest non-Communist trade fair since its founding.[117]

Chinese traders sought to expand contact with traders in other markets as well. In January 1964, Ministry of Foreign Trade officials capped a month-long trade fair in Mexico City, the PRC's first in Latin America.[118] In February 1964, de Gaulle's government in France appointed a chargé d'affaires in Beijing, Paris's first real step toward a restoration of Sino–French diplomatic relations. At the same time, French industrialists were planning an exposition that would open in Beijing later that year. French organizers forecast that France would be able to capture at least a US$200 million market share in China.[119]

All of these efforts produced results. In 1963, the Ministry of Foreign Trade reported that China's exports to capitalist markets had reached US$842 million, a 36 percent increase above the previous year and 112 percent of the ministry's revised target for 1963.[120] In 1964, China's total foreign trade volume climbed to US$3.34 billion, with both imports and exports exceeding the annual plan targets. Trade with capitalists accounted for 70 percent of this volume, up from 58 percent the previous year and far greater than its roughly 18 percent share just nine years earlier, in 1955.[121]

These upward trends emerged in a moment when Li Xiannian, Ye Jizhuang, the Ministry of Foreign Trade, and the State Planning Commission all had more political space for prudence. In the spring of 1961, Mao had "retreated" to the "second line" of Party leadership, leaving Liu Shaoqi to implement the Party's Eight-Character Plan of "adjustment, consolidation, supplementation, and rising standards" (*tiaozheng, gonggu, chongshi, tigao*). This new program amounted to a repudiation of the Great Leap euphoria inspired by Mao.[122] The chairman's influence declined further during a central work conference in early 1962. The meeting, known as the Seven Thousand Cadres Conference, became a month-long venue for venting and catharsis. One by one, Party leaders repudiated the Great Leap Forward, though often in terms that "implicated all while pinpointing none," as one scholar put it.[123] Neither Zhou Enlai nor Chen Yun nor anyone else used the occasion to pin the disasters of the Leap on Mao personally, a fateful decision that left open the door for his resurgence. Still, Mao's own speech during the conference on January 30, 1962, coy and restrained though it was, came closest to a self-criticism from the chairman since the founding of the People's Republic.[124] His influence and prestige had clearly been dented.

This criticism suggested that the Party had begun to atone for its rashness during the Great Leap Forward. The political winds began to favor expertise over redness, creating protection for cadres working at CNTIC and other Ministry of Foreign Trade offices in Beijing, in trade institutions elsewhere in China, and in embassies and offices abroad. These officials had room to use their expertise, more space to carry out guidance from Li Xiannian, Lu Xuzhang, and other top trade officials seeking to restore the stability that had been lost during the Leap. To many, it appeared that the People's Republic of China had embarked on a new path.

"Hot" Thinking

Years earlier, in 1958, as the Great Leap Forward was gaining momentum, the economist Xue Muqiao urged Chen Yun to meet with Mao for a private talk. Xue worried that the Chinese economy had begun to overheat, and he hoped Chen would discuss with Mao how to cool things down before the Leap got out of hand. Although Chen was sympathetic to Xue's concerns, he balked at intervening. "It isn't that Mao alone is hot now [i.e., feverish about rapid growth], many leaders across the country are also hot," he told Xue. Nobody wanted to hear about moderation. It would take a setback to break the fever, Chen believed. He told Xue, if the Chinese people "do not eat a little bitterness, these words [of caution] cannot be heard."[125] With the benefit of hindsight, and a clearer understanding of the bitter toll of the Great Leap Forward, Chen's words can seem callous, even craven. But he was partly right.

Just as Chen Yun predicted, China's fever broke in the early 1960s. But the consequences were larger than Chen could have foreseen in 1958. Beyond the tragedy of starvation and death, the famine and the Sino–Soviet fallout also undermined a specific mode of Chinese socialist development by challenging two convictions that had guided economic work in Mao's China. First, the idea that China could transform itself economically overnight through breakneck expansion of imports and exports had been damaged, though not entirely discredited.[126]

Second, Khrushchev's withdrawal of economic assistance in the summer of 1960 killed the idea that solidarity among socialist markets could serve as the mainstay of China's international trade program. The irony of turning to capitalist markets for salvation in this moment unsettled earlier expectations about how China would relate to what had long been viewed as two contending developmental paths to modernity: one socialist, one capitalist. The contrast between socialist treachery and the benefits of access to capitalist markets called for increasing flexibility in China's own relationships to these two ostensibly alternative development paradigms. This flexibility, in turn, chipped away at the relevance of the distinctions between socialism and capitalism in the context of development through foreign trade.

Zhou Enlai tried to place some of these changes into context in April 1962. In an address to the National People's Congress, he told delegates that China was crossing uncharted terrain. The construction of socialism was a new undertaking, he said. During China's first Five-Year Plan, China had no experience conducting large-scale construction, so it learned from the experiences of the Soviet Union and other socialist states, he said. China also accumulated its own experience along the way. "Blindness" (*mangmuxing*) to objective laws had marred China's socialist construction, he acknowledged, and it was only through practice that the Chinese people, from cadres and the masses up to the top leaders, could gradually recognize and master these objective rules.[127]

Zhou's real argument became clearer as he continued. He told the congress that China's "great achievements" in socialist construction over the past few years had proven that the general political line was absolutely correct. Mistakes arose when the Party deviated from this general line, and the consequences of these missteps only reinforced the correctness of the general line itself.[128] The Great Leap Forward represented a failure in the implementation of certain policies, in other words, not a fundamental flaw in China's approach to socialist construction or political economy.

This was a liberating, if dubious, argument. It freed the CCP to retain its claim to be the sole legitimate voice in the assessment of socialist construction in China despite the blatant failures of the Great Leap Forward. In Zhou's account, recent economic failures resulted from a mix of natural calamities and the misapplication of principles, but the principles themselves nevertheless remained valid for China's unique national circumstances. Nothing in this account suggested a flawed conceptualization, nor did it legitimate the "revisionist" methods of economic construction that were then being implemented in the Soviet Union and Eastern Europe. Zhou's analysis framed the Great Leap Forward as a painful but still progressive learning experience, a time to "eat bitterness," as Chen Yun had put it. It was a corrective process. Looking to the future, he promised that China would continue to pursue its own form of socialist construction, and it would rely on its unique experiences along the way.[129]

Zhou's emphasis on failures of implementation, rather than flaws in principle, also freed the Party leadership from having to accept full blame for the Great Leap Forward. "It is important for leaders themselves to gain experience," he said, "however, solely leaders having experience is not enough, vast numbers of cadres and the broad masses must also gain experience."[130] By implication, "blindness" to objective laws had afflicted not just the top leaders in Beijing, but everyone. And if everybody was responsible, nobody was responsible.

This reasoning revealed a tragic dynamic at work in CCP decision making. Party leaders saw no way to retain legitimacy without clinging to a monopoly on truth, a limited vision that pressed Zhou and the rest of the leadership to account for misguided policies by presenting them as temporary or partial failures of implementation. Yet by failing to denounce fully the failures of the Great Leap Forward, Zhou kept alive the prospect of a return to "hot" thinking in the years ahead.

This was dangerous for workers at the Ministry of Foreign Trade. The Party had yet to synthesize fully the tensions surrounding trade officials' interactions with capitalist markets, and it remained unclear how China's traders would balance the political demands of the revolution with the economic prerogatives of capitalist trade in the future. In 1964, ministry officials had plenty of external challenges to address. The PRC found itself aloof from the two centers of world power. Beijing's economic relations with Moscow and much of the socialist bloc remained strained, and despite recent gains, China's future commercial relations with the capitalist world were still constrained by thin finances and hostility to the world's largest capitalist economy. But the bigger challenge ultimately proved to be internal. The unresolved tension between redness and expertise heightened the vulnerability of the Ministry of Foreign Trade and professionals throughout the Chinese government to the brutality of Mao's next mobilizing campaign—the Great Proletarian Cultural Revolution.

7

MARKETS AND THE RISE AND FALL OF REDNESS

MAO HAD TANGLED MOTIVATIONS FOR launching the Cultural Revolution. A septuagenarian in declining health, he worried about challengers to his authority. He was concerned about his legacy. He also feared that bureaucratic inertia and bourgeois thought might someday smother the revolution and open the door to capitalist restoration in China.[1] These were not distinct concerns in Mao's mind, which makes it difficult to determine precisely which of these considerations, individually or in combination, caused the Cultural Revolution. But the effects of the movement were clearer, particularly for the nation's professional class. The Cultural Revolution again forced workers away from expertise and toward redness. Women and men rushed to demonstrate their allegiance to Mao and revolutionary principles at the expense of stability and prudence. This was a trained response; they remembered the atmosphere of the late 1950s, when the Anti-Rightist Movement convulsed state bureaucracies. In this sense, the Cultural Revolution was familiar, almost episodic—the next surge of redness through the nation's expertise. But the scale and degree of this latest campaign far surpassed anything that preceded it.

Still, it was ultimately the failures of the Cultural Revolution, which were becoming clear by the end of the 1960s, that had the more lasting impact. At the Ministry of Foreign Trade, the obvious shortcomings of the campaign helped to discredit elements of the Chinese revolution that had valorized redness at the expense of expertise, clearing space for the pursuit of proficiency in the ranks of the nation's trade officials. More broadly, the failure of Mao's "last revolution" combined with changes in the international environment to reaffirm for many the importance of deepening China's engagement with global markets. By the early 1970s, it was becoming an increasingly accepted view among CCP leaders that capitalist markets abroad were not just important to the construction of a strong and modern Chinese socialist state; they were essential.

New Depths

Like the Anti-Rightist Movement of 1957, the Cultural Revolution began with warming weather. In late May 1966, teachers at Beijing University displayed a poster denouncing the university administration at the urging of Cao Yi'ou, the wife of Kang Sheng, a Politburo member who would go on to play a leading role in the Cultural Revolution.[2] More criticisms followed, and soon teachers and students across Beijing were publicly attacking university administrations, egged on by a June 1 editorial in the *People's Daily* calling for the masses to "Sweep Away All Monsters and Demons!" The author of the editorial was Chen Boda, Mao's sometime ghostwriter and now the head of the Party's new Cultural Revolution Group. Chen's editorial was a call to arms against familiar targets: "bourgeois specialists," "scholarly authorities," and "venerable masters" who occupied "ideological" and "cultural" positions—those who, by virtue of their expertise and standing, were best positioned to subvert the revolution with rightist inclinations and counterrevolutionary notions.[3] These bourgeois frauds, all bent on deceiving the people and consolidating their own power, had to go. The fate of the revolution seemed to hinge again on a purge, but this time there was something more visceral, almost carnal in the destruction that ensued.

The early violence of the Cultural Revolution shocked firsthand observers. A Swiss diplomat in Beijing reported witnessing "despicable scenes of sadistic juvenile crime."[4] He saw young people looting, smashing shrines, and desecrating religious sites. Mao urged radicals to "bombard the headquarters," by which he meant attack the Party and the state to root out closeted capitalists and other threats to the revolution. Many young citizens eagerly complied. "Red Guards," the shock troops of the Cultural

Revolution, harangued, mocked, brutalized, and "struggled" against officials, teachers, and other authority figures. Much of the enthusiasm behind it all was fueled by a years-long indoctrination movement called the Socialist Education Movement, which the Party launched in the fall of 1962 to teach people the benefits of socialism but also, ominously, to remind them that class enemies still lurked in China's cities and villages. Mao's call to arms in the summer of 1966 tapped into this current of suspicion and encouraged people to eliminate these latent threats.

Still, despite its destructiveness, the Cultural Revolution was never meant to unravel the nation's economy. The official view—from Mao himself—held that the Cultural Revolution would spur production by revitalizing the masses. He still clung to the idea that enthusiasm alone could fire economic development if sufficiently stoked. He indulged in this faith, despite the tragic evidence to the contrary just a few years earlier, partly because no one had uprooted it in the aftermath of the Great Leap Forward. As Zhou Enlai had explained, that fiasco grew from failures of implementation, not flaws in principle. Now, in the summer of 1966, Mao returned to old principles, and once again, these principles put China on a path to disaster.

Outside China, it was unclear at first how the Cultural Revolution would affect China's trade. Foreign observers picked up mixed signals. In November 1966, the Associated Press reported that Ye Jizhuang, China's longtime minister of foreign trade who had done so much to steer the ministry through past upheavals, had been purged.[5] Beijing also recalled China's commercial counsellor in London. Other trade officials began to disappear.[6] So did diplomats. In early 1967, Zhou Enlai ordered the recall of all but one of China's ambassadors and nearly two-thirds of China's embassy staff abroad.[7] Nobody seemed to know precisely why, but it suggested a worrying shift. Clouding the view was the fact that certain trading activities continued unhindered. The fall session of the Canton Trade Fair convened in 1966 as usual and without major disturbances, although some griped about unsolicited lectures on Mao Zedong Thought and the Cultural Revolution.[8] Bargaining at the fair seemed tougher than usual to some, but that may have been unrelated to the campaign. A correspondent for the *Globe and Mail* attributed it to competition among traders rather than political imperatives.[9]

Nothing in the early trade statistics suggested a grievous problem, either. In December 1966, British officials observed that exports to China had actually increased in the first ten months of the year and were well above 1964 levels.[10] Later, as the Cultural Revolution continued, others detected disruptions in China's trade during the most chaotic years, from 1966 to 1968, but even these figures seemed mild in relation to the chaos roiling China. CIA estimates from 1972 indicated that China's total trade volume declined by roughly 8 percent in 1967 and 3 percent in 1968.[11] These were significant declines, but not catastrophic. They also were not caused solely by the Cultural Revolution. Strong domestic harvests in 1967 cut China's demand for grain imports by 20 percent.[12] Egypt's decision to close the Suez Canal at the start of the Six-Day War in June 1967 raised global freight rates, which increased the cost of fertilizer and other Chinese imports from Europe. The Suez closure also made Chinese agricultural exports less competitive on global markets, further diminishing China's trade.[13] All things considered, the Ministry of Foreign Trade appeared to be coping with the instability of the Cultural Revolution quite well. Even the CIA thought so. "Given the self-imposed problems confronting China in 1967," analysts wrote that year, "the trade performance was a remarkably successful one."[14]

Maybe so, but the early years of the Cultural Revolution *felt* more like disaster than success. The potential for crisis seemed ubiquitous. In the summer of 1966, just as the Cultural Revolution was getting underway, Li Xiannian dispatched a work team of Party officials to restore order at the campus of the Foreign Trade Institute in Beijing, where students had toppled the school administration, as they had done at other schools and universities in the capital. But the students had no intention of backing down. Li's team found that some students had posted big-character posters around the school accusing the team of "suppressing the masses." The students became so aggressive that the team soon fled for safety.[15] On June 11, Li also tried to tamp down on the "rebel groups" (*zaofan pai*) that had begun to form inside some departments. The temperature of the masses is high enough, he said. We can let them cool off a bit.[16]

But Li's troubles only mounted over the summer. His decision to send the work team to the Foreign Trade Institute sprang from his mistaken assessment that this latest campaign would be circumscribed, but he soon realized his mistake. Attempting to place limits on the Cultural Revolution had put him at odds with the same radical youth whom Mao intended to use to drive the campaign forward. Li wasn't the only top official to make this mistake. The Party's central leadership—operating without instructions from Mao, who was away from the capital—had sent work teams to restore order on other campuses in Beijing and in other major cities. But when Mao returned to the capital in mid-July, he told Liu Shaoqi that it was wrong to dispatch the work teams. On July 25, Mao said the mistake was an "error of political line" and ordered all the work teams withdrawn.[17]

By early August, Li was apologizing for having misread the situation. He conceded that he had committed errors in "direction" and that he was having trouble keeping up with the situation.[18] He continued to make self-criticisms and began to project a more accommodating stance with the radicals inside the nation's trade institutions. On the evening of August 15, he visited the Ministry of Foreign Trade with Yao Yilin to view big-character posters. In September, he attended a "mass meeting" of rebels from the Foreign Trade Institute in Beijing and again took responsibility for having sent the work team to campus in June.[19]

None of it seemed to help. Rebels continued to criticize Li, Yao Yilin, and other senior economic officials.[20] By the spring of 1967, rebels were calling openly for the masses to "bombard Li Xiannian." On April 14, an association of rebel organizations in Beijing hauled several leaders from trade and finance departments to a public rally, during which the rebels claimed to have uncovered a "capitalist restoration countercurrent" embedded within the trade and finance system.[21]

The chaos threatened to spread directly into China's commercial dealings with foreign capitalists. Just days before the Canton Fair was scheduled to open in April 1967, Red Guards descended on the buildings where the fair was usually held. There they found Buddhist statues, figurines, and other "counterrevolutionary" products on display for export, all of which the Red Guards intended to destroy. They also seized and "struggled against" trade officials and others working at the fair. When Zhou Enlai heard about the disruption, he decided to fly down to Guangzhou himself to mediate between the cadres working at the fair and the Red Guards besieging them. Zhou's plane left Beijing for Guangzhou on April 14, the same day that rebels in Beijing were publicly announcing that a "capitalist restoration countercurrent" lurked inside the nation's economic institutions. It was also the day before the Canton Fair was scheduled to open.[22]

When Zhou arrived in Guangzhou, he tried to diffuse the tension by reorienting the debate (see Figure 7.1). He framed the Canton Fair as a critical front in China's revolutionary struggle rather than a departure from it. It was the same logic Zhou had used to frame capitalist trade in Moscow in 1952 and again in Geneva in 1954. He told the Red Guards and their victims they should view the spring fair as a "new battle campaign" that had to succeed.[23]

The tactic worked. The spring fair opened as planned and Zhou's personal visit gave it the political cover it needed. In June, the Ministry of Foreign Trade reported to Zhou and Li Xiannian that the fair had been a success. More than 7,800 visitors attended from sixty-two different nations, and each attendee was presented with his own Mao badge and copy of "Quotations from Chairman Mao."[24] The disruptions that foreigners did witness during the fair, including lectures on Mao Zedong Thought and coerced attendance at "model theater" performances, were not unchecked excesses of the Cultural Revolution but rather negotiated limits, the product of countervailing pressures behind the scenes and inside the revolution. Zhou had tried to limit how and how much Red Guards could "make revolution" at the expense of trade with capitalists in Canton. He did not insist on total civility. Nor did he demand that the Ministry of Foreign Trade be spared the violence of the Cultural Revolution. Zhou either could not or would not offer such protection, as some officials from the Ministry of Foreign Trade discovered.

Ye Jizhuang was the most prominent trade official to suffer during the Cultural Revolution. When "rebels" persecuted Ye, he was already in his midseventies and in poor health. His attackers accused him of being a counterrevolutionary and stripped him of his official positions. They also searched his home, convinced he had stockpiled "foreign goods" over the years through his contact with foreigners. Finding nothing of interest, the rebels concluded that Ye had hidden his treasures with family members, so they sent representatives to his hometown in Guangdong. There, they ransacked the grave of Ye's father, who had been dead for years. Again, the rebels found nothing. But the trauma of the ordeal worsened Ye's condition, and he died not long after, in June 1967, at the age of seventy-four.[25]

Other trade officials suffered similar fates. Those who were involved in trade with capitalists often fared the worst. Qin Bangli, the founder of China Resources, was accused of espionage, separated from his family, and investigated in the spring of 1968. He also died several months later, at the

Figure 7.1   Zhou Enlai (left) trying to salvage the Canton Fair, April 1967.
Ministry of Commerce, People's Republic of China.

age of sixty, ostensibly of a heart attack. An autopsy ordered by Zhou Enlai
revealed signs of head trauma and other injuries.[26]

Yet Zhou did intervene elsewhere to shield some trade officials from the
worst excesses of the Cultural Revolution. He defended Li Xiannian against
rebel attacks on several occasions.[27] In early June 1967, a few weeks before
Ye Jizhuang died, Zhou also coordinated with Li Xiannian and Li Fuchun
to allow certain officials to live temporarily inside Zhongnanhai, where they
would be safe from rebel attacks. Among this group were Liao Chengzhi,
Yao Yilin, and Qian Zhiguang, all cadres whose longtime ties to trade, finance, and economic affairs marked them as prime targets. It must have
been a relief for these officials to rest, but it was always temporary. They
left the compound eventually, back into the maw, no doubt wondering
whether they would suffer the same fates as Ye and Qin.

Three Shifts

As China turned inward, the world outside was also changing in ways
that would eventually modulate Chinese politics and policies as the 1970s

began. In particular, three interrelated shifts raised fundamental questions that created the need for a new world outlook. These shifts also produced opportunities to develop new policies to suit the changing international environment.

First, Sino–Soviet tensions increased to the point of military conflict between the two socialist powers. The Chinese and Soviet governments had been militarizing the border since the mid-1960s, and skirmishes between the two sides had occurred as early as November 1967. In early January 1968, four Chinese were killed in a clash that raised tensions higher.[28] Both sides prepared for potential conflict. Then, in March 1969, serious fighting erupted over control of a small island on an isolated stretch of the Ussuri River along the eastern reach of the Sino–Soviet border. At least thirty-one Soviet soldiers died in the fight over the island, called Zhenbao in Chinese and Damanskii in Russian. The number of Chinese fatalities remains unknown.[29] Another clash occurred in mid-August 1969.[30] The fighting would never escalate beyond these controlled skirmishes, but neither side knew that at the time. Moscow hinted at a nuclear strike, among other potential responses, and the leadership in Beijing took these threats seriously. Mao concluded that China had to mobilize for war. "No matter the year, we should be prepared for war," he said at the first plenum of the Ninth Central Committee on April 28, 1969. "No matter whether he [the Soviet enemy] comes or not, we should prepare."[31]

The standoff between Moscow and Beijing influenced a second shift in international relations during the early 1970s: China's rapprochement with the United States. As war with the Soviet Union appeared more likely, it became increasingly difficult for the CCP leadership to maintain the same level of discord with the United States. The combined threat to China's national security was simply too great.[32]

Mao had already begun to restrain the excesses of the Cultural Revolution in 1968, a decision that reflected in part the increasing fear in Beijing of war with the Soviet Union.[33] But it also reflected a change in Mao's mind-set. After two years of upheaval, the Cultural Revolution had failed to produce the new revolutionary state and society he had expected. When Red Guards shot at one of his own propaganda teams in Beijing in the summer of 1968, Mao decided it was time to dismantle the Red Guard movement. He also stopped emphasizing the importance of tension in building revolutionary enthusiasm at home and instead began to stress the need to "consolidate" the achievements of the Cultural Revolution, by which he meant consolidating his own power and authority.[34] This shift toward a stability-oriented mode of politics in the late 1960s signaled Mao's increasing willingness to live within the status quo political order, both at home and abroad, rather than strive continuously to challenge it.[35] The revolution was fading, and this opened space for a new relationship with the United States to counter the perceived threat from the Soviet Union.

A third shift, more sudden and jarring, heightened this sense of change in Chinese politics during the early 1970s. On the night of September 12–13, near the village of Undurkhaan in eastern Mongolia, Lin Biao—Mao's "closest comrade in arms" and heir apparent, a hero of the revolution and renowned general—died with his wife and son in a plane crash, allegedly while fleeing to the Soviet Union. The circumstances surrounding Lin's death remain murky to this day, but the sanctioned view among CCP historians is that Lin fled China after he and his son, Lin Liguo, failed in an attempted coup.[36]

Party insiders knew that relations between Lin Biao and Mao had deteriorated sharply before the crash, although none of this was made public at the time. The relationship between the two men had even reached "crisis proportions" by the summer of 1970, according to Mao's personal physician.[37] Mao distrusted Lin and likely viewed him as a potential usurper. Allegedly, the chairman had been warned of a cabal organized by Lin Liguo to seize power.[38] Whether this was true or whether Lin Biao himself was involved in such a plot may never be known.[39] But the allegations of Lin's betrayal, and the news of his death, shocked China.

Mao's face reportedly "collapsed" when he learned that Lin had fled. Soon afterward he became depressed and his health began to deteriorate.[40] Other Party leaders and the public were equally stunned when they learned of Lin's "plot" later that fall, after the Central Committee decided to divulge the news.[41] How could a man so close to Mao, so trusted by the CCP leadership and so vaunted by the Party for so many years, have been a traitor all along? How could Mao have misjudged Lin for so long? What did this say about Mao's fallibility? What did it say about the Party's claims to insight and truth? Such heretical questions likely would have arisen under any circumstances following the revelation of Lin's defection, but increasing disillusionment over the excesses of the Cultural Revolution practically encouraged such cynicism, and it wasn't hard to read Lin's death as an indictment of the Cultural Revolution itself. As Mao's official biographer put it, the Lin Biao incident "proclaimed the theoretical and practical failure of the 'Great Proletarian Cultural Revolution.'"[42]

The Party leadership tried to use Lin as a scapegoat to bolster its legitimacy and its policies. He was accused of having sympathized with Soviet revisionism—why else would he flee north, toward Moscow, after his plot was exposed? The Party also charged Lin with attempting to overturn the dictatorship of the proletariat in China, striving to restore capitalism, and capitulating to Soviet "revisionist-socialist-imperialism."[43] After Nixon's visit to China in February 1972, Lin was further denounced for having opposed rapprochement with the United States and for advocating unity with the revisionist Soviet Union.[44] The logic behind these accusations was easy to comprehend: if a known traitor conspired with the Soviets and resisted a thaw in relations with the United States, surely the Party was correct in resisting the Soviets and relaxing relations with the United States.

Using the downfall of an official to generate support for a new political objective was not a new CCP technique. But in this case, the method posed risks. The more the Party discredited Lin by pointing to his treachery, which it did by launching a campaign to "Criticize Lin and Conduct Rectification," the more it tacitly acknowledged its own obtuseness. Lin's deceitfulness clearly managed to thrive for years undetected at the apex of Party power, and the depth of his deception only became apparent after he stole a state plane and flew for Moscow with his wife, son, and several aids. That the Party leadership seemed unable to stop Lin, despite his proximity to power, suggested limits to the CCP's competence.

It also raised larger questions about the Party's ability to guide China through a particularly fluid moment. The possibility of war with the Soviet Union, warmer relations with the United States, Mao's shifting mindset away from revolution and toward accommodation with the status quo—these developments seemed to question some of the core premises of the Chinese revolution. The historian Chen Jian has argued that this moment, when the Soviet Union and China fought each other while China sought rapprochement with the United States, buried the shared consciousness among communists and their sympathizers around the world that communism offered a solution to the problems created by modernization. It became a "crucial root" of the collapse of the Communist bloc and, years later, the end of the Cold War.[45] Yet just as this moment signaled the start of an end, it also represented the beginning of something new. Because the moral foundation of communism had begun to crack, and China's existing path to modernity no longer seemed as viable as it once had, cadres now had more space and incentives to begin to consider other possibilities for China's future, and they did so by drawing from aspects of the Chinese revolution that had existed all along but were often overshadowed.

The Making of the "Four-Three Program"

The Ministry of Foreign Trade struggled to adapt to all these changes in the short term. Of the three shifts, the conflict with the Soviet Union presented the fewest problems. Relations with Moscow had been sour since the Great Leap Forward, and the recent military clashes along the border signaled an acceleration of an existing trend rather than a fundamental shift in policy. In a March 1973 analysis of the changing international context, the Ministry of Foreign Trade identified the "revisionist" Soviet Union as China's greatest threat, alongside the United States. This stance aligned with what had been the Party's position for years; in April 1969, the CCP had identified the Soviet Union and the United States as China's primary enemies during the Party's Ninth National Congress.[46] More difficult to explain was President Nixon's visit to China just weeks earlier and its implications for the future of Sino–American relations.

The Ministry of Foreign Trade explained this shift by stressing that it was not as dramatic as it might seem. The United States remained an imperialist threat, despite the US president's visits to Beijing and Shanghai. "Nixon and his counselors certainly don't have any warm feelings for China," the ministry said. The Americans simply needed China. They were overstretched and needed a way out. In Vietnam, they had spent so much money and lost so many lives over so many years that Washington had no choice but to reconsider its policies, particularly in light of the fact that the missteps in Southeast Asia had created opportunities for the Soviet Union. The Americans believed that better relations with China might create opportunities to stanch the bleeding, but the United States itself hadn't changed. "Imperialism is still imperialism," the ministry said, "there certainly has not been any change in its nature."[47]

Even more difficult to explain was the fallout from the Lin Biao affair. In late January 1972, the Ministry of Foreign Trade sent a report to senior leaders and various offices and agencies to document its total support for the Party's new line on Lin. The report explained that cadres at the ministry used "Marxism-Leninism and Mao Zedong Thought as weapons" to dissect the counterrevolutionary actions of Lin Biao and other "revisionists" and to criticize their betrayals.[48] It was an awkward document for anyone who had worked at the ministry longer than a year. Just the previous spring, during an export meeting in Guangzhou, ministry officials had extoled the "brilliant leadership" of both Mao and Lin.[49] Now, in January 1972, some of the same officials gathered for nine days to catalog Lin's sins and denounce his deception.[50] The assembled cadres managed this shift as artfully as they could by reaffirming their support for Mao's leadership and the rule of the Chinese Communist Party.

In the context of these political shifts, China's economic planners predicted steady growth in the nation's trade with capitalist markets. A draft of the fourth Five-Year Plan (1971–1975) written in January 1972 shows that the Ministry of Foreign Trade anticipated a sizeable increase in the volume of China's trade with foreign capitalists. State planners predicted exports to capitalist markets would increase from US$1.71 billion in 1970 to between US$2.75 billion and US$3.1 billion in 1975. Imports would rise from US$1.99 billion in 1970 to between US$2.2 billion and US$2.45 billion in 1975.[51] As in the past, these increases would occur within the framework of *zili gengsheng*. "Our socialist construction relies principally on *zili gengsheng*," the ministry wrote in March 1972, "but we must also exchange important materials and introduce new technologies [into China] through foreign trade to help us strengthen our capacity for *zili gengsheng* [and to] expedite socialist construction."[52]

This sounded like more of the same, but it was being voiced in a new political environment. The death and discrediting of Lin Biao opened the door for Zhou Enlai to take control of the Central Committee's daily workflow, thus establishing an advocate for broader, stabler engagement with capitalist markets at a key spot in the Party bureaucracy, just as the "leftism" associated with Lin Biao was in retreat.[53] Zhou began to repopulate the nation's bureaucracies with the professionals who had been purged during the early years of the Cultural Revolution. In March 1972, he submitted a list of over four hundred names of senior officials for rehabilitation, which Mao approved.[54]

A few months later, in August, Li Xiannian recommended that the Ministry of Foreign Trade expand its ranks of trained professionals. He suggested assigning to the ministry young people—women and men in their twenties, thirties, and forties—who had foreign-language abilities and other relevant skills. He proposed recruiting them from the Party's "May Seventh" cadre schools, where intellectuals and professionals had been "sent down" during the Cultural Revolution to learn from peasants through reeducation.[55] These personnel changes did more than redress some of the injustices of the Cultural Revolution. They also filled a growing need. The Ministry of Foreign Trade needed young, skilled personnel to implement the kind of long-term, market-oriented trade agenda that was forming in the minds of top Party leaders.

Li Xiannian drove much of this emerging agenda. In January 1972, he received a briefing on economic affairs that convinced him now was the time for China to take advantage of the economic "crisis" afflicting the capitalist West, where producers were driving down the price of certain goods in a desperate search for export markets. Specifically, Li had in mind imports of complete plants for manufacturing artificial fibers and chemical fertilizers, an idea with clear connections to similar imports during the early and mid-1960s. Poor harvests and revolutionary unrest had created a shortfall of cotton fiber in China, and insufficient fertilizer still hampered agricultural output in the countryside.[56] If the Ministry of Foreign Trade could obtain the right plants and technologies at the right price, China could achieve solutions to these two persistent problems.

Li moved the idea forward in late January 1972 when he endorsed a proposal from the State Planning Commission to import four complete sets of equipment for manufacturing artificial fibers and two for making chemical fertilizers. It was an expensive project. Altogether, the equipment would cost around US$400 million—more than a fifth of China's budget for imports from capitalist nations in 1972. It was also a long-term investment. Li believed that if the relevant ministries remained focused, the new facilities might be operational by 1977 or 1978.[57] In the softening revolutionary context of early 1972, the proposal met little opposition. Zhou Enlai approved it after securing Mao's agreement on February 5, and Li remained alert for similar opportunities.[58]

By summer, Li Xiannian was shepherding another set of large-scale imports through the bureaucracy. On August 6, the State Planning Commission submitted a proposal to import a set of rolling steel mills. The Ministry of Metallurgy had requested the equipment because it didn't have the capacity to roll enough steel to keep up with China's domestic production needs. This, too, was an expensive proposition. The mills, which worked like rolling pins to flatten metal stock to proper thickness, would cost approximately US$200 million each. But they would save money in the long run. The State Planning Commission calculated that without the new mills, China would have to spend approximately US$300 million to import three million tons of steel sheets annually to meet construction needs.[59] Li approved the proposal and forwarded it to Zhou for review, who ordered Li on August 21 to begin the program immediately. That same day, the Central Committee and the State Council approved the importation of 1.7-meter wide rolling steel mills from West Germany and Japan.[60]

Other ministries and bureaus dealing with shortfalls observed the progress of these proposals and soon began to submit requests of their own. Some asked to import new technologies and equipment; others sought permission to conduct overseas fact-finding trips and feasibility studies in capitalist nations to lay the groundwork for future imports. Proposals arrived from various ministries, including metallurgy, light industry, aviation, hydropower, and railways.[61]

In December, Zhou Enlai instructed the State Planning Commission to draft a report to integrate these proposals, and to distill the enthusiasm behind them into coherent rationales for a renewed push into capitalist markets. In its report, the State Planning Commission explained that now was the time to launch a capitalist import drive because of rapid improvements in China's diplomatic standing, the breakdown of imperialist and "socialist-imperialist" embargoes targeting China, and the deepening crisis of the imperialist world, which compelled capitalist firms to seek markets and investments abroad. The State Planning Commission wrote that seizing this opportunity to broaden China's economic exchanges would benefit not only China's international political struggle; it would also accelerate the nation's economic construction.[62]

Ye Jizhuang could have written this report, had he survived. He would have recognized the State Planning Commission's analysis of the fraying China embargo and capitalism in crisis. As minister of foreign trade, he had made similar arguments about capitalist trade furthering China's international political struggle. Rather than break new ground, the State Planning Commission's December report mostly presented already accepted arguments about the benefits of trading with capitalists.

The rationales hadn't changed much since Ye's day, but the climate had. The failure of the Cultural Revolution had punctured China's enthusiasm for redness. The Sino–Soviet conflict and Sino–American rapprochement raised fundamental questions about the legitimacy of socialism as a viable path to modernity. Lin Biao's downfall had undermined the legitimacy of the CCP itself. All of these changes coincided with the People's Republic of China joining the United Nations, assuming a seat on the UN Security Council, and establishing ambassador-level diplomatic relations with sixteen capitalist nations.[63] These changes cast new light on established ideas about the merits of trading with the capitalist world.

As Zhou Enlai had instructed, the State Planning Commission report combined many of the proposals for imports that had been circulating for months, which made for an unwieldy program. Li Xiannian acknowledged this in a note to Zhou Enlai and Ji Dengkui, a member of the Politburo and the Professional Work Office (Yewu Zu), a State Council entity responsible for overseeing economic affairs and daily administration. The plan would "certainly change a lot" during implementation, Li wrote. Officials would have to study as they worked. Still, the State Planning Commission had a clear enough vision to estimate the cost of the program: US$4.3 billion.[64]

The final, formal version of the plan, soon dubbed the "Four-Three Program," was submitted to leaders at the State Council just after the new year, on January 2, 1973. It quickly circulated for approvals from top leaders, including Li Xiannian, Zhou Enlai, and Mao himself, and on March 22, the State Council approved it with revisions.[65] Like the draft from December, the final report framed the program in familiar terms. It explained that imperialism and socialist-imperialism wanted to "isolate" China, a stunning assertion from a state whose own unyielding zealotry had singlehandedly upended nearly all of its diplomatic relationships during the early years of the Cultural Revolution.[66] But conjuring this sense of victimization helped to portray a dramatic increase in imports from the capitalist world as fighting against imperialism rather than consorting with it, a line of argument that stretched back to the Moscow Conference of 1952.

The title of the proposal, "Report and Request to Increase Equipment Imports and Expand Economic Exchanges," didn't capture its scale or scope. Over four billion US dollars would be spent on more than two dozen complete plants and factories.[67] The new facilities would support a host of technical industries, ranging from petrochemicals and electric power generation to steel, fertilizer, and synthetic fiber production. They would also be dispersed across China. Some plants were slated for installation along the coast, where infrastructure was relatively well developed and certain raw materials were accessible. In Tianjin, for example, the State Planning Commission proposed building a petrochemical textile factory to manufacture polyester, nylon, and other synthetic fabrics, all of which required abundant petroleum and water to produce. Other projects were destined for deep within China's interior, such as a natural gas chemical plant in Shuifu Country, in northeastern Yunnan.[68] Despite the breadth and complexity of the proposal, the State Planning Commission predicted all of it could be done in three to five years.[69]

It was an unrealistic schedule. In fact, the projected speed and size of the Four-Three Program echoed the impatience of *dajin dachu* during the Great Leap Forward just a few years earlier, although the new initiative lacked the same degree of decentralized, pell-mell expansionism of the earlier campaign. In its relatively controlled approach, the new program resembled instead the smaller-scale technical imports from Japan and capitalist Europe just before the Cultural Revolution.

Still, many of the problems encountered by *dajin dachu* and other previous import drives resurfaced during the Four-Three Program. Foremost among these was the question of finance. How would China pay for everything? Part of the answer lay in stringing out payments over time. The State Planning Commission proposed deferred-payment schemes, similar to the ones it had used with Japanese and European firms during the early 1960s, whereby China would pay for imports in regular installments that would delay full repayment until—in the case of "medium-term" agreements— about eight years after the equipment was delivered. Payment plans for "long-term" agreements might stretch out as far as twenty or even thirty years after the equipment was received, the planners estimated, another bold proposition given the Party's long-standing apprehensions about debt, its vulnerabilities, and its implications for China's international standing.[70]

Even with deferred payments, China would have to increase its exports considerably to pay for the plants, the equipment, the installation fees, and the interest on the delayed payments. Foreign exchange would be tight in the coming two years, the State Planning Commission conceded. But the planners believed that increasing exports of industrial and mining products, such as tin, coal, and petroleum, could play a crucial role in bankrolling the program. The newly imported equipment and plants, once operational, would also help to increase the production of exports over time.[71]

State planners saw especially strong potential for China's future oil earnings. That central planners expected petroleum to fund much of China's imports was already reflected in planning documents for the fourth Five-Year Plan, which predicted the volume of petroleum exports would increase by more than 1,000 percent from 1970 to 1975.[72] This ambitious projection seemed sound to many in the State Planning Commission at the time, especially to the director, Yu Qiuli, a former minister of the petroleum industry who had risen to national prominence in the 1960s for his role in transforming Daqing, a city in western Heilongjiang Province, into a petroleum powerhouse. China's national oil output, much of it from Daqing, had increased steadily since Yu's tenure there. "Our nation is rich in petroleum resources," state planners had written in a February 1970 report. At the time, geologists had surveyed only a tenth of China's four million square kilometers of sedimentary bedrock. But even this limited exploration had identified some 1,500 geological formations that might contain oil or gas, the planners wrote, and only 200 of these sites had been drilled. Half contained oil.[73] All of this justified the rosy projections. The Soviets had also shown that it could be done by ramping up their own oil production in the 1950s and 1960s.[74]

Exports of other goods would have to increase, too, so the Ministry of Foreign Trade reemphasized the logic of *yijin yangchu*. Officials proposed to buy raw materials that China could then process into finished goods for export, which could be another source of hard currency earnings.[75] Along similar lines, in October 1972 Li Xiannian had endorsed the idea of building special factories, workshops, and "bases" for producing exports in line with international standards—a sort of proto–Special Economic Zone that would help to raise production quality in the rest of the nation. This concept, too, had antecedents in the early 1960s.[76]

A further complication was the fact that leaders in Beijing were also facing a more fluid international financial environment than had existed just a few years earlier. The collapse of the Bretton Woods system in the early 1970s ended on-demand convertibility of US dollars into gold at a fixed price; it also unraveled the system of pegged exchange rates that stabilized the relative values of major world currencies. These shifts brought new volatility, and corresponding risks, into trade planners' work in Beijing.

In the new, post–Bretton Woods environment, for example, foreign exchange holdings became a less stable store of value. Now, when the State Planning Commission proposed spending foreign currency deposits on European equipment, officials had to consider that the value of these deposits fluctuated as the Swiss franc, deutschmark, and other currencies floated more freely against each other.[77] China's trade officials would also need to develop a nimbler approach to price setting that could account for this fluid environment, particularly if exports were to fund a substantial share of Four-Three Program imports.[78]

Other economic headwinds compounded these challenges. In 1974, inflationary pressures in rich capitalist nations raised the price of China's imports. A worldwide recession also depressed demand for many of China's traditional exports. This combination of pressures produced a balance-of-payments problem just as the Four-Three Program was getting underway.[79]

Logistics posed still more problems. The architects of the Four-Three Program worried about whether the nation's traders, technicians, workers, and managers had the knowledge and experience to buy, build, and operate plants equipped with the latest technology, a concern that had also surfaced inside the ministry ten years earlier during talks with European and Japanese firms. To address this knowledge gap, in 1974 the Chinese government signed more than seventy contracts to bring more than two thousand technology workers into China from capitalist nations, most of whom were expected to live and work at project sites in areas previously closed to foreigners, including "Third Front" military-industrial complexes built in the interior.[80] This guest worker program served as a capitalist counterpart to the influx of Soviet advisors and technicians who deployed to Chinese factories and construction sites during the high tide of Sino–Soviet cooperation in the 1950s.

Perhaps most seriously, ideological questions also still loomed over the Four-Three Program. The worst of the Cultural Revolution violence had subsided by the mid-1970s, but memories of the abuse suffered by those with ties to foreigners and capitalism remained fresh in the minds of trade officials and other technocrats. Prominent voices in the Party still rejected the notion that China needed foreign technology to develop its own productive capacities. Mao's wife, Jiang Qing, excoriated the Four-Three Program. She attacked Zhou Enlai, Li Xiannian, and the Yewu Zu specifically, accusing them all of "blindly worshipping all things foreign."[81]

Despite these many challenges, trade officials began to negotiate with foreign firms right away, signing sixteen contracts in 1973 and another five the following year. Construction began in July on the first new project under the Four-Three Program, a fertilizer factory in the Hebei city of Cangzhou. By the end of 1974, construction was underway at twenty different sites.[82]

Just as Li Xiannian had anticipated, cadres had to study and adapt as they worked. Roughly two-thirds of the program's projects encountered delays for various reasons.[83] Sometimes it was funding. Li Xiannian received a report in August 1974 that China's foreign trade deficit may have climbed as high as US$1.4 billion. Alarmed, he instructed state planning officials to investigate and confirm that the deficit had indeed climbed so high. If so, cutbacks and delays would be necessary.[84] Construction setbacks also plagued projects. New equipment sometimes didn't work properly. Oftentimes supporting infrastructure and resources failed to materialize on time.[85]

All of these shortcomings produced complications and delays. Still, by the end of 1979, when Reform and Opening was just taking off, twenty of the projects had already been built and were operational.[86] By 1982, all of the twenty-six large industrial projects outlined in the Four-Three Program had been completed.[87] All of the facilities included in the 1973 plan had been imported from capitalist states: Holland, France, Japan, West Germany, Italy, Switzerland, and the United States—many of the same nations that Mao had urged Central Committee members not to forget, twenty-three years earlier, as they compiled the new Chinese state's first comprehensive trade plan. Back then, in the winter of 1949–1950, Mao had been preoccupied with building economic ties to the leader of the socialist world, and capitalist trade occupied an important but marginal position in the Maoist commercial outlook. Now, in 1973, it was central. China's trade was "leaning" to the side of capitalism.

EPILOGUE

ON A WARM BEIJING MORNING in June 1973, six months after the State Planning Commission submitted its proposal for the Four-Three Program, Chen Yun reflected on the shifting economic landscape. He was chatting in his home on Beichang Street, just west of the Forbidden City, with a group of banking officials, including an old comrade, Chen Xiyu, a former vice minister of finance who was now head of the People's Bank of China.[1] "In the past[,] 75 percent of our foreign trade was oriented toward the Soviet Union and Eastern European nations, and 25 percent with capitalist nations," he told his guest. "Now [this] has changed so that 75 percent [lies with] the capitalist world and 25 percent with the Soviet Union [and] Eastern Europe." He wondered aloud whether this new trend was fixed. "I think it is fixed," he said, not bothering to wait for an answer.[2]

Any lingering expectation Chen Yun may have had for a full resurrection of socialist trade was gone. His faith in Chinese socialism itself remained intact, but Chen had begun to consider that China's path to a modern, powerful socialist state was more complex, and more circuitous, than he and many others had first believed. He recognized, too, that China still had a long way to go. "Lenin once said, [when we] arrive at the age of communism, [we] will build some public toilets with gold," he told Chen Xiyu. "As I see it, China is still quite far from that era."[3] No doubt there was little in the modern Chinese condition of June 1973 that resembled the land of social justice, industry, strength, and abundance that Chen and the CCP envisioned for China's socialist modernization. Not a single golden toilet graced even the stalls of Zhongnanhai.

Amid these disappointments and unexpected turns, Chen Yun's instincts told him that China's position in the world hinged on whether the Chinese people could develop a deeper understanding of global capitalism. "[If we] don't study capitalism," he told Chen Xiyu, "we'll lose out." Unless China developed a deeper grasp of capitalism—and by this he meant global market prices, international finance, currencies, and the economic "laws" of capitalism—"then don't [even] think about occupying the position we should hold in world markets."[4] He meant a much larger presence in world markets, a goal the State Planning Commission had identified two weeks earlier, on May 25, when it said that China's annual trade volume would double—to US$16 billion—by 1976 or 1978.[5] The political implications of this larger presence remained uncertain, but Chen Yun was not calling for an unqualified embrace of global markets. China's socialist revolution may be faltering, and it may take unanticipated turns, but Chen and many of his contemporaries remained convinced, as they had been since the 1930s, that unchecked markets posed an existential threat to the Chinese Communist Party and the "new" China it had created.

Still, Chen's thinking in June 1973 did signal a break with the past. During the mid-twentieth century, Mao and his top lieutenants believed that participating in international capitalist markets would hasten the demise of capitalism itself, a conviction that congealed into state policy during the Korean War but that had roots in the "united front" tactics of the Pacific War in the 1930s and the Party leadership's faith in Marxism-Leninism. PRC trade policy was predicated on the idea that selective commerce would foment discord within the capitalist camp while furnishing China with the technology and equipment it needed to industrialize at home. The idea was to participate in capitalism to precipitate its demise, to exacerbate its contradictions while reaping its resources.

This ambition died with Mao. But the notion that trade could induce the collapse of global capitalism, or that socialist–capitalist divisions should even play a meaningful role in shaping PRC trade policy, had clearly come into question during Mao's lifetime, and not just by Chen Yun. Between 1973 and 1974, the chairman himself began to articulate a fluid vision of world affairs that downplayed capitalist–socialist cleavages and instead emphasized economic development as a central concern in Chinese foreign policy. In what became known as his "three-worlds thesis," Mao carved the globe into three camps, or "worlds." He grouped the United States and the Soviet Union together in the "first world" because they were rich and because they had large stockpiles of nuclear weapons. The "second world" included Japan, Europe, Australia, and Canada. These were wealthy states, some of them had nuclear weapons, but they could not compete with first-world economic and nuclear clout. The "third world" encompassed the rest: Africa, Asia—excluding Japan but including China, and Latin America.[6] Mao still invoked the language and concepts of class struggle, oppression, and imperialism in this new conceptual framework, but he had begun to let go of the view that the main contradictions and conflicts would necessarily revolve around the axis of Cold War bipolarity, just as Chen Yun had. By the late summer of 1974, Mao's development-oriented worldview was already being studied and discussed by officials at the Ministry of Foreign Trade, the State Council, and other trade-related institutions.[7]

Deng Xiaoping was thinking through similar ideas. China's future paramount leader and champion of Reform and Opening played no role in the drafting or approving of the Four-Three Program or any other trade policies during the early 1970s. He was repairing tractor parts in a plant in Jiangxi Province, having been purged in the late 1960s, and did not return to Beijing until February 1973. But the Party leadership's emerging emphasis on development over revolution coincided with Deng's pragmatic streak. On March 1, 1975, while Mao was frail but still alive and in Beijing, Deng told Congo's Prime Minister Henri Lopez bluntly that the socialist camp no longer existed and that the "two-camp" Cold War concept failed to fit contemporary reality. It was out of date, Deng argued, and it made little sense to rely on distinctions between socialism and capitalism when identifying friends and foes.[8]

Mao's death less than two years after Deng's meeting with Henri Lopez, and Deng's subsequent consolidation of power, paved the way for the outward-oriented trade and development policy that helped to underwrite China's transformation in the closing decades of the twentieth century. The post-Mao Party leadership emphasized what capitalist trade could contribute to the nation's economic development, but jettisoned talk of how such trade would undermine the stability of international capitalism itself. Gone was the sense of destruction and impermanence that surrounded capitalist trade during Mao's lifetime. Instead, China became increasingly entrenched in global markets.

Debates persisted among Party leaders over the proper pace and degree of this entrenchment, particularly during the late 1970s and early 1980s.[9] In 1977, under the leadership of Hua Guofeng but also with support from Deng Xiaoping, China launched an even larger import program, dubbed the "Foreign Leap Forward" (Yang Yuejin), which proved so costly and unrealistic that Deng had to pull back by breaking many of the contracts China had signed with foreign firms.[10] In the 1980s, with Reform and Opening underway, some Party leaders worried that China was embracing capitalist markets too enthusiastically. Chen Yun, cautious and scarred by the heedlessness of past economic campaigns, urged moderation when developing ties with foreign capitalists, a position that increasingly put him at odds with Deng. But beneath these disagreements lay the consensus, born of experience and shared by Deng, Li Xiannian, Chen Yun, and other top leaders, that a policy of "opening up" to capitalist markets abroad would benefit China.[11]

On the basis of this consensus, and in the wake of broad domestic reforms, China's trade with foreign capitalists swelled to a scale that would have astonished officials at the Ministry of Foreign Trade in the 1950s, 1960s, and even 1970s.[12] Already by the mid-1990s, China had become one of the world's top trading nations.[13] Its accession to the World Trade Organization in 2001 represented a major step toward embedding the nation into the institutional structures of global capitalism, a decision that fueled further growth in trade during the first decades of the twenty-first century. In 2013, China's reported annual trade in goods surpassed US$4 trillion, making it the world's largest trading nation. The CCP heralded this new role as cause for celebration. "This is a landmark milestone for our nation's foreign trade development," a spokesman for China's customs administration told reporters.[14] China had become one of the largest participants of the very capitalist system that Mao and the CCP once set out to destroy.

Lurking beneath this postrevolutionary transformation in trade and investment, however, were deep continuities that reached back to the Mao era. Much of this continuity endured at the level of personal experience. Many of the individuals who first cut their teeth in capitalist trade during the early Maoist period went on to guide the post-Mao era of Reform and

Opening. For decades, Chen Yun and other top economic officials had emphasized the benefits of capitalist trade. This background shaded the way these leaders understood China's options as the geopolitical landscape shifted in the mid-1970s. Certainly, the Sino–Soviet split, the PRC's admission to the United Nations, Nixon's visit to China, and Sino–Japanese rapprochement all helped to create a political and strategic context conducive to a lasting economic reorientation toward the capitalist world. A general thickening of East–West trade ties in the early 1970s contributed to this context, including a push by Moscow to expand its own commercial relations with capitalist nations.[15] Chinese leaders, including Zhou Enlai, had also taken notice of the export-led growth policies of other Asian nations.[16] But the experience required to conceive and implement China's own shift, as Chen Yun did in June 1973, and to view it as an opportunity rather than defeat, had emerged over decades. Like Chen Yun, Li Xiannian drew from decades of personal experience with capitalist trade policy while he helped to oversee Reform and Opening under Deng Xiaoping. When Li met with a delegation of Americans in July 1979 to solicit investment and encourage them to establish joint ventures, for example, he admitted that China had little experience with these specific issues. But he and other CCP officials had been in this position before, pushing into new corners of capitalist markets, and Li was able to draw from his firsthand experience during the Four-Three Program and, even earlier, his work guiding China toward capitalist markets for grain, technology, and factory equipment after the fallout from the Great Leap Forward.[17]

These continuities at the elite level mattered not just because they contributed to the intellectual and experiential foundation for Reform and Opening, but also because they linked capitalist trade to Mao's imprimatur.[18] So-called first-generation leaders could personally attest to an established tradition of seeking out trade with capitalists that began under Mao's own watch. Deng Xiaoping did so on September 16, 1978, when he reminded senior Party officials from Jilin Province that "when Comrade Mao Zedong was alive, we also wanted to expand economic and technological exchanges between China and the outside world, including developing economic and trade relations with some capitalist nations, and even the introduction [into China] of foreign capital, joint ventures, etc."[19] Connections like these allowed Deng and others to frame expanded capitalist trade as a refinement of Maoist policy rather than a departure from it, which helped to inoculate the "opening" component of Reform and Opening against resurgent opposition.

This Maoist legitimacy was reinforced by the practices and rationales that had developed over decades at the working level. Day in and day out, CCP traders had refined techniques and norms to guide commerce with capitalists amid shifting political, economic, and social conditions at home and abroad. Although capitalist trade was sanctioned and organized by the Party itself, it nevertheless remained a fraught undertaking throughout the mid-twentieth century. Recurring political campaigns, such as the Three and Five Anti Campaigns in 1951–1952, the Anti-Rightist Movement of 1957, the Double-Anti Movement of 1958, and the Cultural Revolution invariably targeted the technocratic market watchers and negotiators at the Ministry of Foreign Trade because these women and men, and the work they performed, provoked troubling questions about the identity of Chinese socialism and its boundaries. Did a record of success in capitalist trade suggest that a cadre had minimized redness for the sake of expertise? At what point did mastery of commodity markets or shrewd advertising begin to alter one's political consciousness? When did the pursuit of profits slide from a revolutionary ambition into a capitalist mentality?

These questions hindered the daily work of CCP capitalist trade, but they also compelled Chinese Communist traders to justify and reaffirm the work they did in acceptable political terms. "United Front" campaigns, "equality and mutual benefit" (*huli pingdeng*), anti-American "depoliticized" trade during the Korean War, the drive for "large-scale imports and exports" (*dajin dachu*), "using imports to yield exports" (*yijin yangchu*)—each of these policy frameworks represented an effort by CCP traders to reconcile capitalist trade to shifting politics at home and abroad. This was an unsteady and often dangerous dynamic for traders at China Resources, inside the Ministry of Foreign Trade, and in China's commercial offices abroad, but each succeeding framework helped to justify the continuation of capitalist trade in support of socialist construction and, by extension, in support of the Chinese revolution itself.

Reaffirmations of this sort helped to sustain a decades-long Maoist experiment in capitalist trade—selectively and at arm's length, for sure, but this was enough to shape policies, institutions, ideology, and even the identities of the CCP and "new" China itself over time. The slow drip of experience left impressions of what China might gain from capitalist trade, and how the PRC might pursue these gains while at the same time safeguarding the Party's political imperatives at home. These impressions accumulated between the 1930s and the 1960s, but it wasn't until the geopolitical landscape shifted in the late 1960s and 1970s that they became truly consequential.

To overlook these Maoist roots is to misunderstand the nature of the historical forces behind China's engagement with global capitalism in the late twentieth and early twenty-first centuries. What China and the world witnessed in the Reform and Opening era and afterward was not simply the rise of capitalism in post-Mao China, but rather the continuation under new historical circumstances of the Party's long-standing willingness to use markets to achieve political aims, foremost among which remained the development of a strong, modern Chinese state capable of "standing up," as Mao said, for its own interests.

There is no question that Mao's China, and Mao himself, fought to achieve a type of Chinese modernity starkly different from the one that emerged after his death. The CCP under Mao aspired to be a China that was self-reliant, egalitarian, steeped in socialist revolutionary consciousness, and forged in heavy industry. Had Mao lived to see the twenty-first century, it is difficult to imagine him celebrating the arc of China's revolution from Yan'an to the center of a global economic system grounded in capitalist norms and practices. But Mao might recognize—and Chen Yun would certainly grasp—the fundamental challenge facing China's leadership today: how to couple the Party's need for control at home with open markets abroad. Mao faced this dilemma in the context of pursuing socialist revolution; China's leaders confront it today as inheritors of a single-party state with no apparent plans to implement meaningful political reform anytime soon. Neither generation of leadership pursued the liberalizing political effects of open-market commercial interactions; both recognized the contributions that such interactions stood to make to the Party's ambition for modernization.

The search for solutions to this dilemma has produced a lasting tension at the heart of the modern political experience under Chinese Communist Party rule: how to use capitalist markets without succumbing to them. During the Maoist era, the Party's search for a resolution to this tension lurched from one direction to another. Today, the CCP's touch is lighter, its approach more nuanced, but the dilemma endures. It remains an open question how the Party will navigate this tension in the years ahead, and the stakes have only grown. Riding on it is the fate not just of the Chinese Communist Party itself, but the nearly 1.4 billion people who live under its rule and the many billions more whose lives are touched in one way or another by the global economy into which China has grown.

ABBREVIATIONS IN THE NOTES

APRF	Archive of the President, Russian Federation
BBC	British Broadcasting Corporation
BLJ	*Balujun Xinsijun Zhu Ge Di Banshi Jigou* (Eighth Route Army and New Fourth Army Administrative Organizations in Various Locations)
CYNP	*Chen Yun Nianpu* (A Chronology of Chen Yun)
CYWX	*Chen Yun Wenxuan* (Selected Works of Chen Yun)
DWMYJ	*Zhonghua Renmin Gongheguo Jingji Dang'an Ziliao Xuanbian, Duiwai Maoyi Juan* (Selection of Materials from the PRC Economic Archives, Foreign Trade Volume)
FMA	Foreign Ministry Archives of the People's Republic of China
FO	Foreign Office, United Kingdom
FPA	Fujian Provincial Archives
FRUS	*Foreign Relations of the United States*
GAC	General Administration of Customs of the PRC
GLF	Great Leap Forward
HPA	Hebei Provincial Archives
HuPA	Hubei Provincial Archives
JAPIT	Japan Association for the Promotion of International Trade
JCIEA	Japan–China Importers and Exporters Association
JDYL	*Jiandang Yilai Zhongyao Wenxian Xuanbian* (Selected Important Documents since the Founding of the Chinese Communist Party)
JETRO	Japan External Trade Organization
JPA	Jilin Provincial Archives
JRJ	*Zhonghua Renmin Gongheguo Jingji Dang'an Ziliao Xuanbian, Jinrong Juan* (Selection of Materials from the PRC Economic Archives, Finance and Banking Volume)
LXNNP	*Li Xiannian Nianpu* (A Chronology of Li Xiannian)

MZDJJNP	*Mao Zedong Jingji Nianpu* (An Economic Chronology of Mao Zedong)
MZDQ J	*Mao Zedong Quanji* (The Complete Works of Mao Zedong)
MZDWJ	*Mao Zedong Wenji* (Collected Works of Mao Zedong)
MZDXJ	*Mao Zedong Xuanji* (Selected Works of Mao Zedong)
RG	Record Group
SMA	Shanghai Municipal Archives
TNA	The National Archives of the United Kingdom
USNA	United States National Archives at College Park, Maryland
WNRC	Washington National Record Center
ZGGCDWX	Zhongguo Gongchandang Wenxian Xinxiku (CCP Literature Database)

NOTES

1. An Jianshe, *Zhou Enlai de Zuihou Suiyue* (1966–1976) [*Zhou Enlai's Final Years* (1966–1976)] (Beijing: Zhongyang Wenxian, 2002), 111; "Li Xiannian Zhuan" Bianxie Zu, *Li Xiannian Zhuan* [A Biography of Li Xiannian], 2 vols. (Beijing: Zhongyang Wenxian, 2009), 2:768–769; Chen Jinhua, *Guoshi Yishu* [Recollections on Affairs of the Nation] (Beijing: Zhonggong Dangshi, 2005), 14. A list of the projects included in the proposal can be found in Chen, *Guoshi Yishu,* 17–19.

2. "Jin Richeng Tongzhi Fabiao Xin Nian Heci[;] Chaoxian Renmin Qianjin Daolu Shang Chongman Shengli he Guangrong" [Comrade Kim Il Sung Issues New Year's Message(;) the Road ahead for the Korean People Is Full of Victory and Glory], *Renmin Ribao* [People's Daily], January 2, 1973, 6. Unless otherwise noted, all English translations throughout the book are my own.

3. "Mao Zhuxi Yulu" [Quotation from Chairman Mao], *Renmin Ribao,* January 2, 1973, 1.

4. Mao Zedong, "Lun Renmin Minzhu Zhuanzheng" [On the People's Democratic Dictatorship], June 30, 1949, in *Mao Zedong Xuanji* [Selected Works of Mao Zedong,], 4 vols. (Beijing: Renmin, 1991) (hereafter cited as *MZDXJ*), 4:1473.

5. Examples include Shen Zhihua, *Mao, Stalin, and the Korean War: Trilateral Communist Relations in the 1950s* (Milton Park, Abingdon: Routledge, 2012); Chen Jian, *Mao's China and the Cold War* (Chapel Hill: University of North Carolina Press, 2001); Lorenz M. Luthi, *The Sino-Soviet Split: Cold War in the Communist World* (Princeton, NJ: Princeton University Press, 2008); Shen Zhihua and Xia Yafeng, *Mao and the Sino-Soviet Partnership, 1945–1959: A New History* (Lanham, MD: Lexington Books, 2015). An exception is Odd Arne Westad, *Restless Empire: China and the World since 1750* (New York: Basic

Books, 2012). Westad focuses on the lived experiences of international affairs, which allows him to capture overlooked ways China absorbed influences from abroad, but he misses China's sustained ties to capitalist markets as a source of these influences.

6. By "commercial relationships" and "commerce," I mean not just trade but the whole range of activities associated with the buying and selling of goods and services, such as advertising and marketing, shipping and transportation, banking, and insurance. I use "capitalism" and "capitalist" here and throughout the book to mean states and places that were not self-avowedly socialist. This is in keeping with contemporary usage by the Chinese Communist Party and throughout Chinese society during the period that concerns this book.

7. One of the most insightful scholars of foreign trade in the Mao era is the economist Alexander Eckstein. Two of his most helpful volumes are *Communist China's Economic Growth and Foreign Trade: Implications for U.S. Policy* (New York: Council on Foreign Relations and McGraw-Hill, 1966), and *China's Economic Development: The Interplay of Scarcity and Ideology* (Ann Arbor: University of Michigan Press, 1975).

8. CIA National Foreign Assessment Center, *China: Foreign Trade Policy in the 1970s,* August 1, 1978, General CIA Records, Freedom of Information Act Electronic Reading Room, CIA-RDP80T00702A000200060012-0, ii.

9. David Zweig, *Internationalizing China: Domestic Interests and Global Linkages* (Ithaca, NY: Cornell University Press, 2002), 4.

10. John King Fairbank, *Trade and Diplomacy on the China Coast: The Opening of the Treaty Ports, 1842–1854* (Cambridge, MA: Harvard University Press, 1964), 21.

11. Oscar Sanchez-Sibony, *Red Globalization: The Political Economy of the Soviet Cold War from Stalin to Khrushchev* (Cambridge: Cambridge University Press, 2014); John R. Lampe, *Yugoslavia as History: Twice There Was a Country* (Cambridge: Cambridge University Press, 2000); Jorge I. Dominguez, *To Make a World Safe for Revolution* (Cambridge, MA: Harvard University Press, 1989); and Alec Nove and Desmond Donnelly, *Trade with Communist Countries* (New York: MacMillan [published for the Institute of Economic Affairs], 1960).

12. Among the Cold War–era economists who did analyze China's trade with capitalists, most focused on the challenges of collecting data and extrapolating insights about the contemporary Chinese economy. Valuable as these studies are, they overlook the deeper changes associated with this trade over time. See Nai-Ruenn Chen and Walter Galenson, *The Chinese Economy under Communism* (Chicago: Aldine, 1969), and Joint Economic Committee of the Congress of the United States, comp., *An Economic Profile of Mainland China* (Washington, DC: US Government Printing Office, 1967). A few historians have analyzed aspects of trade between Mao's China and foreign capitalists, but these studies are less concerned with the deeper effects on China of sustained

commerce with capitalists over decades. See Shu Guang Zhang, *Economic Cold War: America's Embargo against China and the Sino-Soviet Alliance, 1949–1963* (Washington, DC: Woodrow Wilson Center Press, 2001); Chad J. Mitcham, *China's Economic Relations with the West and Japan, 1949–1979: Grain, Trade and Diplomacy* (London: Routledge, 2005); Min Song, "A Dissonance in Mao's Revolution: Chinese Agricultural Imports from the United States, 1972–1978," *Diplomatic History* 38, no. 2 (2014): 409–430; Mao Lin, "Traders as Diplomats: Trade and Sino-American Rapprochement, 1971–1978," *International Journal of Social Science Studies* 5, no. 10 (2017): 52–66.

13. Julia Lovell, *Maoism: A Global History* (New York: Alfred A. Knopf, 2019); Philip Thai, *China's War on Smuggling: Law, Economic Life, and the Making of the Modern State, 1842–1965* (New York: Columbia University Press, 2018), especially 241–271.

1. OPENING A CAPITALIST WINDOW

1. This account of the *Aldan's* arrival in Hong Kong draws from Yuan Chaojun and Le Shuo, "Huarun: Zai Dajuezhan Zhong Chuangye" [China Resources: Entrepreneurship in Armageddon], *Hongyan Chunqiu* [Annals of the Red Crag] 2 (1998): 33–49. Yuan Chaojun was one of the four men on the *Aldan* that day.

2. Yuan and Le, "Huarun: Zai Dajuezhan Zhong Chuangye," 38. A description of the HSBC building in Hong Kong can be found in Frank H. H. King, Catherine E. King, and David J. S. King's *The Hongkong Bank between the Wars and the Bank Interned, 1919–1945: Return from Grandeur* (Cambridge: Cambridge University Press, 1988), 252–256. The description here also draws from "The Hong Kong and Shanghai Banking Corporation[,] Head Office," photograph album, ca. 1935, HSBC London Archives Center, HQ HSBCPH 0140-0002-0003-B-0214.

3. Li Fuchun, "Guanyu Dongbei Caijing Gongzuo Wenti de Baogao" [Report on Issues in Northeast Financial and Economic Work], October 30, 1947, in *Li Fuchun Xuanji* [Selected Works of Li Fuchun] (Beijing: Zhongguo Jihua, 1992), 49.

4. Akira Iriye, "Japanese Aggression and China's International Position, 1931–1939," in *The Cambridge History of China*, vol. 13, *Republican China, 1912–1949,* part 2, ed. John K. Fairbank and Albert Feuerwerker (Cambridge: Cambridge University Press, 1986), 499.

5. Akira Iriye, "Japanese Aggression," 513–514; Michael Sheng, *Battling Western Imperialism: Mao, Stalin, and the United States* (Princeton, NJ: Princeton University Press, 1997), 32.

6. For the Nanjing Massacre and its legacies, see Joshua A. Fogel, ed., *The Nanjing Massacre in History and Historiography* (Berkeley: University of California Press, 2000).

7. Jonathan Spence, *The Search for Modern China* (New York: W. W. Norton, 1999), 423.

8. Alexander V. Pantsov and Steven I. Levine, *Mao: The Real Story* (New York: Simon & Schuster, 2012), 305–306.

9. Pantsov and Levine, *Mao: The Real Story,* 295.

10. For a concise discussion of the Xi'an crisis, see Spence, *The Search for Modern China,* 403–409.

11. Chen Yung-fa, "The Blooming Poppy under the Red Sun: The Yan'an Way and the Opium Trade," in *New Perspectives on the Chinese Communist Revolution,* ed. Tony Saich and Hans van de Ven (Armonk, NY: M.E. Sharpe, 1995), 267.

12. Mao Zedong, "Mao Zedong Guanyu Nanjing Dangju Buchong Balujun Jingfei Ji Yiwu, Danyao Qingkuang Deng Zhi Pan Hannian Dian" [Cable from Mao Zedong to Pan Hannian Regarding Nanjing Authorities' Eighth Route Army Supplemental Outlays and the Situation [with] Clothing, Ammunition, Etc.], August 31, 1937, in Zhongguo Renmin Jiefangjun Lishi Ziliao Congshu Bianshen Weiyuanhui [Chinese People's Liberation Army Historical Information Series Editorial Committee], *Balujun Xinsijun Zhu Ge Di Banshi Jigou* [Eighth Route Army and New Fourth Army Administrative Organizations in Various Locations], 5 vols. (Beijing: Junshi Kexue, 1999–2009) (hereafter cited as *BLJ*), 1:583.

13. Yang Kuisong, "Gongchan Guoji Wei Zhonggong Tigong Caizheng Yuanzhu Qingkuang Zhi Kaocha" [Investigation into the Circumstances of Communist International (Comintern) Financial Assistance to the Chinese Communist Party], *Dangshi Yanjiu Ziliao* [Party History Research Materials] 1 (2004): 1–37.

14. Before the United Front, the CCP funded its trade deficits mainly by depreciating its own currency; confiscating the assets of landlords, usurers, and other "exploiters"; and spending its own hard currency. See Peter Schran, *Guerrilla Economy: The Development of the Shensi-Kansu-Ninghsia Border Region, 1937–1945* (Albany: State University of New York Press, 1976), 169–170.

15. For locations and operating dates of the offices, see *BLJ,* 1:454–457. Not all of the offices operated concurrently. The Nanjing Office, for example, remained open only from August until December 1937.

16. Chen Guomin, "Zhou Enlai yu Kangzhan Shi de Balujun Banshichu" [Zhou Enlai and Eighth Route Army Offices during the War against Japan], *Juewu* [Consciousness] 3 (2015): 36; Lyman Van Slyke, "The Chinese Communist Movement during the Sino-Japanese War, 1937–1945," in *The Cambridge History of China,* vol. 13, *Republican China, 1912–1949,* part 2, 659.

17. Gu Longsheng, ed., *Mao Zedong Jingji Nianpu* [An Economic Chronology of Mao Zedong] (Beijing: Zhonggong Zhongyang Dangxiao, 1993) (hereafter cited as *MZDJJNP*), 106.

18. For Ye's contributions to the negotiations, see "Ye Jianying Zhuan" Bianxie Zu, *Ye Jianying Zhuan* [A Biography of Ye Jianying] (Beijing: Dangdai Zhongguo, 1995), 238–252.

19. *MZDJJNP*, 106–107.

20. *MZDJJNP*, 109, 114, 117–118.

21. *BLJ*, 1:583.

22. *MZDJJNP*, 107.

23. Zhou Enlai, "Zhou Enlai Guanyu Ying Su Jiejue Balujun Dongzhuang Wenti Zhi Mao Zedong, Zhang Wentian Dian" [Cable from Zhou Enlai to Mao Zedong and Zhang Wentian Regarding the Need to Quickly Resolve the Issue of Eighth Route Army Winter Clothing], August 30, 1937, *BLJ*, 3:61.

24. Benjamin Schwartz, *Chinese Communism and the Rise of Mao* (Cambridge, MA: Harvard University Press, 1979), 203–204.

25. Mao Zedong, "Zhongguo Gongchandang Zai Kangri Shiqi de Renwu" [The Duties of the Chinese Communist Party during the Period of Japanese Resistance], May 3, 1937, in Zhonggong Zhongyang Wenxian Yanjiushi [CCP Central Literature Research Office], *Jiandang Yilai Zhongyao Wenxian Xuanbian, 1921–1949* [Selected Important Documents since the Founding of the Chinese Communist Party, 1921–1949], 26 vols. (Beijing: Zhongyang Wenxian, 2011) (hereafter cited as *JDYL*), 14:178–179.

26. Niu Jun, *From Yan'an to the World: The Origin and Development of Chinese Communist Foreign Policy* (Norwalk, CT: Eastbridge, 2005), 12–14.

27. It remains unclear precisely when the CCP leadership learned the details of the Comintern Seventh Congress. Zhang Hao, a CCP envoy to the Comintern, returned to northern Shaanxi in November 1935, but there are indications that news of the congress had reached Yan'an before Zhang's arrival. See Tony Saich, ed., *The Rise to Power of the Chinese Communist Party: Documents and Analysis* (Armonk, NY: M.E. Sharpe, 1996), 659.

28. Niu, *From Yan'an to the World*, 15–16.

29. Mao Zedong, "Fandui Riben Jingong de Fangzhen, Banfa he Qiantu" [Policies, Measures, and Prospects for Resisting the Japanese Invasion], July 23, 1937, *MZDXJ*, 2:347. In the late 1930s, CCP leaders generally characterized economic relations with capitalists as aid or assistance rather than trade. This reflected, in part, the Party's limited ability to produce its own exports for trade. In other words, trade with capitalists was possible only when it could be financed by aid.

30. Framing *zili gengsheng* as a policy has led many to question its coherence over time. Stuart Schram, for example, has argued that although there may have been existential continuity between *zili gengsheng* in the context of Yan'an and the new policies adopted in the post-1949 era, intellectual continuity cannot be said to have existed. But this misses the intellectual continuity that existed in *zili gengsheng* as a framework, a way of conceiving the merits and vulnerabilities of economic exchange. For Schram's argument, see Stuart R. Schram, *The Thought of Mao Tse-Tung* (Cambridge: Cambridge University Press, 1989), 93.

31. Kenneth Lieberthal interprets the term similarly to mean the Party must retain the initiative. See Kenneth Lieberthal, *Governing China: From Revolution through Reform* (New York: W. W. Norton, 1995), 76.

32. *BLJ,* 4:707.

33. Tie Zhuwei, *Liao Chengzhi Zhuan* [A Biography of Liao Chengzhi] (Beijing: Renmin, 1998), 156.

34. Kurt Warner Radtke, *China's Relations with Japan, 1945–1983: The Role of Liao Chengzhi* (New York: Manchester University Press, 1990), 23. For Liao Zhongkai's life and career, see Fook-lam Gilbert Chan, "A Chinese Revolutionary: The Career of Liao Chung-K'ai (1878–1925)" (PhD diss., Columbia University, 1975).

35. The first woman to join the Revolutionary Alliance was the writer Qiu Jin. See Helen Foster Snow, *The Chinese Communists: Sketches and Autobiographies of the Old Guard* (Westport, CT: Greenwood, 1972), 30.

36. Snow, *The Chinese Communists,* 26.

37. Radtke, *China's Relations with Japan,* 13.

38. Hans van de Ven, "The Kuomintang's Secret Service in Action in South China: Operational and Political Aspects of the Arrest of Liao Chengzhi (1942)," *Intelligence and National Security* 16, no. 4 (2004): 224.

39. The quotations are from Tie, *Liao Chengzhi Zhuan,* 156.

40. Chinese sources provide conflicting dates for the meeting between Zhou and Clark Kerr. According to Zhou Enlai's chronology (*nianpu*), which Party historians compiled with privileged access to CCP archives, the meeting occurred in January 1938. See Zhonggong Zhongyang Wenxian Yanjiushi, *Zhou Enlai Nianpu, 1898–1949* [A Chronology of Zhou Enlai, 1898–1949] (Beijing: Zhongyang Wenxian, 1990), 402. An official history of the CCP's wartime supply system dates the meeting to late December 1937. See *BLJ,* 4:841. Both sources are almost certainly incorrect. Ambassador Clark Kerr didn't reach China until February 1938, when he arrived in Shanghai after a brief stop in Hong Kong. See "Extract from 'Chung Kuo Jih Pao' of 26th February, 1938," Archive of Archibald Clark Kerr, Baron Inverchapel, Oxford,

Bodleian Library, MS. 12101 / 27, folder 2, [n.p.]. British sources provide little clarification. I was unable to locate any records of a February or March 1938 meeting between Zhou and Clark Kerr in the ambassador's papers at Bodleian Library, Oxford University, nor did I uncover any records at the British National Archives. The earliest meeting between the two men noted in the ambassador's 1938 diary was on April 22. See Archive of Archibald Clark Kerr, Baron Inverchapel, Oxford, Bodleian Library, MS. 12101 / 43, [n.p.].

41. Ferdinand Kuhn Jr., "British Plan 'Appropriate' Steps; Await Details of Attack on Envoy," *New York Times,* August 27, 1937, 1, 3.

42. Janice R. and Stephen R. MacKinnon, *Agnes Smedley: The Life and Times of an American Radical* (Berkeley: University of California Press, 1988), 202–203.

43. For statistics on arms and ammunition shipments through the colony in 1936, see Governor of Hong Kong, "Transit of Arms and Ammunition through Hong Kong to China," March 3, 1937, National Archives of the United Kingdom (hereafter cited as TNA), Foreign Office (hereafter cited as FO) 371 / 20976, 2316/130/10.

44. Shanghai Office of Jardine Matheson & Co., Ltd., to Hong Kong Office, as quoted in Under-Secretary of State, Foreign Office, "Supply of Munitions to Nanking Government," August 27, 1937, TNA, FO 371 / 20976, 5809 / 130 / 10.

45. Colonial Office, "Memorandum on the Position of Hong Kong," September 6, 1937, TNA, FO 371 / 20976, 6164 / 130 / 10.

46. Colonial Office, "Memorandum," September 6, 1937.

47. Nanking (Gage) to Foreign Office, September 6, 1937, TNA, FO 371 / 20976, 6262/130/10.

48. Nanking (Gage) to Colonial Office, September 4, 1937, TNA, FO 371 / 20976, 6149/130/10.

49. CCP Central Secretariat, "Zhonggong Zhongyang Shujichu Guanyu Muqian Xingshi de Zhishi" [CCP Central Secretariat Instruction on the Current Situation], July 21, 1937, *JDYL,* 14:386–387.

50. Yuan and Le, "Huarun: Zai Dajuezhan Zhong Chuangye," 36; Chen Dunde, *Ba Lu Jun Zhu Xianggang Banshichu Jishi* [True Record of the Eighth Route Army Office in Hong Kong] (Hong Kong: Zhonghua Shuju, 2010), 24–25.

51. *BLJ,* 4:707, 841.

52. Far Eastern Department, Foreign Office, to Cabinet Committee on the Far Eastern Situation, "Position of Hong Kong in Relation to the Present Sino-Japanese Dispute," September 14, 1937, TNA, FO 371 / 20977, 6664/130/10.

53. Frank Welsh, *A Borrowed Place: The History of Hong Kong* (New York: Kodansha International, 1993), 408.

54. Wu Xuewen and Wang Junyan, eds., *Liao Chengzhi yu Riben* [Liao Chengzhi and Japan] (Beijing: Zhonggong Dangshi, 2007), 68.

55. *BLJ,* 4:707.

56. Chen, *Ba Lu Jun Zhu Xianggang Banshichu Jishi,* 34.

57. *BLJ,* 4:709–710. For united-front activities undertaken by the Eighth Route Army Office in Hong Kong, see Wu and Wang, *Liao Chengzhi yu Riben,* 67–112.

58. Tokyo (Dodds) to Foreign Office, September 1, 1937, TNA, FO 371 / 20976, 5968/130/10.

59. The Consul General at Hong Kong (Southard) to the Secretary of State, April 1, 1938, *Foreign Relations of the United States* (hereafter cited as *FRUS*), vol. 3, *The Far East* (Washington, DC: US Government Printing Office, 1938), 132.

60. "Memorandum Prepared in the Division of Far Eastern Affairs," April 20, 1938, *FRUS,* 1938, vol. 3, *The Far East,* 597–598.

61. Liao Chengzhi, "Liao Chengzhi Guanyu Yuehua Gongsi Bei Soucha Ji Keneng Bei Poli Gang Zhi Zhonggong Zhongyang, Nanfang Ju Dian" [Cable from Liao Chengzhi to CCP Central Committee and Southern Bureau Regarding the Search of Yuehua and Possible Pressure to Leave Hong Kong], March 14, 1939, *BLJ,* 4:734; Chen, *Ba Lu Jun Zhu Xianggang Banshichu Jishi,* 35.

62. Liao Chengzhi, "Liao Chengzhi Guanyu Yuehua Gongsi Bei Soucha Yuanyin Ji Yingfu Cuoshi Zhi Zhonggong Zhongyang, Nanfang Ju Dian" [Cable from Liao Chengzhi to CCP Central Committee and Southern Bureau Regarding the Search of Yuehua Company and Measures in Response], March 16, 1939, *BLJ,* 4:736.

63. Liao Chengzhi, "Liao Chengzhi Guanyu GangYing Zhengfu Banbu Jiancha Mishe Diantai Ling Deng Zhi Zhonggong Zhongyang, Nanfang Ju Dian" [Cable from Liao Chengzhi to CCP Central Committee and Southern Bureau Regarding the British Hong Kong Government Issuance of Orders Regarding Inspections for Secretly Installed Transmitter-Receivers, Etc.], June 24, 1939, *BLJ,* 4:742.

64. Sui-jeung Chan, *East River Column: Hong Kong Guerrillas in the Second World War and After* (Hong Kong: Hong Kong University Press, 2009), 29.

65. Central Southern Bureau, "Zhonggong Zhongyang Nanfangju Guanyu Baozhang Banshichu Gongzuo de Jueding Zhi Ge Banshichu Bing Bao Zhongyang Dian" [Cable from the CCP Central Southern Bureau to (Subordinate) Offices and Copied to Central Committee Regarding Decisions to Safeguard Office Work], April 1, 1939, *BLJ,* 1:200.

66. CCP Central Secretariat, "Zhonggong Zhongyang Shujichu Guanyu Mimi Gongzuo de Jueding" [CCP Central Secretariat Resolution Regarding Secret Work], April 12, 1939, *JDYL,* 16:163.

67. Zhu De, Peng Dehuai, and Yang Shangkun, "Zhu De Deng Guanyu Kefu Caizheng Jingji Kunnan gei Nie Rongzhen de Dianbao" [Cable from Zhu De and Others to Nie Rongzhen on Overcoming Financial and Economic Difficulties], April 13, 1939, *JDYL,* 16:165.

68. Wu et al., *Hongse Huarun* [Red China Resources] (Beijing: Zhonghua, 2010), 5.

69. Zhou Yan, "Hongse 'Huarun' de Shouwei Zhangmenren Yang Lin" [Yang Lin, the First Head of Red "Huarun"], *Shiji* [Century] 3 (2007): 13.

70. Zhou Yan, "Yang Lin," 13–14. The CCP employed other undercover commercial operators in Shanghai during the late 1930s and 1940s. Allison Rottmann, "Resistance, Urban Style: The New Fourth Army and Shanghai, 1937–1945" (PhD diss., University of California, Berkeley, 2007), 358.

71. Qin Fuquan, *Bo Gu he Mao Zedong* [Bo Gu and Mao Zedong] (Hong Kong: Dafeng, 2009), 191.

72. Wu et al., *Hongse Huarun,* 12.

73. Wu et al., 14, 19.

74. Wu et al., 17, 19.

75. CCP Central Secretariat, "Zhonggong Zhongyang Shujichu Guanyu Dui Diren Jingji Douzheng de Zhishi" [CCP Central Secretariat Instruction Regarding the Economic Struggle against the Enemy], March 23, 1940, available at Zhongguo Gongchandang Wenxian Xinxiku [CCP Literature Database], http://data.people.com/cn (hereafter cited as ZGGCDWX).

76. CCP Central Secretariat, "Zhonggong Zhongyang Shujichu dui Puxi Bei Caijing Zhengce de Zhishi" [CCP Central Secretariat Instruction to Northwestern Shanxi [Regarding] Financial and Economic Policies], May 18, 1940, ZGGCDWX. See also Northern Bureau, untitled instruction, April 1, 1940, ZGGCDWX.

77. Harold M. Tanner, *Where Chiang Kai-shek Lost China: The Liao-Shen Campaign, 1948* (Bloomington: Indiana University Press, 2015), 36.

78. Spence, *The Search for Modern China,* 469.

79. Mao Zedong, "Lun Lianhe Zhengfu" [On Coalition Government], April 24, 1945, *MZDXJ,* 3:1038–1039, 1094.

80. Mao Zedong, "Zhi Dongbei Ju Dian" [Cable to Northeast Bureau], October 22, 1946, in *Mao Zedong Quanji* [Complete Works of Mao Zedong], ed. Zhang Dijie, 52 vols. (Hong Kong: Rundong, 2013) (hereafter cited as *MZDQJ*), 22:193.

81. Mao Zedong, "Di Qiang Wo Ruo Bixu Zhunbei Changqi Douzheng" [The Enemy Is Strong, We Are Weak, (We) Must Prepare for Protracted Struggle], October 25, 1946, *MZDQJ,* 22:195.

82. CCP Central Committee, "Zhonggong Zhongyang Guanyu Jiefangqu Waijiao Fangzhen de Zhishi" [Instruction from the Central Committee Regarding Foreign Relations Guidelines for Liberated Areas], May 3, 1946, *JDYL,* 23:243.

83. *JDYL,* 23:243.

84. Soren Clausen and Stig Thogersen, *The Making of a Chinese City: History and Historiography in Harbin* (Armonk: M.E. Sharpe, 1995), 151.

85. Treaty of Friendship and Alliance between the Republic of China and the U.S.S.R., Moscow, August 14, 1945, Agreement Concerning Dairen. See *Chronology of International Events and Documents* 1, no. 5 (August 27–September 9, 1945): 118–126.

86. The Consul General at Dairen (Benninghoff) to the Secretary of State, January 17, 1947, *FRUS,* 1947, vol. 7, *The Far East: China,* 484.

87. The Consul General at Dairen (Benninghoff) to the Chargé in China (Robertson), April 27, 1946, *FRUS,* 1946, vol. 10, *The Far East: China,* 1163; Ambassador in China (Stuart) to the Secretary of State, April 20, 1947, *FRUS,* 1947, vol. 7, *The Far East: China,* 514–515.

88. Dalian Shi Shizhi Bangongshi [Dalian City Historical Records Office], ed., *Zhonggong Dalian Difang Shi* [Chinese Communist Party Local History of Dalian] (Dalian: Dalian, 1996), 160–161, 163–164. For a firsthand account of one such firm, see Xie Qian, "Zai Dalian Gong'an Zongju de Houqin Zhanxian Shang" [On the Logistics Front of the Dalian Public Security Bureau], in *Jiefang Chuqi de Dalian: Jinian Dalian Jiefang Sishi Zhounian* [Dalian at Liberation's Beginning: Remembering the Fortieth Anniversary of the Liberation of Dalian], ed., Zhonggong Dalian Shiwei Dangshi Ziliao Zhengji Bangongshi [CCP Dalian Municipal Committee Office for the Collection of Party Historical Materials] (Dalian: [s.n.], 1985), 81–92.

89. The Consul General at Dairen (Benninghoff) to the Ambassador in China (Stuart), March 18, 1947, *FRUS,* 1947, vol. 7, *The Far East: China,* 503–505.

90. Dalian Shi Shizhi Bangongshi, *Zhonggong Dalian Difang Shi,* 164; Wu Xiuquan, "Jiefang Zhanzheng Qijian Dalian de Jungong Shengchan" [Military Production in Dalian during the War of Liberation], in *Jiefang Chuqi de Dalian,* 111.

91. The Consul General at Dairen (Benninghoff) to the Ambassador in China (Stuart), March 18, 1947, 504.

92. Li Zhuping, "Huadong Ju Caiwei Zhu Dalian Banshichu he Jianxin Gongsi" [The Northeast Bureau Finance Committee Office in Dalian and the Jianxin Company], in *Jiefang Chuqi de Dalian,* 118.

93. Zhu Jianhua et al., eds., *Dongbei Jiefang Qu Caizheng Jingji Shigao, 1945. 8–1949.9* [A Financial (and) Economic History of the Northeast China

Liberated Areas, August 1945–September 1949] (Harbin: Heilongjiang Renmin, 1987), 413.

94. Dalian Shi Shizhi Bangongshi, *Zhonggong Dalian Difang Shi,* 160.

95. Zhu Jiamu and Liu Shukai, eds., *Chen Yun Nianpu, 1905–1994* [A Chronology of Chen Yun, 1905–1994], 3 vols. (Beijing: Zhongyang Wenxian, 2000) (hereafter cited as *CYNP*), 1:459, 463–464.

96. Zhu, *Dongbei Jiefang Qu Caizheng Jingji Shigao,* 339.

97. *CYNP,* 1:465.

98. John R. Stewart, "Manchuria: The Land and Its Economy," *Economic Geography* 8, no. 2 (April 1932): 135, 141.

99. Zhu, *Dongbei Jiefang Qu Caizheng Jingji Shigao,* 338.

100. Osawa Takehiko and Qiao Jun, trans., "Jiefang Zhanzheng Shiqi Zhongguo Gongchandang Dui Dongbei de Guanli yu Dui Su Maoyi" [Chinese Communist Party Management of Northeast China and Trade with the Soviet Union during the War of Liberation], *Zhonggong Dangshi Ziliao* [CCP Party History Materials] 1 (2007): 179.

101. Zhu, *Dongbei Jiefang Qu Caizheng Jingji Shigao,* 338–339.

102. The Northeast Bureau established the Pyongyang office in July 1946. Wu, *Hongse Huarun,* 37.

103. *CYNP,* 1:468, 470.

104. Wu, *Hongse Huarun,* 22.

105. Wu, 23.

106. Wu, 23–24.

107. Yuan and Le, "Huarun: Zai Dajuezhan Zhong Chuangye," 44.

108. Wu, *Hongse Huarun,* 23; Yuan and Le, "Huarun: Zai Dajuezhan Zhong Chuangye," 37.

109. Wu, *Hongse Huarun,* 23.

110. For Yuan's service in Guiyang, see *BLJ,* 1:453, table: "Balujun Zhu Ge Di Banshi Jigou Yilanbiao" [Table of Eighth Route Army Administrative Offices in Various Locations]. For his experience in Shanghai, see Yuan and Le, "Huarun: Zai Dajuezhan Zhong Chuangye," 33–35. On Yuan's Hong Kong arrival in April 1947, see Wu Hesong, ed., *Qian Zhiguang Zhuan* [A Biography of Qian Zhiguang] (Beijing: Zhonggong Dangshi, 2011), 290.

111. Yuan and Le, "Huarun: Zai Dajuezhan Zhong Chuangye," 37. For Liu's work in Guilin, see *BLJ,* 4:422, table: "Balujun Guilin Banshichu Ganbu Minglu" [Directory of Cadres (at the) Eighth Route Army Office in Guilin]. For his role as shipping director in the Chongqing Eighth Route Army Office, see *BLJ,*

1:915, table: "Balujun Zhu Chongqing Banshichu Ganbu Minglu" [Directory of Cadres (at the) Eighth Route Army Office in Chongqing].

112. Wu, *Qian Zhiguang Zhuan,* 285; Wu, *Hongse Huarun,* 35.

113. Wu, *Qian Zhiguang Zhuan,* 286; Wu, *Hongse Huarun,* 38. Wang Huasheng had been a branch manager in the Eighth Route Army Office in Chongqing. *BLJ,* 1:915, table: "Balujun Zhu Chongqing Banshichu Ganbu Minglu" [Directory of Cadres (at the) Eighth Route Army Office in Chongqing].

114. Wu, *Qian Zhiguang Zhuan,* 286.

115. Wu, *Hongse Huarun,* 39.

116. Yuan and Le, "Huarun: Zai Dajuezhan Zhong Chuangye," 39.

2. CLOSING THE OPEN DOOR

1.   Mao Zedong, "Lun Renmin Minzhu Zhuanzheng" [On the People's Democratic Dictatorship], June 30, 1949, *MZDXJ,* 4:1473.

2.   Ministry of Foreign Trade, "Guanyu Guoqu Gongzuo Jiben Zongjie Ji Jinhou Gongzuo Zhishi" [Instruction Concerning a Basic Summary of Past and Future Work], August 1953, in Ministry of Foreign Trade General Office, *Duiwai Maoyi Bu Zhongyao Wenjian Huibian, 1949 Nian—1955 Nian* [Compilation of Important Documents of the Ministry of Foreign Trade, 1949–1955], October 1956, Hebei Provincial Archives (hereafter cited as HPA), F752.0-1, 1.

3.   None of the most influential works on CCP foreign relations during the founding of the People's Republic analyzes trade with capitalists in depth. Most focus instead on ideology, security, and politics. See Michael Hunt, *The Genesis of Chinese Communist Foreign Policy* (New York: Columbia University Press, 1996); Chen Jian, *China's Road to the Korean War: The Making of the Sino-American Confrontation* (New York: Columbia University Press, 1994); Dorothy Borg and Waldo Heinrichs, eds., *Uncertain Years: Chinese-American Relations, 1947–1950* (New York: Columbia University Press, 1980). Nancy Tucker has analyzed US trade interests in China during this period, but she is concerned with how American businesses influenced Truman administration policy. See Nancy Bernkopf Tucker, *Patterns in the Dust: Chinese-American Relations and the Recognition Controversy, 1949–1950* (New York: Columbia University Press, 1983). Shu Guang Zhang has examined Chinese trade with capitalists during this period from the Chinese perspective, but his work concerns the effects of sanctions on Chinese trade policy rather than the wider experiences and deeper influences of the Party's trade with capitalists. See Zhang, *Economic Cold War: America's Embargo against China and the Sino-Soviet Alliance 1949–1963* (Washington, DC: Woodrow Wilson Center Press, 2001), especially 50–112. For scholarship on Sino–Soviet trade during the late 1940s and early 1950s, see Shen Zhihua, *ZhongSu Tongmeng de Jingji*

Beijing: 1948–1952 [The Economic Background of the Sino–Soviet Alliance: 1948–1952] (Hong Kong: Chinese University of Hong Kong, Hong Kong Institute of Asia Pacific Studies, 2000), and William C. Kirby, "China's Internationalization in the Early People's Republic: Dreams of a Socialist World Economy," *China Quarterly* 188 (2006): 870–890.

4. Mao Zedong, "Lun Renmin Minzhu Zhuanzheng," in *MZDXJ,* 4:1473.

5. Clayton Gleysteen to Paul Paddock, "Junk Traffic to & from Dairen," July 8, 1948, General Records of the Department of State, US National Archives, College Park, MD (hereafter cited as USNA), Record Group (hereafter cited as RG) 84, Dairen Consulate, Box 1, File 1.

6. Paul Paddock, *China Diary: Crisis Diplomacy in Dairen* (Ames: Iowa State University, 1977), 137.

7. Gary J. Bjorge, *Moving the Enemy: Operational Art in the Chinese PLA's Huai Hai Campaign* (Fort Leavenworth, KS: Combat Studies Institute Press, 2004), 15–16, 43.

8. Mao Zedong, "Jiefang Zhanzheng Di Er Nian de Zhanlüe Fangzhen" [Strategic Policies for the Second Year of the War of Liberation], September 1, 1947, *MZDXJ,* 4:1230.

9. Gu Shiming, Li Qiangui, and Sun Jianping, *Li Fuchun Jingji Sixiang Yanjiu* [Studies in the Economic Thought of Li Fuchun] (Xining: Qinghai Renmin, 1992), 35.

10. Harold M. Tanner, *Where Chiang Kai-shek Lost China: The Liao-Shen Campaign, 1948* (Bloomington: Indiana University Press, 2015), 133.

11. Gu, Li, and Sun, *Li Fuchun Jingji Sixiang Yanjiu,* 35.

12. Li Fuchun, "Guanyu Dongbei Caijing Gongzuo Wenti de Baogao" [Report on Financial and Economic Work Issues in Dongbei], October 30, 1947, in *Li Fuchun Xuanji* [Selected Documents of Li Fuchun] (Beijing: Zhongguo Jihua, 1992), 57.

13. Li Fuchun, "Guanyu Dongbei Caijing Gongzuo Wenti de Baogao," 58.

14. Li Fuchun, 58.

15. Tanner, *Where Chiang Kai-shek Lost China,* 133.

16. Zhu Jianhua et al., eds., *Dongbei Jiefang Qu Caizheng Jingji Shigao, 1945.8–1949.9* [A Financial (and) Economic History of the Northeast China Liberated Areas, August 1945–September 1949] (Harbin: Heilongjiang Renmin, 1987), 339.

17. Mao Zedong, "Zhongguo de Shehui Jingji Xingtai, Jieji Guanxi he Renmin Minzhu Geming" [China's Socioeconomic Forms, Class Relations, and the People's Democratic Revolution], February 15, 1948, in *Mao Zedong Wenji* [The Collected Works of Mao Zedong], 8 vols. (Beijing: Renmin, 2009) (hereafter cited as *MZDWJ*), 5:57.

18. CCP Central Committee, "Zhonggong Zhongyang Gongzuo Weiyuanhui Guanyu Shoufu Shijiazhuang Jingyan de Jieshao" [CCP Central Committee Working Group Introduction Regarding Experiences (Gained from) the Recapture of Shijiazhuang], February 19, 1948, in CCP Central Committee Central Policy Institute, Northeast Bureau, *1948 Nian Yilai de Zhengce Huibian (Shang Ce)* [Compilation of Policies since 1948 (first volume)], HPA, D22-32-1, 96.

19. CCP Central Committee, "Zhonggong Zhongyang Guanyu Chengshi Gongzuo de Zhishi" [CCP Central Committee Instruction on Urban Work], February 1948, in Northeast Bureau, *1948 Nian Yilai de Zhengce Huibian,* 93.

20. CCP Central Committee, "Zhonggong Zhongyang Guanyu Chengshi Gongzuo de Zhishi," 94.

21. Tan Deshan and Bian Yanjun, eds., *Dong Biwu Nianpu* [A Chronology of Dong Biwu] (Beijing: Zhongyang Wenxian, 2007), 309. For Xu's residence in Hong Kong, see Fang Zhuofen, *Huiyi Xu Dixin: Yi Wei Bisheng Jianchi, Tansuo he Kaituo de Makesi Zhuyi Jingji Xuejia* [Remembering Xu Dixin: A Marxist Economist Who Has Persevered, Explored, and Pioneered throughout His Life] (Shenzhen: Haitian, 2002), 183.

22. Fang, *Huiyi Xu Dixin,* 183; Tan and Bian, *Dong Biwu Nianpu,* 309.

23. Jiang Guansheng, *Zhonggong Zai Xianggang (1921–1949)* [The CCP in Hong Kong (1921–1949)], 2 vols. (Hong Kong: Tiandi Tushu, 2011), 1:245.

24. "Provisional Regulations Covering the Control over Overseas Remittance" and "Organizational Regulations of the Oversea Remittance Association," translations of documents from Ka Yan to Li Yee Lam, n.d., TNA, CO 537 / 4815; "The Concessions Obtained by the British and American Merchants Trading in China," translated document, n.d., TNA, CO 537 / 4815.

25. "The Establishment of the Trade Bureau and Its Working Principles," translated document from Ka Yan to Lee Mee Lan, n.d., TNA, CO 537 / 4815.

26. Security Intelligence Far East, GHQ FARELF (Singapore), to Commissioner-General's Office, "South China Bureau (Ho Kai Ming—Documents 2, 3 and 4)," May 19, 1949, TNA, 537 / 4815, n.p.; Governor of Hong Kong to the Secretary of State for the Colonies, "Communist Documents Seized in Hong Kong," May 26, 1949, TNA, CO 537 / 4815, 1.

27. CCP Central Committee, "Zhonggong Dongbei Yangyang [*sic*] Ju Guanyu Baohu Xin Shoufu Chengshi de Zhishi" [CCP Central Northeast Bureau Instruction on Safeguarding Newly Recovered Cities], June 10, 1948, in Northeast Bureau, *1948 Nian Yilai de Zhengce Huibian,* 101.

28. Pang Xianzhi and Zhongyang Wenxian Yanjiushi, eds., *Mao Zedong Nianpu, 1893–1949* [A Chronology of Mao Zedong, 1893–1949], 3 vols. (Beijing: Zhongyang Wenxian, 2002), 3:430.

29. Mao Zedong, "Xin Minzhu Zhuyi Lun" [On New Democracy], January 9, 1940, *MZDXJ,* 2:662–709.

30. Zhou Enlai, "Women de Waijiao Fangzhen he Renwu" [Our Diplomatic Guidelines and Tasks], April 30, 1952, HPA, 1057-8-44, 13.

31. Lu Zhenyang, "Guanyu Xin Zhongguo San Tiao Waijiao Fangzhen de Zhiding" [On the Formulation of New China's Three Foreign Policy Guidelines], *Dang de Wenxian* [Party Literature] 1 (1995): 51. For the directive, see CCP Central Committee, "Zhongyang Guanyu Waijiao Gongzuo de Zhishi" [CCP Central Committee Directive on Foreign Affairs Work], January 19, 1949, in Zhongyang Dang'anguan Bian [Central Archives, ed.], *Zhonggong Zhongyang Wenjian Xuanji (1921–1949)* [Anthology of Chinese Communist Party Central Committee Documents (1921–1949)], 18 vols. (Beijing: Zhonggong Zhongyang Dangxiao, 1992), 18:44–49.

32. Shi Zhe and Li Haiwen, *Zai Lishi Juren Shenbian: Shi Zhe Huiyilu* [At the Side of History's Giants: The Memoir of Shi Zhe] (Beijing: Jiuzhou, 2015), 275.

33. Associated Press, "ECA Halts Flour Dole to China; Pengpu Falls," *Daily Boston Globe,* January 17, 1949, 1–2.

34. A. T. Steele, "Tientsin's Fall Further Hurts Chiang's Cause, but Reds May Find City a Liability until They Can Restore Its Trade," *New York Herald Tribune,* January 17, 1949, 7.

35. Pang Xianzhi and Zhongyang Wenxian Yanjiushi, *Mao Zedong Nianpu,* 3:429.

36. CCP Central Committee, "Zhonggong Zhongyang Guanyu Waijiao Gongzuo de Zhishi," January 19, 1949, Zhongyang Dang'anguan Bian, *Zhonggong Zhongyang Wenjian Xuanji (1921–1949),* 18:45–46.

37. Pang Xianzhi and Zhongyang Wenxian Yanjiushi, *Mao Zedong Nianpu,* 3:440–441.

38. Liu Shaoqi drafted both documents on behalf of the Central Committee. See Liu Chongwen et al., eds., *Liu Shaoqi Nianpu (1898–1969)* [A Chronology of Liu Shaoqi (1898–1969)], 2 vols. (Beijing: Zhongyang Wenxian, 1996), 2:180.

39. CCP Central Committee, "Zhonggong Zhongyang Guanyu Duiwai Maoyi Jiben Fangzhen de Zhishi" [CCP Central Committee Instruction on Basic Foreign Trade Principles], February 16, 1949, *JDYL,* 26:137.

40. "Memorandum of Conversation between Anastas Mikoyan and Mao Zedong," January 31, 1949, translated by Sergey Radchenko, History and Public Policy Program Digital Archive, Archive of the President, Russian Federation (hereafter cited as APRF): F. 39, Op. 1, D. 39, Ll. 7-16, as reprinted in Andrei Ledovskii, Raisa Mirovitskaia, and Vladimir Miasnikov, *Sovetsko-Kitaiskie Otnosheniia,* vol. 5, book 2, 1946–February 1950 (Moscow: Pamiatniki Istoricheskoi Mysli, 2005), 37–43, http://digitalarchive.wilsoncenter.org/document/112436.

41. CCP Central Committee, "Zhonggong Zhongyang Guanyu Duiwai Maoyi Jiben Fangzhen de Zhishi," *JDYL*, 26:137–138.

42. Recipients included the Tianjin and Beiping CCP municipal committees, the North China Bureau, Lin Biao, and Luo Rongheng. The Central Committee also instructed recipients to pass the instructions to central and branch Party offices. CCP Central Committee, "Zhonggong Zhongyang Guanyu Duiwai Maoyi de Jueding" [CCP Central Committee Resolution Concerning Foreign Trade], February 16, 1949, *JDYL*, 26:133.

43. CCP Central Committee, "Zhonggong Zhongyang Guanyu Duiwai Maoyi de Jueding," *JDYL*, 26:133.

44. CCP Central Committee, "Zhonggong Zhongyang Guanyu Duiwai Maoyi de Jueding," *JDYL*, 26:133–136.

45. CCP Central Committee, "Zhonggong Zhongyang Guanyu Duiwai Maoyi he Yinhang Waihui Guanli Deng Wenti gei Tianjin Shiwei Deng de Dianbao" [CCP Central Committee Cable to the Tianjin Municipal Committee and Others Concerning Foreign Trade, Bank Management of Foreign Exchange, Etc.], February 20, 1949, *Dang de Wenxian* 3 (2009): 8.

46. CCP Central Committee, "Zhonggong Zhongyang Dui Tianjin Shi Chengli Duiwai Maoyi Ju de Zhishi" [CCP Central Committee Instruction on the Establishment of the Tianjin Municipal Foreign Trade Bureau], March 1, 1949, *Dang de Wenxian* 3 (2009): 10.

47. S. L. Burdett to Wang Zhenbo, "Memorandum," September 13, 1949, TNA, FO 371 / 75867, F15297/1153/10.

48. Chen Nailiang, *Shangjie Qiren: Chen Zupei* [A Business Talent: Chen Zupei] (Guangzhou: Yangcheng Wanbao, 2000), 72–73.

49. CCP Central Committee, "Zhonggong Qi Jie Er Zhong Quanhui Jueyi" [Resolution of the Second Plenum of the Seventh CCP Central Committee], March 13, 1949, *JDYL*, 26:206.

50. Zhu, *Dongbei Jiefang Qu Caizheng Jingji Shigao*, 410–411.

51. Zhu, 411–412; Tan Tianyu and Yin Xin, "20 Shiji Shang Ban Ye E Shang Zai Hua Qiye Yanjiu—Yi Qiulin Gongsi Wei Li" [A Study of Russian Businessmen in China in the First Half of the Twentieth Century—Taking the Qiulin Company as an Example], *Taiyuan Chengshi Zhiye Jishu Xueyuan Bao* [Journal of the Taiyuan City Professional and Technical College] 103, no. 2 (2010): 86–87.

52. Ren Bishi to Ren Yuanzhi, untitled letter, October 6, 1948, in Zhonggong Zhongyang Wenxian Yanjiushi, *Ren Bishi Shuxin Xuanji* [Selected Letters of Ren Bishi] (Beijing: Zhongyang Wenxian, 2014), 69.

53. Ren Bishi, "Zai Zhonggong Qi Jie Er Zhong Quanhui Shang de Fayan" [Speech during the Second Plenum of the Seventh CCP Central Committee], March 13, 1949, *JDYL*, 26:183.

54. Mao Zedong, "Zai Zhongguo Gongchandang Di Qi Jie Zhongyang Weiyuanhui Di Er Ci Quanti Huiyi Shang de Baogao" [Report during the Second Plenum of the Seventh CCP Central Committee], March 5, 1949, *JDYL,* 26:165.

55. Sheng, *Battling Western Imperialism: Mao, Stalin, and the United States* (Princeton, NJ: Princeton University Press, 1997), 184–185.

56. Sir R. Stevenson (Nanking) to Foreign Office, "Attitude towards Chinese Communists," April 22, 1949, TNA, FO 371 / 75865, F5746/1153/10.

57. *CYNP,* 1:563; Jiang Changqing, "Wo Shi Suanzhang Pai: Chen Yun Jingji Guanli de Zhongyao Fangfa" [I Am the Account Settlement Party: Important Methods of Chen Yun's Economic Management], in *Chen Yun yu Dangdai Zhongguo* [Chen Yun and Contemporary China], ed. Zhu Jiamu (Beijing: Dangdai Zhongguo, 2014), 739.

58. *CYNP,* 1:563.

59. Chen Yun, "Guanyu Tong Zhang Naiqi Deng Ren Tanhua Qingkuang gei Zhou Enlai de Xin" [Letter to Zhou Enlai Regarding Discussions with Zhang Naiqi and Others], May 21, 1949, and "Guanyu Gou Mian Wenti gei Zhou Enlai de Xin" [Letter to Zhou Enlai on the Purchase of Cotton], May 23, 1949, *Chen Yun Wenji* [The Collected Works of Chen Yun], 3 vols. (Beijing: Zhongyang Wenxian, 2005), 1:673–676.

60. Cao Yingwang, "1949 Nian Chen Yun Shouming Zujian Zhongcaiwei" [Chen Yun's 1949 Orders to Form the Finance and Economics Committee], in *Dangshi Bolan* [Party History Exposition], August 18, 2006, http://cpc.people .com.cn/GB/68742/69118/69660/4718608.html. For Stalin's input on the new economic governance structure, see Stalin to Mao Zedong (via Kovalev), untitled cable, May 26, 1949, translated by Sergey Radchenko, History and Public Policy Program Digital Archive, APRF: F. 45, Op. 1, D. 331, L1.73–75, as reprinted in Ledovskii, Mirovitskaia, and Miasnikov, *Sovetsko-Kitaiskie Otnosheniia,* vol. 5, book 2, 136–138, http://digitalarchive.wilsoncenter.org/ document/113370.

61. *CYNP,* 1:565.

62. Chen Yun, "Guanyu Chengli Zhongyang Caizheng Jingji Weiyuanhui" [On the Establishment of the Central Finance and Economics Committee], June 4, 1949, in *Chen Yun Wenxuan* [Selected Works of Chen Yun], 3 vols. (Beijing: Renmin, 1995) (hereafter cited as *CYWX*), 1:388–389.

63. Patrick O'Donovan, "Shanghai Key to Trade Prospects; Communists' Many Problems," *The Scotsman,* May 27, 1949, 5.

64. A. T. Steele, "Shanghai Likely to Set Pattern of U.S. Trade Contact with Reds: City Depends on Oil, Food and Cotton from Allies, Reds Must Weigh Economics vs. Ideology," *New York Herald Tribune,* May 1, 1949, 16.

65. O'Donovan, "Shanghai Key to Trade Prospects," 5.

66. Steele, "Shanghai Likely to Set Pattern," 16.

67. Walter Sullivan, "Reds in Shanghai Issue Trade Rules," *New York Times,* June 9, 1949, 17.

68. A. T. Steele, "Shanghai to Be Proving Ground for Reds' Relations with West," *New York Herald Tribune,* May 27, 1949, 10.

69. Chen Yi, "Rucheng Jilü Shi gei Xinqu Chengshi Renmin de Jianmian Li" [Discipline When Entering the City Is a Gift to the People of the New City], May 10, 1949, in Chen Yi, *Chen Yi Junshi Wenxuan* [Selected Military Documents of Chen Yi] (Beijing: Jiefangjun, 1996), 501.

70. CCP Central Committee, as quoted in Liu Mianyu, ed., *Zhongguo Gongchandang Jingji Zhengce Fazhanshi* [The History of the Development of Chinese Communist Party Economic Policy] (Changsha: Hunan Renmin, 2001), 157–158.

71. CCP Central Committee, "Zhonggong Zhongyang Guanyu Shanghai Deng Shi Ying Ji Sheli Duiwai Maoyi Guanli Chu de Zhishi" [CCP Central Committee Instruction on Immediately Establishing Foreign Trade Management Offices in Shanghai and Other Locations], June 4, 1949, *Dang de Wenxian* 3 (2009): 13.

72. Sullivan, "Reds in Shanghai Issue Trade Rules," 17.

73. Randall Gould, "Shanghai: Communists Release Imports, Cut Red Tape in Move to Restore Trade," *Christian Science Monitor,* June 2, 1949, 9.

74. Interview with Jerome K. Holloway, June 16, 1989, *Frontline Diplomacy: The Foreign Affairs Oral History Collection of the Association for Diplomatic Studies and Training* (Arlington, VA: Association for Diplomatic Studies and Training, 1998), http://hdl.loc.gov/loc.mss/mfdip.2004hol04.

75. United Press, "New Trade Rules Announced," *New York Times,* June 7, 1949, 6.

76. Sullivan, "Reds in Shanghai Issue Trade Rules," 17.

77. Untitled Information Circular Airgram, March 30, 1949, RG 84, Box 11, WNRC (Washington National Record Center, in Suitland), as cited in Sheng, *Battling Western Imperialism,* 181.

78. The Consul General at Peiping (Clubb) to the Secretary of State, April 30, 1949, *FRUS,* 1949, vol. 9, *The Far East: China,* 976–977.

79. Yao Jin, *Yao Yilin Bai Xi Tan* [Yao Yilin: One Hundred Evening Chats] (Beijing: Zhonggong Dangshi, 2008), 176.

80. Stalin to Kovalev, telegram no. 1828, April 19, 1949, translated by Sergey Radchenko, History and Public Policy Program Digital Archive, APRF, F. 45, Op. 1, D. 331, L1. 24–25, and RGASP1, f. 558, op. 11, d. 331, II. 0024-0025, as reprinted in Ledovskii, Mirovitskaia, and Miasnikov, *Sovetsko-Kitaiskie Otnosheniia,* vol. 5, book 2, 120–121, http://digitalarchive.wilsoncenter.org/document/113356; Stalin to Kovalev, untitled cable, April 26, 1949, translated by

Sergey Radchenko, History and Public Policy Program Digital Archive, APRF: F. 45, Op. 1, D. 3331 [*sic,* likely 331], L. 3, as reprinted in Ledovskii, Mirovitskaia, and Miasnikov, *Sovetsko-Kitaiskie Otnosheniia,* vol. 5, book 2, 126, http:// digitalarchive.wilsoncenter.org/document/113357.

81. Michael Hunt, "Mao Tse-tung and the Issue of Accommodation with the United States, 1948–1950," in *Uncertain Years: Chinese-American Relations, 1947–1950,* ed. Dorothy Borg and Waldo Heinrichs (New York: Columbia University Press, 1980), 208–209.

82. Northeast Bureau, "Dongbei Ju Guanyu Duiwai Maoyi Wenti gei Zhongyang de Dianbao" [Northeast Bureau Cable to the Central Committee Regarding Foreign Trade Issues], May 25, 1949, *Dang de Wenxian* 3 (2009): 12.

83. For Zhou's authorship of the Central Committee's response, see Zhonggong Zhongyang Wenxian Yanjiushi, *Zhou Enlai Nianpu, 1898–1949* [A Chronology of Zhou Enlai, 1898–1949] (Beijing: Zhongyang Wenxian, 1990), 829.

84. CCP Central Committee, "Zhonggong Zhongyang Guanyu Dui Ri Maoyi Wenti gei Dongbei Ju de Zhishi" [CCP Central Committee Instruction to the Northeast Bureau Regarding the Issue of Trading with Japan], June 2, 1949, *Dang de Wenxian* 3 (2009): 12.

85. CCP Central Committee, "Zhonggong Zhongyang Guanyu Dui Ri Maoyi Wenti gei Dongbei Ju de Zhishi," 12.

86. Mr. Nathan (Chinese Engineering and Mining Co.) to Mr. Scarlett, untitled letter, March 10, 1949, TNA, FO 371/75865, F3972/1153/10.

87. Leo Wertheimer to Minerals Office of the Export Department, Foreign Trade Office of East China, untitled letter, July 11, 1949, Shanghai Municipal Archives (hereafter cited as SMA), B230-2-671.

88. Paul H. Pearson (US Consulate General, Hong Kong) to Sam Cheong Company, untitled letter, August 3, 1949, USNA, RG 84, Hong Kong Consulate General, General Records, 1936–1963, Box 137, File 510.2.

89. Mr. Han to United States Consulate General, untitled letter, July 26, 1949, USNA, RG 84, Hong Kong Consulate General, General Records, 1936–1963, Box 137, File 510.

90. For Frost's role in arranging meetings with Yao, see L. G. Frost to Yao Yee Lin, Esq., untitled letter, July 15, 1949, TNA, FO 371/75866, F12554/1153/10.

91. *CYNP,* 1:570.

92. *CYNP,* 1:570.

93. R. Stevenson (Nanking) to Foreign Office, "Following Received from Tientsin," August 19, 1949, TNA, FO 371/75866, F12434/1153/10.

94. L. G. Frost to Yap [*sic*] Yee Lin, Esquire, "Visit to Peiping from Shanghai of Mr. John Keswick and Jardines' Specialized Executives. Also Mr Stacey,

Hongkong & Shanghai Banking Corporation," August 11, 1949, TNA, FO 371 / 75867, F15011/1153/10.

95. R. W. Urquhart (Shanghai) to J. C. Hutchison, Esq (Nanjing), untitled letter, November 9, 1949, TNA, FO 371 / 75868, F18655/1153/10.

96. Consul General (Shanghai) to Foreign Office, untitled telegram, November 5, 1949, TNA, FO 371 / 75868, F16653/1153/10.

97. R. W. Urquhart (Shanghai) to J. C. Hutchison, Esq (Nanjing), untitled letter, November 9, 1949.

98. John Keswick [unsigned], untitled memorandum, [n.d.], enclosed within R. W. Urquhart (Shanghai) to J. C. Hutchison, Esq (Nanjing), untitled letter, November 9, 1949.

99. Consul General (Shanghai) to Foreign Office, untitled telegram, November 5, 1949.

100. Hutchison (Nanking) to Foreign Office, untitled telegram, October 29, 1949, TNA, FO 371 / 75868, F16273/1153/10.

101. For a detailed examination of how this "squeeze" unfolded in Shanghai, see Jonathan J. Howlett, "'The British Boss Is Gone and Will Never Return': Communist Takeovers of British Companies in Shanghai (1949–1954)," *Modern Asian Studies* 47, no. 6 (November 2013): 1941–1976.

102. Chen Yun, "Kefu Caizheng Jingji de Yanzhong Kunnan" [Overcome Severe Challenges in Economics and Finance], August 8, 1949, *CYWX,* 2:2.

103. *CYNP,* 1:572. The mass of a quintal, or hundredweight, varies depending on the local base unit used for weight measurement. Chen was probably referring to a British Imperial quintal, which is just over fifty kilograms.

104. Mao Zedong to Rao Shushi, "Bixu Weichi Shanghai, Tongchou Quanju" [Preserve Shanghai, Coordinate the Overall Situation], September 2, 1949, *MZDWJ,* 5:335.

105. Chen, "Kefu Caizheng Jingji de Yanzhong Kunnan," 2.

106. Chinese People's Political Consultative Conference, "Zhongguo Renmin Zhengzhi Xieshang Huiyi Gongtong Gangling" [Common Program of the Chinese People's Political Consultative Conference], September 29, 1949, *JDYL,* 26:768.

107. Chen Yun, "Jianshe Renmin de Xin Haiguan" [The Construction of the People's New Customs Administration], *CYWX,* 2:24.

108. Mao Zedong, "Zhongguo Ren Congci Zhanqi Laile" [Henceforth the Chinese People Have Stood Up], September 21, 1949, *MZDWJ,* 5:343–344.

109. Mikoyan arrived in Xibaipo on January 31, 1949. Shi and Li, *Zai Lishi Juren Shenbian,* 270.

110. "Memorandum of Conversation between Anastas Mikoyan and Zhou Enlai," February 1, 1949, translated by Sergey Radchenko, History and Public Policy

Program Digital Archive, APRF: F. 39, Op. 1, D. 39, Ll. 25–30, as reprinted in Ledovskii, Mirovitskaia, and Miasnikov, *Sovetsko-Kitaiskie Otnosheniia,* vol. 5, book 2, 48–51, http://digitalarchive.wilsoncenter.org/document/113317; "Memorandum of Conversation between Anastas Mikoyan and Mao Zedong," February 6, 1949, translated by Sergey Radchenko, History and Public Policy Program Digital Archive, Ledovskii, Mirovitskaia, and Miasnikov, *Sovetsko-Kitaiskie Otnosheniia,* vol. 5, book 2, 81–87, http://digitalarchive.wilsoncenter.org/document/113352.

111. Mao Zedong, untitled cable to Stalin, January 8, 1949, translated by Sergey Radchenko, History and Public Policy Program Digital Archive, APRF: F. 39, Op. 1, D.37, L.1, Ledovskii, Mirovitskaia, and Miasnikov, *Sovetsko-Kitaiskie Ostnosheniia,* vol. 5, book 2, 10, http://digitalarchive.wilsoncenter.org/document/112232.

112. Mao had broached a US$300 million loan with Mikoyan in Xibaipo on February 6, 1949. "Memorandum of Conversation between Anastas Mikoyan and Mao Zedong," February 6, 1949, History and Public Policy Program Digital Archive, 81–87. For a record of Stalin's conversation with Liu Shaoqi and the CCP delegation on June 27, see "Memorandum of Conversation between Stalin and CCP Delegation," June 27, 1949, translated by Sergey Radchenko, History and Public Policy Program Digital Archive, APRF: F. 45, Op. 1, D.329, L1. 1–7, Ledovskii, Mirovitskaia, and Miasnikov, *Sovetsko-Kitaiskie Otnosheniia,* vol. 5, book 2, 148–151, http://digitalarchive.wilsoncenter.org/document/113380.

113. Zhang Shu Guang, *Beijing's Economic Statecraft during the Cold War, 1949–1991* (Washington, DC: Woodrow Wilson Center Press, 2014), 37.

114. Odd Arne Westad, "Fighting for Friendship: Mao, Stalin, and the Sino-Soviet Treaty of 1950," *Cold War International History Project Bulletin,* no. 8/9 (Winter 1996): 224.

115. Mao Zedong, "Guanyu Zhunbei Dui Su Maoyi Tiaoyue Wenti gei Zhongyang de Baogao" [Report to the CCP Central Committee Concerning Issues Related to Preparations for the Soviet Trade Treaty], December 22, 1949, in Zhonggong Zhongyang Wenxian Yanjiushi, *Jianguo Yilai Mao Zedong Wengao* [Mao Zedong's Manuscripts since the Founding of the People's Republic of China], 13 vols. (Beijing: Zhongyang Wenxian, 1987), 1:197.

116. Chen Yun and Bo Yibo, untitled telegram to Mao Zedong, January 20, 1950, *Chen Yun Wenji,* 2:69–71.

3. THE KOREAN WAR AND THE FIGHT FOR TRADE

1. Mao Zedong, untitled cable, January 2, 1950, in Zhonggong Zhongyang Wenxian Yanjiushi, *Jianguo Yilai Mao Zedong Wengao* [Mao Zedong's Manuscripts since the Founding of the People's Republic of China], 13 vols. (Beijing: Zhongyang Wenxian, 1987), 1:211–212.

2. Mao Zedong, "Guanyu Churukou Maoyi Wenti gei Zhou Enlai de Dianbai" [Telegram to Zhou Enlai Concerning Import / Export Trade Issues], January 7, 1950, in *Jianguo Yilai Mao Zedong Wengao,* 1:218.

3. Shi Zhe and Li Haiwen, *Zai Lishi Juren Shenbian: Shi Zhe Huiyilu* [At the Side of History's Giants: The Memoir of Shi Zhe] (Beijing: Jiuzhou, 2015), 320.

4. I. V. Stalin and Chairman of the Central People's Government of the People's Republic of China, Mao Zedong, untitled record of conversation, December 16, 1949, translated by Danny Rozas, History and Public Policy Program Digital Archive, APRF, fond (f.) 45, opis (op.) 1, delo (d.) 329, listy (ll.) 9–17, http://digitalarchive.wilsoncenter.org/document/111240.

5. Alexander V. Pantsov and Steven I. Levine, *Mao: The Real Story* (New York: Simon & Schuster, 2012), 367–373.

6. Zhang Shu Guang, *Beijing's Economic Statecraft during the Cold War, 1949–1991* (Washington, DC: Woodrow Wilson Center Press, 2014), 37.

7. Lorenz M. Luthi, *The Sino-Soviet Split: Cold War in the Communist World* (Princeton, NJ: Princeton University Press, 2008), 37.

8. "Zhonghua Renmin Gongheguo Zhongyang Renmin Zhengfu Suwei'ai Shehui Zhuyi Gongheguo Lianmeng Zhengfu Guanyu Daikuan gei Zhonghua Renmin Gongheguo de Xieding" [Central People's Government of the People's Republic of China (and the) Union of Soviet Socialist Republics Agreement on Loan to the People's Republic of China], *Renmin Ribao,* February 15, 1950, 2; "Zhong-Su Youhao Hezuo de Xin Shidai" [A New Era of Friendly Cooperation between China and the Soviet Union], *Renmin Ribao,* February 15, 1950, 3.

9. *CYNP,* 2:31–32.

10. Chen Yun, "Caijing Gongzuo Renyuan Yao Tigao Zijuexing" [Finance and Economics Personnel Must Raise (Their Political) Consciousness], February 13, 1950, *CYWX,* 2:60–62.

11. *CYNP,* 2:43.

12. For the problems, see British Chamber of Commerce in Shanghai to the China Association, untitled telegram relayed by Shanghai Consul General to Foreign Office, March 16, 1950, TNA, FO 371 / 83344, FC 1106 / 26, 1.

13. Chen Yun, "Muqian Jingji Xingshi he Tiaozheng Gongshangye, Tiaozheng Shuishou de Cuozhe" [The Current Economic Situation and Policies for Adjusting Business and Taxation], June 15, 1950, *CYWX,* 2:100.

14. Chen Jian, *China's Road to the Korean War: The Making of the Sino-American Confrontation* (New York: Columbia University Press, 1994), 125.

15. For scholarship on the broader significance of the Korean War, see Masuda Hajimu, *Cold War Crucible: The Korean Conflict and the Postwar World* (Cambridge, MA: Harvard University Press, 2015); Sheila Miyoshi Jager, *Brothers at War: The Unending Conflict in Korea* (New York: W. W. Norton,

2013); Steven Casey, ed., *The Korean War at Sixty: New Approaches to the Study of the Korean War* (New York: Routledge, 2012); and William Stueck, ed., *The Korean War in World History* (Lexington: University Press of Kentucky, 2004). For works that emphasize the view from Beijing during the war, see Chen Jian, *Mao's China and the Cold War* (Chapel Hill: University of North Carolina Press, 2001), especially chap. 4, and Chen Jian, *China's Road to the Korean War*. Several scholars have written about the influence of the war on China's economic relations with the capitalist world. These works tend to examine exclusively post-1949 trade policy, however, rather than the impact of the war on deeper CCP trade traditions that began before the founding of the People's Republic of China. See Shu Guang Zhang, *Economic Cold War: America's Embargo against China and the Sino-Soviet Alliance, 1949–1963* (Washington, DC: Woodrow Wilson Center Press, 2001), especially 79–112; Gu Xiaoying, "Jianguo Chuqi de 'Jinyun' he 'Fan Jinyun'" ['Embargo' and 'Anti-Embargo' during the Early PRC (Period)], *Shanghai Daxue Xuebao (Shehui Kexue Ban)* [Journal of Shanghai University (Social Sciences Edition)] 6 (1995): 48–52; Guo Youxin, "1949–1954 Nian Meiguo Dui Xianggang de Jingji Fangwei Zhengce" [US Economic Defense Policies toward Hong Kong, 1949–1954], *Dongbei Shida Xuebao (Zhexue Shehui Kexue Ban)* [Journal of Northeast Normal University (Philosophy and Social Sciences Edition)] 6, no. 188 (2000): 56–61.

16. Gao Feng, *Lin Haiyun Zhuan: Cong Hongjun Zhanshi Dao Gongheguo Haiguan Zongshu Shuzhang, Waimao Bu Buzhang* [A Biography of Lin Haiyun: From Red Army Soldier to (People's) Republic (of China) Customs Director, Director of the Ministry of Foreign Trade] (Beijing: Duiwai Jingji Maoyi Daxue, 2000), 207.

17. Gao, *Lin Haiyun Zhuan,* 207.

18. Gao, 208.

19. Gao, 209.

20. Zhongguo Zhonggong Dangshi Renwu Yanjiu Hui, *Zhonggong Dangshi Renwu Zhuan* [Biographies from Chinese Communist Party History], 89 vols. (Beijing: Zhongguo Renmin Daxue, 2017), 45:229.

21. Gao, *Lin Haiyun Zhuan,* 209. For biographical information on Lei Renmin and Sha Qianli, see C. D. W. O'Neill to Selwyn Lloyd, "China: Personalities Report for 1957," June 3, 1957, 18, 30, TNA, FO 371 / 127263, FC 1012 / 1.

22. For Soviet influences on the Ministry of Trade, see Gao, *Lin Haiyun Zhuan,* 209.

23. Gao, 210.

24. Central People's Government Ministry of Trade, "Zhongyang Renmin Zhengfu Maoyi Bu Guowai Maoyi Si Gongzuo Tiaoli" [Central People's Government Ministry of Trade Foreign Trade Division Work Regulations], 1951, in Zhongguo Shehui Kexueyuan and Zhongyang Dang'anguan, comps., *Zhonghua Renmin Gongheguo Jingji Dang'an Ziliao Xuanbian, 1949–1952,*

Duiwai Maoyi Juan [Selection of Materials from the PRC Economic Archives, 1949–1952, Foreign Trade Volume] (Beijing: Jingji Guanli, 1994) (hereafter cited as *DWMYJ, 1949–1952*), 81. The Office of European and American Trade coordinated trade with Australia.

25. Central Ministry of Trade Foreign Trade Division, "Maoyi Guanli Chu Banshi Xize" [Trade Management Office Work Rules and Regulations], 1951, *DWMYJ, 1949–1952,* 93.

26. Central People's Government Ministry of Trade, "Zhongyang Renmin Zhengfu Maoyi Bu Guowai Maoyi Si Gongzuo Tiaoli," 80.

27. Central People's Government Ministry of Trade, "Zhongyang Renmin Zhengfu Maoyi Bu Guowai Maoyi Si Gongzuo Tiaoli," 82.

28. Gao, *Lin Haiyun Zhuan,* 211, 213.

29. Gao, 213.

30. China International Trade Association, Shanghai Branch, "Zhongguo Guoji Maoyi Yanjiu Hui Shanghai Fenhui Choubeihui Gongzuo Baogao" [China International Trade Association Shanghai Branch Preparatory Meeting Work Report], n.d. [1952], SMA, B171-1-3.

31. Charles E. Egan, "US Forbids Its Ships 'Anywhere' to Carry Key Goods to Red Areas," *New York Times,* December 8, 1950, 1.

32. For the US politics surrounding the embargo, see Kailai Huang, "American Business and the China Trade Embargo in the 1950s," *Essays in Economic and Business History* 19 (2001): 33–48; Zhang, *Economic Cold War,* 17–48.

33. United States Congress, *Technology and East-West Trade* (Washington, DC: Congress of the United States, Office of Technology Assessment, 1979), 113, 153.

34. For the logic behind the creation of CHINCOM, see Jeffrey A. Engel, "Of Fat and Thin Communists: Diplomacy and Philosophy in Western Economic Warfare Strategies toward China (and Tyrants, Broadly)," *Diplomatic History* 29, no. 3 (2005): 445–474.

35. International Cooperation Administration, "East-West Trade Controls" (statement prepared for delivery by Walter S. DeLany [Deputy Director for Mutual Defense Assistance Control] before the Subcommittee on Foreign Economic Policy of the Joint Committee on the Economic Report, 84th US Congress, November 16, 1955), General CIA Records, Freedom of Information Act Electronic Reading Room, CIA- RDP61S00527A000100180167-4, 5.

36. Ye Jianying to Zhou Enlai, untitled telegram, August 19, 1950, Guangdong Provincial Archive, 204-1-247; Zhou Enlai and Bo Yibo to Ye Jianying and Fang Fang, untitled telegram, August 27, 1950, Guangdong Provincial Archive, 204-1-247, both as cited in Zhang, *Beijing's Economic Statecraft during the Cold War,* 26.

37. Zhou Enlai and Bo Yibo to Ye Jianying and Fang Fang, untitled telegram, August 27, 1950, Guangdong Provincial Archive, 204-1-247, as cited in Zhang, *Beijing's Economic Statecraft during the Cold War,* 26.

38. US Consulate Hong Kong to the Department of State, "Hong Kong's Trade with Communist Controlled Areas (Period December 4–9, 1950)," January 5, 1951, USNA, RG 84, Records Re Hong Kong Trade with Communist Controlled Areas, 1950–1954, Box 1, File 1, 2.

39. *CYNP,* 2:74–75.

40. Central Finance and Economic Committee, "Meidi Duiwo Jingji Fengsuo Xin Zhengce Ji Wo Tiyi Zhi Duice" [The American Imperialists' New Economic Blockade against Us and Our Proposed Countermeasures], December 15, 1950, HPA, 855-1-20-12, [n.p.].

41. Zhang, *Economic Cold War,* especially 79–112; Wu et al., *Hongse Huarun* [Red China Resources] (Beijing: Zhonghua, 2010), 179.

42. Wu et al., *Hongse Huarun,* 179.

43. CFEC, "Zhongcaiwei Guanyu Chuli Bei Dongjie Meihui de Jueding" [CFEC Decision Regarding the Handling of Frozen US Currency], June 7, 1952, in Zhongguo Shehui Kexueyuan and Zhongyang Dang'anguan, comps., *Zhonghua Renmin Gongheguo Jingji Dang'an Ziliao Xuanbian, 1953–1957, Jinrong Juan* [Selection of Materials from the PRC Economic Archives, 1953–1957, Finance Volume] (Beijing: Zhongguo Wujia, 2000) (hereafter cited as *JRJ*), 943. For internal CCP import statistics in 1950, see Ministry of Foreign Trade, *Duiwai Maoyi Youguan Ziliao Huibian, Di Yi Fen Ce* [Compilation of Information on Foreign Trade, volume 1], May 1956, Fujian Provincial Archives (hereafter cited as FPA), quanzong ziliao, mulu 35, [8], figure 6.

44. Ministry of Trade, "Guanyu Chukou Guanli Ji Xiang Yuanze de Zhishi" [Instruction on Several Principles of Export Management], October 7, 1950, in Ministry of Foreign Trade General Office, *Duiwai Maoyi Bu Zhongyao Wenjian Huibian, 1949 Nian—1955 Nian* [Compilation of Important Documents of the Ministry of Foreign Trade, 1949–1955], October 1956, HPA, F752.0-1, 170.

45. Ministry of Trade, "Guanyu Chukou Guanli Ji Xiang Yuanze de Zhishi," 170.

46. Ministry of Trade, 170.

47. CFEC, "Zhongcaiwei Dui Zhongyang Maoyi Bu Baogao de Pifu" [Central Finance and Economics Committee Reply to Central Ministry of Trade Report], November 6, 1950, *DWMYJ, 1949–1952,* 103.

48. Fang Zhong, "Gongheguo Jingji Fengyun Zhong de Chen Yun yu Yao Yilin" [Chen Yun and Yao Yilin amid Economic Instability in the Republic], *Jiang Huai Wenshi* [Jianghuai Culture History] 5 (2012): 48.

49. China Committee for the Promotion of International Trade, "Guanyu Zhaoji Gedi Zhongguo Guoji Maoyi Yanjiu Hui Gongzuo Huiyi de Jihua" [Regarding the Plan to Convene a Work Meeting of China International Trade Association (Branches) from Various Regions], March 20, 1953, *DWMYJ, 1949–1952*, 126.

50. China Committee for the Promotion of International Trade, "Guanyu Zhaoji Gedi Zhongguo Guoji Maoyi Yanjiu Hui Gongzuo Huiyi de Jihua," 126–127.

51. China International Trade Association, "Zhongguo Guoji Maoyi Yanjiuhui Zhangcheng: Jianyi Xiuzheng Cao'an" [China International Trade Association Constitution: Draft Suggested Amendments], n.d. [1951], SMA, B171-1-1.

52. China International Trade Association, "Zhongguo Guoji Maoyi Yanjiuhui Zhangcheng: Jianyi Xiuzheng Cao'an," SMA, B171-1-1.

53. China International Trade Association, SMA, B171-1-1.

54. China Committee for the Promotion of International Trade, "Ge Di Fen (Zhi) Hui Huiyuan Tongji" [Membership Statistics for Branches (Divisions) in Various Regions], March 20, 1953, *DWMYJ, 1949–1952,* 128.

55. China International Trade Association, "Zhongguo Guoji Maoyi Yanjiu Hui Shanghai Fenhui Choubei Weiyuan Hui Mingdan" [China International Trade Association Shanghai Branch Preparatory Committee (Member) List], n.d. [likely September 1951], SMA, B171-1-4.

56. General Administration of Customs (GAC), "Haiguan Tongji Nianbao 1951 Nian Juan" [Customs Statistics Annual Report, 1951 volume], 1951, *DWMYJ, 1949–1952,* 622–623.

57. Ministry of Trade, "San Nian Lai Woguo Dui Dongnan Ya Ge Guo Maoyi Jiankuang Ji Xianggang Zhuankou Wenti" [Briefing on PRC Trade with Southeast Asian Countries during the Past Three Years and the Hong Kong Re-export Problem], July 1952, *DWMYJ, 1949–1952,* 625.

58. Wang Hongxu, "Lei Renmin yu Mosike Guoji Jingji Huiyi" [Lei Renmin and the Moscow International Economic Conference], *Bai Nian Chao* [Hundred Year Tide] 4 (2001): 41–42.

59. South China Finance Committee, "Huanan Caiwei Guanyu Chengli Duiwai Maoyi Lianhe Banshichu" [South China Finance Committee Resolution to Establish Joint Foreign Trade Offices], Guangdong Provincial Archive, 206-1-3-48, as cited in Ouyang Xiang, "20 Shiji 50 Niandai Xin Zhongguo Zai Xiang'Ao Diqu Kaizhan de Shichang Zhengduo Zhan" [The Struggle for Markets Launched by New China in Hong Kong and Macao during the 1950s], *Dang de Wenxian* 2 (2014): 72.

60. The Ministry of Trade issued the instructions on August 19, 1950. See Zhang, *Economic Cold War,* 81–82.

61. CIA, "Smuggling Trade from Hong Kong to Communist China via Macao," October 23, 1951, General CIA Records, Freedom of Information Act Electronic Reading Room, CIA-RDP82-00457R008900230003-0, 1.

62. CIA, "Chinese Communist Economic Activities, Hong Kong and Macao," October 4, 1951, General CIA Records, Freedom of Information Act Electronic Reading Room, CIA-RDP82-00457R008800530016-4, 1.

63. CIA, "1. Procurement of War Materials for Communist China[;] 2. Leftist Labor in Hong Kong," August 31, 1951, General CIA Records, Freedom of Information Act Electronic Reading Room, CIA-RDP82-00457R008500420001-5, 1.

64. CIA, "Chinese Communist Economic Activities, Hong Kong and Macao," October 4, 1951, 1-2.

65. CIA, "Smuggling from Hong Kong to Communist China," December 10, 1951, General CIA Records, Freedom of Information Act Electronic Reading Room, CIA-RDP82-00457R009400070006-9.

66. CIA, "Chinese Communist Government Opium Regulation," May 9, 1951, General CIA Records, Freedom of Information Act Electronic Reading Room, CIA-RDP82-00457R007500390013-0, 1-2.

67. Governor of Hong Kong to the Secretary of State for the Colonies, untitled Savingram, September 11, 1951, TNA, FO 371 / 92385, FC 1905 / 9.

68. H. P. Hall to N. C. C. Trench, untitled letter, September 27, 1951, TNA, FO 371 / 92385, FC 1905 / 9.

69. Washington (Department of Commerce) to Hong Kong Consulate, untitled telegram, November 18, 1949, USNA, RG 84, Records Re Hong Kong Trade with Communist Controlled Areas, 1950–1954, Box 1, File 1.

70. For examples, see USNA, RG 84, Records Re Hong Kong Trade with Communist Controlled Areas, 1950–1954, Box 1, File 1.

71. US Consulate, "Hong Kong's Trade with Communist Controlled Areas (Period December 4–9, 1950)," January 5, 1951, USNA, RG 84, Records Re Hong Kong Trade with Communist Controlled Areas, 1950–1954, Box 1, File 1; US Consulate, "Hong Kong's Trade with Communist Controlled Areas (Period March 25–31, 1951)," April 19, 1951, USNA, RG 84, Records Re Hong Kong Trade with Communist Controlled Areas, 1950–1954, Box 1, File 2.

72. US Consulate (Rankin) to Secretary of State, untitled telegram, November 9, 1949, USNA, RG 84, Records Re Hong Kong Trade with Communist Controlled Areas, 1950–1954, Box 1, File 1.

73. US Consulate Hong Kong (Rankin) to the Secretary of State, untitled telegram, February 21, 1950, USNA, RG 84, Records Re Hong Kong Trade with Communist Controlled Areas, 1950–1954, Box 1, File 1.

74. Hong Kong Colonial Secretariat (Nicoll) to Colonial Office (Sidebotham), untitled letter, April 23, 1951, TNA, FO 371/92385, FC 1905/6.

75. Wu et al., *Hongse Huarun,* 180, 183.

76. [Ministry of Trade,] "Zhonghua Renmin Gonghe Guo Zhu Ouzhou Shangwu Daibiao Chu Zuzhi yu Gongzuo Zanxing Tiaoli (Cao'an)" [Provisional Regulations on the Organization and Work of People's Republic of China Commercial Representation Offices in Europe (Draft)], 1951, *DWMYJ, 1949–1952,* 87.

77. "Zhonghua Renmin Gonghe Guo Zhu Ouzhou Shangwu Daibiao Chu Zuzhi yu Gongzuo Zanxing Tiaoli (Cao'an)," 88–89

78. "Zhonghua Renmin Gonghe Guo Zhu Ouzhou Shangwu Daibiao Chu Zuzhi yu Gongzuo Zanxing Tiaoli (Cao'an)," 87–88.

79. "Zhonghua Renmin Gonghe Guo Zhu Ouzhou Shangwu Daibiao Chu Zuzhi yu Gongzuo Zanxing Tiaoli (Cao'an)," 89.

80. Committee for the Promotion of International Trade, *International Economic Conference in Moscow, April 3–12, 1952* (Moscow: Committee for the Promotion of International Trade, 1952), 9.

81. During a February 1951 meeting in Berlin, members of the Soviet-backed World Peace Council had also proposed a conference of technical experts, economists, industrialists, agricultural specialists, and businesspeople from socialist and capitalist countries to discuss trade. The Council planned to hold the conference in Moscow in October 1951, but it never materialized. See Wang, "Lei Renmin yu Mosike de Guoji Jingji Huiyi," 42. For the World Peace Council and its antinuclear campaign during the early Cold War, see Lawrence S. Wittner, *The Struggle against the Bomb: A History of the World Nuclear Disarmament Movement, 1954–1970,* vol. 2, *Resisting the Bomb* (Stanford, CA: Stanford University Press, 1997), 307–317.

82. Wang, "Lei Renmin yu Mosike de Guoji Jingji Huiyi," 43.

83. Wang, 43. For Ji Chaoding's training in the United States, see Gregory S. Lewis, "Shades of Red and White: The Life and Political Career of Ji Chaoding, 1903–1963" (PhD diss., Arizona State University, 1999), 46.

84. Wang, "Lei Renmin yu Mosike de Guoji Jingji Huiyi," 43.

85. Lewis, "Shades of Red and White," 243.

86. Wang Jinyuan and Shao Xianli, "Lü Dang Da Ren[,] Bu Ru Shiming: Lei Renmin Zai Jianshe Xin Zhongguo de Gangwei Shang" [Assuming Major Roles Time and Again(,) Never Dishonoring the Mission: Lei Renmin at Post in the Building of New China], *Dangshi Wenhui* [Corpus of Party History] 7 (2004): 26.

87. Wang and Shao, "Lü Dang Da Ren[,] Bu Ru Shiming," 26.

88. C. D. W. O'Neill to Selwyn Lloyd, "China: Personalities Report for 1957," June 3, 1957, TNA, FO 371/127263, FC 1012/1, 18.

89. For a concise analysis of the Three and Five Anti Campaigns, see Karl Gerth, *Unending Capitalism: How Consumerism Negated China's Communist Revolution* (Cambridge: Cambridge University Press, 2020), 58–64.

90. Wang, "Lei Renmin yu Mosike de Guoji Jingji Huiyi," 42.

91. Wang and Shao, "Lü Dang Da Ren[,] Bu Ru Shiming," 26.

92. Wang Jinyuan and Shao Xianli have written that Zhou selected Lei Renmin as Nan Hanchen's deputy for the conference and Ji Chaoding as the group secretary. See Wang and Shao, "Lü Dang Da Ren[,] Bu Ru Shiming," 26. But Gregory Lewis has argued, based on interviews with Chinese officials, that Zhou approved a delegation list that identified Ji Chaoding as Nan's second-in-command, not Lei, a decision that rankled Lei for years after the conference. See Lewis, "Shades of Red and White," 242, 326. Contemporaneous CIA reporting claimed Ji was the de facto head of the delegation and that he took orders from Zhang Wentian, Beijing's ambassador in Moscow. CIA, "Chinese Communist Trade Agreement at Moscow Economic Conference," May 6, 1952, General CIA Records, Freedom of Information Act Electronic Reading Room, CIA-RDP82-00457R01190010006-5.

93. Wang and Shao, "Lü Dang Da Ren[,] Bu Ru Shiming," 26.

94. Wang and Shao, 26.

95. Wang and Shao, 26–27.

96. Zhang Peisen, ed., *Zhang Wentian Nianpu* [A Chronology of Zhang Wentian], 2 vols. (Beijing: Zhonggong Dangshi, 2000), 2:928.

97. Wang, "Lei Renmin yu Mosike de Guoji Jingji Huiyi," 44.

98. Special to the *New York Times,* "Economic Parley Opens in Moscow; 3 U.S. Businessmen There—U.N. Touches Seen in Press and Translation Systems," *New York Times,* April 4, 1952, 9.

99. "Conference Diary," *International Economic Conference Information Bulletin,* no. 7 (April 10, 1952), CIA, "World Economic Conference Information Bulletins," June 20, 1952, General CIA Records, CIA-RDP83-00415R012000020001-4, 1, 4–5. The CIA collected and distributed copies of the *International Economic Conference Information Bulletin* to US government officials.

100. United Press, "Moscow Economic Conclave Called 'Spurious' by Achcson," *Washington Post,* March 15, 1952, 3.

101. Harry Schwartz, "Many in U.S. Spurn Moscow Talk Bids," *New York Times,* March 16, 1952, 24; C. L. Sulzberger, "Moscow's Parley on Trade Shunned," *New York Times,* April 3, 1952, 11.

102. Schwartz, "Many in U.S. Spurn Moscow Talk Bids," 24.

103. Lei Renmin, untitled remarks, April 7, 1952, Committee for the Promotion of International Trade, *International Economic Conference in Moscow,* 115.

104. Deputy Director (Plans) to the Director of Central Intelligence, "PSB [Psychological Strategy Board] Panel on Psychological Aspects of East-West Trade," April 23, 1952, General CIA Records, CIA-RDP80R01731R0033 00070004-9.

105. Nan Hanchen, untitled remarks, April 4, 1952, Committee for the Promotion of International Trade, *International Economic Conference in Moscow,* 47.

106. Lei Renmin, untitled remarks, April 7, 1952, Committee for the Promotion of International Trade, *International Economic Conference in Moscow,* 113.

107. Wang and Shao, "Lü Dang Da Ren[,] Bu Ru Shiming," 27.

108. Chinese Delegation (to the Moscow Conference), "Canjia Mosike Guoji Jingji Huiyi Maoyi Gongzuo de Zongjie Baogao" [Summary Report on Trade Work during Attendance at the Moscow International Economic Conference], 1952, *DWMYJ, 1949–1952,* 616.

109. Shen Jueren et al., *Dangdai Zhongguo Duiwai Maoyi* [Contemporary Chinese Foreign Trade], 2 vols. (Beijing: Dangdai Zhongguo, 1992), 1:402.

110. Xinhua, "Nan Hanchen Tan Guoji Jingji Huiyi de Chengjiu; Ge Guo Daibiao Yizhi Renwei Yinggai Quxiao Fengsuo yu Jinyun Jinliang Fazhan Guoji Maoyi; Wo yu Ying Fa Deng Guo Shangye Jia Qianding Jinchukou yu Yi Liu Qian Wan Mei Yuan de Xieding" [Nan Hanchen Discusses the Successes of the International Economic Conference; Country Delegates Unanimously Believe Embargoes and Blockades Should Be Canceled [to] Develop International Trade as Much as Possible; Our Country Signs Import–Export Contracts with Businessmen from England, France, and Other Countries Worth over 160 Million US Dollars], *Renmin Ribao,* April 16, 1952, 1.

111. Xinhua, "Nan Hanchen Tan Guoji Jingji Huiyi de Chengjiu," 1.

112. Renmin Ribao Shelun, "Jinian 'Wuyi' Guoji Laodong Jie Wei Shijie Chijiu Heping Er Fendou" [Remember "May First" International Labor Day, Struggle for Lasting International Peace], *Renmin Ribao,* May 1, 1952, 1.

113. GAC, "Yi Jiu Wu Er Nian Di Er Ji Dui Ziben Zhuyi Guojia Maoyi Gaikuang" [Overview of Trade with Capitalist Nations during the Second Quarter of 1952], July 1952, *DWMYJ, 1949–1952,* 613–614.

114. GAC, "Yi Jiu Wu Er Nian Di Er Ji Dui Ziben Zhuyi Guojia Maoyi Gaikuang," 614.

115. Central Ministry of Trade, "Yi Jiu Wu Er Nian Shangban Nian Maoyi Gongzuo Baogao" [Report on Trade Work during the Second Half of 1952], August 28, 1952, HPA, 684-1-549-27.

116. Ministry of Trade (forwarded by the CFEC), "Shi Yi, Shi Er Yue Fen Gongzuo Baogao" [Work Report for November and December], March 4, 1953, *DWMYJ, 1949–1952,* 616.

117. Zhou Enlai, "Women de Waijiao Fangzhen he Renwu" [Our Diplomatic Guidelines and Tasks], April 30, 1952, HPA, 1057-8-44, 16–17.

118. Zhou Enlai, "Women de Waijiao Fangzhen he Renwu," 17.

119. Committee for the Promotion of International Trade, "Establishment of the Committee for the Promotion of International Trade," in *International Economic Conference in Moscow*, 307.

120. Wang Jinyuan and Shao Xianli identify the founding date of the Chinese Committee for the Promotion of International Trade as May 24, 1952. See Wang and Shao, "Lü Dang Da Ren[,] Bu Ru Shiming," 27. This is most likely a mistake. Official Chinese sources identify the founding date as May 4. See Ministry of Foreign Trade General Office, "Guanyu Duiwai Maoyi Ruogan Wenti he Woguo Shehui Zhuyi Chengjiu Fangmian de Cankao Ziliao (1960 Nian Buchong Ben)" [Reference Materials on Various Issues in China's Foreign Trade and Aspects of China's Socialist Achievements (1960 supplementary edition)], 1960, *DWMYJ, 1949–1952*, 129.

121. China Committee for the Promotion of International Trade, "Guanyu Zhaoji Gedi Zhongguo Guoji Maoyi Yanjiu Hui Gongzuo Huiyi de Jihua," 127.

122. China International Trade Association, Shanghai Branch, "Zhongguo Guoji Maoyi Yanjiuhui Shanghai Fenhui Choubeihui Gongzuo Baogao" [China International Trade Association Shanghai Branch Preparatory Meeting Work Report], n.d. [1952], SMA, B171-1-3.

123. China Committee for the Promotion of International Trade, "Guanyu Guoji Jingji Yanjiu Jinxing Fengong de Yijian" [Suggestions on the Division of Labor in International Economics Research], July 4, 1952, *DWMYJ, 1949–1952*, 129.

124. China Committee for the Promotion of International Trade, "Guanyu Guoji Jingji Yanjiu Jinxing Fengong de Yijian," 129–130.

125. China Committee for the Promotion of International Trade, "Zhongguo Guoji Maoyi Cujin Weiyuanhui Liang Nian Lai de Gongzuo" [The Work of the China Committee for the Promotion of International Trade during the Past Two Years], 1954, *DWMYJ, 1949–1952*, 132.

126. Hua-Yu Li, "Mao, Stalin, and Changing Course: Building Socialism in China, 1948–1953," (PhD diss., Columbia University, 1997), 143.

127. Su Shangyao and Han Wenwei, *Zhonghua Renmin Gongheguo Zhongyang Zhengfu Jiguan, 1949–1990 Nian* [Central Government Agencies of the People's Republic of China, 1949–1990] (Beijing: Jingji Kexue, 1993), 405.

128. The Ministry of Foreign Trade assumed control of China Resources in October 1952. Prior to that, the company reported to the Central Committee's General Office. See Wu et al., *Hongse Huarun*, 7.

129. World Bank, *China: Socialist Economic Development,* vol. 9, *Annex H: External Trade and Finance,* Report 3391-CHA (Washington, DC: World Bank Group, 1981), 18–19.

130. Kenneth Wang, "Foreign Trade Policy and Apparatus of the People's Republic of China," *Law and Contemporary Problems* 38, no. 2 (1973), 193–194.

131. For a full list of China's foreign trade corporations by the late 1950s, including their lines and locations, see China Committee for the Promotion of International Trade, *Foreign Trade of the People's Republic of China* 3 (September 1959) [n.p.]. For the original foreign trade corporations and their founding dates, see "Guoying Duiwai Maoyi Zhuanye Gongsi Chengli Qingkuang" [The Establishment of State-Owned Foreign Trade Companies], 1951, *DWMYJ, 1949–1952,* 133–134.

132. Wang, "Lei Renmin yu Mosike de Guoji Jingji Huiyi," 42; Wang and Shao, "Lü Dang Da Ren[,] Bu Ru Shiming," 27.

133. CIA, "China National Import Export Corporation," May 23, 1956, General CIA Records, Freedom of Information Act Electronic Reading Room, CIA-RDP79T01049A001600310002-8, 1.

134. Wang, "Lei Renmin yu Mosike de Guoji Jingji Huiyi," 42.

135. Wang, 47.

136. British Council for the Promotion of International Trade, *China's Foreign Trade: An Analysis and Guide for the British Business Man* (London: British Council for the Promotion of International Trade, 1954), 51.

137. British Council for the Promotion of International Trade, *China's Foreign Trade,* 55.

138. CIA, "China National Import Export Corporation," May 23, 1956, 2.

139. CIA, May 23, 1956, 3.

4. COMMERCE IN THE MAKING OF "PEACEFUL COEXISTENCE"

1.   On the Korean armistice as a catalyst for the protracted militarization of the Korean Peninsula and the region, see Steven Lee, "The Korean Armistice and the End of Peace: The US-UN Coalition and the Dynamics of War-Making in Korea, 1953–1976," *Journal of Korean Studies* 18, no. 2 (2013): 183–224.

2.   Korean War Armistice Agreement, July 27, 1953, Article IV, 25, United Nations Peace Agreements Database, https://peacemaker.un.org/sites/peacemaker.un.org/files/KP%2BKR_530727_AgreementConcerningMilitaryArmistice.pdf.

3.   Zhou Enlai, "Preliminary Opinions on the Assessment of and Preparation for the Geneva Conference," March 2, 1954, translated by Chen Zhihong, History and Public Policy Program Digital Archive, PRC FMA (Foreign

Ministry Archives of the People's Republic of China; hereafter cited as FMA) 206-Y0054, http://digitalarchive.wilsoncenter.org/document/111963.

4. John Foster Dulles, "Text of Report by Dulles to Nation on Four-Power Conference in Berlin," *New York Times,* February 25, 1954, 2.

5. For Dulles's suggestion that the PRC was simply "evil," see John F. Dulles, "Statement at Berlin," January 26, 1954, in US Department of State Publication Services Division, "Four Power Discussions at Berlin," *Department of State Bulletin* 30, no. 763, Publication 5369, February 8, 1954, 181. For charges that the Geneva Conference was a "Far Eastern Munich," see Gordon H. Chang, *Friends and Enemies: The United States, China, and the Soviet Union, 1949–1972* (Stanford, CA: Stanford University Press, 1990), 101.

6. Shu Guang Zhang, "Constructing 'Peaceful Coexistence': China's Diplomacy toward the Geneva and Bandung Conferences, 1954–1956," *Cold War History* 7, no. 4 (November 2007): 509–528; Tao Wang, "Neutralizing Indochina: The 1954 Geneva Conference and China's Efforts to Isolate the United States," *Journal of Cold War Studies* 19, no. 2 (Spring 2017): 3–42; Pei Jianzhang, *Zhonghua Renmin Gongheguo Waijoshi* [Diplomatic History of the People's Republic of China] (Beijing: Shijie Zhishi, 1994), 220–230; Zhai Qiang, "China and the Geneva Conference of 1954," *China Quarterly* 129 (1992): 103–122; Kuo-kang Shao, "Zhou Enlai's Diplomacy and the Neutralization of Indo-China, 1954–1955," *China Quarterly* 107 (1986): 483–504; Chen Jian, *Mao's China and the Cold War* (Chapel Hill: University of North Carolina Press, 2001), 138–144; and Shi Zhe and Li Haiwen, *Zai Lishi Juren Shenbian: Shi Zhe Huiyilu* [At the Side of History's Giants: The Memoir of Shi Zhe] (Beijing: Jiuzhou, 2015), 384–405.

7. Xiong Huayuan, *Zhou Enlai Chudeng Shijie Wutai* [Zhou Enlai Debuts on the World Stage] (Shenyang: Liaoning Renmin, 1999), 8.

8. Zhou, "Preliminary Opinions on the Assessment of and Preparation for the Geneva Conference," March 2, 1954.

9. Shi and Li, *Zai Lishi Juren Shenbian,* 390.

10. Wang Jinyuan and Shao Xianli, "Lü Dang Da Ren[,] Bu Ru Shiming: Lei Renmin Zai Jianshe Xin Zhongguo de Gangwei Shang" [Assuming Major Roles Time and Again(,) Never Dishonoring the Mission: Lei Renmin at Post in the Building New China], *Dangshi Wenhui* 7 (2004): 27. For the PRC delegation list, see "Zhonghua Renmin Gongheguo Canjia Rineiwa Huiyi Daibiao Tuan Mingdan" [List of Names from People's Republic of China's Geneva Conference Delegation], n.d., FMA 206-Y0001, in Zhonghua Renmin Gongheguo Waijiao Bu Dang'anguan, ed., *Zhonghua Renmin Gongheguo Waijiao Dang'an Xuanbian (di yi ji), 1954 Nian Rineiwa Huiyi* [Selections from the People's Republic of China Ministry of Foreign Affairs Archive (first collection), the Geneva Conference of 1954] (Beijing: Shijie Zhishi, 2006), 15.

11. Barbara Barnouin and Yu Changgen, *Zhou Enlai: A Political Life* (Hong Kong: Chinese University Press, 2006), 152.

12. Wang and Shao, "Lü Dang Da Ren[,] Bu Ru Shiming," 27.

13. Zhou Enlai, "Guanyu Waijiao Wenti de Baogao" [Report on Diplomatic Issues], August 12, 1954, FPA, 101-5-542, 3.

14. Lei Renmin, "Huiyi Zhou Zongli Duiwai Maoyi Gongzuo de Guanhuai he Zhidao" [Recalling the Care and Guidance in Premier Zhou's Foreign Trade Work], in *Bujin de Sinian* [Endless Longing], ed. Zhonggong Zhongyang Wenxian Yanjiushi (Beijing: Zhongyang Wenxian, 1987), 250.

15. Lei, "Huiyi Zhou Zongli Duiwai Maoyi Gongzuo de Guanhuai he Zhidao," 250; Zhou, "Guanyu Waijiao Wenti de Baogao," August 12, 1954, FPA, 101-5-542, 1.

16. Peter Tennant, "Talks on Trade with China, May 6th–7th, 1954," n.d., TNA, FO 371 / 110289, folder 3, FC 1151 / 55, 1; Chu Siyi, "Lei Renmin Huijian Du Weilian, Tai Luntuo Tanhua Jilu" [Transcript of Meeting between Lei Renmin, Trevelyan, and Tennant], May 6, 1954, FMA 206-C053, in *Zhonghua Renmin Gongheguo Waijiao Dang'an Xuanbian (di yi ji), 1954 Nian Rineiwa Huiyi,* 408–410.

17. Tennant, "Talks on Trade with China, May 6th–7th, 1954," n.d., 1.

18. Chu Siyi, "Lei Renmin Huijian Du Weilian, Tai Luntuo Tanhua Jilu," May 6, 1954, 408–409.

19. Chu Siyi, 409.

20. Tennant, "Talks on Trade with China, May 6th—7th, 1954," n.d., 3.

21. Tennant, 3, 6.

22. Peter Tennant, "Report on Trade Talks with Chinese in Geneva, May 26–28, 1954," n.d., TNA, FO 371 / 110289, folder 3, FC 1151 / 72, 1, 3–4.

23. Tennant, "Report on Trade Talks with Chinese in Geneva, May 26–28, 1954," n.d., 4.

24. Tennant, "Talks on Trade with China, May 6th–7th, 1954," n.d., 4–5.

25. Humphrey Trevelyan (Geneva) to Foreign Office (London), untitled dispatch, May 6, 1954, TNA, FO 371 / 110289, folder 3, FC 1151 / 57, 2.

26. Tennant, "Talks on Trade with China, May 6th–7th, 1954," n.d., 5.

27. Tennant, "Talks on Trade with China, May 6th–7th, 1954," n.d., 7.

28. Chu Siyi, "Lei Renmin Huijian Du Weilian, Tai Luntuo Tanhua Jilu," May 6, 1954, FMA 206-C053, in *Zhonghua Renmin Gongheguo Waijiao Dang'an Xuanbian (di yi ji), 1954 Nian Rineiwa Huiyi,* 410.

29. Tennant, "Talks on Trade with China, May 6th–7th, 1954," n.d., 4.

30. Tennant, "Talks on Trade with China, May 6th–7th, 1954," n.d., 7–8.

31. Tennant, "Report on Trade Talks with Chinese in Geneva, May 26–28, 1954," n.d., 1–2.

32. Foreign Office (London) to UK Delegation (Geneva), untitled dispatch, June 2, 1954, TNA, FO 371 / 110289, folder 3, FC 1151 / 72.

33. Sir Roger Makins (Washington) to Foreign Office (London), untitled dispatch, May 20, 1954, TNA, FO 371 / 110289, folder 3, FC 1151 / 64.

34. Humphrey Trevelyan (Geneva) to Foreign Office (London), untitled dispatch, May 19, 1954, TNA, FO 371 / 110289, folder 3, FC 1151 / 63.

35. Foreign Office (London) to UK Delegation (Geneva), untitled dispatch, June 2, 1954; Foreign Office (London) to UK Delegation (Geneva), untitled dispatch, June 10, 1954, TNA, FO 371 / 110289, folder 3, FC 1151 / 82. For the exclusion of Lei Renmin, see Foreign Office (London) to UK Delegation (Geneva), untitled dispatch, June 10, 1954.

36. Foreign Office (London) to UK Delegation (Geneva), untitled dispatch, June 3, 1954, TNA, FO 371 / 110289, folder 3, FC 1151 / 81, 1–2.

37. Zhang Wentian to Li Kenong, "Concerning the Soviet Suggestion on Propaganda Work at Geneva," April 6, 1954, translated by Chen Zhihong, History and Public Policy Program Digital Archive, PRC FMA 206-00004-04, http://digitalarchive.wilsoncenter.org/document/110596.

38. D. R. Mankekar, "China Ready to Trade with Any Country, All Facilities Offered," *Times of India News Service,* May 17, 1954, 11.

39. Mankekar, "China Ready to Trade with Any Country," 11.

40. Mankekar, 11.

41. Robert Alden, "Red China Makes Bid for U.S. Trade," *New York Times,* 15 May 1954, 9. A reporter for the Associated Press agreed. See Associated Press, "Red China Seeks Trade with West," *Washington Post and Times Herald,* May 15, 1954, M5.

42. Alden, "Red China Makes Bid for U.S. Trade," 9.

43. The Hongkong and Shanghai Banking Corporation, "Chairman's Statement," March 11, 1955, January 11, 1955–December 20, 1955, Minutes of the Board of Directors, HK 0104 / 0005, the Hongkong and Shanghai Banking Corporation Archives, Asia Pacific (Hong Kong), 3.

44. Ministry of Foreign Trade, *Duiwai Maoyi Youguan Ziliao Huibian, Di Yi Fen Ce* [Compilation of Information on Foreign Trade, volume 1], May 1956, FPA, quanzong ziliao, mulu 35, [n.p.].

45. International Cooperation Administration, "East-West Trade Controls" (statement prepared for delivery by Walter S. DeLany [Deputy Director for

Mutual Defense Assistance Control] before the Subcommittee on Foreign Economic Policy of the Joint Committee on the Economic Report, 84th US Congress, November 16, 1955), General CIA Records, Freedom of Information Act Electronic Reading Room, CIA- RDP61S00527A000100180167-4, 10–11, and chart 4 [n.p.].

46. Alden, "Red China Makes Bid for U.S. Trade," 9.

47. Zhou Enlai, "Guanyu Waijiao Wenti de Baogao" [Report on Diplomatic Issues], August 12, 1954, FPA, 101-5-542, 1.

48. Zhonggong Zhongyang Wenxian Yanjiushi, *Zhou Enlai Nianpu, 1949–1976* [A Chronology of Zhou Enlai, 1949–1976], 3 vols. (Beijing: Zhongyang Wenxian, 1999), 1:373. Lei Renmin had discussed a commercial office in London during a meeting with Wilson and Robson-Brown on May 28. Wang and Shao, "Lü Dang Daren[,] Bu Ru Shiming," 28. For the Chinese minutes from the May 30 meeting, see "Zhou Enlai Huijian Yingguo Yiyuan Wei'erxun, Luo Boxun-Bulang Tanhua Jiyao" [Minutes from Talks during Zhou Enlai's Meeting with Representatives Wilson and Robson-Brown], May 30, 1954, FMA 206-Y0009, in *Zhonghua Renmin Gongheguo Waijiao Dang'an Xuanbian (di yi ji), 1954 Nian Rineiwa Huiyi,* 412–414.

49. Zhou Enlai to Mao Zedong, Liu Shaoqi, and the Central Committee, "Zhou Enlai Guanyu Daibiao Tuan yu Yingfang Jiechu Qingkuang Zhi Mao Zedong, Liu Shaoqi Bing Bao Zhongyang de Dianbao" [Cable from Zhou Enlai to Mao Zedong, Liu Shaoqi, and the Central Committee Concerning the (Chinese) Delegation's Contact with the British], June 1, 1954, FMA 206-Y0004, in *Zhonghua Renmin Gongheguo Waijiao Dang'an Xuanbian (di yi ji), 1954 Nian Rineiwa Huiyi,* 415.

50. UK Delegation (Geneva) to Foreign Office (London), "Anglo-Chinese Trade," May 31, 1954, TNA, FO 371 / 110289, folder 3, FC 1151 / 75.

51. Wang and Shao, "Lü Dang Daren[,] Bu Ru Shiming," 28; "Lei Renmin Huijian Yidali Gongshangjie Daibiao Tanhua Jiyao" [Minutes from Talks during Lei Renmin's Meeting with Italian Business Representatives], June 13, 1954, FMA 206-C052, in *Zhonghua Renmin Gongheguo Waijiao Dang'an Xuanbian (di yi ji), 1954 Nian Rineiwa Huiyi,* 436–436.

52. The London Chamber of Commerce (Inc), "Visit of Chinese Trade Mission," appendix to "Sino–British Trade Committee," June 26, 1954, TNA, FO 371 / 110291, FC 1151 / 119.

53. Sino–British Trade Committee, "Report on Visit of Chinese Mission," n.d., TNA, FO 371 / 110291, FC 1151 / 121, 3.

54. The CCP adopted the idea of "peaceful coexistence" from the Soviets, as Mao explained at a Politburo meeting on July 7, 1954. Mao Zedong, "Tong Yiqie Yuanyi Heping de Guojia Tuanjie Hezuo" [Unite and Cooperate with All

Nations Desiring Peace], July 7, 1954, *MZDWJ*, 6:334. Zhou first identified the five principles—mutual respect for sovereignty and territorial integrity, nonaggression, noninterference in other countries' internal affairs, equality and mutual benefit, and peaceful coexistence—during a meeting with Indian officials on December 31, 1953. See Zhou Enlai, "Heping Gongchu Wuxiang Yuanze" [Five Principles of Peaceful Coexistence], December 31, 1953, in *Zhou Enlai Waijiao Wenxuan* [Selected Diplomatic Works of Zhou Enlai] (Beijing: Zhongyang Wenxian, 1990), 63.

55. Zhou Enlai, "Nihelu Fanghua Qian Zhou Zongli Guanyu Waijiao Wenti de Baogao" [Premier Zhou Enlai's Report on Diplomatic Issues on the Eve of Nehru's Visit to the People's Republic of China], October 18, 1954, FPA, 101-5-542, 1-3.

56. Zhou, "Nihelu Fanghua Qian Zhou Zongli Guanyu Waijiao Wenti de Baogao," 3–4, 9.

57. Zhou, 6.

58. Zhou, 9.

59. Zhou, 9.

60. Zhou, 9.

61. Li Fuchun, "Di Yi ge Wunian Jihua de Fangzhen yu Renwu" [Guidelines and Tasks of the First Five-Year Plan], July 5, 1955, in Li Fuchun, *Li Fuchun Xuanji* [Selected Works of Li Fuchun] (Beijing: Zhongguo Jihua, 1992), 133–134.

62. Mao Zedong, "Women Yinggai Zai Hezuo Zhong Zengjin Liaojie" [We Should Enhance Mutual Understanding through Cooperation], December 1, 1954, in *Mao Zedong Waijiao Wenxuan* [Selected Diplomatic Works of Mao Zedong] (Beijing: Zhongyang Wenxian, 1994), 179.

63. Chen, *Mao's China and the Cold War,* 169.

64. Yang Kuisong and Mao Sheng have emphasized Mao's emotions in precipitating the crisis, particularly his sense of victimhood. See Kuisong Yang and Sheng Mao, "Unafraid of the Ghost: The Victim Mentality of Mao Zedong and the Two Taiwan Strait Crises in the 1950s," *China Review* 16, no. 1 (Spring 2016): 1–34. Michael Sheng argues that Mao may have been motivated by fear of a US attack. See Michael M. Sheng, "Mao and China's Relations with the Superpowers in the 1950s: A New Look at the Taiwan Strait Crises and the Sino-Soviet Split," *Modern China* 34, no. 4 (October 2008): 480–487.

65. Yang Kuisong and Mao Sheng, "Unafraid of the Ghost," 11–12.

66. The US defense commitment applied only to the island of Taiwan and the Pescadores, not the Nationalist-controlled islands nearer the mainland coast. Mutual Defense Treaty between the United States and the Republic of China,

December 2, 1954, *Yale Law School Avalon Project: Documents in Law, History and Diplomacy,* http://avalon.law.yale.edu/20th_century/chin001.asp#1.

67. Chen, *Mao's China and the Cold War,* 169–170.

68. Central Ministry of Foreign Trade Leading Party Group, "Zhongyang Duiwai Maoyi Bu Dangzu Guanyu Waihui Wenti de Baogao" [Central Ministry of Foreign Trade Leading Party Group Report on Foreign Currency Issues], February 9, 1954, *JRJ, 1953–1957,* 892–894.

69. State Planning Commission, "1953–1957 Nian Dui Ziben Zhuyi Guojia Waihui Pingheng Shisuanbiao" [Trial Balance (Sheet) of Foreign Exchange Balances with Capitalist Countries(,) 1953–1957], March 30, 1954, *JRJ, 1953–1957,* 899; Central Ministry of Foreign Trade Leading Party Group, "Zhongyang Duiwai Maoyi Bu Dangzu Guanyu Waihui Wenti de Baogao" [Central Ministry of Foreign Trade Leading Party Group Report on Foreign Currency Issues], February 9, 1954, *JRJ, 1953–1957,* 887.

70. "Zhongyang Ji Yi Jiu Wu San Nian Du Shiyong Fei Jinkou Waihui Zhifu Fenmu Tongjibiao" [Subheading (of) Statistical Table for Central Nonimport Foreign Currency Payments in 1953], January 29, 1954, *JRJ, 1953–1957,* 890.

71. Central Ministry of Foreign Trade Leading Party Group, "Zhongyang Duiwai Maoyi Bu Dangzu Guanyu Waihui Wenti de Baogao," February 9, 1954, *JRJ, 1953–1957,* 887.

72. Zhonggong Zhongyang Wenxian Yanjiushi, *Zhou Enlai Nianpu, 1949–1976,* 1:554.

73. Zhonggong Zhongyang Wenxian Yanjiushi, *Zhou Enlai Nianpu, 1949–1976,* 1:554.

74. Mao Zedong, "Mao Zedong Zai 1956 Nian 4 Yue 25 Ri Zhongyang Zhengzhi Ju Kuoda Huiyi Shang de Baogao (biji)" [(Notes from) Mao Zedong's Report during the April 25, 1956, Enlarged Central Political Bureau Meeting], April 25, 1956, Gansu Provincial Archives, 91-018-0495, 13.

75. Li Zheren, "Duiwai Maoyi Bu Gongzuo Huibao" [Ministry of Foreign Trade Work Report], March 21, 1956, FPA, quanzong ziliao, mulu 232, 1.

76. Li, "Duiwai Maoyi Bu Gongzuo Huibao," 27.

77. Li, 3, 30.

78. Li, 14.

79. Li, 19, 22.

80. Editorial Board, "Editorial Note," *Foreign Trade of the People's Republic of China* 1 (May 1956): [n.p.].

81. Editorial Board, "Editorial Note," 3; Koo I-fan, "For Trade and Friendship," *Foreign Trade of the People's Republic of China* 1 (May 1956): 7; Tsao Kaung-po,

"How China's Foreign Trade Is Conducted," *Foreign Trade of the People's Republic of China* 3 (May 1957): 6.

82. Tsao Kaung-po, "How China's Foreign Trade Is Conducted," 6.

83. "The Development of China's Economy and Her Foreign Trade in 1956," *Foreign Trade of the People's Republic of China* 2 (November 1956): 3.

84. The Soviets also moved past this interpretation and used advertising in the early postwar era. See James W. Markham, "Is Advertising Important in the Soviet Economy?" *Journal of Marketing* 28, no. 2 (April 1964): 31–37.

85. China was simultaneously moving toward a socialist aesthetic in advertising during the 1950s. See Karl Gerth, "Compromising with Consumerism in Socialist China: Transnational Flows and Internal Tensions in 'Socialist Advertising,'" *Past & Present* 218, supplement 8 (2013): 203–232. For continuities in Chinese domestic advertising before and after 1949, see Karl Gerth, *Unending Capitalism: How Consumerism Negated China's Communist Revolution* (Cambridge: Cambridge University Press, 2020), 101–117.

86. Koo I-fan, "For Trade and Friendship," *Foreign Trade of the People's Republic of China* 1 (May 1956): 6–7.

87. Zhou Enlai to Pan Hannian, "Tongyi Zai Shanghai Xinjian Zhanlan Hu-ichang" [Agreement on New Construction of an Exhibition Site in Shanghai], December 28, 1953, in Zhou Enlai, *Zhou Enlai Shuxin Xuanji* [Selected Letters of Zhou Enlai] (Beijing: Zhongyang Wenxian, 1988), 498.

88. Gao Feng, *Lin Haiyun Zhuan: Cong Hongjun Zhanshi Dao Gongheguo Haiguan Zongshu Shuzhang, Waimao Bu Buzhang* [A Biography of Lin Haiyun: From Red Army Soldier to (People's) Republic (of China) Customs Director, Director of the Ministry of Foreign Trade] (Beijing: Duiwai Jingji Maoyi Daxue, 2000), 289.

89. Chen Leigang, "Zhou Enlai yu 'Zhongguo Diyi Zhan' de Lishi Qingyuan" [Fateful Ties between Zhou Enlai and "China's First Exhibition"], *Zhongshan Fengyu* [Zhongshan Wind and Rain] 2 (2014): 4; Wu et al., *Hongse Huarun* [Red China Resources] (Beijing: Zhonghua, 2010), 268.

90. Ouyang Xiang, "Cong Guangjiaohui de Chuangban Kan Er Shi Shiji Wushi Niandai Zhongqi Zhongguo Wai Jingmao Fazhan de Zhanlüe Tiaozheng," [Readjustments to the Strategy of China's Foreign Trade Development in the Mid-1950s as Seen from the Launch of the Guangzhou Export Commodities Fair], *Zhonggong Dangshi Yanjiu* [Studies in CCP Party History] 9 (2011): 35.

91. Chen, "Zhou Enlai yu 'Zhongguo Diyi Zhan' de Lishi Qingyuan," 4.

92. Li Zheren, "Duiwai Maoyi Bu Gongzuo Huibao," 25–26.

93. The US Consulate in Hong Kong was still monitoring for PRC smuggling in the colony. American Consulate General (Hong Kong) to Department of State

(Washington), "Communists' Demand for Petroleum," April 7, 1955; US Army Liaison Officer (Hong Kong), "Smuggling of Diesel Oil and Kerosene to Communist China," n.d. [1955], both in USNA, RG 84, Hong Kong Classified General Records, Box 22, File 511.2.

94. On the Ministry of Foreign Trade's push to minimize "nontrade" (*fei maoyi*) spending of foreign currencies, see Ministry of Foreign Trade Leading Party Group, "Zhongyang Duiwai Maoyi Bu Dangzu Guanyu Waihui Wenti de Baogao," February 9, 1954, *JRJ, 1953–1957,* 888.

95. China Committee for the Promotion of International Trade, *Foreign Trade of the People's Republic of China* 5 (September 1958): 1.

96. "The Chinese Export Commodities Fairs: A Retrospect," in Ta Kung Pao, *The Chinese Export Commodities Fair* (Hong Kong: Ta Kung Pao, 1960), 11.

97. Percy Timberlake, *The 48 Group: The Story of the Icebreakers in China* (London: The 48 Group Club, 1994), 38.

98. Shu Guang Zhang, *Economic Cold War: America's Embargo against China and the Sino-Soviet Alliance, 1949–1963* (Washington, DC: Woodrow Wilson Center Press, 2001), 192.

99. Timberlake, *The 48 Group,* 41.

5. A "GREAT LEAP" IN TRADE

1. Ye Jizhuang, "Ye [Ji] Zhuang Buzhang Zai Waimao Juzhang Huiyi Shang de Zongjie Jianghua (Jilu Gao)" [Summary Remarks by Minister Ye [Ji] Zhuang at the Foreign Trade Bureau Chiefs' Meeting (Transcript)], December 14, 1957, in Zhongguo Shehui Kexueyuan and Zhongyang Dang'anguan, comps., *Zhonghua Renmin Gongheguo Jingji Dang'an Ziliao Xuanbian, 1958–1965, Duiwai Maoyi Juan* [Selection of Materials from the PRC Economic Archives, 1958–1965, Foreign Trade Volume] (Beijing: Zhongguo Caizheng Jingji, 2011) (hereafter cited as *DWMYJ, 1958–1965*), 4–5.

2. Ministry of Foreign Trade Leading Party Group, "Duiwai Maoyi Bu Dangzu Guanyu Jinhou Duiwai Maoyi Fazhan Qushi, Renwu, Fangzhen Zhengce he Zhongyao Cuoshi gei Zhongyang de Baogao" [Ministry of Foreign Trade Leading Party Group Report to the CCP Central Committee on Future Foreign Trade Development Trends, Tasks, Policies, and Important Measures], May 11, 1958, *DWMYJ, 1958–1965*, 11.

3. Wu et al., *Hongse Huarun* [Red China Resources] (Beijing: Zhonghua, 2010), 284.

4. Wu et al., *Hongse Huarun,* 285–286.

5. Ye Jizhuang, "Ye [Ji] Zhuang Buzhang Zai Waimao Juzhang Huiyi Shang de Zongjie Jianghua (Jilu Gao)," December 14, 1957, 3–4.

6. Mao Zedong, untitled speech at Moscow meeting of representatives of Communist and Workers' Parties, November 18, 1957, *MZDWJ,* 7:321.

7. Kenneth Lieberthal, "The Great Leap Forward and the Split in the Yan'an Leadership, 1958–1965," in *The Politics of China: Sixty Years of the People's Republic of China,* ed. Roderick MacFarquhar (Cambridge: Cambridge University Press, 2011), 93.

8. Mao's impatience with slow growth had increased by 1957 but was not new. He had long pushed for rapid industrialization and economic transformation. See Andrew G. Walder, *China under Mao: A Revolution Derailed* (Cambridge, MA: Harvard University Press, 2015), 124.

9. Lorenz M. Luthi, *The Sino-Soviet Split: Cold War in the Communist World* (Princeton, NJ: Princeton University Press, 2008), 76.

10. Tong Xiaopeng, *Feng Yu Sishi Nian* [Forty Years of Wind and Rain], 2 vols. (Beijing: Zhongyang Wenxian, 1997), 2:350.

11. Mao Zedong, "Mao Zedong Zai Ba Jie San Zhong Quanhui Shang de Jianghua" [Address by Mao Zedong at the Third Plenary Session of the Eighth CCP Central Committee], October 9, 1957, Jilin Provincial Archives (hereafter cited as JPA) 1-13/1-1957.64, 7.

12. Frederick C. Teiwes, "Mao Texts and the Mao of the 1950s," *Australian Journal of Chinese Affairs* 33 (1995): 144.

13. Mao, "Mao Zedong Zai Ba Jie San Zhong Quanhui Shang de Jianghua," October 9, 1957, 6.

14. "Bixu Jianchi Duo Kuai Hao Sheng de Jianshe Fangzhen" [(We) Must Adhere to the Construction Policy of More, Faster, Better, More Economical], *Renmin Ribao,* December 12, 1957, 1.

15. Tong, *Feng Yu Sishi Nian,* 2:355.

16. Tong, 2:355–356. See also Jin Chongji, *Zhou Enlai Zhuan* [A Biography of Zhou Enlai], 4 vols. (Beijing: Zhongyang Wenxian, 2018), 3:1234–1235. Opposition to "rash advance" began to gain steam in the spring of 1956 when excessive capital investment, the ballooning cost of wage reforms, rapid expansion of the urban workforce, overextended credit, and deficit spending prodded Zhou to argue that opposition to "rightism" and "conservatism" had gone on long enough. See Frederick C. Teiwes and Warren Sun, *China's Road to Disaster: Mao, Central Politicians, and Provincial Leaders in the Unfolding of the Great Leap Forward, 1955–1959* (Armonk, NY: M.E. Sharpe, 1999), 29.

17. Teiwes, "Mao Texts," 146.

18. Mao Zedong, "Mao Zedong Zhuxi Zai Chengdu Hankou Huiyi Shang de Jianghua (Jilu)" [Chairman Mao Zedong's Addresses in Chengdu and Hankou (Wuhan) (transcript)], March 9, 1958, HPA, 855-4-1265-3, 2.

19. Mao Zedong, "Gongzuo Fangfa Liu Shi Tiao (Cao'an)" [Sixty Articles on Working Methods (Draft)], January 31, 1958, *MZDWJ,* 7:344–364.

20. Mao, "Gongzuo Fangfa Liu Shi Tiao (Cao'an)," January 31, 1958, 349–350.

21. Mao, 351.

22. Mao, 351–352. For the origins of "red and expert," see Richard D. Baum, "'Red and Expert': The Politico-Ideological Foundations of China's Great Leap Forward," *Asian Survey* 4, no. 9 (September 1964): 1048–1057.

23. Mao, "Gongzuo Fangfa Liu Shi Tiao (Cao'an)," January 31, 1958.

24. General Office of the CCP Central Committee, "Zhongyang Bangong Ting Guanyu 'Gongzuo Fangfa Liu Shi Tiao (Cao'an)' de Yuedu, Taolun Fanwei he Taolun Fangfa Guiding de Tongzhi" [Central Committee General Office Instruction with Stipulations for the Scope and Discussion Methods for Reading 'Sixty Articles on Working Methods' (Draft)], February 8, 1958, HPA, 855-4-1268-38, 1.

25. Ministry of Foreign Trade, "Waimao Bu Dui Dang Nei Cuowu Sixiang de Fenxi" [Ministry of Foreign Trade Analysis of Internal Party Erroneous Thought], in Central Ministry of Propaganda, ed., *Xuanjiao Dongtai* [Trends in Propaganda and Education] 313 (October 29, 1957), HPA, 864-2-430, 7.

26. "Fan Langfei Fan Baoshou Shi Dangqian Zhengfeng Yundong de Zhongxin Renwu" [Anti-Waste, Anti-Conservatism Is the Central Task of the Current Rectification Movement], *Renmin Ribao*, February 18, 1958, 1.

27. Higher Education Office, "Waimao Xueyuan Shuangfan Yundong de Yixie Qingkuang" [Certain Circumstances in the Institute of Foreign Trade Double-Anti Movement], in Central Ministry of Propaganda, ed., *Xuanjiao Dongtai* 365 (March 13, 1958), HPA, 864-2-440, 3.

28. British Broadcasting Corporation (BBC) Monitor Report, "Setting Up of an Institute of Foreign Trade in Peking," August 31, 1954, TNA, FO 371 / 110279, FC 1126 / 1; Kenneth Wang, "Foreign Trade Policy and Apparatus of the People's Republic of China," *Law and Contemporary Problems* 38, no. 2 (1973): 193–194.

29. Higher Education Office, "Waimao Xueyuan Shuangfan Yundong de Yixie Qingkuang," 4.

30. In early 1958, Mao presided over a national public health campaign that aimed to eliminate the "four pests": mosquitoes, flies, rats, and sparrows. For the context of the campaign, see Roderick MacFarquhar, *The Origins of the Cultural Revolution*, vol. 2, *The Great Leap Forward, 1958–1960* (New York: Published for the Royal Institute of International Affairs, the East Asian Institute of Columbia University, and the Research Institute on Communist Affairs of Columbia University by Columbia University Press, 1974), 21–24; Judith Shapiro, *Mao's War against Nature: Politics and the Environment in Revolutionary China* (Cambridge: Cambridge University Press, 2001), 86–89.

31. Students also spent eighteen hours in class each week, six hours on "labor," and four hours on other Party and Communist Youth League activities (*dangtuan huodong*). Higher Education Office, "Waimao Xueyuan Shuangfan Yundong de Yixie Qingkuang," 4.

32. Qu Yun, "Preface," *DWMYJ, 1958–1965,* 2.

33. Ministry of Foreign Trade, "Quan Guo Waimao Juzhang Huiyi Cankao Wenjian Zhi Si: Guqi Geming Ganjin Wei Wancheng Yi Jiu Wu Ba Nian Dui Ziben Zhuyi Guojia Chukou Liu Yi Dao Qi Yi Mei Yuan de Guangrong Renwu Er Nuli" [Nationwide Foreign Trade Bureau Directors' Conference Document No. 4: Muster the Motivation to Strive to Complete the Glorious Mission of Exporting US$600–700 million to Capitalist Nations in 1958], February 3, 1958, *DWMYJ, 1958–1965,* 397.

34. Ministry of Foreign Trade, "Quan Guo Waimao Juzhang Huiyi Cankao Wenjian Zhi Si," 401–402.

35. Jin, *Zhou Enlai Zhuan,* 3:1256–1257.

36. Jin, 1250.

37. Zhou Enlai, "Zai Zhongguo Gongchandang Di Ba Jie Quan Guo Daibiao Dahui Di Er Ci Huiyi Shang de Fayan" [Remarks at the Second Session of the Eighth National Congress of the Chinese Communist Party], May 1958, HPA, 855-18-543-3, 1–2.

38. Bo Yibo, "Bo Yibo Tongzhi de Fayan" [Comrade Bo Yibo's Remarks], May 1958, HPA, 855-18-543-4, 2.

39. Chen Yun, "Zai Zhongguo Gongchandang Di Ba Jie Quan Guo Daibiao Dahui Di Er Ci Huiyi Shang de Fayan" [Remarks at the Second Session of the Eighth National Congress of the Chinese Communist Party], May 21, 1958, HPA, 855-18-543-1, 4.

40. Li Xiannian, "Guanyu Caizheng Gongzuo Ruhe Zhixing Duo Kuai Hao Sheng Fangzhen de Wenti" [On the Issue of How Financial Work Can Implement the Policy of More, Faster, Better, More Economical], May 1958, HPA, 855-18-543-5, 3.

41. Ye Jizhuang, "Guanyu Duiwai Maoyi Fazhan Wenti" [On Issues in the Development of Foreign Trade], May 1958, HPA, 855-18-543-11, 6.

42. Ye, "Guanyu Duiwai Maoyi Fazhan Wenti."

43. In October 1954, for example, Zhou Enlai argued that the capitalist world was "old," riddled with contradictions, and dying. See Zhou Enlai, "Nihelu Fanghua Qian Zhou Zongli Guanyu Waijiao Wenti de Baogao" [Premier Zhou Enlai's Report on Diplomatic Issues on the Eve of Nehru's Visit to the People's Republic of China], October 18, 1954, FPA, 101-5-542, 1, 3.

44. Ye, "Guanyu Duiwai Maoyi Fazhan Wenti," 7.

45. Ye, 7–8.

46. Mao Zedong, "Lun Shi Da Guanxi" [On the Ten Major Relationships], April 25, 1956, *MZDWJ*, 7:32.

47. Ye, "Guanyu Duiwai Maoyi Fazhan Wenti," 12–13.

48. Ye, 13.

49. Ministry of Foreign Trade Leading Party Group, "Duiwai Maoyi Bu Dangzu Guanyu Jinhou Duiwai Maoyi Fazhan Qushi, Renwu, Fangzhen Zhengce he Zhongyao Cuoshi gei Zhongyang de Baogao" [Ministry of Foreign Trade Leading Party Group Report to Central Authorities on Future Foreign Trade Trends, Tasks, Policies, and Important Measures], May 11, 1958, *DWMYJ, 1958–1965*, 11.

50. Ministry of Foreign Trade Leading Party Group, "Duiwai Maoyi Bu Dangzu Guanyu Jinhou Duiwai Maoyi Fazhan Qushi, Renwu, Fangzhen Zhengce he Zhongyao Cuoshi gei Zhongyang de Baogao," 11–17.

51. Jardine, Matheson & Company, *China Trade Bulletin,* no. 32 (April 12, 1958), as enclosed in US Consulate General (Hong Kong) to Department of State (Washington), "Jardine, Matheson & Co, Ltd. China Trade Bulletin No. 32," April 29, 1958, USNA, RG 59, Far East Trade, Box 2047, File 493.00/3-355, 6–7.

52. Chicago Daily News Foreign Service, "China Gives France $12 Million Order," *Washington Post and Times Herald,* March 30, 1958, A12.

53. Jardine, Matheson & Company, *China Trade Bulletin,* no. 32 (April 12, 1958), 1.

54. British Embassy (Beijing) to Foreign Office (Far Eastern Department), "China: Economic Report," no. 3 (March 26, 1958), TNA, FO 371 / 133392, FC 1101 / 3, 2.

55. Memorandum from the Assistant Secretary of Commerce (Kearns) to the Chairman of the Council on Foreign Economic Policy (Randall), "Review of Foreign Assets Control Regulations and Their Effect on American-Owned Subsidiaries and Other Foreign Firms," July 7, 1958, *FRUS,* 1958–1960, vol. 4, *Foreign Economic Policy* (Washington, DC: US Government Printing Office, 1958–1960), 720–721.

56. Tillman Durdin, "Red China Buying Canadian Wheat," *New York Times,* April 1, 1958, 11.

57. This question had also surfaced in recent exchanges with Ford of Canada; Ford of England; Quaker Oats of Canada; American Cyanimid of Canada; the Canadian subsidiary of Joy Manufacturing; Robin Hood Flour Mills of

Montreal, a subsidiary of International Milling Company; Cargill Company; and International Harvester Company. Memorandum from the Assistant Secretary of Commerce (Kearns) to the Chairman of the Council on Foreign Economic Policy (Randall), "Review of Foreign Assets Control Regulations and Their Effect on American-Owned Subsidiaries and Other Foreign Firms," July 7, 1958, *FRUS,* 1958–1960, vol. 4, *Foreign Economic Policy,* 722.

58. Associated Press, "U.S. May Ease China Trade Ban," *Baltimore Sun,* July 11, 1958, 1.

59. "A Break in the Chinese Trade Wall," *Los Angeles Times,* July 12, 1958, B4.

60. Wall Street Journal News Roundup, "Canadian Units of U.S. Auto Makers Willing to Sell to Red China," *Wall Street Journal,* July 14, 1958, 20.

61. Dewey W. Smith to US Embassy Ottawa, untitled letter, September 3, 1958, USNA, RG 59, Far East Trade, Box 2051, File 493.119 / 1-1758, 1.

62. Memorandum of Conversation, "U.S. Policy toward the Export of U.S. Origin Transport Aircraft to Communist China," September 22, 1958, USNA, RG 59, Far East Trade, Box 2051, File 493.119 / 1-1758, 1.

63. The CCPIT signed the deal with the Japan Association for the Promotion of International Trade (JAPIT), the Diet Members' League for the Promotion of Sino–Japanese Trade, and the Japan–China Importers and Exporters Association (JCIEA). See Amy King, *China-Japan Relations after World War Two: Empire, Industry, and War, 1949–1971* (Cambridge: Cambridge University Press, 2016), 135.

64. "Tokyo Approves Red China Trade," *New York Times,* April 10, 1958, 3.

65. Jerome Alan Cohen, *The Dynamics of China's Foreign Relations* (Cambridge, MA: East Asian Research Center, Harvard University; Distributed by Harvard University Press, 1970), 44.

66. Ministry of Foreign Trade, "Quan Guo Waimao Juzhang Huiyi Cankao Wenjian Zhi Si," 400; Jardine, Matheson & Company, *China Trade Bulletin,* no. 32 (April 12, 1958), 1–2.

67. Kurt Werner Radtke, *China's Relations with Japan, 1945–1983: The Role of Liao Chengzhi* (Manchester: Manchester University Press, 1990), 123–124.

68. Many of the disagreements that surfaced during the negotiations had roots in the third Sino–Japanese trade agreement, which was signed in 1955. These included Beijing's demand for an intergovernmental trade agreement, a payment agreement between state banks, permanent trade missions endowed with diplomatic immunity, an end to Japan's trade embargo against China, and the abandonment of the practice of fingerprinting Chinese trade officials who intended to stay in Japan longer than two months. See Gene T. Hsiao, *The*

Foreign Trade of China: Policy, Law, and Practice (Berkeley: University of California Press, 1977), 42.

69. Hsiao, *The Foreign Trade of China,* 45-46.

70. Editorial, "The Two Sides of Chinese Communist-Japanese Trade" (in Chinese), *Zhongyang Ribao* [Central Daily News] (Taipei), March 12, 1958, 2, as cited in Hsiao, *The Foreign Trade of China,* 46n21.

71. Hsiao, *The Foreign Trade of China,* 46.

72. Memorandum of Conversation between US and KMT officials, "Exchange of Views," March 14, 1958, *FRUS,* 1958–1960, vol. 19, *China,* 9–10.

73. Wu Xuewen and Wang Junyan, eds., *Liao Chengzhi yu Riben* [Liao Chengzhi and Japan] (Beijing: Zhonggong Dangshi, 2007), 253.

74. Tillman Durdin, "Red Chinese Halt Mission to Japan," *New York Times,* April 5, 1958, 3.

75. "Tokyo Approves Red China Trade," *New York Times,* April 10, 1958, 3.

76. Hsiao, *The Foreign Trade of China,* 48.

77. Greg MacGregor, "Red China Spurns Tokyo Trade Pact," *New York Times,* April 14, 1958, 1, 3.

78. Hsiao, *The Foreign Trade of China,* 49.

79. Wu and Wang, *Liao Chengzhi Yu Riben,* 257.

80. Associated Press, "Red China Bars Trade with Japan," *New York Herald Tribune,* May 11, 1958, 9.

81. Ye Jizhuang, "Guanyu Duiwai Maoyi Fazhan Wenti" [On Issues in the Development of Foreign Trade], May 1958, HPA, 855-18-543–11, 12.

82. Mayumi Itoh, *Pioneers of Sino-Japanese Relations: Liao and Takasaki* (New York: Palgrave MacMillan, 2012), 109. For Saionji's ties to Soviet intelligence, see Edward M. Collins, *Myth, Manifesto, Meltdown: Communist Strategy, 1848– 1991* (London: Praeger, 1998), 61–62.

83. CCP Central Investigation Department, "Zuijin Riben Zhengfu Dui Zhong-Ri Maoyi he Zhong-Ri Maoyi Tanpan de Taidu" [The Japanese Government's Recent Attitude toward Sino–Japanese Trade and Sino–Japanese Trade Talks], *Diaocha Ziliao* [Investigation Materials] 43 (October 10, 1957), HPA, D5-5-1, 1–2.

84. CCP Central Investigation Department, "Riben Jingji Qingkuang Ji Zhong-Ri Maoyi Quxiang" [Recent Developments in the Japanese Economy and Sino–Japanese Trade Trends], *Diaocha Ziliao* 7 (February 28, 1958), HPA, D5-5-2, 1–4.

85. CCP Central Investigation Department, "Riben Jingji Shuaitui de Fazhan Qushi Ji Qi Yingxiang" [Development Trends in the Decline of Japan's Economy and Their Effects] *Diaocha Ziliao* 11 (April 26, 1958), HPA, D5-5-2, 1.

86. Editorial Board, "Riben Dui Wo Zuijin Dui Ri Zhengce de Yixie Neimu Fanying" [Some Insider Reactions in Japan to Our Recent Policies Toward Japan], *Qingbao Jianxun* [Intelligence Newsletter] 22 (June 4, 1958), HPA, D5-4-1, 1.

87. Editorial Board, "Riben Jiji Tanxun Ying-Fa Dui Wo Guo Maoyi de Taidu" [Japan Actively Makes Inquiries about Britain's and France's Attitudes Toward Trade with China], *Qingbao Jianxun* 25 (June 12, 1958), HPA, D5-4-1, 1.

88. Chinese statistics show that Sino–Japanese trade ceased entirely from 1959 to 1960, but Japanese sources reveal that some trade did occur. See Shen Jueren et al., *Dangdai Zhongguo Duiwai Maoyi* [Contemporary Chinese Foreign Trade], 2 vols. (Beijing: Dangdai Zhongguo, 1992), 2:371, appendix 3. See also Japan External Trade Organization (JETRO), *Chū-Nichi Bōeki Geppō* [Sino–Japanese Trade Monthly Report], no. 11 (1964): 20–21, table 1, JETRO Business Library and Archive, Tokyo, Japan, no. 304, 0003347370.

89. Ministry of Foreign Trade Leading Party Group, "Duiwai Maoyi Dangzu Guanyu Zai Di San Jidu Difang Zanshi Tingzhi Dui Ziben Zhuyi Guojia Xin de Dinghuo de Qingshi Baogao" [Ministry of Foreign Trade Leading Party Group Report Requesting Instructions on Localities Temporarily Ceasing New Orders for Goods from Capitalist Nations during the Third Quarter], August 4, 1958, *DWMYJ, 1958–1965,* 404.

90. CCP Central Committee, "Zhongyang Pizhuan Duiwai Maoyi Bu Dangzu Guanyu Zai Di San Jidu Difang Zanshi Tingzhi Dui Ziben Zhuyi Guojia Xin de Dinghuo de Qingshi Baogao" [Central Committee Endorsement and Distribution of Ministry of Foreign Trade Leading Party Group Report Requesting Instructions on Localities Temporarily Ceasing New Orders for Goods from Capitalist Nations during the Third Quarter], August 10, 1958, *DWMYJ, 1958–1965,* 404.

91. CCP Central Committee, "Zhonggong Zhongyang Guanyu Duiwai Maoyi Bixu Tongyi Duiwai de Jueding (Cao'an)" [CCP Central Committee Resolution on the Necessity of Foreign Trade (Work) Unifying (When Facing) Abroad (Draft)], August 15, 1958, HPA, 855-18-555-32, 1.

92. The Central Committee's resolution also complained about problems in trade with socialist nations, such as work units negotiating deals without approvals from the center. CCP Central Committee, "Zhonggong Zhongyang Guanyu Duiwai Maoyi Bixu Tongyi Duiwai de Jueding (Cao'an)," 1.

93. Ye Jizhuang, "Ye Jizhuang Buzhang Zai Quan Guo Duiwai Maoyi Juzhang Huiyi Shang de Jielun" [Concluding Remarks by Minister Ye Jizhuang at a Nationwide Meeting of Foreign Trade Bureau Chiefs], July 19, 1958, *DWMYJ, 1958–1965,* 21.

94. CCP Central Committee, "Zhonggong Zhongyang Guanyu Duiwai Maoyi Bixu Tongyi Duiwai de Jueding (Cao'an)," 2.

95. CCP Central Committee, 3.

96. CCP Central Committee, 1.

97. British Consulate General, Shanghai (J. H. Wright) to British Embassy
    (K. G. Ritchie), untitled letter, October 15, 1958, TNA, FO 371 / 133394, FC
    1121 / 13.

98. Foreign Office Working Group on Chinese Exports, "Chinese Exports to South
    East Asia: Memorandum by the Joint Intelligence Bureau with Appendix by the
    Colonial Office," October 15, 1958, TNA, FO 371 / 133394, FC 1121 / 15.

99. Reuters, "China Sales Policy Irks Japanese," *Washington Post and Times Herald,*
    June 9, 1958, A21.

100. "Red China Intensifies Trade War in Asia: Sato," *Japan Times,* July 17, 1958, 1,
     as reported in British Embassy (Tokyo) to the Far Eastern Department, Foreign
     Office, untitled dispatch, July 21, 1958, TNA, FO 371 / 133394, FC 1121 / 6.

101. "China Sales Policy Irks Japanese," A21.

102. "Red China Intensifies Trade War in Asia: Sato," *Japan Times,* July 17, 1958,
     1; P. K. Padmanabhan, "Trade War in Asia," *Los Angeles Times,* August 3,
     1958, B5.

103. British Embassy (Bangkok) to Far Eastern Department, Foreign Office,
     untitled dispatch, October 2, 1958, TNA, FO 371 / 133399, FC 11323 / 2.

104. "Red China Intensifies Trade War in Asia," 1.

105. US Consulate General (Hong Kong) to Department of State (Washington),
     "Conversation with Japan Manager of Bank of Tokyo on Chinese Commu-
     nist Trade Offensive in Southeast Asia," August 14, 1958, USNA, RG 84,
     Hong Kong Classified General Records, Box 24, File 510.1–China,
     P.R. / Japan, 1.

106. British Embassy (Djakarta) to Far Eastern Department, Foreign Office,
     untitled dispatch, December 17, 1958, TNA, FO 371 / 133399, FC 11323 / 5.
     "Cost and freight" refers to transactions in which the seller, in this case a
     Chinese state company, pays for the shipment of goods to the port of destina-
     tion, Jakarta, and provides the Indonesian buyer with documents necessary to
     take possession of the goods from the shipper.

107. P. K. Padmanabhan, "Trade War in Asia," B5.

108. British Embassy (Bangkok) to Far Eastern Department, Foreign Office,
     untitled dispatch, October 2, 1958.

109. Radtke, *China's Relations with Japan, 1945–1983,* 151n61. See also Sudhakar
     Bhat, "Bid to Capture Asian Markets: China Launches Economic War against
     Japan," *Times of India,* July 14, 1958, 7, and Walter Briggs, "Tokyo Calm to
     Threats of Red China," *New York Herald Tribune,* July 9, 1958, 2.

110. British Embassy (Saigon) to Far Eastern Department, Foreign Office, untitled dispatch, August 29, 1958, TNA, FO 371 / 133399, FC 11323 / 1A; British Embassy (Vientiane) to Far Eastern Department, Foreign Office, untitled dispatch, August 22, 1958, TNA, FO 371 / 133399, FC 11323 / 1B; British Embassy (Phnom Penh) to Far Eastern Department, Foreign Office, untitled dispatch, August 30, 1958, TNA, FO 371 / 133399, FC 11323 / 1C; British Embassy (Bangkok) to Far Eastern Department, Foreign Office, untitled dispatch, September 22, 1958, TNA, FO 371 / 133399, FC 11323 / 1D; British Embassy (Rangoon) to Far Eastern Department, Foreign Office, untitled dispatch, October 7, 1958, TNA, FO 371 / 133399, FC 11323 / 3; British Embassy (Manila) to Far Eastern Department, Foreign Office, untitled dispatch, November 12, 1958, TNA, FO 371 / 133399, FC 11324; British Embassy (Djakarta) to Far Eastern Department, Foreign Office, untitled dispatch, December 17, 1958.

111. Chen Jian, *Mao's China and the Cold War* (Chapel Hill: University of North Carolina Press, 2001), 64.

112. Thomas J. Christensen, *Useful Adversaries: Grand Strategy, Domestic Mobilization, and Sino-American Conflict, 1947–1958* (Princeton, NJ: Princeton University Press, 1996), 199; Chen, *Mao's China and the Cold War,* 72–78.

113. Mao Zedong, "Tong Sulian Zhu Hua Dashi Youjin de Tanhua" [Conversation with Soviet Ambassador to China (Pavel) Yudin], July 22, 1958, in *Mao Zedong Waijiao Wenxuan* [Selected Diplomatic Works of Mao Zedong] (Beijing: Zhongyang Wenxian, 1994), 322–333.

114. Gong Li, "Tension across the Taiwan Strait in the 1950s: Chinese Strategy and Tactics," in *Re-Examining the Cold War: U.S.-China Diplomacy, 1954–1973,* ed. Robert S. Ross and Jiang Changbin (Cambridge, MA: Harvard University Asia Center, distributed by Harvard University Press, 2001), 158.

115. Chen, *Mao's China and the Cold War,* 163–204.

116. Chen, 175.

117. Zhou Enlai et al., untitled minutes from meeting on foreign trade work, November 8, 1958, HPA, 855-4-1273-6, 1–2.

118. Zhou et al., untitled minutes, November 8, 1958, 2–3.

119. Jin, *Zhou Enlai Zhuan,* 3:1281–1282.

120. Ministry of Foreign Trade, "Guanyu Guoqu Gongzuo Jiben Zongjie Ji Jinhou Gongzuo Zhishi" [Instruction Concerning a Basic Summary of Past and Future Work], August 1953, in Ministry of Foreign Trade General Office, *Duiwai Maoyi Bu Zhongyao Wenjian Huibian, 1949 Nian—1955 Nian* [Compilation of Important Documents of the Ministry of Foreign Trade, 1949–1955], October 1956, HPA, F752.0-1, 7.

121. Zhou et al., untitled minutes, November 8, 1958, 3.

122. Zhou et al., 3, 5, 2.

123. Zhou et al., 7.

124. Zhou et al., 7.

125. Zhou et al., 8.

126. Zhou et al., 8.

127. Zhou et al., 6.

128. Zhou et al., 10.

129. Zhou et al., 11.

130. Zhou Enlai, "Zhou Zongli Guanyu Duiwai Maoyi Fangzhen Zhengce de Zhishi Jiyao" [Summary Instructions from Premier Zhou on Foreign Trade Policy], November 23, 1958, HPA, 855-4-1273-8, 1.

131. Zhou, "Zhou Zongli Guanyu Duiwai Maoyi Fangzhen Zhengce de Zhishi Jiyao," November 23, 1958, 2.

132. Zhou, 1.

133. Zhou, 1.

134. Zhou Enlai, "Zhou Zongli Jiejian Waimao Bu Kou'an Waimao Juzhang Zuotanhui Daibiao de Jianghua" [Remarks by Premier Zhou during Meetings with Representatives at a Forum of Ministry of Foreign Trade Port-Level Foreign Trade Chiefs], December 23, 1958, HPA, 855-4-1273-10, 4, 10.

135. Zhou, "Zhou Zongli Jiejian Waimao Bu Kou'an Waimao Juzhang Zuotanhui Daibiao de Jianghua," December 23, 1958, 1. For past references to "commercial war," see Li Zheren, "Duiwai Maoyi Bu Gongzuo Huibao" [Ministry of Foreign Trade Work Report], March 21, 1956, FPA, quanzong ziliao, mulu 232, 27.

136. Zhou, "Zhou Zongli Jiejian Waimao Bu Kou'an Waimao Juzhang Zuotanhui Daibiao de Jianghua," December 23, 1958, 1–2.

137. Zhou, 6.

138. Zhou, 10–11.

139. Mao Zedong and other top leaders knew of instances of famine as early as 1958. Jeremy Brown, "Great Leap City: Surviving the Famine in Tianjin," in *Eating Bitterness: New Perspectives on China's Great Leap Forward and Famine,* ed. Kimberley Ens Manning and Felix Wemheuer (Vancouver: UBC Press, 2011), 227.

140. Ministry of Foreign Trade Leading Party Group, "Duiwai Maoyi Bu Dangzu Guanyu Yi Jiu Wu Jiu Nian Jinchukou Huodan Tiaozheng Yijian de Qingshi Baogao" [Ministry of Foreign Trade Leading Party Group Report Requesting

Instructions on Proposed Adjustments to the 1959 Import and Export Manifests], January 23, 1959, Hubei Provincial Archive (hereafter HuPA), SZ77-01-0058-001, 2.

141. US Assistant Secretary of State for Far Eastern Affairs (Robertson) to Hong Kong Consul (Dillon), "Growing Dependence of the Chinese Mainland Economy on Free World Imports and Prospective Payments Difficulties," February 16, 1959, USNA, RG 59, Far East Trade, Box 2047, File 493.00/3-355, 2.

142. US Consulate in Hong Kong (Dillon) to Secretary of State, untitled telegram, March 25, 1959, USNA, RG 84, Hong Kong Classified General Records, Box 25, File 510.1–Trade Agreements Hong Kong and Other Countries.

143. O. Edmund Clubb, *Twentieth Century China* (New York: Columbia University Press, 1964), 375.

144. US Consulate in Hong Kong (Steeves) to Secretary of State, untitled telegram, April 2, 1959, USNA, RG 84, Hong Kong Classified General Records, Box 25, File 510.1–Trade Agreements China, P.R. and Other Countries 1959-60–61.

145. Ministry of Foreign Trade Leading Party Group, "Duiwai Maoyi Bu Dangzu Guanyu Zhixing Duiwai Maoyi Jihua Zhong Cunzai Wenti de Qingshi Baogao" [Ministry of Foreign Trade Leading Party Group Report Requesting Instructions Concerning Existing Problems in the Implementation of the Foreign Trade Plan], March 11, 1959, HuPA, SZ77-01-0058-004, 2.

146. Li Xiannian, "Li Xiannian Tongzhi Zai Quan Guo Caimao Shuji Huiyi Shang de Zongjie Fayan" [Concluding Remarks by Comrade Li Xiannian at a Nationwide Meeting of Finance and Trade Secretaries], May 12, 1959, *DWMYJ, 1958–1965,* 29.

147. Li Rui, *Lushan Huiyi Shilu* [A True Account of the Lushan Conference] (Hong Kong: Tiandi Tushu, 2015), 117.

148. Luthi, *The Sino-Soviet Split,* 127; MacFarquhar, *The Origins of the Cultural Revolution,* 2:213.

149. MacFarquhar, *The Origins of the Cultural Revolution,* 2:234.

150. As quoted in Harrison E. Salisbury, *The New Emperors: China in the Era of Mao and Deng* (Boston: Little, Brown, 1992), 181.

151. Gao Feng, *Lin Haiyun Zhuan: Cong Hongjun Zhanshi Dao Gongheguo Haiguan Zongshu Shuzhang, Waimao Bu Buzhang* [A Biography of Lin Haiyun: From Red Army Soldier to (People's) Republic (of China) Customs Director, Director of the Ministry of Foreign Trade] (Beijing: Duiwai Jingji Maoyi Daxue, 2000), 355.

152. CCP Central Committee, "Zonggong Zhongyang Pizhuan Duiwai Maoyi Bu Dangzu 'Guanyu Jin Nian Duiwai Maoyi Shougou, Chukou Jihua Zhixing

Qingkuang he Wancheng Quan Nian Renwu de Yijian de Baogao'" [CCP Central Committee Endorsement and Distribution of the Ministry of Foreign Trade Leading Party Group's 'Report on Recommendations Concerning Implementation of This Year's Foreign Trade Procurement (and) Export Plan and Completion of Annual Tasks'], October 7, 1959, HPA, 910-1-27-5, 2.

153. Ministry of Foreign Trade Leading Party Group, "Guanyu Jin Nian Duiwai Maoyi Shougou, Chukou Jihua Zhixing Qingkuang he Wancheng Quan Nian Renwu de Yijian de Baogao" [Report on Recommendations Concerning Implementation of This Year's Foreign Trade Procurement (and) Export Plan and Completion of Annual Tasks], September 30, 1959, HPA, 910-1-27-5, 2.

154. Ministry of Foreign Trade Leading Party Group, "Shi Wu Zhong Zhuyao Shangpin Chukou Xieyi Zhixing Qingkuang Biao" [Table (Showing) Implementation of Fifteen Major Types of Commodity Export Agreements], in "Guanyu Jin Nian Duiwai Maoyi Shougou, Chukou Jihua Zhixing Qingkuang he Wancheng Quan Nian Renwu de Yijian de Baogao," September 30, 1959, 6. These figures represented the fulfillment levels of socialist export agreements and planned exports to capitalist markets for 1959, as well as commitments to socialist nations from 1958 that had not yet been fulfilled.

155. CCP Central Committee and the State Council, "Zhonggong Zhongyang, Guowuyuan Guanyu Lizheng Wancheng Jin Nian Duiwai Maoyi de Shougou Renwu he Chukou Renwu de Jinji Zhishi" [CCP Central Committee and State Council Urgent Instruction on Striving to Fulfill This Year's Foreign Trade Procurement and Export Tasks], October 26, 1959, HuPA, SZ77-01-0061-006, [n.p.].

156. Ministry of Foreign Trade, "Guanyu Jianjue Guanche 'Zhonggong Zhongyang, Guowuyuan Guanyu Lizheng Wancheng Jin Nian Duiwai Maoyi de Shougou Renwu he Chukou Renwu de Jinji Zhishi' de Zhishi" [Directive Concerning the Resolute Implementation of "CCP Central Committee and State Council Urgent Instruction on Striving to Fulfill This Year's Foreign Trade Procurement and Export Tasks"], November 4, 1959, HuPA, SZ77-01-0061-004, 1.

157. Gao, *Lin Haiyun Zhuan,* 356–357.

158. Ministry of Foreign Trade Leading Party Group, "Duiwai Maoyi Bu Dangzu Guanyu 1960 Nian Duiwai Maoyi Jihua he Guobie Kongzhi Shuzi de Qingshi Baogao" [Ministry of Foreign Trade Leading Party Group Report Requesting Instructions on the 1960 Foreign Trade Plan and National (Trade) Control Figures], December 20, 1959, in CCP Central Committee, "Zhongyang Yuanze Tongyi Duiwai Maoyi Bu Dangzu Guanyu 1960 Nian Duiwai Maoyi Jihua de Qingshi Baogao" [Central Committee Agreement in Principle to Ministry of Foreign Trade Leading Party Group Report Requesting Instructions on the 1960 Foreign Trade Plan], HPA, 855-18-655-24, 2.

159. Ministry of Foreign Trade Leading Party Group, "Duiwai Maoyi Bu Dangzu Guanyu 1960 Nian Duiwai Maoyi Jihua he Guobie Kongzhi Shuzi de Qingshi Baogao," December 20, 1959, 9.

160. Ministry of Foreign Trade Leading Party Group, 7.

6. TRADING FOR SALVATION

1. "Grain Output in '59 below China's Goal," *New York Times,* January 21, 1960, 5.

2. "Li Xiannian Zhuan" Bianxie Zu, *Li Xiannian Nianpu* [A Chronology of Li Xiannian], 6 vols. (Beijing: Zhongyang Wenxian, 2011) (hereafter cited as *LXNNP*), 3:205; State Council Office of Finance and Trade, "Guowuyuan Caimao Bangongshi Guanyu Yi Jiu Wu Jiu Nian Duiwai Maoyi Shougou Renwu he Chukou Renwu Chao'e Wancheng de Baogao" [State Council Office of Finance and Trade Report Regarding Surpassed Completion of Foreign Trade Procurement and Export Tasks in 1959], January 6, 1960, *DWMYJ, 1958–1965,* 104–105.

3. "Li Xiannian Zhuan" Bianxie Zu, *Li Xiannian Zhuan* [A Biography of Li Xiannian], 2 vols. (Beijing: Zhongyang Wenxian, 2009), 1:467; Jin Chongji, *Zhou Enlai Zhuan* [A Biography of Zhou Enlai], 4 vols. (Beijing: Zhongyang Wenxian, 2018), 3:1391.

4. Thomas P. Bernstein, "Mao Zedong and the Famine of 1959–1960: A Study in Willfulness," *China Quarterly* 186 (June 2006): 422.

5. This scene was recounted by Huang Da, Li Xiannian's personal secretary from 1953 to 1964. Gao Yuanrong and Liu Xueli, "Li Xiannian: Gongheguo Er Shi Liu Nian de Fu Zongli—Jinian Li Xiannian Danchen Yi Bai Zhou Nian Fangtan Lu" [Li Xiannian: Twenty-Six-Year Vice Premier of the Republic—Interviews to Commemorate the 100th Anniversary of Li Xiannian's Birth], *Zhonggong Dangshi Yanjiu* 6 (2009): 103.

6. Li Xiannian, "Li Xiannian Tongzhi Zai Quan Guo Caimao Shuji Huiyi Shang de Zongjie Fayan" [Comrade Li Xiannian's Concluding Remarks during the National Conference of Finance and Trade (Party) Secretaries], February 28, 1960, HPA, 855-5-1805-1, 14.

7. CCP Central Committee, "Zhongyang Pizhuan Li Xiannian Tongzhi Guanyu Anpai Nongcun Renmin Shenghuo Wenti he Jixu Kaizhan Aiguo Shou Mian Yundong de Baogao" [Central Committee Endorsement and Distribution of Comrade Li Xiannian's Report on Problems Concerning the Organization of Rural People's Livelihoods and Continued Development of the Patriotic Cotton Sales Campaign], January 21, 1960, as cited in "Li Xiannian Zhuan" Bianxie Zu, *Li Xiannian Zhuan,* 1:467.

8. Li Xiannian, "Guanyu Kaizhan Jinji Diaoyun Liangshi de Tuji Yundong de Baogao" [Report on the Campaign to Conduct Emergency Food Transfers],

February 18, 1960, in Li Xiannian, *Jianguo Yilai Li Xiannian Wengao* [Li Xiannian's Manuscripts since the Founding of the People's Republic], 4 vols. (Beijing: Zhongyang Wenxian, 2011), 2:116.

9. Li, "Guanyu Kaizhan Jinji Diaoyun Liangshi de Tuji Yundong de Baogao," 116–117.

10. Droughts in the north and floods in the south exacerbated these shortfalls. Philip Short, *Mao: A Life* (New York: Henry Holt, 1999), 502.

11. Fang Weizhong and Jin Chongji, eds., *Li Fuchun Zhuan* [A Biography of Li Fuchun] (Beijing: Zhongyang Wenxian, 2001), 540.

12. Jin, *Zhou Enlai Zhuan,* 3:1392–1393.

13. As quoted in "Shanghai Huiyi Jieshu Shi Jianghua Jiyao" [Summary of Shanghai Meeting Concluding Remarks], June 17, 1960, HPA, 855-5-1793-5, 1–2.

14. Fang and Jin, *Li Fuchun Zhuan,* 541.

15. The original totals are provided in *jin,* or Chinese catties, in Fang and Jin, 541. The figures here are based on calculations at two thousand *jin* per metric ton.

16. CCP Central Committee, "Zhonggong Zhongyang Pizhuan Shaanxi Sheng Wei Guanyu Pubian de Shenru de Jiancha Duiwai Maoyi Shougou Gongzuo de Baogao" [CCP Central Committee Endorsement and Distribution of Shaanxi Provincial Committee Report on General and In-Depth Investigations of Foreign Trade Procurement Work], April 10, 1960; CCP Shaanxi Provincial Committee, "Zhonggong Shaanxi Sheng Wei Pizhuan Sheng Shangye Ting Dangzu Guanyu Jin Nian Yi, Er Yue Fen Waimao Shougou Qingkuang de Jianbao" [CCP Shaanxi Provincial Committee Endorsement and Distribution of Provincial Department of Commerce Leading Party Group Brief Report on the Circumstances of Foreign Trade Procurement in January and February of this Year], March 29, 1960, both in *DWMYJ, 1958–1965,* 112.

17. Ministry of Foreign Trade Leading Party Group, "Duiwai Maoyi Bu Dangzu Guanyu Yi Jiu Liu Ling Nian Duiwai Maoyi Jihua Zhixing Qingkuang de Qingshi Baogao" [Ministry of Foreign Trade Leading Party Group Report and Request for Instructions on the Implementation of the 1960 Foreign Trade Plan], June 3, 1960, *DWMYJ, 1958-1965,* 113.

18. CCP Central Committee, "Yi Jiu Liu Ling Nian Liu Yue Er Shi Liu Ri Zhaokai de Dianhua Huiyi—Tan Zhenlin[,] Li Xiannian Tongzhi Jiang Xiashou Xiazhong he Liangshi Diaoyun Wenti Jilu" [Telephone Conference Convened on June 26, 1960—Comrades Tan Zhenlin and Li Xiannian Discuss the Summer Harvest and Grain Transportation Issues], June 26, 1960, HPA, 855-5-1801-5, 18.

19. Short, *Mao: A Life*, 503; Chen Jian, "The Tibetan Rebellion of 1959 and China's Changing Relations with India and the Soviet Union," *Journal of Cold War Studies* 8, no. 3 (2006): 54–101.

20. Short, *Mao: A Life*, 503.

21. Wu Lengxi, *Shi Nian Lunzhan: 1956–1966 Zhong-Su Guanxi Huiyi Lu* [Ten Years of Polemics: A Memoir of Sino–Soviet Relations, 1956–1966], 2 vols. (Beijing: Zhongyang Wenxian, 1999), 1:251–252, and Alexander Pantsov and Steven Levine, *Deng Xiaoping: A Revolutionary Life* (Oxford: Oxford University Press, 2015), 206. For the colloquial meaning of "galoshes," see William Taubman, *Khrushchev: The Man and His Era* (New York: W. W. Norton, 2003), 394.

22. Editorial Department, "Yanzhe Weida Liening de Daolu Qianjin" [Along the Great Path of Lenin], *Renmin Ribao,* April 22, 1960, 1.

23. Lu Dingyi, "Zai Liening de Geming Qizhi Xia Tuanjie Qilai—1960 Nian 4 Yue 22 Ri Zai Liening Dansheng Jiushi Zhou Nian Jinian Dahui Shang de Baogao" [Unite under the Revolutionary Banner of Lenin—Report during Meeting Commemorating the Ninetieth Anniversary of the Birth of Lenin], *Renmin Ribao,* April 23, 1960, 1. For an inside account of how the CCP coordinated this propaganda attack, see Wu, *Shi Nian Lunzhan,* 1:258–266.

24. Odd Arne Westad, introduction to *Brothers in Arms: The Rise and Fall of the Sino-Soviet Alliance, 1945–1963,* ed. Odd Arne Westad (Washington, DC: Woodrow Wilson Center Press, 1998), 25.

25. US Consulate Hong Kong (Holmes) to the Secretary of State (Herter), untitled telegram, March 30, 1960, USNA, RG 84, Hong Kong Classified General Records, Box 25, File 510.1–Trade Agreements China, P.R. and Other Countries 1959-60-61.

26. CCP Central Committee, "Yi Jiu Liu Ling Nian Liu Yue Er Shi Liu Ri Zhaokai de Dianhua Huiyi," 1.

27. CCP Central Committee, "Yi Jiu Liu Ling Nian Liu Yue Er Shi Liu Ri Zhaokai de Dianhua Huiyi," 18.

28. State Council Office of Finance and Trade, "Guanyu Yaoqiu Quan Dang Zhuajin Liangshi Diaoyun, Zhuajin Chukou Shougou, Zhuajin Fushipin Shengchan he Gongying de Baogao" [Report Requesting the Entire Party Grasp Firmly Grain Transportation(,) Export Procurement(,) Food Production and Supplies (Work)], June 15, 1960, HPA, 999-4-29-12, 2.

29. CCP Central Committee, "Yi Jiu Liu Ling Nian Liu Yue Er Shi Liu Ri Zhaokai de Dianhua Huiyi," 18.

30. Jin, *Zhou Enlai Zhuan,* 3:1396.

31. Jin, 3:1396; Shu Guang Zhang, "The Sino-Soviet Alliance and the Cold War in Asia, 1954–1962," in *The Cambridge History of the Cold War,* vol. 1, *Origins,* ed. Melvyn P. Leffler and Odd Arne Westad (New York: Cambridge University Press, 2009), 371.

32. Zhang, "The Sino-Soviet Alliance and the Cold War in Asia, 1954–1962," 371.

33. Zhang, 371.

34. CCP Central Committee, "Zhongyang Guanyu Quan Dang Dagao Duiwai Maoyi Shougou he Chukou Yundong de Jinji Zhishi" [Central Committee Emergency Instructions Regarding the Entire Party Vigorously Conducting the Campaign for Foreign Trade Procurement and Exports], August 10, 1960, HPA, 855-5-1813-9, 2–3.

35. Gao Feng, *Lin Haiyun Zhuan: Cong Hongjun Zhanshi Dao Gongheguo Haiguan Zongshu Shuzhang, Waimao Bu Buzhang* [A Biography of Lin Haiyun: From Red Army Soldier to (People's) Republic (of China) Customs Director, Director of the Ministry of Foreign Trade] (Beijing: Duiwai Jingji Maoyi Daxue, 2000), 362.

36. CCP Central Committee, 1, 3.

37. CCP Central Committee, 1–2.

38. CCP Central Committee, 2.

39. On the likelihood that Mao knew about Stalin's larger loan to Poland in 1949, see Lawrence C. Reardon, *The Reluctant Dragon: Crisis Cycles in Chinese Foreign Economic Policy* (Seattle: University of Washington Press, 2002), 50.

40. Mao Zedong to Central Committee, January 3, 1950, as translated and reproduced in Zhang Shu Guang and Chen Jian, eds., *Chinese Communist Foreign Policy and the Cold War in Asia: New Documentary Evidence, 1944–1950* (Chicago: Imprint, 1996), 132–133; Anastas Mikoyan and Mao Zedong, untitled memorandum of conversation, February 6, 1949, translated by Sergey Radchenko, History and Public Policy Program Digital Archive, APRF: F. 39, Op. 1, D. 39, Ll. 78–88, as reprinted in Andrei Ledovskii, Raisa Mirovitskaia, and Vladimir Miasnikov, *Sovetsko-Kitaiskie Otnosheniia,* vol. 5, book 2, 1946–February 1950 (Moscow: Pamiatniki Istoricheskoi Mysli, 2005), 81–87, http://digitalarchive.wilsoncenter.org/document/113352.

41. CCP Central Committee, "Zhongyang Guanyu Quan Dang Dagao Duiwai Maoyi Shougou he Chukou Yundong de Jinji Zhishi," 2.

42. Shen Jueren et al., *Dangdai Zhongguo Duiwai Maoyi* [Contemporary Chinese Foreign Trade], 2 vols. (Beijing: Dangdai Zhongguo, 1992), appendix 3, 2:383.

43. Benjamin Schwartz, *Chinese Communism and the Rise of Mao* (Cambridge, MA: Harvard University Press, 1979), 203–204.

44. Alexander V. Pantsov and Steven I. Levine, *Mao: The Real Story* (New York: Simon & Schuster, 2012), 476; Frank Dikotter, *Mao's Great Famine: The History of China's Most Devastating Catastrophe, 1958–1962* (New York: Walker, 2010), 116.

45. Li Xiannian, "Li Xiannian Tongzhi Zai Ba Yue Er Shi Wu Ri Dianhua Huiyi Shang de Jianghua" [Remarks by Comrade Li Xiannian During the August 25 (1960) Telephone Conference], in CCP Central Committee, "Yi Jiu Liu Ling Nian Ba Yue Er Shi Wu Ri Zhaokai de Dianhua Huiyi—Li Xiannian[,] Liao Luyan[,] Tan Zhenlin Tongzhi Jiang Nongchanpin Shougou he Shenghuo Anpai Wenti Huiyi Jilu" [Telephone Conference Convened on August 25, 1960—Comrades Li Xiannian, Liao Luyan, and Tan Zhenlin Discuss the Matters of Agricultural Procurement and Arrangements for (People's) Livelihood], August 25, 1960, HPA, 855-5-1802-3, 2.

46. The Central Committee also began to relax some of the most harmful domestic policies associated with the Great Leap Forward. A November 3 emergency directive permitted villagers to maintain private plots, engage in small sideline occupations, and participate in newly revived rural markets (*nongcun jishi*). CCP Central Committee, "Zhonggong Zhongyang Guanyu Nongcun Renmin Gongshe Dangqian Zhengce Wenti de Jinji Zhishi Xin" [CCP Central Committee Emergency Instruction Letter Concerning the Issue of Current Policies for Rural People's Communes], November 3, 1960, HPA, 940-4-511-8.

47. "Li Xiannian Zhuan" Bianxie Zu, *Li Xiannian Zhuan*, 1:481; Shang Chang-feng, "1961 Nian Zhongguo Liangshi Jinkou Yanjiu" [Analysis of China's 1961 Grain Imports], *Zhonggong Dangshi Ziliao* [CCP Party History Materials] 3 (2009): 155.

48. Chad J. Mitcham, *China's Economic Relations with the West and Japan, 1949–1979: Grain, Trade and Diplomacy* (London: Routledge, 2005), 4.

49. Shang, "1961 Nian Zhongguo Liangshi Jinkou Yanjiu," 154.

50. *LXNNP,* 3:258; Zhang Suhua, "'Bu Diaocha Qingchu, Ta Jiu Bu Jianghua'—Ganwu Liu Shi Niandai Chu de Chen Yun" ["If (He) Doesn't Investigate Clearly, He Does Not Speak"—Coming to Grips with Chen Yun in the Early 1960s], *Dang de Wenxian* 4 (2005): 122–123.

51. Zhou Enlai to Mao Zedong and the Central Committee, untitled memorandum, October 23, 1960, HPA, 855-18-692-9, [n.p.].

52. Ye Jizhuang, "Waimao Bu Ye Jizhuang Buzhang Guanyu Zhong-Su Maoyi Wenti Yuejian Sulian Dashi he Sulian Shangwu Daibiao de Tanhua Gao" [Draft Remarks by MOFT Minister Ye Jizhuang on Sino–Soviet Trade Issues (for) an Appointment with the Soviet Ambassador and the Soviet Commercial Representative], October 1960, HPA, 855-18-692-9, 1–2.

53. Ye, "Waimao Bu Ye Jizhuang Buzhang Guanyu Zhong-Su Maoyi Wenti Yuejian Sulian Dashi he Sulian Shangwu Daibiao de Tanhua Gao," 2–4.

54. Ye, 4.

55. Ye, 5–6.

56. Chinese Embassy in Moscow to Ministry of Foreign Affairs and Ministry of Foreign Trade, "Sugong Zhongyang Taolun 1961 Nian Duiwai Yuanzhu he Maoyi Wenti" [Communist Party of the Soviet Union Central Committee Discusses Foreign Aid and Trade Issues for 1961], November 14, 1960, FMA, 109-02076-04(1), 101.

57. Chinese Commercial Office (Moscow) to the Ministry of Foreign Trade, "Su 1961 Nian Duiwai Maoyi Tanpan Qingkuang" [The Circumstances of the Soviet Union's 1961 Foreign Trade Talks], December 21, 1960, FMA, 109-02076-04(1), 104.

58. "Li Xiannian Zhuan" Bianxie Zu, *Li Xiannian Zhuan,* 1:481–482.

59. Gao, *Lin Haiyun Zhuan,* 365.

60. Mitcham, *China's Economic Relations with the West and Japan,* 39; British Chargé d'Affaires in Beijing (R. D. Clift) to Far Eastern Department, Foreign Office, untitled letter, June 3, 1960, TNA, FO 371 / 150449, FC 1121 / 7; British Embassy in Beijing (A. H. Campbell) to Peter G. F. Dalton, Foreign Office, untitled letter, March 15, 1957, TNA, FO 371 / 127322, FC 1122 / 3.

61. Li Xiannian also worked with Minister of Foreign Trade Ye Jizhuang, Minister of Grain Chen Guodong, Niu Peicong, and Ma Dingbang. See "Li Xiannian Zhuan" Bianxie Zu, *Li Xiannian Zhuan,* 1:482.

62. Wu et al., *Hongse Huarun* [Red China Resources] (Beijing: Zhonghua, 2010), 301, 305.

63. Ministry of Foreign Trade Leading Party Group, "Dangqian Duiwai Maoyi Shougou he Chukou Qingkuang de Baogao" [Report on the Current Circumstances of Foreign Trade Procurement and Exports], November 14, 1960, HPA, 855-5-1813-13, 3–4.

64. State Council Office of Finance and Trade, "Caimao Bangongshi Guanyu 1961 Nian Liangshi he Shichang Wenti de Anpai Yaodian" [Finance and Trade Office on Key Points Concerning the Disposition of Grain and Market Issues for 1961], December 22, 1960, *DWMYJ, 1958–1965,* 124.

65. One *liang* was equivalent to 50 grams based on the PRC's standard mass units, which were recalibrated in 1959.

66. State Council Office of Finance and Trade, "Caimao Bangongshi Guanyu 1961 Nian Liangshi he Shichang Wenti de Anpai Yaodian," 124.

67. Gao and Liu, "Li Xiannian: Gongheguo Er Shi Liu Nian de Fu Zongli—Jinian Li Xiannian Danchen Yi Bai Zhou Nian Fangtanlu," 107.

68. Li Xiannian, "Li Xiannian Tongzhi Fayan Yaodian: Di Er ge Wenti Chukou yu Waihui" [Key Remarks by Comrade Li Xiannian: The Second Problem(,) Exports and Foreign Exchange], March 20, 1961, *DWMYJ, 1958–1965,* 128.

69. Li Xiannian, "Zuohao Jinkou Liangshi de Jiexie, Zhuanyun Gongzuo" [Complete the Work of Receiving, Unloading, and Distributing Imported Grain], January 27, 1961, in *Li Xiannian Lun Caizheng Jinrong Maoyi, 1950–1991 Nian* [Li Xiannian on Finance, Banking, (and) Trade, 1950–1991], 2 vols. (Beijing: Zhongguo Caizheng Jingji, 1992), 1:441.

70. Li, *Li Xiannian Lun Caizheng Jinrong Maoyi, 1950–1991 Nian,* 1:441.

71. Wu et al., *Hongse Huarun,* 303.

72. Wu et al., 303.

73. CCP Central Committee, "Zhongyang Pizhuan Caimao Bangongshi Guanyu Yi Jiu Liu Yi Nian Duiwai Maoyi Ruogan Wenti de Qingshi Baogao" [Central Committee Endorsement and Distribution of Finance and Trade Office Report and Request for Instructions on Several Issues in Foreign Trade for 1961], February 7, 1961, HPA, 855-6-2032-13, 2.

74. Frederick Nossal, "China Seeks Credit Deal in Wheat," *Globe and Mail,* April 6, 1961, 1; Wu et al., *Hongse Huarun,* 302.

75. Bruce MacDonald, "Canadian Goods Sought after 3 Years: China Trade Team Arrives: Wheat Considered Principal Interest," *Globe and Mail,* December 29, 1960, 1.

76. Bruce MacDonald, "China Signs Barley Deal with Canada," *Globe and Mail,* January 24, 1961, 1.

77. "Canada Makes Big Grain Deal with Red China," *Chicago Daily Tribune,* February 3, 1961, 14.

78. "Canada Makes Big Grain Deal with Red China," 14.

79. Wu et al., *Hongse Huarun,* 305.

80. Raymond Daniell, "Canada to Sell China 362 Million in Grain," *New York Times,* May 3, 1961, 1.

81. Bruce MacDonald, "China Buys $362,000,000 Grain," *Globe and Mail,* May 3, 1961, 1.

82. "Red China Top Wheat Buyer," *Los Angeles Times,* September 12, 1961, 12.

83. Shang, "1961 Nian Zhongguo Liangshi Jinkou Yanjiu," 157.

84. Raymond Daniell, "Canada to Sell China 362 Million in Grain," 2.

85. State Council Office of Finance and Trade, "Guanyu Yi Jiu Liu Yi Nian Duiwai Maoyi Ruogan Wenti de Qingshi Baogao" [Report and Request for Instructions on Several Issues in Foreign Trade for 1961], January 18, 1961, in CCP Central Committee, "Zhongyang Pizhuan Caimao Bangongshi Guanyu Yi Jiu Liu Yi Nian Duiwai Maoyi Ruogan Wenti de Qingshi Baogao," February 7, 1961, HPA, 855-6-2032-13, 4, 6.

86. Following suggestions from Li Xiannian in March 1961, the central government began to offer grain incentives to producers of six key export products: tea, silk, peppermint oil, apples, oranges, and shelled walnuts. By 1962, the state's foreign trade companies could offer cigarettes, silk, and other scarce goods to induce farmers to produce lucrative export commodities. See Lawrence C. Reardon, "Learning How to Open the Door: A Reassessment of China's 'Opening' Strategy," *China Quarterly* 155 (1998): 485.

87. State Council Office of Finance and Trade, "Guanyu Yi Jiu Liu Yi Nian Duiwai Maoyi Ruogan Wenti de Qingshi Baogao," 7.

88. Li Xiannian to Chairman Mao and the Central Committee, "Guanyu Liangshi Wenti de Yi Feng Xin" [A Letter on the Grain Issue], July 30, 1961, HPA, 855-6-2031-6, 2.

89. Li Xiannian to Chairman Mao and the Central Committee, "Guanyu Liangshi Wenti de Yi Feng Xin," July 30, 1961, 5, 8.

90. Gao, *Lin Haiyun Zhuan,* 405. See also Qu Yun, "Preface," *DWMYJ, 1958–1965,* 5.

91. Chen Yun, "Zuohao Waimao Gongzuo" [Perform Foreign Trade Work Well], May 30, 1961, *CYWX,* 3:157–158.

92. Zhu De, excerpts from untitled remarks in Guangzhou, March 30, 1960, as quoted in "'Yi Jin Yang Chu' he 'Yi Chu Dai Jin,'" *Dang de Wenxian* 6 (2006): 7.

93. Zhu De, "'Yi Jin Yang Chu' he 'Yi Chu Dai Jin,'" 9.

94. Ministry of Foreign Trade, "Jin Ji Nian Lai Duiwai Maoyi Ji ge Zhuyao Bianhua de Ziliao" [Data for Several Major Changes in Foreign Trade during the Past Few Years], August 1, 1962, *DWMYJ, 1958–1965,* 70.

95. On this point, see State Planning Commission and State Council Office of Finance and Trade, "Guojia Jihua Weiyuanhui, Guowuyuan Caimao Bangongshi Guanyu Yi Jiu Liu Si Nian Duiwai Maoyi Jihua Anpai Yijian de Baogao" [Report by the State Planning Commission and the State Council Office of Finance and Trade on Suggestions for Foreign Trade Planning Arrangements for 1964], November 8, 1963, *DWMYJ, 1958–1965,* 157.

96. For population increases in China from 1958 to 1965 and the corresponding drop in per capita grain production, see Colin A. Carter and Fu-Ning Zhong, "China's Past and Future Role in the Grain Trade," *Economic Development and Cultural Change* 39, no. 4 (July 1991): 792.

97. State Planning Commission and Ministry of Foreign Trade, "Guojia Jiwei, Duiwai Maoyi Bu Guanyu Xiang Xi Ou Guojia Goumai Huafei, Huaxian, Lianyou Chengtao Shebei he Zhuanli de Qingshi Baogao" [Report from the State Planning Commission and the Ministry of Foreign Trade Requesting Instructions on the Purchase of Chemical Fertilizer, Chemical Fiber, and Oil Refining Equipment and Patents from Western European Nations], October 13, 1962, *DWMYJ, 1958–1965,* 417.

98. State Planning Commission and Ministry of Foreign Trade, "Guojia Jiwei, Duiwai Maoyi Bu Guanyu Xiang Xi Ou Guojia Goumai Huafei, Huaxian, Lianyou Chengtao Shebei he Zhuanli de Qingshi Baogao," 417–419.

99. State Planning Commission and Ministry of Foreign Trade, 418. For the estimated cost of each project, see State Planning Commission and Ministry of Foreign Trade, 421, schedules 1 and 2.

100. State Planning Commission and Ministry of Foreign Trade, 417.

101. Zhou Enlai, "Guanyu Cujin Zhong-Ri Guanxi de Zhengzhi San Yuanze he Maoyi San Yuanze" [Three Political Principles and Three Trade Principles Concerning the Promotion of Sino–Japanese Relations], August 27, 1960, *DWMYJ, 1958–1965,* 466.

102. Amy King, *China-Japan Relations after World War Two: Empire, Industry, and War, 1949–1971* (Cambridge: Cambridge University Press, 2016), 178.

103. King, *China-Japan Relations after World War Two,* 183.

104. State Planning Commission, "Guojia Jiwei Guanyu Yi Jiu Liu San Nian Ba Yue Zhi Yi Jiu Liu Si Nian San Yue Cong Ziben Zhuyi Guojia Jinkou Chengtao Shebei de Qingkuang" [State Planning Commission (Report) on the Circumstances Surrounding Imports of Complete Sets of Equipment from Capitalist Countries from August 1963 to March 1964], March 17, 1964, *DWMYJ, 1958–1965,* 432–433.

105. Board of Trade, "Brief for the Official Visit of Mr. Lu Hsu-Chang, Vice Minister of Foreign Trade of the People's Republic of China, 21st March to 12th April, 1963," TNA, FO 371 / 170691, FC 1151 / 42.

106. Board of Trade, "Visit to Britain of Mr. Lu Hsu-Chang, Vice-Minister of Foreign Trade of the People's Republic of China," TNA, FO 371 / 170691, FC 1151 / 45.

107. Jean Polaris, "The Sino-Soviet Dispute: Its Economic Impact on China," *International Affairs* 40, no. 4 (October 1964): 651.

108. State Planning Commission, "Guojia Jiwei Guanyu Yi Jiu Liu San Nian Ba Yue Zhi Yi Jiu Liu Si Nian San Yue Cong Ziben Zhuyi Guojia Jinkou Chengtao Shebei de Qingkuang," *DWMYJ, 1958–1965,* 432, 435.

109. CIA, "Communist China[:] Organization for the Conduct of Foreign Trade," January 1962, General CIA Records, Freedom of Information Act Electronic Reading Room, CIA-RDP78-02646R000500150001-6, 28.

110. Ministry of Foreign Trade General Office, "Duiwai Maoyi Bu Bangong Ting: Guanyu Wo Yi Xiang Liu ge Ziben Zhuyi Guojia Dingtuo Shi Wu Xiang Chengtao Shebei he Xin Jishu" [Ministry of Foreign Trade General Office: (Report) Concerning (That) We Have Already Ordered Fifteen Complete Sets of Equipment and New Technologies from Six Capitalist Countries], December 4, 1964, *DWMYJ, 1958–1965,* 460.

111. For Zhou's role in the creation of these two groups, see Liu Yang, "20 Shiji 60 Niandai Cong Xifang Guojia Yinjin Chengtao Shebei he Jishu dui Zhongguo Keji Fazhan Yingxiang Yanjiu" [Analysis of the Effect of the Introduction of Complete Sets of Western Equipment and Technology from Western Countries on China's Scientific and Technological Development in the 1960s], *Zhongguo Keji Shi Zazhi* [Chinese Journal for the History of Science and Technology] 39, no. 2 (2018): 171.

112. Chemical Fertilizer Group and Chemical Fiber Group, "Huafei Xiaozu, Huaxian Xiaozu Guanyu Cong Xi Ou he Riben Qiagou Chengtao Shebei Gongzuo de Jinzhan Qingkuang he Wenti Xiang Jiwei he Zhongyang de Baogao" [Chemical Fertilizer Group (and) Chemical Fiber Group Report to the State Planning Commission and the Central Committee on the Progress and Problems of Negotiating the Purchase of Complete Equipment Sets from Western Europe and Japan], March 7, 1963, *DWMYJ, 1958–1965,* 423.

113. Ministry of Foreign Trade General Office, "Duiwai Maoyi Bu Bangong Ting: Guanyu Wo Yi Xiang Liu ge Ziben Zhuyi Guojia Dingtuo Shi Wu Xiang Chengtao Shebei he Xin Jishu," 460.

114. New Technology Import Group, "Xin Jishu Jinkou Xiaozu Guanyu Yinjin Xin Jishu Gongzuo Ji ge Zhuyao Wenti de Baogao" [New Technology Import Group Report on Several Major Issues in the Work of Importing New Technology], March 8, 1965, *DWMYJ, 1958–1965,* 463.

115. New Technology Import Group, "Xin Jishu Jinkou Xiaozu Guanyu Yinjin Xin Jishu Gongzuo Ji ge Zhuyao Wenti de Baogao," 465.

116. Office of the British Chargé d'Affaires in Beijing (L. S. Ross) to M. R. L. Robinson of the De La Rue Company, untitled letter, May 23, 1963, TNA, FO 371 / 170717, FC 1861 / 12, 1; Office of the British Chargé d'Affaires in Beijing (L. S. Ross) to Foreign Office, Far Eastern Department (H. B. McKenzie-Johnston), untitled letter, August 27, 1963, TNA, FO 371 / 170717, FC 1861 / 20, 2.

117. Flora Lewis, "Britain Pushing China Trade: Sending $3 Million in Samples to Trade Fair in Peking," *Washington Post,* October 23, 1964, A17.

118. "Peking Ends Fair in Mexico," *New York Times,* January 7, 1964, 14.

119. Drew Middleton, "French Diplomat Gets Peking Post: Chargé d'Affaires Chosen—Trade Goal Outlined," *New York Times,* February 13, 1964, 1. China

ultimately imported US$64.64 million worth of goods from France in 1964. Ministry of Foreign Trade General Office, "Zhong-Fa Maoyi Qingkuang he Dangqian Cunzai de Zhuyao Wenti" [The Sino-French Trade Situation and Current Main Issues], *Waimao Diaoyan* [Foreign Trade Research] 36, November 20, 1965, as reproduced in *DWMYJ, 1958–1965,* 490.

120. Ministry of Foreign Trade, "Duiwai Maoyi Bu Guanyu Yi Jiu Liu San Nian Ji Xiang Zhuyao Gongzuo de Zonghe Baogao" [Ministry of Foreign Trade Composite Report Concerning Several Important (Types of) Work in 1963], December 28, 1963, *DWMYJ, 1958–1965,* 148.

121. Ministry of Foreign Trade Leading Party Group, State Planning Commission Leading Party Group, State Council Office of Finance and Trade, "Duiwai Maoyi Bu Dangzu, Guojia Jihua Weiyuanhui Dangzu, Guowuyuan Caimao Bangongshi Guanyu 1965 Nian Duiwai Maoyi Jihua Anpai Yijian de Baogao" [Ministry of Foreign Trade Leading Party Group, State Planning Commission Leading Party Group, State Council Office of Finance and Trade (Joint) Report on Suggested Arrangements for the 1965 Foreign Trade Plan], February 18, 1965, as cited in Qu Yun, "Preface," *DWMYJ, 1958–1965,* 6; Ministry of Foreign Trade, "Duiwai Maoyi You Guan Ziliao Huibian, Di Yi Fen Ce" [Compilation of Information on Foreign Trade, volume 1], May 1956, FPA, quanzong ziliao, mulu 035, 1.

122. The CCP adopted Li's Eight-Character Plan during the Ninth Plenum of the Eighth National Party Congress in January 1961. See Lawrence C. Reardon, *The Reluctant Dragon: Crisis Cycles in Chinese Foreign Economic Policy,* 105.

123. Roderick MacFarquhar, *The Origins of the Cultural Revolution,* vol. 3, *The Coming of the Cataclysm, 1961–1966* (Oxford: Oxford University Press, 1974), 178.

124. Roderick MacFarquhar and Michael Schoenhals, *Mao's Last Revolution* (Cambridge, MA: The Belknap Press of Harvard University Press, 2006), 8. For an excerpt of Mao's speech, see Zhonggong Zhongyang Wenxian Yanjiushi, *Mao Zedong Zhuan, 1949–1976* [A Biography of Mao Zedong, 1949–1976], 2 vols. (Beijing: Zhongyang Wenxian, 2004), 2:1202.

125. Zhang Suhua, "'Bu Diaocha Qingchu, Ta Jiu Bu Jianghua'—Ganwu Liushi Niandai Chu de Chen Yun," 122.

126. The concept of rapid transformation through trade would reemerge in the late 1970s under the leadership of Hua Guofeng. For an overview, see Barry Naughton, *The Chinese Economy: Transitions and Growth* (Cambridge, MA: MIT Press, 2007), 77–79.

127. Zhou Enlai, "Zai Di Er Jie Quan Guo Renmin Daibiao Dahui Di San Ci Huiyi Bimu Huishang de Jianghua" [Closing Remarks for the Third Session of the Second National People's Congress], April 16, 1962, HPA, 855-6-2289-5, 2.

128. Zhou, "Zai Di Er Jie Quan Guo Renmin Daibiao Dahui Di San Ci Huiyi Bimu Huishang de Jianghua," April 16, 1962, 3.

129. Zhou, 2, 4.

130. Zhou, 2.

7. MARKETS AND THE RISE AND FALL OF REDNESS

1.   The most comprehensive account of the origins of the Cultural Revolution remains Roderick MacFarquhar's three-volume series, *The Origins of the Cultural Revolution* (New York: Published for the Royal Institute of International Affairs, the East Asian Institute of Columbia University, and the Research Institute on Communist Affairs of Columbia University by Columbia University Press, 1974–1997).

2.   Roderick MacFarquhar, *The Origins of the Cultural Revolution,* vol. 3, *The Coming of the Cataclysm, 1961–1966* (Oxford: Oxford University Press, 1997), 461.

3.   Frank Dikotter, *The Cultural Revolution: A People's History, 1962–1976* (New York: Bloomsbury, 2016), 56–57.

4.   Arnold Hugentobler, "Mao verschreibt Terror zum Bruch mit der Vergangenheit" [Mao Prescribes Terror to Break with the Past], August 31, 1966, Swiss Federal Archives E2001-05#1979/137#36*, as cited in Ariane Knüsel, "The Swiss Witnesses to China's Cultural Revolution," Sources and Methods, June 19, 2017, https://www.wilsoncenter.org/blog-post/the-swiss-witnesses-to -chinas-cultural-revolution.

5.   Associated Press, "Red China Purges Trade Minister," *Boston Globe,* November 17, 1966, 54.

6.   "Unrest Threatens U.K. Trade Links," *Times of London,* September 1, 1966, clipping included in TNA, BT 11/6726.

7.   John W. Garver, *China's Quest: The History of the Foreign Relations of the People's Republic of China* (New York: Oxford University Press, 2016), 272.

8.   "Chinese Trade Fair Falls below Standard: Business Hampered by Lectures on Mao," *Times of London,* November 16, 1966, clipping included in TNA, BT 11/6726.

9.   David Oancia, "Peking Wants More Canadian Trade: Hard-Driving Bargainers, These Chinese," *Globe and Mail,* December 7, 1966, B5.

10. Far Eastern Department, Foreign Office, "Trade with China," December 21, 1966, TNA, BT 11/6726, 1.

11. CIA, "China: Prospects for Foreign Trade in 1972," July 1, 1972, General CIA Records, Freedom of Information Act Electronic Reading Room, CIA-RDP85T00875R001700030106-0, 18.

12. CIA, "Communist China: Foreign Trade 1967 and Prospects for 1968," May 1, 1968, General CIA Records, Freedom of Information Act Electronic Reading Room, CIA-RDP85T00875R001600010004-6, 2.

13. CIA, Central Intelligence Bulletin, June 7, 1968, General CIA Records, Freedom of Information Act Electronic Reading Room, CIA-RDP79T00975A011400010001-3, 7.

14. CIA, "Communist China: Foreign Trade 1967 and Prospects for 1968," 2.

15. Li also sent a work team to the Central School of Finance in Beijing. "Li Xiannian Zhuan" Bianxie Zu, *Li Xiannian Zhuan* [A Biography of Li Xiannian], 2 vols. (Beijing: Zhongyang Wenxian, 2009), 1:604.

16. *LXNNP,* 4:345.

17. Philip Short, *Mao: A Life* (New York: Henry Holt, 1999), 537–539.

18. *LXNNP,* 4:356.

19. *LXNNP,* 4:359, 366.

20. For criticisms of Yao Yilin, see *LXNNP,* 4:389.

21. *LXNNP,* 4:423. For calls to "bombard Li Xiannian," see *LXNNP,* 4:421.

22. Wu et al., *Hongse Huarun* [Red China Resources] (Beijing: Zhonghua, 2010), 337–338; Ouyang Xiang, "'Wen Ge' Dongluan he Ji 'Zuo' Luxian Dui Guangjiao Hui de Ganrao yu Pohuai—Jian Lun 'Wen Ge' Shiqi Guomin Jingji Zhuangkuang de Pingjia Wenti" [Disruption and Destruction by "Cultural Revolution" Turmoil and the Ultra "Left" Line at the Canton Fair—Also an Evaluation of the National Economic Situation during the "Cultural Revolution"], *Hong Guang Jiao* [Red Wide Angle] 4 (2013): 4–5.

23. Wu et al., *Hongse Huarun,* 338; Chen Yangyong, *Kucheng Weiju: Zhou Enlai Zai 1967* [Struggling to Steady a Perilous Situation: Zhou Enlai in 1967] (Chongqing: Chongqing Publishing, 2008), 330.

24. Wu et al., *Hongse Huarun,* 339.

25. Song Fengying, "'Hongse Guanjia' Ye Jizhuang," ["The Red Housekeeper" Ye Jizhuang], *Dangshi Zonglan* [Party History Survey] 3 (2011): 41; Li Huimin, He Jinzhou, eds., *Ye Jizhuang Zhuan* [A Biography of Ye Jizhuang] (Beijing: Zhonggong Dangshi, 2010), 220.

26. Wu et al., *Hongse Huarun,* 494.

27. For examples, see *LXNNP,* 4:396, 417, 439.

28. Lorenz Luthi, "Restoring Chaos to History: Sino-Soviet-American Relations, 1969," *China Quarterly* 10 (2012): 382; Yang Kuisong, "The Sino-Soviet Border Clash of 1969: From Zhenbao Island to Sino-American Rapprochement," *Cold War History* 1, no. 1 (August 2000): 24.

29. Lorenz M. Luthi, *The Sino-Soviet Split: Cold War in the Communist World* (Princeton, NJ: Princeton University Press, 2008), 340.

30. Luthi, "Restoring Chaos to History," 390.

31. Mao Zedong, "Mao Zhuxi Zai Zhongguo Gongchandang Di Jiu Jie Zhong-yang Weiyuanhui Di Yi Ci Quanti Huiyi Shang de Jianghua" [Chairman Mao's Speech at the First Plenary Session of the CCP's Ninth Central Committee], April 28, 1969, in Central Cultural Revolution Group, "Mao Zhuxi de Liang Pian Zhongyao Jianghua" [Two Important Speeches by Chairman Mao], May 9, 1969, HPA, 919-1-186-1, 12.

32. For an analysis of rapprochement that stresses security considerations, see Henry Kissinger, *Diplomacy* (New York: Simon & Schuster, 1994), 703–732.

33. Odd Arne Westad, *Restless Empire: China and the World since 1750* (New York: Basic Books, 2012), 360.

34. Chen Jian, *Mao's China and the Cold War* (Chapel Hill: University of North Carolina Press, 2001), 244.

35. Chen, *Mao's China,* 244.

36. Zhonggong Zhongyang Wenxian Yanjiushi, *Mao Zedong Zhuan, 1949–1976* [A Biography of Mao Zedong, 1949–1976], 2 vols. (Beijing: Zhongyang Wenxian, 2004), 2:1556–1604.

37. Li Zhisui and Anne F. Thurston, *The Private Life of Chairman Mao: The Memoirs of Mao's Personal Physician* (New York: Random House, 1994), 528.

38. Li and Thurston, *The Private Life of Chairman Mao,* 533.

39. Several scholars have questioned the feasibility of such a plot. Qiu Jin, for example, the daughter of Lin Biao's Air Force chief, Wu Faxian, argues that Lin never intended to challenge Mao. Qiu Jin, *The Culture of Power: The Lin Biao Incident in the Cultural Revolution* (Stanford, CA: Stanford University Press, 1999).

40. Li and Thurston, *The Private Life of Chairman Mao,* 536, 542.

41. The Central Committee decided in late October 1971 that news of the Lin Biao "incident" would be communicated to the masses. Guo Jian, Yongyi Song, and Yuan Zhou, *Historical Dictionary of the Chinese Cultural Revolution* (Lanham, MD: Scarecrow Press, 2006), 59.

42. Zhonggong Zhongyang Wenxian Yanjiushi, *Mao Zedong Zhuan, 1949–1976,* 2:1605.

43. Ministry of Foreign Trade, "Waimao Jihua Zuotanhui Jianbao, di 11 qi" [Foreign Trade Plan Symposium Bulletin, issue number 11], January 27, 1972, HPA, 926-2-10-5, 1–2, 10.

44. Ministry of Foreign Trade, "Guanyu Dangqian Guoji Xingshi de Ji ge Wenti" [Regarding Several Issues in the Current International Situation], March 23, 1972, HPA, 926-2-15-3, 6.

45. Chen, *Mao's China and the Cold War,* 276.

46. Ministry of Foreign Trade, "Guanyu Dangqian Guoji Xingshi de Ji ge Wenti," March 23, 1972, 3–4.

47. Ministry of Foreign Trade, 3.

48. Ministry of Foreign Trade, "Waimao Jihua Zuotanhui Jianbao, di 11 qi," January 27, 1972, 1–2.

49. Ministry of Foreign Trade, "Quan Guo Waimao Dui Zi Chukou Gongzuo Huiyi Jiyao" [Minutes from the National Foreign Trade Conference on Work (Relating to) Exports to Capitalist (Nations)], April 4, 1971, in Ministry of Foreign Trade, "Waimao Bu Yinfa Duiwai Chukou Maoyi de Ruogan Juti Zhengce he Zuofa" [Ministry of Foreign Trade Printing and Distribution (of) Several Specific Policies and Practices for Foreign Export Trade], May 24, 1971, HPA, 926-2-9-5, 11.

50. Ministry of Foreign Trade, "Waimao Jihua Zuotanhui Jianbao, di 11 qi," January 27, 1972, 1.

51. Ministry of Foreign Trade, "Di Si ge Wu Nian: Fazhan Duiwai Maoyi Chukou Guihua Zhuyao Shangpin Chubu Shexiang (Caogao)" [Fourth Five-Year (Plan): Preliminary Thoughts on Major Goods in the Development of Foreign Trade Export Planning (Draft)], January 1972, HPA, 926-2-10-2, 1.

52. Ministry of Foreign Trade, "Di Si ge Wu Nian Ji Hua Qijian Fazhan Duiwai Maoyi Chukou Guihua de Chubu Shexiang (Cao'an)" [Preliminary Thoughts on Developing Foreign Trade Export Planning during the Fourth Five-Year Plan], March 21, 1972, in Ministry of Foreign Trade, "Guanyu Waimao Jihua Zuotanhui Qingkuang de Baogao" [Report on the Situation of the Foreign Trade Plan Symposium], March 21, 1972, HPA, 926-2-10-16, 8.

53. Tian Songnian, "'Si Wu' Jihua Shulüe" [Brief Narrative of the 'Four(th) Five'(-Year) Plan], *Dang de Wenxian* 2 (2000): 31; Chen Donglin, "Qi Shi Niandai Qianqi de Zhongguo Di Er Ci Duiwai Yinjin Gaochao" [Early 1970s China's Second High Tide of Imports], *Zhonggong Dangshi Yanjiu* 2 (1996): 78.

54. Ezra Vogel, *Deng Xiaoping and the Transformation of China* (Cambridge, MA: Belknap Press of Harvard University Press, 2011), 64.

55. *LXNNP,* 5:211.

56. Chen Donglin, "Qi Shi Niandai Qianqi de Zhongguo Di Er Ci Duiwai Yinjin Gaochao," 78.

57. *LXNNP,* 5:169–170. As of January 1972, the Ministry of Foreign Trade expected to spend US$1.9 billion on imports from capitalist markets during the year. See Ministry of Foreign Trade, "Di Si ge Wu Nian: Fazhan Duiwai Maoyi Chukou Guihua Zhuyao Shangpin Chubu Shexiang (Caogao)," January 1972, 1.

58. *LXNNP,* 170; Zhonggong Zhongyang Wenxian Yanjiushi, *Chen Yun Zhuan* [A Biography of Chen Yun], 4 vols. (Beijing: Zhongyang Wenxian, 2015), 3:1412.

59. "Li Xiannian Zhuan" Bianxie Zu, *Li Xiannian Zhuan,* 2:766–767.

60. *LXNNP,* 5:208–209.

61. "Li Xiannian Zhuan" Bianxie Zu, *Li Xiannian Zhuan,* 2:764–765.

62. "Li Xiannian Zhuan" Bianxie Zu, 767–768.

63. Alexander Pantsov and Steven Levine, *Deng Xiaoping: A Revolutionary Life* (Oxford: Oxford University Press, 2015), 276.

64. "Li Xiannian Zhuan" Bianxie Zu, *Li Xiannian Zhuan,* 2:768.

65. Ji Dengkui and Hua Guofeng also participated in the approval process. See Chen Jinhua, *Guoshi Yishu* [Recollections on Affairs of the Nation] (Beijing: Zhonggong Dangshi, 2005), 14. For Mao's involvement, see An Jianshe, *Zhou Enlai de Zuihou Suiyue* (1966–1976) [Zhou Enlai's Final Years (1966–1976)] (Beijing: Zhongyang Wenxian, 2002), 111.

66. State Planning Revolutionary Committee, "Guanyu Zengjia Shebei Jinkou, Kuoda Jingji Jiaoliu de Qingshi Baogao" [Report and Request to Increase Equipment Imports and Expand Economic Exchanges], January 2, 1973, *Zhonggong Dangshi Ziliao* 2 (2004): 12.

67. Supplemental requests increased the size of the plan to US$5.18 billion. See "Li Xiannian Zhuan" Bianxie Zu, *Li Xiannian Zhuan,* 2:768.

68. Chen Jinhua, "Huigu Xin Zhongguo Di Er Ci Da Guimo Chengtao Jishu Shebei de Yinjin," [Looking Back on the Importation of Large-Scale Complete Sets of Technical Equipment into New China], *Zhonggong Dangshi Ziliao* 2 (2004): 35, 36.

69. State Planning Revolutionary Committee, "Guanyu Zengjia Shebei Jinkou, Kuoda Jingji Jiaoliu de Qingshi Baogao," 14.

70. State Planning Revolutionary Committee, 17.

71. State Planning Revolutionary Committee, 18.

72. Officials estimated that petroleum exports would climb from 209,000 tons in 1970 to over 2.7 million tons in 1975. Ministry of Foreign Trade, "Di Si ge Wu Nian: Fazhan Duiwai Maoyi Chukou Guihua Zhuyao Shangpin Chubu Shexiang (Caogao)," January 1972, 11.

73. State Planning Commission, "Jihua Huiyi Wenjian: 1970 Nian he Di Si ge Wu Nian Guomin Jingji Jihua Baogao (Gong Taolun Xiugai Gao)" [Planning Meeting Document: 1970 and the Fourth Five-Year National Economic Planning Report (For Discussion and Revision)], February 15, 1970, State Planning Commission Archives, (70) 001, no. 0000103, 24.

74. Barry Naughton, *Growing Out of the Plan: Chinese Economic Reform, 1978–1993* (Cambridge: Cambridge University Press, 1995), 69. For the growth of China's oil expansion in the 1960s and 1970s, see Katsuhiko Hama, "The Daqing Oil Field: A Model in China's Struggle for Rapid Industrialization," *Developing Economies* 18, no. 2 (1980): 184.

75. State Planning Commission Core Small Group, "Guanyu Guomin Jingji Jihua Wenti de Baogao" [Report on National Economic Plan Issues], May 25, 1973, HPA, 855-20-1846-13, 19.

76. *LXNNP,* 5:224.

77. *LXNNP,* 5:314.

78. Chen Yun and Li Xiannian regularly discussed the challenge of export pricing in this new environment during internal CCP meetings in 1973. For examples, see *LXNNP,* 5:266–267, 295, 328; Zhonggong Zhongyang Wenxian Yanjiushi, *Chen Yun Zhuan,* 3:1424–1425, 1429.

79. Carl Riskin, *China's Political Economy: The Quest for Development since 1949* (Oxford: Oxford University Press, 1987), 193.

80. [Ministry of Foreign Trade], "Jiedai Waiguo Jishu Renyuan Gongzuo Zuo-tanhui Jiyao (Caogao)" [Minutes of the Symposium on Receiving Foreign Technicians (Draft)], September 1974, HPA, 1057-1-9-3, 1.

81. "Li Xiannian Zhuan" Bianxie Zu, *Li Xiannian Zhuan,* 2:777.

82. For contract and construction details, see Chen Jinhua, "Huigu Xin Zhongguo Di Er Ci Da Guimo Chengtao Jishu Shebei de Yinjin," 35–36 and 38–39, respectively.

83. Liu Bingfeng, "Mao Zedong yu 'Si San Fang'an' de Zhiding Shishi" [Mao Zedong and the Formulation (and) Implementation of the "Four-Three" Program], *Wenshi Tiandi* [Literature and History of the World] 7 (2017): 23.

84. Li Xiannian, excerpt of letter to Yu Qiuli, Gu Mu, and the State Planning Commission, August 21, 1974, in *Jianguo Yilai Li Xiannian Wengao* [Li Xiannian's Manuscripts since the Founding of the People's Republic], 4 vols. (Beijing: Zhongyang Wenxian, 2011), 3:304.

85. Liu Bingfeng, "Mao Zedong yu 'Si San Fang'an' de Zhiding Shishi," 23.

86. Chen Donglin, "Kaifang de Qianzou: 'Si San Fang'an' Ji Qi Dui Gaige Kaifang de Yingxiang" [A Prelude to Opening Up: The Four-Three Program and Its Influence on Reform and Opening], *Zhongguo Guojia Bowuguan Guankan* [Journal of the National Museum of China] 186, no. 1 (2019): 18.

87. Chen Donglin, "Qi Shi Niandai Qianqi de Zhongguo Di Er Ci Duiwai Yinjin Gaochao," 82.

EPILOGUE

1. Zhonggong Zhongyang Wenxian Yanjiushi, *Chen Yun Zhuan* [A Biography of Chen Yun], 4 vols. (Beijing: Zhongyang Wenxian, 2015), 3:1417.

2. Chen Yun, "Yao Yanjiu Dangdai Ziben Zhuyi" [(We) Must Study Modern Capitalism], June 7, 1973, *CYWX,* 3:217–218. This wasn't a passing thought.

Chen mentioned this shift—75 percent capitalist, 25 percent socialist—several times in mid-1973. Zhonggong Zhongyang Wenxian Yanjiushi, *Chen Yun Zhuan,* 3:1417, 1419.

3. Chen Yun, "Yao Yanjiu Dangdai Ziben Zhuyi," 218. Chen was referencing Lenin's "The Importance of Gold Now and after the Complete Victory of Socialism." See V. I. Lenin, *Lenin's Collected Works* (Moscow: Progress, 1965).

4. Chen Yun, "Yao Yanjiu Dangdai Ziben Zhuyi," 218. See also Dong Zhikai, "Chen Yun Duidai Ziben yu Ziben Shichang de Sixiang Shijian Tanxi" [Chen Yun's Approach to Capital and Capital Markets in Theory and Practice], *Zhonggong Dangshi Yanjiu* 8 (2010): 77. For Chen's emphasis on prices, finance, currencies, and capitalist economic "laws," see Zhonggong Zhongyang Wenxian Yanjiushi, *Chen Yun Zhuan,* 3:1419–1426.

5. State Planning Commission Core Small Group, "Guanyu Guomin Jingji Jihua Wenti de Baogao" [Report on National Economic Plan Issues], May 25, 1973, HPA, 855-20-1846-13, 19.

6. Chen Jian, "China's Changing Policies toward the Third World and the End of the Global Cold War," in *The End of the Cold War and the Third World: New Perspectives on Regional Conflict,* ed. Artemy M. Kalinovsky and Sergey Radchenko (New York: Routledge, 2011), 101–121.

7. [Ministry of Foreign Trade], "Jiedai Waiguo Jishu Renyuan Gongzuo Zuo-tanhui Jiyao (Caogao)" [Minutes of the Symposium on Receiving Foreign Technicians (Draft)], September 1974, HPA, 1057-1-9-3, 1.

8. Zhang Shu Guang, *Beijing's Economic Statecraft during the Cold War, 1949–1991* (Washington, DC: Woodrow Wilson Center Press, 2014), 263.

9. For the contours of these debates, see Frederick C. Teiwes and Warren Sun, "China's Economic Reorientation after the Third Plenum: Conflict Surrounding 'Chen Yun's' Readjustment Program, 1979–1980," *China Journal* 70 (July 2013): 163–187; Dorothy J. Solinger, "The Fifth National People's Congress and the Process of Policy Making: Reform, Readjustment, and the Opposition," *Asian Survey* 22, no. 12 (December 1982): 1238–1275; and David Bachman, "Differing Visions of China's Post-Mao Economy: The Ideas of Chen Yun, Deng Xiaoping, and Zhao Ziyang," *Asian Survey* 26, no. 3 (March 1986): 292–321.

10. Ezra Vogel, *Deng Xiaoping and the Transformation of China* (Cambridge, MA: Belknap Press of Harvard University Press, 2011), 424–435.

11. On the consensus between Deng Xiaoping and Chen Yun on the need for China to "open up," see Zhu Jiamu, *Lun Chen Yun* [On Chen Yun] (Beijing: Zhongyang Wenxian, 2010), 359–360.

12. For a concise overview of early reforms within China's foreign trade system after 1979, see Weijian Shan, "Reforms of China's Foreign Trade System: Experiences and Prospects," *China Economic Review* 1, no. 1 (1989): 35–55.

13. Nicholas Lardy, "The Role of Foreign Trade and Investment in China's Economic Transformation," *China Quarterly* 144 (December 1995): 1065.

14. Angela Monaghan, "China Surpasses U.S. as World's Largest Trading Nation," *Guardian,* January 10, 2014.

15. Richard N. Cooper, "Economic Aspects of the Cold War, 1962–1975," in *The Cambridge History of the Cold War,* vol. 2, *Crises and Détente,* ed. Melvyn P. Leffler and Odd Arne Westad (Cambridge: Cambridge University Press, 2010), 55; Daniel Yergin, "Politics and Soviet-American Trade: Three Questions," *Foreign Affairs* 55, no. 3 (April 1977): 521; Barry Naughton, *Growing Out of the Plan: Chinese Economic Reform, 1978–1993* (Cambridge: Cambridge University Press, 1995), 63.

16. For example, see Zhou Enlai, "Xunqiu Butong Zhengzhi Zhidu Xia Youliyu Shuangfang Fazhan Maoyi de Banfa" [Seeking Methods to Develop Mutually Beneficial Trade under Different Political Systems], June 29, 1973, *Zhou Enlai Jingji Wenxuan* [Selected Economic Works of Zhou Enlai] (Beijing: Zhongyang Wenxian, 1993), 645.

17. *LXNNP,* 6:54–55. For Li's involvement in China's import of technology and factory equipment from Japan and Europe during the early 1960s, see "Li Xiannian Zhuan" Bianxie Zu, *Li Xiannian Zhuan* [A Biography of Li Xiannian], 2 vols. (Beijing: Zhongyang Wenxian, 2009), 1:572. For a discussion of his broader contributions to trade and foreign policy during Reform and Opening, see Cheng Zhensheng, "Li Xiannian yu Gaige Kaifang Chuqi de Duiwai Gongzuo" [Li Xiannian and Foreign Affairs Work during the Early Phase of Reform and Opening], *Zhonggong Dangshi Yanjiu* 6 (2009): 93–102.

18. Outside influences also shaped Reform and Opening as Chinese politicians and intellectuals sought insights from foreign economic thinkers in Europe, the United States, and elsewhere. See Julian Gewirtz, *Unlikely Partners: Chinese Reformers, Western Economists, and the Making of Global China* (Cambridge, MA: Harvard University Press, 2017).

19. Deng Xiaoping, *Deng Xiaoping Wenxuan* [Selected Works of Deng Xiaoping], 3 vols. (Beijing: Renmin, 1994), 2:127. Li Xiannian also used Mao's approval of trade with capitalists to support broader commercial engagement with the capitalist world in the late 1970s. Li Xiannian, "Guanyu Jiakuai Guomin Jingji Fazhan de Ji ge Wenti" [On Several Issues in the Acceleration of National Economic Development], March 18, 1977, as quoted in "Deng Xiaoping Deng Lao Yi Bei Gemingjia Guanyu Jingji Jianshe he Fazhan Wenti de Yizu Jianghua, Pishi (Yi Jiu Qi Qi Nian San Yue—Yi Jiu Qi Ba Nian Si Yue)" [A Collection of Speeches and Instructions from Deng Xiaoping and Other Older-Generation Revolutionaries Regarding Economic Construction and Development Issues (March 1977–April 1978)], *Dang de Wenxian* 2 (2009): 5.

ACKNOWLEDGMENTS

Many people and organizations provided support and encouragement during the years I spent writing this book. At Cornell, where I first started my research and writing, I couldn't have asked for a better committee. Chen Jian, my chair, supported the project from the outset. I'm grateful for his generosity, his unerringly sound advice, and his contagious enthusiasm for history, all of which have shaped my view of what a model teacher and scholar should be. Fred Logevall inspired me to push for clear thinking through clear writing—a lifelong project, it turns out—and I couldn't be more thankful for so many hours spent talking about history and writing with someone whose work I admire so much. Vic Koschmann taught me more about teaching and collegiality than perhaps he realizes. Our directed reading in the spring of 2014 was one of the highlights of my time at Cornell, and I'll never forget it. Karl Gerth, who joined my committee once the project had picked up steam, offered invaluable feedback as the work was coming into its final form. I can't thank him enough for his many helpful questions and critiques.

At Cornell, I also benefited from the wisdom and advice of many faculty and fellow graduate students. I am particularly indebted to Sherman Cochran, Chen Zhihong, Durba Ghosh, Victor Seow, Jiang Huajie, Wang Yuanchong, Matts Fibiger, Kaitlin Pontzer, Chris Tang, Zhou Taomo, Jack Chia, Wah Guan Lim, Shiau-Yun Chen, and Fritz Bartel for helpful comments and camaraderie. After Cornell, I was fortunate to spend time as an Ernest May Fellow in History and Policy at the Harvard Kennedy School, an ideal environment for working on the project. I am grateful to the faculty and fellows at the Belfer Center for their support—particularly to

Graham Allison and Fred Logevall for welcoming me back for a second year following an abrupt change of plans. Special thanks to Arne Westad for valuable feedback, and to Calder Walton, my former officemate, for encouragement and occasional commiseration. Thanks also to Moshik Temkin, Alex Keyssar, David Allen, Alexandra Tejblum Evans, Julian Gewirtz, and Yakov Feygin for suggestions on portions of earlier drafts. Scholars elsewhere also shared ideas, sources, and contacts to help the project along. My thanks in particular go to Elizabeth Remick, Philip Thai, Fei-Hsien Wang, Steven Pieragastini, Wang Tao, Giles Chance, Doug Irwin, Dex Wilson, Sally Paine, Bob Flynn, Chen Bo, and Wu'er Beimi. Greg Lewis not only invited me to Utah to read through his collection of materials on the life of Ji Chaoding but was also kind enough to insist that I stay with him during my trip.

For the past two years, the US Naval War College has provided a stimulating and supportive environment in which to finish the book. I am particularly grateful to my civilian and military colleagues in the Department of Strategy & Policy and to my students, whose experience and professionalism are an inspiration. I am equally indebted to friends and former colleagues serving elsewhere in the US government for doing so much to shape my understanding of diplomacy, trade, and international relations in practice. To my Chinese teachers at Yale, Princeton in Beijing, and the Inter-University Program (IUP) for Chinese Studies at Qinghua: thank you for your enthusiasm, your rigor, and your bottomless patience.

I could not have written this book without the help of the archivists, librarians, researchers, and staff at Cornell University's Rare and Manuscript Collections; the Fung Library at Harvard University; the Baker Library Historical Collections at the Harvard Business School; the Universities Service Center for China Studies at the Chinese University of Hong Kong; the East China Normal University (ECNU) Center for Cold War International History Studies; the US National Archives at College Park, Maryland; the Diplomatic Archives of the Japanese Ministry of Foreign Affairs; the Japan External Trade Organization Business Library and Archives in Tokyo; the Hongkong and Shanghai Banking Corporation (HSBC) Archives in London and Hong Kong; the National Archives at Kew; and Bodleian Archives & Manuscripts at Oxford University. I am especially thankful to Garfield Lam at the HSBC Archive in Hong Kong,

Helen Ceci and Susan Gentles at the HSBC Archive in London, Svenja Kunze with Special Collections at Bodleian Libraries, and Nancy Hearst of the Fairbank Center for Chinese Studies at Harvard. Nancy came to the rescue—more than once—when I was scrambling to find a document or volume in the midst of a global pandemic. Once again, you saved the day, Nancy. Special thanks, also, to the many helpful archivists and librarians in China for their assistance and for all the challenging and important work they do.

Kathleen McDermott, my editor at Harvard University Press, took an early interest in the project and provided expert guidance as I revised. My thanks also to Kathi Drummy and the staff at the Press for their support and assistance, and to the anonymous reviewers for reading the draft manuscript so carefully and providing such detailed and constructive suggestions. Cheryl Hirsch ensured the production process went smoothly, Isabelle Lewis created the map and the graphs, and Sue Sakai copyedited the draft manuscript. Any errors or missteps are my own.

Generous funding from many sources supported me throughout my research and writing. I am grateful for financial support from the US Naval War College, the Naval War College Foundation, the John A. van Beuren Chair of Asia-Pacific Studies at the Naval War College, the Ernest May Fellowship in History and Policy at the Harvard Kennedy School, the Hu Shih Fellowship in Chinese Studies at Cornell University, the Mario Einaudi Center International Research and Travel Grant, the Cornell East Asia Program Japan Studies Travel Grant, the Judith Reppy Institute Graduate Fellows Program at Cornell, the Cornell University Sage Fellowship, the Association for Asian Studies China and Inner Asia Council Research Grant, the US Department of Education Foreign Language and Area Studies Fellowship program, and the Kathryn Davis Fellowship for Peace.

Fellowships and grants generously paid for the airline tickets, the rooms, the copies, and the meals away, but it was my family that sustained me through it all. Love and thanks to both sides—in California, in Maine, and in between—for all the support over the years. Mary C. Drury, who taught me so much, asked about the book nearly every time we talked. I miss our conversations and I wish she were here to read it. Finally, my deepest gratitude goes to Rebecca and Abigail. Becca read every page, offered thoughtful suggestions, picked up the slack when I was away or sequestered to write, and still managed to pursue a successful career, all while making motherhood look easy. Amazing. Abigail, who has grown up with this book, has kept my feet on the ground by always knowing precisely when it's time for a break. Thank you both for your support, your patience, and your love, and for helping me to keep the big picture in view. I couldn't have done this without you.

INDEX

Page numbers in italics refer to illustrations